DOING

SCIENCE

RESEARCH

DOING
SOCIAL
SCIENCE
RESEARCH

Simeon J. Yates

SAGE Publications
London • Thousand Oaks • New Delhi   *in association with*

The Open
University

First published 2004

SAGE Publications Ltd
6 Bonhill Street
London EC2A 4PU

SAGE Publications Inc
2455 Teller Road
Thousand Oaks, California 91320

SAGE Publications India Pvt Ltd
B–42 Panchsheel Enclave
Post Box 4109
New Delhi 110 017

British Library Cataloguing in Publication data

A catalogue record for this book is
available from the British Library

ISBN 0 7619 6797 4
ISBN 0 7619 6798 2 (pbk)

Library of Congress Control Number: 2003102948

Typeset by M Rules
Printed in Great Britain by Cromwell Press Ltd, Trowbridge, Wiltshire

Contents

Readings   vi
Acknowledgements   vii

PART I DOING SOCIAL RESEARCH

Introduction   1
1   Social Research as Practice   3

PART II QUANTITATIVE RESEARCH METHODS

Introduction   5
2   General Research Process   7
3   Survey Research   21
4   Experimental Research   65
5   Numerical Data Analysis   78

PART III QUALITATIVE RESEARCH METHODS

Introduction   133
6   Positioning Qualitative Work   135
7   Collecting Qualitative Data   155
8   Analysing Qualitative Data   188
9   Discourse Analysis   233

PART IV SELECTING AND EVALUATING METHODS

10   Selecting and Evaluating Methods   279
     References   287

Readings

Reading A   Data Analysis and the Research Process
Alan Bryman and Duncan Cramer   14

Reading B   Lessons from the Electorate: What the 1992 British General
Election Taught British Pollsters about the Conduct of
Opinion Polls
Robert M. Worcester   36

Reading C   Studying Sexual Lifestyles
Julia Field, Anne Johnston, Jane Wadsworth and Kaye Wellings   48

Reading D   Studying Sexual Lifestyles: Long Questionnaire
Julia Field, Anne Johnston, Jane Wadsworth and Kaye Wellings   57

Reading E   Age Differences in Source Forgetting: Effects on Reality
Monitoring and on Eyewitness Testimony
Gillian Cohen and Dorothy Faulkner   71

Reading F   Causality and Research Design
Alan Bryman and Duncan Cramer   117

Reading G   The Visual Life History Interview
Annabel Tomas   141

Reading H   What is Qualitative Data?
Ian Dey   147

Reading I   Thinking through Fieldwork (1)
Judith Okely   175

Reading J   Thinking through Fieldwork (2)
Judith Okely   179

Reading K   Selecting a Case
Simeon J. Yates   180

Reading L   Thinking through Fieldwork (3)
Judith Okely   193

Reading M   Qualitative Analysis for Social Scientists
Anselm Strauss   197

Reading N   Thinking through Fieldwork (4)
Judith Okely   211

Reading O   'Becoming a Mother' - Developing a New Theory of
Early Motherhood
Frances Rogan, Virginia Shmied, Lesley Barclay,
Louise Everitt and Aileen Wyllie   215

Reading P   Analyzing Discourse (1)
Jonathan Potter and Margaret Wetherell   246

Reading Q   Analyzing Discourse (2)
Jonathan Potter and Margaret Wetherell   249

Reading R   Analyzing Discourse (3)
Jonathan Potter and Margaret Wetherell   251

Reading S   From the Street to the Screen: *Breadline Britain* and the
Semiotics of Poverty
Ulrike Meinhof   262

Acknowledgements

Grateful acknowledgement is made to the following sources for permission to reproduce material in this book:

Readings A and F: Bryman, A. and Cramer, D. (1990) *Quantitative Data Analysis for Social Scientists*. Routledge; **Reading B**: Worcester, R.M. (1995) 'Lessons from the electorate: what the 1992 British General Election taught British pollsters about the conduct of opinion polls', *International Social Science*, 14(4), © UNESCO, Blackwell Publishers Ltd, Table 8. MORI/Sunday Times; **Readings C and D**: Field, J., Johnson, A., Wadsworth, J. and Wellings, K. (1994) *Sexual Behaviour in Britain*. Penguin Books Ltd, by permission of Peters, Fraser and Dunlop; **Reading E**: Cohen, G. and Faulkner, D. (1989) 'Age differences in source forgetting: effects on reality monitoring and on eyewitness testimony', *Psychology and Aging*, 4(1): 10, 14–17, American Psychological Association; **Reading G**: Tomas, A. (1997) The visual life history interview, © Annabel Tomas. **Reading H**: Dey, I. (1993) *Qualitative Data Analysis*, pp. 9–17, Routledge; **Readings I, J, L and N**: Okely, J. (1994) 'Thinking through fieldwork', in Bryman, A. and Burgess, R.G. (eds) *Analyzing Qualitative Data*. Routledge; **Reading M**: Strauss, A. (1987) *Qualitative Analysis for Social Scientists*. Cambridge University Press, also with permission of the author; **Reading O**: Rogan, F, Shmied, V., Barclay, L., Everitt, L. and Wyllie, A. (1997) '"Becoming a mother": developing a new theory of early motherhood', *Journal of Advanced Nursing*, 25: 877–85, Blackwell Science Ltd, also with permission of the authors; **Readings P, Q and R**: Potter, J. and Wetherell, M. (1994) 'Analyzing discourse', in Bryman, A. and Burgess, R.G. (eds) *Analyzing Qualitative Data*. Routledge; **Reading S**: Meinhof, U. (1994) 'From the street to the screen: *Breadline Britain* and the semiotics of poverty', in Meinhof, U. and Richardson, K. (eds) *Text, Discourse and Content. Representations of Poverty in Britain*. Longman Group Limited, reprinted by permission of Addison Wesley Longman Ltd.

PART I
DOING SOCIAL RESEARCH

Introduction

This book is a basic introduction to *empirical* research methods. It examines a range of methods that try to deal with primary sources of information about the social world – actual people and events that can inform us about the processes, practices 1, 2, 3 and ideas in the social world around us. Working with secondary sources – writings and materials produced by other social researchers – is of course a central aspect of being a researcher and doing research. Skills in using secondary sources are an essential complement to empirical research and you can find guidance on this aspect of research in a range of other texts (see, for example, Hart, 1998).

As you work through this book you will come to realise that the term 'empirical' has a broad range of meanings. Above I linked it to the use of 'primary sources' – the collection of 'new information' about people and societies. Unfortunately what is counted as useful, relevant, 'reliable' and 'usable' *data* is not so easy to define. In fact what we will often explore in this book are the ways in which social researchers come to decide what is (and is not) good data. Therefore things other than the topic under study often define 'empirical research'. Very often social scientists rely upon philosophical ideas about 'science' and 'knowledge' to help resolve these questions. For philosophers a focus on the 'empirical' may imply a philosophical position of *empiricism* which is often connected to *positivism* . Here the social research methods often rely upon numerical and statistical methods. Such methods are often called 'quantitative' methods. At the other end of the range 'the empirical' is used to denote any methods that are reliant upon primary source information – very often the 'data' is not numerical. Such research does not use statistics and is often called 'qualitative' research. By the time you have worked through this book it should be clear to you that it is possible to engage in empirical research without having to be an 'empiricist'. In other words the philosophical position of *empiricism* fails to capture the breadth and depth of social science research practice.

The book introduces you to some of the key ideas and methods available to contemporary social scientists; it does not attempt to provide a complete introduction to all forms of social research. The intention is to provide you with enough information about research methods to allow you to start thinking about your own research projects as well as understand and critique the methods described in research publications. The book is split into four parts. Part I is this brief introduction. Following on from our discussion above the next two parts focus on 'Quantitative' and 'Qualitative' methods. In this book I will also use the phrases 'Numerical' and 'Textual' methods as well as 'Quantitative' and 'Qualitative'. My main reason for doing this is to remind you that some methods produce 'numbers' – they attempt to measure the social world. Others focus on 'meanings' – they produce descriptions and 'understandings' of social life. Part II focuses on quantitative research. It introduces the basic ideas behind survey and experimental methods. It also provides a 'walk through' for examples of the three main 'types' of statistical test. Part III is concerned with qualitative and textual research, focusing on interview, ethnographic and discourse analytic methods. It includes an opportunity to qualitatively 'code' a text and to examine a piece of 'interaction'. Part IV concludes the book by briefly considering the question of how to select a research method.

Using this Book

This book is designed to be used alongside one or more texts that specifically examine the philosophical basis of social research. A selection of useful and relevant texts of this kind is given in the further reading section at the end of this part. Some discussion of the philosophical, or to be precise 'epistemological' issues behind social research will take place at various points but this book is not an introduction to this topic. When discussing these issues I will mostly reference Smith (1998), which provides a full discussion of links between research methods and philosophical positions and social theories. This book and Smith (1998) were developed together and we hope that readers will find them complementary. I will also indicate the points where other texts provide useful and relevant comment.

A large part of the teaching in this book takes place through self-assessment tasks and questions (SAQs). They direct you to read extracts from various social science research publications, consider important questions, or practise specific skills. Bear in mind that if you skip the SAQs you will be limiting your learning about research methods. The extracts, headed Reading A, B, C, etc., appear after the main text of Parts II and III. Suggested solutions to the SAQs are provided at the end of Parts II, III and IV.

1   *Social Research as Practice*

Empirical social research is a practical activity. It involves the collection, exploration and reporting of information about people and societies. While this book concentrates on methods – that is, on how one goes about these basic tasks – you will need to keep in mind the various influences that have, over time, affected the development of these methods. The most important of these influences are:

- *philosophical ideas about science and social science*. Philosophy has provided a great number of models of the process of doing research which have been drawn upon by social scientists when developing research methods.
- *theories and findings from social science*. Because social science is a very 'reflexive' activity, new findings often lead to new ideas about how to go about researching the social world.
- *practical constraints on conducting actual research*. Whatever the philosophical position we might start from, or the social science idea that informs our research, or the tools we use, we are faced with the practical task of actually doing research. This experience, and the need to work within the constraints of an actual research context, can alter our choice and application of methods, and it can also inform our philosophical models of the research process itself.

One social scientific way in which we might view this is to consider social research as a 'social practice' that is influenced by this set of three related and competing factors. The idea of viewing 'social research' in this way is relatively new and flows from a specific set of philosophical perspectives. These positions can be described as 'idealist' or 'relativist' (see Smith, 1998: Chapters 1, 4, 6 and 7). For each of the methods examined I will try to comment upon the ways in which these three factors influence the practices of social researchers.

Whatever the specific influences on a particular research method there is an overall structure to nearly all types of social research. This structure involves five 'stages'. First, there is the reasoning behind the social research project itself. Social research is done for a number of reasons. In most cases researchers are attempting to explore a new theory or social context; in some cases the goal is to 'test' the theory, in others to bring to light the details of some aspects of social life. Second, whatever the method used, the next main step is the collecting of information and evidence – what can be generally described as 'data'. Third, the researcher will also explore, or analyse, the collected data. Fourth, the results of this exploration are interpreted, which involves linking them back to the ideas which formed the reasoning for the research. Last, these interpretations are usually presented to a particular audience, usually in the form of a written/published text.

Try to keep these five stages in mind as you work through this book. In studying each method you need to consider the philosophical and social science ideas that have influenced its development, the practical problems that need to be overcome and the ways in which the method addresses the different stages of the research process. You may wish to refer to more general works on the philosophy of the social sciences as you go along. Along the way I have indicated some relevant parts of Smith (1998). You might wish to use another text. Some possible candidates are indicated in the further reading.

Further Reading

Crotty, M. (1998), *The Foundations of Social Research: Meaning and Perspective in the Research Process*. London: Sage.
Martin, M. and McIntyre, L.C. (eds) (1994) *Readings in the Philosophy of Social Science*. London: MIT Press.
Smith, M. (1998) *Social Science in Question*. London: Sage.

PART II
QUANTITATIVE
RESEARCH METHODS

Introduction

This part introduces you to two methods of conducting empirical social research: survey research and experimental research. After a brief introduction to the general process of conducting quantitative research I will introduce the main elements of each method and their strengths and weaknesses. You will then work through examples of a statistical analysis to gain a general understanding of this technique and the contexts in which it can be applied.

There are a number of reasons why these two empirical research methods have been placed together. First, both are most often associated with 'natural science' based approaches to social research. In the history of social research there has been a two-way flow of ideas, if not always a perfect one, between the practical realities of research and the philosophy of the social sciences. Surveys and experiments are often described both proudly and derogatively, depending upon who is speaking, as being positivist and/or empiricist (see Smith, 1998: Chapters 2 and 3).

This part weighs up this association with the natural sciences against the actual day-to-day workings of research methods, arguing that methods are influenced by philosophical arguments about social science, but that they are also influenced by the practicalities of doing research. This often leads to a complex situation. In the case of the quantitative and numerical methods discussed here you will find that the practicalities of conducting research have an impact on the application of positivist ideas. In many cases, though the research might be categorised as 'positivist', and may, in fact, be designed to reflect the goals of positivist thinking, it will also be limited by the need to develop practically useful methods. It is important to engage in empirical work, but that empirical work does not by definition have to be empiricist or positivist to be useful and valid.

A second reason why these methods have been brought together is the extent to which they often rely upon quantitative, essentially numerical, evidence. Smith (1998) points out that one key element of 'natural' science, or positivist, approaches, is their belief that social science can 'measure' social phenomena. Both survey and experimental research methods often make extensive use of various forms of social measurement. The third reason for bringing these methods together relates to the issue of 'control'. An important element of attempts to re-create natural science methods in the social sciences concerns the ability to control the elements under examination. This control is achieved through the construction of 'closed systems'. Survey research attempts to gain closure by the use of sampling, experimental research in the design of the experiment. In both cases statistics are often used to complete the process (see Smith, 1998: Chapters 2 and 3).

2   *General Research Process*

All social science research goes through some form of overall process by which information is collected and related to the ideas or goals of the researcher. Many quantitative researchers describe this process in a manner which combines elements of both **inductive** and **falsificationist** methods, and which is seen to reflect the process of natural science research. Bryman and Cramer (1990) provide the following diagram to explain the process.

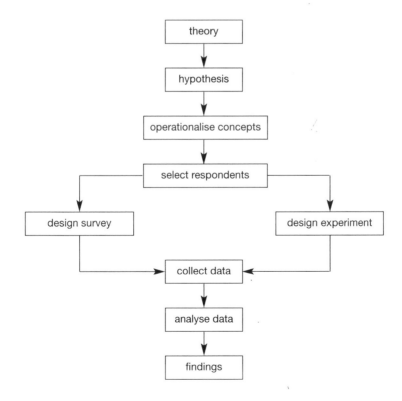

Figure 2.1 *Quantitative research process (adapted from Bryman and Cramer, 1990: 3)*

There are eight parts to the process of conducting quantitative research as presented in this figure:

1   Theory
2   Hypothesis
3   Operationalisation of concepts
4   Selection of respondents or cases
5   Research design
6   Collection of data
7   Analysis of data
8   Findings

We will examine this process in detail in the rest of this section by looking at several examples of survey and experimental methods. Along the way we will explore the key elements of each method and consider how they go about attempting to achieve some form of closure.

Study Comment
Please ensure that you attempt each of the self-assessment questions (SAQs), as a large part of the teaching takes place in these set tasks. If you leave out the SAQs you will limit your learning of the material.

SAQ 2.1

Turn to Reading A, 'Data analysis and the research process', which is an extract from Bryman and Cramer's discussion of Figure 2.1. After you have read each section, from the one headed 'Theory' onwards, answer the section-relevant questions below. There is no section on collecting data as Bryman and Cramer do not touch on this process.

Theory

1   Describe in one or two sentences the type of theory Bryman and Cramer see as being 'most likely to receive empirical attention'.
2   Can you name two or three such theories from your own study of social science?

Hypothesis

3   Write down in one or two sentences how hypotheses are related to theory.
4   Write down in two sentences what Bryman and Cramer see as being the benefits and problems of formulating an hypothesis.

Operationalisation of concepts

5   Which natural science do Bryman and Cramer claim that the term 'Operationalisation' is derived from?
6   Write down in one or two sentences how Hirschi operationalised the concept of 'commitment to conventional society'.

Selection of respondents or cases

7   Write down in one or two sentences the way in which Hirschi selected respondents in order to ensure that the findings would hold true in general.

Setting up a research design

8   Write down the two types of research design which Bryman and Cramer claim are most common in psychology and sociology.
9   Write down a few of the differences between these designs as described by Bryman and Cramer.
10 Which of these categories of design does Hirschi's work fit into?

Analysing data

11 Write down the names for the three types of data analysis pointed out by Bryman and Cramer.
12 Write down in one or two sentences the difference between an 'experimental' and a 'control' group.

Findings

13 Write down in two or three sentences the ways in which the results from analysing data relate to the hypothesis and to the original theory.

Here you have met most of the terms and issues that will be dealt with in the following sections. Some of the more important terms and issues are:

- theory
- measure
- sample
- experimental design
- univariate

- hypothesis
- variable
- random sample
- survey design
- bivariate

- concept
- observation
- representative sample
- multivariate

Don't worry if you have not met some of these before, or if you are not yet comfortable with how to apply them; we will discuss them in depth during your study of this part. Before moving on to the discussion of survey and experimental methods we need to consider the argument of Bryman and Cramer in relation to questions of philosophy or epistemology.

Natural Science and Quantitative Data Analysis

It is clear from Figure 2.1 and the references to natural science methods in the Bryman and Cramer reading that the process of quantitative social research can be seen as similar to if not the same as that of the natural sciences. Social scientists can draw on natural science ideas in two main ways.

- First, they can use natural science models as *metaphors* for social phenomena. For example we can find in the history of social science many ways of 'explaining' phenomena by using models or metaphors from other sciences. We can often find arguments that social phenomena are like biological phenomena. They 'evolve', or have an organisation like an 'organic system'. We can even find engineering or computing metaphors.
- Second, they can attempt to replicate the *methods* used in the natural sciences. Though much research that uses 'natural science methods' may also use 'natural science metaphors' we will concentrate in this section on how social scientists have tried to replicate or transfer natural science methods to social research.

The main manner in which social scientists attempt to do this is through the production of 'closed systems' (see Smith, 1998: Chapter 2). Closed systems are ones where no 'external factors' influence the ways in which the system functions. Most natural science experiments try to create such situations. For example, in chemistry an experimenter will make sure that the laboratory and the equipment are very clean. They will measure out exact proportions of the chemicals, etc. By doing this they can be sure that the product of an experiment has come from the reaction between the chemicals they used. No other factors (such as a dirty test tube) affected the results. A closed system therefore allows the observer to test out their predictions about the relationships between the various elements within the system without having to worry that some other factor might influence the result. The researcher employs various controls that remove or minimise the effect of external factors. The opposite to a closed system is an open system. Here there are so many factors at work and there are no 'controls' on how they interact. In fact nearly all 'real' systems in the world (things like societies, the weather, the galaxy) are open systems. Table 2.1 is taken from Smith (1998) and distinguishes the features of open and closed systems.

Table 2.1 *Features of open and closed systems*

	Closed systems	Open systems
Simplicity and complexity	A limited number of measurable variables are involved to increase the possibility of identifying and predicting clear relationships	A state of complexity is acknowledged as the condition of one's objects of analysis and the relations between them
External boundary	Exclusion clauses ensure that the confusing mass of possible influences are screened out	No external boundary is assumed to exist so that each object can be part of multiple causal relations and one cannot predict an outcome with any degree of certainty
Intrinsic properties	All objects of analysis are taken at face value so that the intrinsic properties of an object are not considered	Open systems analysis recognises that all objects have intrinsic properties and structures which affect their performance in different conditions

Smith (1998) describes three types of closure:

- Experimental
- Theoretical
- Statistical

Table 2.2 details these three methods of gaining 'closure' available to social researchers.

Table 2.2 *Methods of closure*

Experimental closure	Theoretical closure	Statistical closure
This is done through the control of specific events, experiences or cases. Very often in psychology experiments, participants are split into separate groups that undergo different experiences. The effects of those differences are then 'measured'	This is about 'modelling' the world, for instance the use of computer models in economics. You control the design of and inputs to the model. If the results are similar to those found in the 'real world' then maybe it is a good model of the real world	This is controlling for chance and other influences by the use of mathematics (statistics). The relationships between numerical measures of some aspects of the social world are assessed to see if something other than chance is at work. It is also the design and use of representative samples to ensure generalisable results

Figure 2.1 therefore highlights the stages that a social researcher might go through to control enough factors in an open system, such as a society, to produce a 'controlled context'. First, the researcher focuses upon an element, factor or variable of the system under study by constructing an hypothesis – a prediction about the system. Second, the researcher finds ways of measuring and categorising the elements of the system by operationalising their theoretical concepts. Third, the researcher controls the elements of the system. In the case of surveys this is done

by careful selection of cases (statistical closure) and careful design of questionnaires. In the case of experiments it is done through the design of the experiment – using experimental closure. Fourth, quantitative researchers can further control and remove the influence of external factors through the use of statistics. Most statistical analyses are designed to separate out 'random' or external effects from those of the system under study. The results of these analyses then confirm or refute the predictions made by the researcher. This is, of course, an idealised version of the process which, as Bryman and Cramer (1990: 7) point out, 'constitutes a model of the research process, which may not always be reproduced in reality. None the less, it does serve to pin-point the importance to the process of quantitative research of developing measures of concepts and the thorough analysis of subsequent data.'

Positivism and Quantitative Research Methods

The obvious question one can ask is this: why should the social sciences use natural science methods? One direct answer is that natural science methods appear to be so successful in their field of use (see Smith, 1998: Chapters 1 and 2). But this is just part of the story. I argued earlier that philosophies of science and knowledge have had a strong influence on the development of social research methods. In particular the broad set of philosophical ideas known as 'positivism' have directly influenced the development of the social sciences from the mid 1800s to the present (see Smith, 1998: Chapter 3). We do not have space here to explore the full nature of positivism but Smith (1998) provides a useful summary of the key assumptions of positivism (see Table 2.3).

Table 2.3 *Main assumptions of positivism*

Assumption	Definition	Implication
Naturalism	Positivists are committed to naturalism, the idea that it is possible to transfer the assumptions and methods of natural sciences to the study of social objects, often referred to as the 'unification of method'.	This means that you would study behaviour, institutions and society in much the same way as studying, for example, chemical processes, hydraulic systems, geological structures. The closed system of a scientific experiment is often taken as a model for knowledge production in the social sciences.
Phenomenalism	Phenomenalism is the assumption that only knowledge gained from observed experience can be taken seriously. If something cannot be directly experienced it is said to be metaphysical – beyond our physical senses.	If we cannot touch it, see it, hear it, taste it or smell it, then an object cannot be said to exist except in so far as it is an idea of something. For example, 'happiness' is something which exists only in people's minds and cannot be directly physically experienced.

Table 2.3 *Cont.*

Assumption	Definition	Implication
Nominalism	Nominalism shares with phenomenalism the argument that concepts must be based upon experience, but it also asserts that concepts have no use other than as names. Words are seen as pure reflections of things. It is, of course, very difficult to do this because the words we use are usually far more than simple descriptions.	All concepts or ideas which are not directly experienced through the senses are meaningless. In a strict sense, concepts such as the 'unconscious' and 'capitalism' are names for things we can't directly experience through our senses. Therefore, by this criterion, such concepts are meaningless.
Atomism	Atomism is a particular approach to the definition of objects. Atomism states that the objects of scientific study are discrete, that is, the objects cannot be broken down into any smaller parts. These objects act as the foundations of a scientific study. Collective objects are thus the sum total of their smaller atomic components.	When approaching any field of study, atomists look for the smallest observable units which cannot be broken down any further. When studying a society the most discrete unit is often taken as the individual. Atomistic explanations of society would start with the individual and regard society as no more than a collection of individuals.
Scientific laws	The purpose of science is to develop laws. To develop a scientific law you start from the observation of a particular set of objects and look for regularities. The regular appearance of two or more things together, or in some kind of sequence, can be called an empirical regularity. This is sometimes described as a constant conjunction of events. You then explore whether the same regularities occur in other similar circumstances. A scientific law is a general statement which describes and explains empirical regularities that occur in different places and at different times.	The search for scientific laws involves finding empirical regularities, such as the well known example of smoking tobacco and developing lung cancer. Social scientists adopting this assumption would look for empirical regularities between, say, poverty and crime, the money supply and price inflation, school class sizes and literacy levels, gender and earnings, and so on. In practice, one is usually taken as the cause of the other. For instance, high levels of poverty are seen as a causal factor in crime levels.
Facts/values	Facts and values are seen as distinct. Only facts can be regarded as scientific. Facts can be empirically verified, that is, observed, measured and explained by reference to observational evidence. Values involve subjective assessments and claims about what ought to be. Thus values cannot be observed, measured or explained.	Social scientists accepting these assumptions would distinguish scientific statements, which describe what is the case, from unscientific value-laden statements. For example, a measure of the number of homeless is often viewed as a fact whereas the statement that homelessness is a social evil is a value statement.

Quantitative or numerical research methods are often associated with the terms 'positivism' and 'empiricism' for a number of reasons. First, by using or replicating methods from the natural sciences they are in line with the assumption of naturalism – that all phenomena can be explained in the same way through the 'scientific method'. Second, many forms of quantitative research rely upon 'observations' of human behaviour. In fact they assume that one can observe and measure the social world directly. This fits the assumption of phenomenalism – that only directly experienced data is relevant to science. Third, many quantitative methods assume that words and terms have universal and fixed meanings. For instance, they may assume that the word 'work' has the same meaning for all respondents to a questionnaire. This fits the assumption of nominalism. Fourth, quantitative methods have a tendency to focus upon individual units of a system and individual respondents (e.g. individual people, individual families, individual factories, etc.). This fits the assumption of atomism. Fifth, a goal of much quantitative research is the production of general statements, or 'laws', which hold across a range of contexts. This fits the assumption of scientific laws. Last, the processes of hypothesis formation, concept operationalisation and research design are intended to limit the impact of the researcher's value system on the research itself. This fits the assumption of a distinction between facts and values. Though one can therefore clearly argue that positivist thinking has influenced quantitative or numerical social research methods we need to be careful how far we take this argument. We need to separate this apparent influence from the actualities of research practice. In the following sections we will consider how and if actual examples of quantitative methods fit positivist criteria. We will now move on to explore two main types of 'quantitative' or numerical methods – surveys and experiments.

Further Reading

Bryman, A. and Cramer, D. (1990) *Quantitative Data Analysis for Social Scientists*. London: Routledge.

Crotty, M. (1998) *The Foundations of Social Research: Meaning and Perspective in the Research Process*. London: Sage.

Halfpenny, P. (1992) *Positivism and Sociology: Explaining Social Life (Modern Revivals in Sociology)*. London: Gregg Revivals.

Kumar, R. (1996) *Research Methodology: A Step by Step Guide for Beginners*. London: Sage.

Martin, M. and McIntyre, L.C. (eds) (1994) *Readings in the Philosophy of Social Science*. London: MIT Press.

Smith, M. (1998) *Social Science in Question*. London: Sage.

Reading A: Data Analysis and the Research Process

Alan Bryman and Duncan Cramer

Why should social-science students have to study quantitative data analysis, especially at a time when qualitative research is coming increasingly to the fore (Bryman, 1988a)? After all, everyone has heard of the ways in which statistical materials can be distorted, as indicated by Disraeli's often-quoted dictum: 'There are lies, damn lies and statistics.' Why should serious researchers and students be prepared to get involved in such a potentially unworthy activity? If we take the first issue – why social-science students should study quantitative data analysis – it is necessary to remember that an extremely large proportion of the empirical research undertaken by social scientists is designed to generate, or draws upon, quantitative data. In order to be able to appreciate the kinds of analyses that are conducted in relation to such data and possibly to analyse their own data (especially since many students are required to carry out projects), an acquaintance with the appropriate methods of analysis is highly desirable for social-science students. Further, although qualitative research has quite properly become a prominent strategy in sociology and some other areas of the social sciences, it is by no means as pervasive as quantitative research, and in any case many writers recognize that there is much to be gained from a fusion of the two research traditions (Bryman, 1988a).

On the question of the ability of statisticians to distort the analyses that they carry out, the prospects for which are substantially enhanced in many people's eyes by books with such disconcerting titles as *How to Lie with Statistics* (Huff, 1973), it should be recognized that an understanding of the techniques to be covered in our book will greatly enhance the ability to see through the misrepresentations about which many people are concerned. Indeed, the inculcation of a sceptical appreciation of quantitative data analysis is beneficial in the light of the pervasive use of statistical data in everyday life. We are deluged with such data in the form of the results of opinion polls, market-research findings, attitude surveys, health and crime statistics, and so on. An awareness of quantitative data analysis greatly enhances the ability to recognize faulty conclusions or potentially biased manipulations of the information. There is even a fair chance that a substantial proportion of the readers of this book will get jobs in which at some point they will have to think about the question of how to analyse and present statistical material. Moreover, quantitative data analysis does not comprise a mechanical application of predetermined techniques by statisticians and others; it is a subject with its own controversies and debates, just like the social sciences themselves. Some of these areas of controversy will be brought to the reader's attention where appropriate.

Quantitative Data Analysis and the Research Process

In this section, the way in which quantitative data analysis fits into the research process – specifically the process of quantitative research – will be explored . . .

Figure [2.1 in main text] provides an illustration of the chief steps in the process of quantitative research. Although there are grounds for doubting whether research always conforms to a neat linear sequence (Bryman, 1988a, 1988b), the components depicted in Figure [2.1] provide a useful model. The following stages are delineated by the model . . .

Theory

The starting-point for the process is a theoretical domain. Theories in the social sciences can vary between abstract general approaches (such as functionalism) and fairly low-level theories to explain specific phenomena (such as voting behaviour, delinquency, aggressiveness). By and large, the theories that are most likely to receive direct empirical attention are those which are at a fairly low level of generality. Merton (1967) referred to these as theories of the middle range, to denote theories that stood between general, abstract theories and empirical findings. Thus,

Hirschi (1969), for example, formulated a 'control theory' of juvenile delinquency which proposes that delinquent acts are more likely when the child's bonds to society are breached. This theory is in large part derived from other theories and also from research findings relating to juvenile delinquency.

Hypothesis

Once a theory has been formulated, it is likely that researchers will want to test it. Does the theory hold water when faced with empirical evidence? However, it is rarely possible to test a theory as such. Instead, we are more likely to find that a hypothesis, which relates to a limited facet of the theory, will be deduced from the theory and submitted to a searching enquiry. Hirschi, for example, drawing upon his control theory, stipulates that children who are tied to conventional society (in the sense of adhering to conventional values and participating or aspiring to participate in conventional values) will be less likely to commit delinquent acts than those not so tied. Hypotheses very often take the form of relationships between two or more entities – in this case commitment to conventional society and juvenile delinquency. These 'entities' are usually referred to as 'concepts' – that is, categories in which are stored our ideas and observations about common elements in the world . . . Although hypotheses have the advantage that they force researchers to think systematically about what they want to study and to structure their research plans accordingly, they exhibit a potential disadvantage in that they may divert a researcher's attention too far away from other interesting facets of the data he or she has amassed.

Operationalization of Concepts

In order to assess the validity of a hypothesis it is necessary to develop measures of the constituent concepts. This process is often referred to as *operationalization*, following expositions of the measurement process in physics (Bridgman, 1927). In effect, what is happening here is the translation of the concepts into variables – that is, attributes on which relevant objects (individuals, firms, nations, or whatever) differ. Hirschi operationalized the idea of commitment to conventional society in a number of ways. One route was through a question on a questionnaire asking the children to whom it was to be administered whether they liked school. Delinquency was measured in one of two ways, of which one was to ask about the number of delinquent acts to which children admitted (i.e. self-reported delinquent acts). In much experimental research in psychology, the measurement of concepts is achieved through the observation of people, rather than through the administration of questionnaires. If the researcher is interested in aggression, for example, a laboratory situation may be set up in which variations in aggressive behaviour are observed. Another way in which concepts may be operationalized is through the analysis of existing statistics, of which Durkheim's (1952/1898) classic analysis of suicide rates is an example . . .

Selection of Respondents or Subjects

If a survey investigation is being undertaken, the researcher must find relevant people to whom the research instrument that has been devised (for example, self-administered questionnaire, interview schedule) should be administered. Hirschi, for example, randomly selected over 5,500 schoolchildren from an area in California.

The fact of random selection is important here because it reflects a commitment to the production of findings that can be generalized beyond the confines of those who participate in a study. It is rarely possible to contact all units in a population, so that a *sample* invariably has to be selected. In order to be able to generalize to a wider population, a *representative sample*, such as one that can be achieved through random sampling, will be required. Moreover, many of the statistical techniques . . . are *inferential statistics*, which allow the researcher to demonstrate the probability that the results deriving from a sample are likely to be found in the population from which the sample was taken, but only if a random sample has been selected . . .

Setting up a Research Design

There are two basic types of research design that are employed by psychologists and sociologists. The former tend to use *experimental* designs in which the researcher actively manipulates aspects of a setting, either in the laboratory or in a field situation, and observes the effects of that manipulation on experimental subjects. There must also be a 'control group' which acts as a point of comparison with the group of subjects who receive the experimental manipulation. With a *survey/correlational* design, the researcher does not manipulate any of the variables of interest and data relating to all variables are collected simultaneously. The term *correlation* also refers to a technique for analysing relationships between variables . . . but is used in the present context to denote a type of research design. The researcher does not always have a choice regarding which of the two designs can be adopted. Thus, for example, Hirschi could not *make* some children committed to school and others less committed and observe the effects on their propensity to commit delinquent acts. Some variables, like most of those studied by sociologists, are not capable of manipulation. However, there are areas of research in which topics and hypotheses are addressed with both types of research design (for example, the study of the effects of participation at work on job satisfaction and performance – see Locke and Schweiger, 1979; Bryman, 1986). It should be noted that in most cases, therefore, the nature of the research design – whether experimental or survey/correlational – is known at the outset of the sequence signified by Figure [2.1], so that research-design characteristics permeate and inform a number of stages of the research process. The nature of the research design has implications for the kinds of statistical manipulation that can be performed on the resulting data. The differences between the two designs are given greater attention in the next section.

Collect Data

The researcher collects data at this stage, by interview, questionnaire, observation, or whatever . . .

Analyse Data

. . . At a minimum, the researcher is likely to want to describe his or her subjects in terms of the variables deriving from the study. The researcher might for example be interested in the proportion of children who claim to have committed no, just one, or two or more delinquent acts . . . However, the analysis of a single variable (sometimes called *univariate analysis*) is unlikely to suffice and the researcher will probably be interested in the connection between that variable and each of a number of other variables, i.e. *bivariate analysis*. The examination of connections among variables can take either of two forms. A researcher who has conducted an experiment may be interested in the extent to which experimental and control groups differ in some respect. The researcher might for example be interested in examining whether watching violent films increases aggressiveness. The experimental group (which watches the violent films) and the control group (which does not) can then be compared to see how far they differ . . . The researcher may be interested in relationships between variables – are two variables connected with each other so that they tend to vary together? Hirschi (1969: 121), for example, presents a table which shows how liking school and self-reported delinquent acts are interconnected. He found that whereas only 9 per cent of children who say they like school have committed two or more delinquent acts, 49 per cent of those who say they dislike school have committed as many delinquent acts . . . Very often the researcher will be interested in exploring connections among more than two variables, i.e. *multivariate analysis* . . . The distinction between studying differences and studying relationships is not always clear-cut. We might find that boys are more likely than girls to commit delinquent acts. This finding could be taken to mean that boys and girls differ in terms of propensity to engage in delinquent acts or that there is a relationship between gender and delinquency.

Findings

If the analysis of the data suggests that a hypothesis is confirmed, this result can be fed back into the theory that prompted it. Future researchers can then concern themselves either with seeking to replicate the finding or with other ramifications of the theory. However, the refutation of a hypothesis can be just as important in that it may suggest that the theory is faulty or at the very least in need of revision. Sometimes, the hypothesis may be confirmed in some respects only. Thus, for example, a multivariate analysis may suggest that a relationship between two variables pertains only to some members of a sample, but not others (for example, women but not men, or younger but not older people). Such a finding will require a reformulation of the theory. Not all findings will necessarily relate directly to a hypothesis. With a social survey, for example, the researcher may collect data on topics whose relevance only becomes evident at a later juncture.

As suggested above, the sequence depicted in Figure [2.1] constitutes a model of the research process, which may not always be reproduced in reality. None the less, it does serve to pin-point the importance to the process of quantitative research of developing measures of concepts and the thorough analysis of subsequent data. One point that was not mentioned in the discussion is the *form* that the hypotheses and findings tend to assume. One of the main aims of much quantitative research in the social sciences is the demonstration of *causality* – that one variable has an impact upon another. The terms *independent variable* and *dependent variable* are often employed in this context. The former denotes a variable that has an impact upon the dependent variable. The latter, in other words, is deemed to be an effect of the independent variable. This causal imagery is widespread in the social sciences and a major role of multivariate analysis is the elucidation of such causal relationships (Bryman, 1988a). The ease with which a researcher can establish cause-and-effect relationships is strongly affected by the nature of the research design . . .

References

Bridgman, P.W. (1927) *The Logic of Modern Physics*. London: Macmillan.

Bryman, A. (1986) *Leadership and Organizations*. London: Routledge.

Bryman, A. (1988a) *Quantity and Quality in Social Research*. London: Unwin Hyman.

Bryman, A. (1988b) 'Introduction: "inside" accounts and social research in organizations', in A. Bryman (ed.) *Doing Research in Organizations*. London: Routledge.

Durkheim, E. (1952) *Suicide: A Study in Sociology*. London: Routledge & Kegan Paul. First published 1898.

Hirschi, T. (1969) *Causes of Delinquency*. Berkeley, CA: University of California Press.

Huff, D. (1973) *How to Lie with Statistics*. Harmondsworth: Penguin.

Locke, E.A. and Schweiger, D.M. (1979) 'Participation in decision-making: one more look', in B.M. Shaw (ed.) *Research in Organizational Behavior*, Vol. 1. Greenwich, CT: JAI Press.

Merton, R.K. (1967) *On Theoretical Sociology*. New York: Free Press.

Source: Bryman and Cramer, 1990: 1–7

Solution to Chapter 2 SAQ

Theory

1   Theories of a fairly low level of generality: between general abstract theories such as functionalism, and specific empirical assertions.

2   Examples I thought of include: Durkheim on suicide; Eysenck on IQ; Barker on new religious movements; Goldthorpe and Lockwood on affluent workers.

Hypothesis

3   Hypotheses tend to be constructed from one facet, one specific aspect, of a theory.

4   An advantage of hypotheses is that they force researchers to think systematically about an aspect of their research. A disadvantage of hypotheses is that they may divert attention from other interesting aspects of the data a researcher collects.

Operationalisation of concepts

5   Physics.

6   Hirschi operationalised this concept by asking children if they liked school. If children liked school they were likely to be committed to the values of school life and therefore society at large.

Selection of respondents or cases

7   Hirschi used 'randomly' selected schoolchildren from one area. Random
    sampling is designed to ensure a representative sample and therefore
    generalisable results.

Setting up a research design

8   Surveys and experiments.
9   In experiments the researcher can control aspects of the situation under
    study; in surveys this is often not the case. Experiments tend to focus upon
    observations of behaviour whilst surveys tend to question subjects directly.
10 Survey research.

Analysing data

11 Univariate, bivariate, multivariate.
12 An experimental group consists of those subjects undergoing some form of
    manipulation (e.g. watching a video). A control group consists of those
    subjects who do not undergo some form of manipulation (e.g. don't watch a
    video!).

Findings

13 Results can support or refute an hypothesis. If an hypothesis is supported this
    lends support to the theory. If an hypothesis is refuted this casts doubt on
    aspects of the theory.

3 Survey Research

Introduction

Nearly all of us will have come across surveys in our everyday life. Consumer surveys and political polls are two very common forms of survey we might have participated in or have seen the results of. In fact survey methods are actively used by nearly all major commercial, government and private organisations the world over. Quantitative methods, especially survey work, are one of the major ways in which these organisations collect the information upon which policy decisions are made. The classic example of such research is the UK National Census, which is collected every ten years and provides much of the data upon which the government makes predictions about the UK population. Such predictions inform decisions on, for example, the allocation of public funds to health care and pensions.

There are three important aspects to the overall design of survey research:

1 measurement
2 sampling
3 questionnaire design and administration.

These three elements are themselves tied to the operationalisation, selection and design stages of the overall process. Though Figure 2.1 (see p. 7) implies this is an essentially linear process, it is often the case that decisions about each stage are interdependent. This will become clearer as you work through the following material.

Measurement

The designing of measures is tightly bound up with the operationalisation of concepts. In many cases social science theories work with quite abstract concepts. Even with everyday concepts such as 'health' or 'work' any attempt to measure runs up against the fact that everyday language use and concepts are quite 'fuzzy'. In operationalising concepts social researchers attempt to make clear the precise aspects of society or social behaviour that relates to their hypothesis and their theory. We will look at an example of a commonly used measure that relates work and work satisfaction later in the chapter but first you will need to complete SAQ 3.1. Smith (1998) discusses the issues of measurement and implications for social research of the 'fuzziness' of concepts and of language (see Smith, 1998: Chapters 4, 6 and 7).

SAQ 3.1

Try to be as precise as possible, but don't spend too long on this SAQ.

Write down the titles of five types of work. Next put these in a ranked order according to a criterion of your choice (e.g. best/most first, worst/least last). Looking at your ranked list, write down in one or two sentences what criteria you used to define 'work'. Then, write down in one or two sentences what criterion you used to rank the five types of work.

There are of course hundreds of different answers to SAQ 3.1. In doing this task you have started to address the issues around the operationalisation of concepts. When constructing any kind of measure, either questionnaire or observation based, you need carefully to take apart the key elements of each concept and focus upon those elements that relate to the research question. You then have to consider how you might implement these either as questions or as types of behaviour you will need to observe. In the case of work, a concept we use in everyday life, we can see that operationalising the concept in ways that can be measured is not straightforward. The next section will give you a clearer idea of how you begin to go about constructing measures.

Measuring Work

The following example of work satisfaction is used by a wide range of social researchers but especially those working in the field of occupational, or work, psychology. To put a framework around this example we might be conducting research on the relationship between type of work and how satisfied people are with their work. A specific hypothesis might be: 'The higher status your job is the more satisfied you will be with the job.' We therefore need to operationalise job status and job satisfaction. You had a go at thinking about ranking jobs, possibly by status, in SAQ 3.1. How might we go about operationalising job satisfaction? There are many things we might equate with job satisfaction, for example good wages and a nice boss. But how do we quantify such things? We could ask people how much they earn. We could see if their manager has been on relevant training courses and also find out how many staff stay in their department, since these could both be used as measures of 'being a good boss'. To do this we would need to know a lot about the job, the worker and the manager in order to ask the right questions, and then *we* would be deciding if the job was satisfying.

A better way would be to start by thinking about the concept of satisfaction. This term is hard to define and relative – a job which one person finds satisfying may not be so for another person. In fact, job satisfaction is both a subjective and a relative concept. We therefore need to operationalise the concept of job satisfaction so that our measure deals with both the subjective nature of satisfaction and the different types of work environment that exist. This is quite a tall order.

Actually, there are many measures of work satisfaction used by occupational psychologists. The example presented here, developed by Warr, Cook and Wall in 1979, is intended to measure overall job satisfaction. It is important to note that this measure was designed to be short (i.e. does not need a lot of data from each participant) and to be easily completed (i.e. does not require lots of time and effort on the part of the participant). These criteria were set because the measure was designed to be applied in predominantly blue-collar, manual work environments. The measure consists of the following instruction and fifteen items:

- The following statements describe features of your job. Please indicate the answer which best describes how satisfied you are with the feature.

1   The physical working conditions.
2   The freedom to choose your own method of working.
3   Your fellow team-members.
4   The recognition you get for good work.
5   Your immediate boss.
6   The amount of responsibility you are given.
7   Your rate of pay.
8   The opportunity to use your ability.
9   Relationships between management and workers in the organisation.
10   Your chance of promotion or progression within the organisation.
11   The way your department is managed.
12   The attention paid to suggestions you make.
13   Your hours of work.
14   The amount of variety in your job.
15   Your job security.

For all the features the respondents reply on the following seven-point scale, with least satisfaction scoring 1 and greatest satisfaction scoring 7:

1   I'm extremely dissatisfied.
2   I'm very dissatisfied
3   I'm moderately dissatisfied.
4   I'm not sure.
5   I'm moderately satisfied.
6   I'm very satisfied.
7   I'm extremely satisfied.

The measure is then scored by simply adding up the scores for each question, giving a range from 15 – extremely dissatisfied with all aspects of work – through to 105 – extremely satisfied with all aspects of work. The measure is also split into two 'sub-scales' that are intended to measure 'extrinsic' features, things outside of the person which affect job satisfaction, and 'intrinsic' features, features tied to the person themselves. The 'extrinsic' features are numbers 1, 3, 5, 7, 9, 11, 13 and 15 and the 'intrinsic' features are 2, 4, 6, 8, 10, 12 and 14.

Let's briefly look at this measure. It is a measure of people's perceived personal satisfaction with their job. For each of the fifteen job features it asks respondents to provide answers that are essentially 'subjective' personal statements about their own satisfaction. None of the questions ask for 'objective' observable facts such as actual wage levels, hours worked, specific measured physical work conditions, etc. The measure is not concerned with the specific type of work, with the place of work, the grade of workers, the social status of the work, the age, sex, ethnicity of the workers and so forth. It is specifically focused upon the self-reported subjective experience of work satisfaction.

SAQ 3.2

Look over the measure above and write down a few short points which answer the following questions.

1 How does the choice of items allow the measure to work for any position in a work hierarchy?
2 How does the measure address general rather than specific aspects of the work environment?
3 Can you note any ways in which the measure reflects the context (blue-collar, manual work) in which it was intended to be used?

There is, of course, much more to the building of measures than simply selecting some good questions. The questions in the measure discussed above were developed over time. The actual use of the measure allowed the effectiveness of items to be tested statistically and such statistical testing points out which questions are most informative. The measures were also statistically compared to other existing and related measures to ensure that they were giving reasonably accurate and consistent results.

The next task in testing the hypothesis that the higher the job status, the more satisfied you will be with the job, is to construct or find a relevant measure of job status along the lines begun in SAQ 3.2. With the two measures – of job status and job satisfaction – we could then construct a questionnaire and begin the process of selecting relevant cases. The process of selecting cases, termed sampling, is dealt with on pp. 25–31.

Measures and Positivism

Before moving on, let's consider the measure of job satisfaction in the light of some of the requirements of positivism. This measure clearly transgresses two of the assumptions of positivism:

- phenomenalism – that data must be from direct experience
- nominalism – that words have fixed meanings

First, it is a measure of something that cannot be directly experienced – we can't directly experience another's 'satisfaction' with their work. Knowledge about 'satisfaction' is therefore metaphysical – not part of the experienced physical world. For a fully paid-up positivist this knowledge should therefore be rejected as bad scientific knowledge as it fails the assumption of phenomenalism. Second, the measure also assumes that levels of 'satisfaction' are relative to the person and context; in other words 'satisfaction' means different things to different people at different times. The term 'satisfaction' is not, therefore, a fixed constant, which is the basis of the assumption of nominalism. Again the adherent to positivism would find this measure lacking 'validity'.

Having said this, the measure does follow the spirit if not the exact letter of these assumptions. It assumes that 'satisfaction', though different in different contexts, is reasonably understood in its general meaning by all participants. The building of the measure itself implies that satisfaction in work is something that can be measured and therefore observed in some way. Yet, one could also argue that the development of the measure itself reflects a set of values about the nature of blue-collar work. Such a claim would question the extent to which the researchers' values influences their means of collecting facts.

Sampling

Once your concepts have been operationalised you need to consider who or what you need to study. The selection of cases or respondents is called sampling. Sampling is one of the key ways in which survey researchers attempt to control the various factors that might influence their research. There is a vast range of methods for conducting sampling and you will be introduced to a number of these. There are two combined purposes of sampling. First, it is very unlikely that you could question or observe all the possible cases which relate to your research question. Second, and given the first condition, sampling is used to ensure that the results you gain are representative of the set of cases you have chosen to study. Like a medical practitioner taking a blood sample as a small but representative and informative selection from the whole, so social researchers can select a set of cases that are representative and informative of a larger group. There will be times where it is possible to question or observe all the possible cases, but this is more often true in smaller scale ethnographic research, which is dealt with in Part III.

Whom you choose to study and how you sample them is tightly bound up with your theory and your hypothesis. Put crudely, there is no point asking unemployed people about their satisfaction with their current job! You therefore need to think about a few basic issues before you design a sample. First, you need to consider which people, groups, organisations, etc. your theory and hypothesis relate to. Second, you need to consider to which cases you can actually gain practical access. Third, you must now choose a method of sampling that will produce the most representative sample. These three stages are termed: the general universe, the working universe and the sample itself (see Sjoberg and Nett, 1968). The overall process is shown in Figure 3.1.

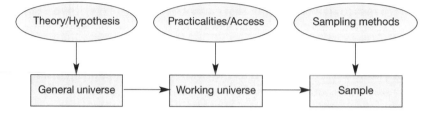

Figure 3.1 *Theory, practicality and sampling*

The theory of sampling is based upon the use of set theory, which you may have met in previous studies, especially in mathematics. The general universe is a set of cases defined by your theory and hypothesis. The working universe is a set of cases defined by your theory and hypothesis and the practicalities of accessing the cases. The sample is a set of cases selected by a chosen method from the working universe.

In the work satisfaction example on p. 22 our theory and hypothesis asserted that the social status of the work and workers' satisfaction with their jobs are interlinked in some way. The general universe is therefore derived from this theory. General universes are themselves only ever theoretical constructs; in this case the general universe is the class of all workers in all jobs. It is highly unlikely that we can question all workers in all jobs. If we were conducting the research in the UK we would have access to UK workers only, and we would be very unlikely to have access to all UK workers. In truth, we are likely to be able to get access to workers in only a limited range of workplaces. For argument's sake, let's assume we have free rein to select workers from two towns, Bolton in Lancashire and Guildford in Surrey. Our working universe is then all workers in Bolton and Guildford. In order to create the actual sample of workers we then need to decide on a specific sampling method.

Sampling can be viewed as a selection from a wider population. The term 'population' can refer to a population in the everyday sense, for example the population of the UK. In research into people's voting habits, the population you would be sampling from would be all people in the UK. But the term 'population' has a specific meaning in relation to sampling. In our example the population that we can actually sample from is defined by our working universe – all workers in Bolton and Guildford. Knowing important features of the population – how many cases there are, how they are distributed according to various criteria and so forth – allows researchers to use statistics to both design and check the reliability of their samples. The statistics involved in this process are beyond the scope of this book, though the basic issues will be raised in Chapter 5 where you will work through three statistical analyses.

There are two broad categories of sampling method: purposive and probability. In your reading of Bryman and Cramer (Reading A) you came across the idea of random sampling. Random sampling is the archetypal form of probability sampling. There are a large number of different specific methods of sampling within each of these two categories. Many of these were designed to get round the practical problems of gaining access to cases in real world research. Some of these methods are described in Tables 3.1 and 3.2.

Purposive Sampling

Purposive samples are those samples where the probability of a case being selected is 0%, 100%, or an unknown. An example of a purposive sample would be all workers in a specific factory. In this case, each worker in the factory has a chance of 100% of being picked, while workers in another factory have 0% chance. An alternative example of purposive sampling would be to wander round some of the factories and pick some workers on a whim. Every worker has some chance of being picked, but the probability is unknown. Because we have no way of quantifying the sampling process, this is *not* a random sample. Table 3.1 provides four examples of purposive sampling.

Table 3.1 *Purposive sampling methods*

Method	Definition	Example
Homogeneous sample	A narrow range based upon one factor	Only and all workers in textile companies in the two towns
Structural sample	A set of related categories	Example cases from each management position in a set of factories
Heterogeneous sample	Based on a broad range of categories	Example cases from all types of jobs in both towns
Quota sample	Representatively structured version of a heterogeneous sample	Example cases from all types of jobs in both towns; numbers of cases from each type of job are in proportion to the total number of people in each type of job

Probability Sampling

Probability samples are those where the cases have a known probability between 0% and 100% of being selected. In these samples all and only the selected cases are used. An example of a probability sample would be to select randomly a quarter of the workers from all factories in, say, Bolton and Guildford. This could be done by randomly selecting a worker from the first four on the factories' staff lists (e.g. by rolling a die) and taking every fourth worker thereafter. Every worker has a

25% chance of being chosen. The researcher can use the selected cases only. If any are unavailable (e.g. the worker is on holiday), the case is marked down as being 'missing data'. A set of probability sampling methods is presented in Table 3.2.

Table 3.2 *Probability sampling methods*

Method	Definition	Example
Simple random	All cases have an equal probability of being selected	A probability of being selected is set – say 10%. Each case is given a number; for example, if you had 100 cases then each case would be allocated a number from 1 to 100. A computer would then generate 10 random numbers between 1 and 100; these will be the cases for the sample. You can also use specially designed lists of random numbers
Systematic sample	Every *n*th case is selected, starting with a specific case	Every 4th worker in all factories starting with the 3rd worker in the first factory
Stratified/ structured random	As in the simple random method, but the population is subdivided according to a set of categories; cases are proportionally selected at random from the subdivisions	The population split between manual and non-manual workers; the proportion of manual to non-manual workers is kept the same after the random sampling
Cluster sample	Cases chosen from randomly selected 'areas' related to some variable	Workers are randomly selected by postcode on the assumption that place of residence relates to average levels of income

In the case of our work satisfaction study we could employ any of these methods. Many of the criteria for selecting a sampling method are tied to decisions about both the likelihood of bias in the sample and keeping the method as simple as possible. Bias occurs when the sampling method results in an unrepresentative sample. In most cases it is not possible to eliminate bias completely but one can put guards against it in place.

The rest of this section consists of two SAQ tasks. You need to work through both of these as they give you the opportunity to work with the idea of sampling and consider the role of bias. SAQ 3.3 is a 'thought experiment' about sampling methods; SAQ 3.4 considers the 1992 UK general election and the reasons why the opinion polls were so wrong in their predictions of the final result.

SAQ 3.3

Read the following story and then by looking over the examples of sampling methods in Tables 3.1 and 3.2 try to answer the questions.

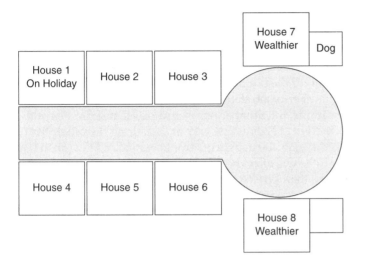

Figure 3.2 *Houses to be sampled*

An interviewer was asked to conduct a questionnaire survey of workers' housing in Bolton. It was decided that she should survey 50% of the houses. Happy with her task she set off down the street shown in Figure 3.2 on a nice sunny day. She first tried house 1 but found no one in because they were on holiday. Moving on to house 2, as this was the closest to house 1, she found people at home and was able to conduct an interview. Leaving house 2 she crossed the road to buy an ice-cream from a van parked outside house 5. After eating the ice-cream she tried houses 5 and 6 and in both cases was able to conduct interviews. She next tried house 7, as she thought she'd better try a house on the other side of the street to 'balance things up'. house 7 was much bigger and had a large dog in the garden. Seeing the dog, she decided to go for house 3 instead, where she successfully conducted an interview. The interviewer now had a sample of four out of eight houses, 50%, and so moved on to the next street.

Now consider:

1 Is this is a 'representative' sample?
2 What factors affected the selection of households?
3 Who was actually controlling the sampling process?
4 Which of the sampling methods in Tables 3.1 and 3.2 might have improved the sampling procedure? How?

SAQ 3.3 makes clear that controlling sampling is essential if the final results are to be at all representative. Choosing the best sampling method provides the social researcher with a better understanding of the population from which they sampled. The more controlled and accurate the sampling method the more representative and reliable the results should be.

There is, of course, more to the overall process than the selection of the best available method. You may have noticed that many reports of surveys quote a margin of error. For example, an opinion poll might give a margin of error of 'plus or minus 3%'. This margin of error tells us how reliable the results are. If one party is found to be supported by 30% of the electorate sampled 'plus or minus 3%', the pollsters are actually saying that the result for the population as a whole is somewhere between 27% and 33%. These margins of error are statistically calculated in a number of ways that relate the size of the sample, the number of cases sampled and the size of the population as a whole. A margin of error is one way of measuring the **reliability** of a sample. As the sample gets bigger, the margin of error gets smaller. How small you need your margin of error to be will affect how large the sample needs to be. To get very low margins of error, less than 1 or 2%, often requires a far greater sample of the population than it is practical to obtain. In the case of the UK electorate, a well designed sample of between 1,000 and 2,000 people should give a margin of error of between 2 and 4%, which is accurate enough for most pollsters.

In SAQ 3.4 you will address this issue of reliability and representativeness by looking at the real case of the 1992 UK general election. In this election the opinion polls were wrong by more than their margin of error, which caused the companies that conducted the survey research to check their sampling methods.

SAQ 3.4

Turn to Reading B, 'Lessons from the electorate: what the 1992 British general election taught British pollsters about the conduct of opinion polls'. While you are reading this extract make notes on these questions:

1 What types of sampling method are mentioned?
2 What numbers of respondents are seen as being enough for a representative sample of the UK population?
3 What causes of the sampling error, the bias, are discussed?
4 What remedies are suggested?

You should now have a basic grasp of samples and sampling methods. After deciding upon your measures and your samples, the next stage is to design your survey questionnaire. In many respects the development of your measures and the factors around which you have structured your sample will form the basis of your questionnaire. Before moving on, however, we will look at sampling from the point of view of positivism.

Sampling and Positivism

Sampling is one of the key ways in which survey research attempts to control for elements of the system under study. In fact sampling falls under the category of statistical closure. As we can see from SAQ 3.3 and SAQ 3.4, sampling methods are far from perfect, and the extent to which they provide a level of closure comparable to that in natural sciences, especially a science such as physics, has to be questioned. From the positivist's perspective this implies that social research that makes use of sampling falls short of the assumption of naturalism – in other words the methods are not the same as (as good as) those in the 'natural sciences'. There can be considerable debate over this claim, especially given that throughout the natural sciences, even in physics, arguments are often based upon very small samples collected using the same sampling theory as social science. We could reverse this criticism and argue that it is positivism's assumption of naturalism – that all scientific methods be the same as in a science such as physics – that is at fault. One might argue that sampling in social research follows the spirit of naturalism, but we cannot assume that methods in the natural sciences are always applicable in social science.

Dealing with the practical issue of selecting cases to study in a reasonably representative manner leads directly to a questioning of the assumptions of positivism as a description of the research process in both natural science and social science. As nearly all branches of social and natural science make use of statistical arguments based on results from samples of larger populations, you might wish to question the models of science and of closure that positivism is based upon. Both natural science and social science have developed a great deal since the early 1900s when positivism reflected many people's perceptions of the scientific process, as it existed at that time.

Questionnaire Design and Administration

There are many ways in which you can design questions to be used in a survey. The choice of topics and content will come from the theory, hypothesis, measures and sample design. The phrasing of the questions and overall structure of the questionnaire will depend upon the means of administering it and the means by which the data will be analysed. There are two main ways of administering a questionnaire: interactively using either a face-to-face or a telephone interviewer; or self-completion by the participants themselves.

Questionnaire Design Contexts

In some respects we have already been considering questionnaire design. SAQ 3.1 and SAQ 3.2 on measuring work satisfaction pointed to the main issues. These include:

- the concepts to be measured/data to be collected;
- the context in which the research is to take place;
- the knowledge and skills of the respondents;
- the time and resources available to both the interviewer and respondent.

SAQ 3.5

Turn to Reading C, 'Studying sexual lifestyles', which is an extract from the introduction to a report on a large national survey. The topic of the survey, sexual behaviour, was not the easiest on which to develop a questionnaire. The goal of the research was to collect reliable data on this issue so as to inform health practitioners and health promotion campaigns, especially in relationship to diseases such as AIDS.

As you read this extract make notes on the following:

1   What were the main policy aims of the research?
2   What was the general theory informing the research?
3   What six things did the researchers specifically want to measure?
4   Why did the researchers decide on a face-to-face interview rather than a postal or telephone-based survey?
5   How did the researchers test their questionnaire before starting the full survey?
6   How did the researchers allow the respondents privacy in answering more sensitive questions?
7   Why did the researchers choose to use 'standard neutral terms' rather than 'vernacular' terms in the questionnaire?

SAQ 3.5 demonstrates how difficult it can be to design a good questionnaire. Sexual behaviour is a very sensitive subject, requiring considerable care and thought. Though most areas of social research may not be as personally sensitive, you must keep in mind many of the same issues. These include:

- *How reliable will the method of administration – face-to-face, telephone, postal, etc. – be?* This question can be answered only by considering both the types of question being asked and the type of population being surveyed. A short questionnaire to find out purchasing preferences could easily be conducted by post. An in-depth interview looking at teachers' perceptions of school management systems might require a lengthy face-to-face interaction.
- *Should the questionnaire be completed by the interviewer or the respondent?* The advantages and disadvantages of these two are made clear in Reading C. An interviewer-completed questionnaire in a telephone or face-to-face context gives the opportunity to offer clarification of the questions and to collect larger amounts and more complex data. It can also ensure that the correct procedure is followed and that the questionnaire for each sampled case is completed. This is a costly option in terms of time and resources, and it also runs the risk of introducing bias due to the interactions of the interviewer and the interviewee (the problem of 'reactivity'). Self-completion provides privacy for the respondent and cuts down the costs of the survey process. It

also removes any influence that an interviewer might have, but response rates to self-completion questionnaires can be poor.

- *What terminology will be used?* Though this issue is very clearly highlighted by the sexual behaviour survey, it applies to all survey research. In the case of the work satisfaction measure (pp. 22–24), terms such as 'work', 'rates of pay', 'boss' were used as these were deemed more relevant to the target respondents than terms such as 'employment', 'salary', 'line manager'.

Designing Questions

We now need to consider designing actual questions. There are essentially two types of survey questions: open and closed. Open questions give the respondent free range to answer. In a face-to-face interview the researcher has to record the answer in some way, either by using audio or video tape or by taking notes. We will look at open-ended questions and their analysis in our discussion of qualitative data analysis in Part III. Closed questions are more commonly used in quantitative survey research. They provide the respondent with a limited number of options from which to choose an answer. The work satisfaction measure (p. 23) is a good example of the use of closed questions.

In designing a closed question you need to keep a number of issues in mind. These include (adapted from Cannel and Kahn, 1968):

- *survey objectives*: put crudely, questions should be relevant to the survey objectives. There is often a desire to add questions 'just in case they are relevant'. Too many 'off topic' questions can make the whole questionnaire hard to administer and serve no great purpose. Look at your theory and hypothesis and keep to questions which directly help to explore those issues.
- *amount of information held by the respondent*: think through how much information the respondent is likely to be able to draw upon. For example, doctors' knowledge of medical risks is likely to be deeper and more complex than that of a lay person.
- *likely structure of the respondents' ideas/concepts*: how complex is your respondent's knowledge likely to be? Doctors may be able to make fine distinctions between types of health risk, whereas lay people may be able to state only if they know something is a risk or not.
- *respondents' motivation*: how much time and effort respondents are likely to put into their responses will affect how you set up the questions. If respondents will have little time available you may need to keep questions short and simple to interpret.
- *prior knowledge of the population under study*: all the previous points imply the need for as good a knowledge of the respondents as you can acquire.

Examples of Closed Questions

The following are some of the more common examples of the many different types of closed questions. The actual questions used in most questionnaires will be variations, even combinations, of these examples.

Direct Questions   These are questions that often have specific numerical answers, such as 'How old are you?' or 'How tall are you?' They can also be simple 'yes/no/don't know' questions such as 'Do you like apples?' Though these questions seem straightforward, you still need to take care with them. In the case of numerical answers respondents may have a good idea, but be able to provide a range only (e.g. 'about 1.5 to 1.6 metres'). In many cases they may not know, so you may need to have a 'don't know' option.

Two-way Questions   These can be simple two-category questions (e.g. yes/no, male/female), but in other cases the middle ground is also presented (e.g. 'Things should: change a lot/change a little/remain the same'). Such questions should be short (less than about 20 words) and direct (e.g. 'Should the government raise taxes?'). Avoid additions to the question (e.g. '. . . or not') as these can cause confusion and lead to a stress on one option over another. If you need to give additional information do so before the question, make sure the information is balanced across both options, and then keep the actual question short and direct. In most cases other than very fixed category questions (e.g. male/female) you should provide a 'don't know' option. If there is the possibility of a middle ground, then provide this as an option. It is essential that the categories be mutually exclusive (e.g. the categories 'employee' and 'manager' are not exclusive as managers are in most cases also employees, whereas 'manual workers' and 'non-manual workers' are exclusive categories) (Smith, 1975: 174–5).

Multiple-choice Questions   These are an extension of the two-way questions. They often begin with a general statement, for example 'The government should raise taxes . . .', followed by a set of statements/questions with mutually exclusive category answers. In this example the questions might be: 'to increase funding to education', 'to increase spending on the military', 'to increase funding in the health service', 'to increase MPs' wages', etc. The options in each case could be 'yes/no/don't know'.

Scaled Questions   These are mostly used as part of designed measures such as the work satisfaction scale. Table 3.3 is an example of a standard form of scale known as a 'Likert scale'. A set of statements are made about an issue or object. In each case you are given certain options, with possible scores allocated as indicated in the table.

Table 3.3 *Likert scale scores*

Answer	strongly agree	agree	uncertain	disagree	strongly disagree
Score	+2	+1	0	−1	−2
Score	+5	+4	+3	+2	+1

The number of items can range from 4 to 7 and the scoring will depend upon the design of the measure. Table 3.3 shows two possible scoring systems.

SAQ 3.6

Turn to Reading D, 'Studying sexual lifestyles: long questionnaire', look at the examples of survey questions, and answer the following:

1 Into which of the categories described above do the questions fall?
2 In which of the questions must the interviewer interpret the answers?
3 Now answer the questions for yourself. Once you have done this make notes on the way you interpreted the questions. Did you already have opinions on these issues or did you form an opinion while answering the question? What limitations can you see with closed questions such as these?

We have now explored the three main areas of survey research – measurement, sampling and questionnaire design – that lead up to the conducting of the survey. The interview process itself raises a wide range of issues, but we will leave these until the discussion of qualitative data collection in Part III. To conclude this discussion of survey methods we need to consider the relationship between the design of questionnaires and positivist arguments.

Questionnaires and Positivism

Most of the issues raised in SAQ 3.5 and the example questions in SAQ 3.6 focus on personal opinions and subjective experiences. We could argue, therefore, that survey work breaks the assumptions of nominalism and phenomenalism: nominalism because we have to deal with the different meanings that respondents will attribute to the words, ideas and terms we use in our questions; phenomenalism because questionnaires often ask questions about beliefs, feelings, attitudes and personal values which are not directly experienced phenomena. If we look back at SAQ 3.5 it is quite clear that one of the main problems facing the researchers was the variation in terms, from the vernacular to the medical, as well as the values people place on these terms. Sexual behaviour is one of the most sensitive and private aspects of people's lives, and nearly all of the issues are therefore tied to personal and cultural values. It is a highly value-laden domain. Rather than being able to reject such values as 'non-scientific' or as 'metaphysical' in some way, the researchers had to deal actively with and attempt to measure these values.

One important lesson to be drawn from this discussion is about the relationship of positivism, as a statement about the nature of science, to social science research, as actually conducted. Because the focus of social research is often upon people's values, it may not be possible or even desirable to adhere to positivist ideas. At the same time, the general approach embodied in survey work was directly inspired by attempts to mirror natural science methods, as described by positivist philosophy. The details of the research method may fail positivism's tests, but the overall programme of survey research is clearly influenced by the general approach associated with positivism. In many respects it is this tension that provides surveys with their usefulness and explanatory power. By combining the goals of positivist ideas with the practical need to deal with actual social practices and values, surveys can provide broad 'social scientific' pictures of the group surveyed.

Further Reading

Fink, A. (2003) *The Survey Kit*, 2nd edition. London: Sage.
Punch, K.F. (2003) *Survey Research: The Basics*. London: Sage.
Sapsford, R. (1999) *Survey Research*. London: Sage.
Thomas, S.J. (1999) *Designing Surveys That Work: A Step-by-Step Guide*. London: Sage.

Reading B: Lessons from the Electorate: What the 1992 British General Election taught British Pollsters about the Conduct of Opinion Polls

Robert M. Worcester

The British have a long history of election polling, a system of national print and broadcast media and an interested and literate audience in the British public. The record of the British polls is a good one, well within the often quoted 'margin of plus or minus three per cent' sampling tolerance range. The most recent British General Election was, however, an exception, when 'the polls got it wrong'.[1] Critics of the polls rushed into print after the April 1992 election to put forward a multiplicity of hypotheses on what went wrong, some fanciful, others more thoughtful. The Market Research Society of Great Britain established an inquiry of professional market researchers, academic psephologists and pollsters to take time to look into all the hypotheses and document why the polls failed to live up to expectations, and in due course report, on the basis of the evidence, on what had gone wrong and why, and what could be done in the future to improve methodology, and the reporting of public opinion polls in the run up to and during General Elections, to ensure that the errors of 1992 were not repeated. Many of the findings of this review have universal application. Much new methodological understanding was obtained . . .

The Record of the British Polls

What is the record of the British polls over the years? On the whole, rather good, until 1992. In 1983, all six were within sampling tolerance, given sample size, three within plus or minus *one per cent*. In 1987, all six were within plus or minus *one and a half per cent*, on average for the share of each party.

Over the thirteen British General Elections since the war up until now, and over the period of election polling, until now, polls have performed, on average, very well and better than could have been expected from statistical theory relating to pure random sampling. The margin of error on the gap (the difference in share between the leading party and the party in second place) should be approximately double that of share (the percentage of public support for each party), according to sampling theory, and indeed it is, according to the empirical evidence of 51 election forecasts over 42 years. About a quarter of the polls since 1945 have been able to estimate the Labour and Conservative share of the vote to within ± 1 per cent, and over 50 per cent have forecast to within ± 2 per cent.

Of these 51 polls, 29 have overestimated the Tory share of the popular vote and

Table 1 *Accuracy of the final polls, 1945–92*

Year	Mean error gap %	Average error per party %	Number of polls
1945	3.5	1.5	1
1950	3.6	1.2	2
1951	5.3	2.2	3
1955	0.3	0.9	2
1959	1.1	0.7	4
1964	1.2	1.7	4
1966	3.9	1.4	4
1970	6.6	2.2	5
1974 Feb.	2.4	1.6	6
1974 Oct.	4.5	1.4	4
1979	1.7	1.0	4
1983	4.5	1.4	6
1987	3.7	1.4	6
Average	3.3	1.4	51
1992	8.7	2.7	5

Source: *The Opinion Polls and the 1992 General Election.* Market Research Society, 1994

29 overestimated the Labour share; 20 underestimated the Tory share and 19 underestimated the Labour share. No sign of any political bias. On average they have marginally underestimated the Tory lead over Labour, but as polls do not measure postal voters and these are generally agreed to favour the Tories – perhaps by as much as 3:1 – the direction of these averages is not surprising, and in any case, the slight bias has been only about half of one per cent in each direction, or an error in the lead of one per cent.

The 1992 British Polls Got It Wrong

The polls in the 1992 British General Election, however, have a lot to answer for. While the five major pollsters, Gallup, Harris, ICM, MORI and NOP, averaged a 1.3 per cent Labour lead, the final result was a 7.6 per cent lead for the Conservatives. The polls backed the wrong winner, by a wider margin than can be accounted for by sampling error, and were widely criticized for their inability to perform to expectation.

Table 2 *Eve of poll polls, April 1992*

Company	Harris	MORI	NOP	Gallup	ICM	GE
Sample	2,210	1,731	1,746	2,478	2,186	
Fieldwork	4th–7th	7th–8th	7th–8th	7th–8th	8th	9th
	%	%	%	%	%	%
Conservative	38	38	39	38.5	38	42.8
Labour	40	39	42	38	38	35.2
Lib Dem	18	20	17	20	20	18.3
Other	4	3	2	3.5	4	3.7
Con lead	−2	−1	−3	+0.5	0	7.6
Error on lead	9.6	8.6	10.6	7.1	7.6	8.7
						Ave
Error on share	2.55	2.75	3.4	2.25	2.4	2.67
						Ave

Source: The Opinion Polls and the 1992 General Election. Market Research Society, 1994

The Campaign Polls

What were the campaign polls showing? A pretty steady picture, steady across company, and, generally, over time. They certainly were not out of line with the final polls – indeed, on average they found a bigger Labour lead. Whatever problems affected the final polls affected the earlier campaign polls as well. The campaign tracking polls were also broadly in line with the two national panel studies published at the same time, and the results of all these face-to-face polls were matched by the small number of telephone polls which were conducted.

What Went Wrong?

Much space in the papers after the General Election was given over to 'POLLSTERS ADMIT ELECTION MISTAKES' (30 April 1992) and 'THE INVISIBLE VOTERS WHO FOOLED THE POLLSTERS' (1 May 1992) (in *The Independent*), as well as to the various letter writers' expressions of their own views.

Just a day or two after the election, letter writers and critics alike were dismissing any 'late swing lame excuses' from the pollsters. There were a number of pundits' and psephologists' commentaries and readers' letters in *The Times, The Daily Telegraph, The Independent, The Guardian, The Financial Times* and elsewhere following the election, expressing various opinions as to why the opinion polls 'got it wrong' on 9 April. Their suggestions are set out – and, for the most part, easily refuted – below.

All the polling companies have, naturally, carried out their own reviews of the problems and an exhaustive, two-year inquiry by a committee set up by the Market Research Society, which consisted of pollsters, academics and other experienced market researchers not involved in opinion polling, reported in July 1994. Their conclusions and recommendations have a great many lessons for both pollsters and poll readers.[2]

Sample Size

One of the most popular knee-jerk reactions to the polls' failure in 1992 was to blame sample size, but it is manifestly apparent that sample size is not the key to quality of findings. The ICM poll taken in the third week of the campaign, among a sample of 10,460 electors in 330 sampling points and taken over nearly a week including a weekend, was almost identical in its voting intention to the findings of a 'smaller' poll conducted over the same period. Interviewing on 31 March–3 April, ICM recorded 36 per cent for the Conservatives, 39 per cent for Labour and 20 per cent for the Liberal Democrats. At the same time, on 31 March–1 April, NOP interviewed 'only' 1,302 electors in 83 sampling points and found 37 per cent, 39 per cent and 19 per cent.

The fact that the final polls of the campaign, all taken a day or two before polling day, were so consistent – all five had the Tories at 38 per cent ± 1 per cent, Labour at 40 per cent ± 2 per cent, and the Liberal Democrats at 18 per cent ± 2 – suggests that neither sample size nor sampling variation were responsible for the magnitude of the difference between the final polls and the actual result. Despite this, the British public remain unconvinced: a Gallup survey in April 1992 found 63 per cent of British adults saying that it is not possible 'from a survey of 1,000 or 2,000 people . . . to give a reliable picture of British public opinion'. This is an area in which the pollsters' biggest challenge is to educate the British public.

Millions of Expatriate Tory Voters?

Another letter writer claimed government by fraud, reporting that one of the first Acts of the 1987 Conservative Government was to give the postal vote to two million expatriate Britons, but ignores the fact that only 34,454 of these expatriates registered to vote. At an average of 53 voters per constituency, they could have made some difference, but not that much – the registered overseas electorate exceeded the majority in only two seats.

The Mendacious British Public?

Another letter writer spoke up confidently to report that there was 'no eleventh-hour swing to the Conservatives', and reported himself to be in a state of profound depression and dismay; no wonder he is depressed, if he is convinced that the British (against all my experience to the contrary) are 'a nation of liars'. One academic critic even included the comment in his paper's title.[3] Other letter writers also suggested millions of people lied to interviewers. In the case of the three panel studies that were undertaken and which had comparable results both before and after the election, this would involve repeated and consistent lying. In the campaign tracking polls, it would have to assume that respondents lied consistently on a bank of other, non-voting, questions that they answered as well, since there is no evidence of inconsistency between voting and attitudinal questions. The MRS Inquiry found no evidence of widespread lying.

The Random Sampling Myth

The leader in *The Independent* on 30 April raised another point, alleging that 'Random polls have proved more accurate' (than quota polls). This is an enduring myth with the polls' critics, but is in fact erroneous. British election polls conducted by random sampling during past national elections where both methods were used (including the 1975 EEC Referendum) were less, not more, accurate, than those conducted by quota, due to poor compilation of registers and late swing after the bulk of the interviewing was done.

Table 3 *The comparative record of random and quota polls in British elections*

| Election | Average error in lead* (Number of polls in brackets) | |
	Random polls	Quota polls
1970	7.3 (3)	5.4 (2)
Feb. 1974	3.7 (2)	1.7 (4)
Oct. 1974	8.0 (2)	3.5 (4)
1975 (Referendum)	10.0 (1)	3.9 (5)
1979	1.6 (1)	1.7 (4)
Mean error 1970–79	6.3	3.0

* Conservative lead over Labour at General Elections. 'Yes' lead over 'No' in referendum.

Source: MORI analysis

Interviewing in Street

Nor is there any evidence that other variations in the sampling design would have improved matters. Differences in interviewing procedures played no role. Although most of the polls were conducted in the streets, a few were conducted partly or exclusively in homes. Near-identical poll results were obtained.

Table 4 *Comparison of in-street and in-home polls: average party shares*

	Con %	Lab %	Lib Dem %	Other %	Con lead %
In street	38	40	18	5	−2
In street and in home	38	40	18	4	−2
In home	39	40	17	5	−1

Source: *The Opinion Polls and the 1992 General Election.* Market Research Society, 1994

Telephone Polling

Although telephone polling in British elections had some problems in its early days, in 1992 the small number that were published found entirely comparable results to the face-to-face polls.

Table 5 *Comparison of phone calls and face-to-face polls: average party shares*

	Con %	Lab %	Lib Dem %	Other %	Con lead %
Phone polls (7)	38.8	39.5	17.3	4.4	−0.7
Face-to-face polls (47)	38.2	40.0	17.7	4.1	−1.8

Source: *The Opinion Polls and the 1992 General Election*. Market Research Society, 1994.

One-day, Two-day and Longer Polls

There was no difference in results between those polls conducted as 'one-day quickies' and those with fieldwork spread over a longer period.

Table 6 *Comparison of one-day, two-day and longer polls*

	Con %	Lab %	Lib Dem %	Other %	Con lead %
All polls (54)	38	40	18	4	−2
All one-day polls (15)	38	40	17	5	−2
All two-day polls (24)	38	40	18	5	−2
All longer polls (15)	38	40	18	4	−2
Excluding telephone polls (47)					
One-day polls (13)	38	40	17	5	−2
Two-day polls (23)	38	40	18	4	−2
Longer polls (11)	38	40	18	4	−2
Excluding telephone polls and later waves of panel studies (44)					
One-day polls (13)	38	40	17	5	−2
Two-day polls (23)	38	40	18	4	−2
Longer polls (8)	39	40	17	4	−1

Source: *The Opinion Polls and the 1992 General Election*. Market Research Society, 1994

Weekend and Weekday Polls

There was no evidence either that it made any difference whether or not fieldwork periods included a weekend.

Table 7 *Weekend and weekday polls: average party shares*

	Con %	Lab %	Lib Dem %	Other %	Con lead %
All polls (54)	38	40	18	4	−2
With some Saturday or Sunday fieldwork (17)	38	40	18	4	−2
With no Saturday or Sunday fieldwork (37)	38	40	18	4	−2
With some Saturday fieldwork (14)	39	39	18	5	0
With some Sunday fieldwork (10)	39	39	18	4	0

Source: *The Opinion Polls and the 1992 General Election*. Market Research Society, 1994

Selection of Sampling Points

But what about the actual constituencies sampled? If they had happened to be biased to Labour, that might have caused an error. The MRS inquiry compared the results in 1987 and 1992 in each polling company's selection of constituencies with the national result. It found that four of the five companies had selections very slightly biased to Labour in 1992, and also that the same bias had existed in those constituencies in 1987 – it was not simply bad luck in picking constituencies which swung unusually. But the average error was barely 1 per cent on Conservative lead over Labour, and most of the potential effect should have been corrected by the operation of the quota system to ensure a representative social profile. Besides, the company whose selection of constituencies *was* representative fared no better than the others in 'predicting' the final result. Plainly this was not a major cause of the error.

Late Swing

The MRS Inquiry isolated three root causes of the discrepancy between the poll findings and the final result. The first of these was late swing.

Polls are snapshots at a point in time, and that point is when the fieldwork was done, not when the results were published. If after that voters change their minds, the 'don't knows' decide to vote after all, and one party's supporters become so apathetic that they stay at home, the polls will 'get it wrong'.

It has become fashionable in certain quarters to decry the late swing explanation,[4] and even to suggest that there was no movement of opinion throughout the campaign. Late swing was not the only problem (or the exit polls should have been spot on), but no-one at the time doubted that it was happening. Forgotten now are the headlines on election day: 'LATE SURGE BY TORIES CLOSES GAP ON LABOUR IN FINAL HOURS OF CAMPAIGN' was the *Times'* banner; 'TORY HOPES RISE AFTER LATE SURGE' was the headline over the 'splash' in *The Guardian*. In *The Daily Telegraph* it was 'TORIES NARROW GAP', and in *The Financial Times* the banner read 'OPINION POLLS INDICATE LAST-MINUTE SWING FROM LABOUR TO TORIES' while *The Daily Express* trumpeted 'TORY SURGE: POLLS SHOW LATE BOOST FOR MAJOR'.

Labour's peak came on 'Sheffield Wednesday', eight days before polling day, with published leads sufficient to give them an overall majority. But Labour's triumphant 'Sheffield Rally' proved the beginning of the end for Labour and its leader Neil Kinnock. From that point on, the campaign went downhill. The Conservatives spent nearly all of their advertising money in the final three days (at a weight greater, annualized, than the spending of Procter & Gamble or Unilever on soap powder), levelling all their guns at the Liberal Democrats' voters 'letting Labour in'. The testimony of the Liberal Democrats' campaign manager was that this did great damage to their support in the final hours of the campaign. The Tory tabloids did all they could on their front pages, as well as the leader columns, to ensure the Conservatives were returned to power. Right to the end of the election, the 'floating voters' were higher than ever before.

The Clues Were There

In retrospect, it might have been possible to guess that a late swing to the Tories was on the cards. The polls themselves unearthed a number of clues. One clue was the image of the leaders. There is a tradition among political scientists in Great Britain to explain patiently to visiting American academics, psephologists, pollsters, politicians and political journalists that one main difference between British and American elections is that in British elections policies, not people, are the deciding factor. MORI research over the past decade has shown a fairly steady 50 per cent policies/30 per cent leader image/20 per cent party image relationship in determinants of voting decision-making. Yet during the 1992 election one striking finding stood out: throughout the election, from the beginning to the end, John Major led Neil Kinnock by between 9 per cent and 13 per cent as the 'most capable' prime ministerial candidate. With hindsight, I believe that this question and its replies consistently gave a guide as to the outcome; we just were not smart enough to see it clearly enough, although the *Times'* Robin Oakley focused an entire article on this early in the campaign.[5]

Another clue was that when asked 'Which two or three issues will be most important to you in helping you to make up your mind on how to vote?', the NHS, education, and unemployment – all Labour issues – led the field. Yet the one time that a different question was asked, 'How much will you be influenced, if at all, in the way you vote at the General Election by the policies of the political parties on taxation?', no fewer than 39 per cent of the electorate said their vote would be influenced 'a great deal'. No lies, no prevarication from this four in ten of the electorate. They told us plainly: 'a great deal', they said. Did we hear clearly enough?

Another key finding was in the post-election wave of the MORI panel survey for the BBC's *On the Record*, a telephone recall on people interviewed throughout the campaign by On-Line Telephone Surveys, a MORI subsidiary. The panel consisted of 'floating voters', and comprised those who after expressing a voting intention said they might change their minds between the time interviewed and polling day, plus the full category usually described as the 'don't knows', which is the 10 per cent who said they would not vote, the 4 per cent who were 'undecided' and the fewer than 1 per cent who were 'undecided' and the fewer than 1 per cent who refused to say how they intended to vote. In all, the 'floaters' represented some 38 per cent of the base-line survey from which the panellists were recruited. On-Line re-interviewed over a thousand (1,090) of the panel on the Friday and Saturday following the election.

When asked, 'Thinking about the way you voted, which was stronger, your liking the party you voted for or your dislike of the other parties?', a majority, 55 per cent said it was antipathy, with only 37 per cent liking the party they voted for, among the 'floating voters' on the panel. Panellists also voted by more than three to one, 56 per cent to 18 per cent, that the Conservative Party rather than Labour could best handle the economy generally. And by four to one, 48 per cent to 12 per cent, they regarded John Major, rather than Neil Kinnock, as the most capable Prime Minister. If pollsters had taken these factors into account before the election, they would have been less surprised by the result.

Of course, the economy is also vital. During the 'autumn election boon' in 1991, ITN had rung us to find out what the Economic Optimism Index was for September. 'Why?' a colleague asked them. 'Because Central Office [Conservative Party headquarters] says they'll call the election if it goes over 15, as they did in '83 and '87', was the reply. It was checked, and they had. The 1992 election was finally called with the index negative. But it was little noticed, except possibly by Central Office and in an article in *The Times*,[6] that in a MORI survey taken on 16 March, a sharp reversal had taken place in the national mood, and the –2 per cent EOI recorded in February had been replaced by +15 per cent, with 36 per cent expressing optimism and only 21 per cent gloom.

Another clue came late in the campaign, replicating findings of a year and more earlier. When asked if they thought a hung Parliament would be good or bad for Britain, a majority, 56 per cent, said 'bad', and they included an astonishing 44 per cent of Liberal Democrats. It was certainly this group who were worried by the Tories' attack on the Liberal Democrats and the prospect of a hung parliament in which Mr Ashdown held the balance of power. Certainly captains of industry were in no doubt; MORI fieldwork for *The Financial Times* at the beginning of the campaign and certainly at the end proved that. In the first wave of the 'captains' panel, six in ten main board directors of the nation's largest companies said that a hung parliament would be bad for their business; by 6–7 April, when just such an outcome seemed the most likely, three-quarters said it would be bad.

A majority, 52 per cent, of the electorate worried about their belief that the Tories would privatize the National Health Service, including 26 per cent of their own supporters. But at the same time, seven in ten of the public, including nearly half, 47 per cent, of Labour supporters believed that most people would pay more taxes under a Labour Government. Another clue was the degree of volatility in the electorate. One thing that the snapshot polls do not show is the movement of the electorate between parties, which largely cancelled itself out, but which reveals the remarkable changeablility of the electorate's political allegiance. The panel surveys provided this information.

The most instructive analysis should come from the panel study which MORI conducted for *The Sunday Times*. The panel was interviewed face-to-face by MORI four times during the campaign, and then re-interviewed after the election by telephone by FDS, an independent market research firm who were sub-contracted to undertake the recalls (the MORI telephone survey subsidiary, On-Line Telephone Surveys, being fully stretched with recalls on the panel for the BBC). FDS, on MORI's behalf, contacted 934 panellists on Friday 10 April, between 10.00 am and 9.00 pm. This represented a 60 per cent recall of the original panel, not bad for a one-day recall, especially when one bears in mind that some 10 per cent of the original 1,544 panel were unavailable because they were not on the telephone. The data were of course weighted to both the demographic and political profile of the original panel.

The MORI/*Sunday Times* panel recall found that only 63 per cent said they had made up their minds before the election had been called, down nearly 20 per cent from the more usual 80 per cent that was measured in previous elections. And, as noted below, 8 per cent said they had made their mind up only in the last 24 hours, and 22 per cent during the last week of the campaign.

As *The Sunday Times* reported week after week, the amount of movement in the electorate – people who switched from one party to another ('switchers') or in and out of don't know ('churners') – was higher than ever before, and as reported in the final article, some 11.1 million electors changed their minds during the campaign out of the 42.58 million in the electorate. The week before polling day, the panellists indicated their voting intention, at that time as a Labour lead of one point; when re-interviewed after the election, their actual votes indicated a 2.5 per cent swing. (The other national panel, conducted by NOP for *The Independent on Sunday*, found an even bigger swing – 4 per cent over the same period.)

Perhaps more relevant, however, is the proportion of the panel that had already switched allegiance *during the campaign* – 21 per cent even before the final week, far more than ever before.

The figures in Table 8 give clear evidence that in 1992 British voters made up their minds later, and shifted their ground in greater numbers, than have been measured in prior elections. After extensive examination the Market Research Society Inquiry concluded: 'After the final interviews there was a . . . swing to the Tories. It seems likely that this was the cause of a significant part of the final error . . . We estimate that late swing . . . probably accounted for between a fifth and a third of the total error'.[7] On the panel evidence, the proportion may have been even higher, perhaps as much as half.

What does this imply for future elections? It will be dangerous to try to second-guess the electorate and 'correct' the figures to reflect changes of mind before they happen. On the other hand, it is probably possible to construct models of behaviour to allow for those 'don't knows' who vote, and certainly all possible methods need to be used to correct for differential turnout by using certainty of voting questions.

Table 8 *Changes of mind during election campaigns 1979–92*

	'Switchers' % of electorate switching between main parties during campaign	'Churners' % of electorate switching to or from others/don't knows	Total % of electorate changing answers during campaign
1979	5.6	6.9	12.5
1983	7.8	7.1	14.9
1987	8.4	10.1	18.5
1992	9.4	11.6	21.0

Source: MORI/+ panels

The 'Spiral of Silence'

One of the more simplistic letter writers explained that the unreliability of the public opinion surveys (and of the media comment on them) is down to ignoring the 'don't knows'. In fact, there were many reports on the 'don't knows', the 'floating voters' and the 'undecideds', including Robin Oakley's pieces on the 'don't knows' and the 'soft' party supporters. One Oakley article, the 'splash' that day, was headlined 'PARTIES MAKE FINAL PUSH TO CAPTURE FLOATING VOTERS' and stated: 'However, 24 per cent of Liberal Democrat supporters said they might yet change their vote. So did a fifth of Conservative supporters and 16 per cent of Labour backers.'

So the 'don't knows' were not ignored. Nevertheless, those who told MORI they didn't know may have contributed to the problem. Investigation has made it plain that there was some differential refusal, the second principal cause. Traditionally, Conservative supporters are somewhat less likely to reveal their loyalties than Labour supporters. This certainly operated through the reluctance of some of those interviewed to reveal their voting intentions, both by outright refusal and by answering 'don't know'. A similar and probably numerically more significant effect probably operated through a refusal by some to be interviewed at all, although there is no solid evidence to support this – consequently the samples interviewed were tilted towards Labour, and Conservative support was underestimated. This probably arose through the operation of what has been described as 'the spiral of silence'.[8] Conservatives, feeling their party was unfashionable and that they were out numbered, were more reluctant to disclose their loyalties. This effect seems to have persisted in the period since the election.

Techniques need to be developed to try to maximize the number of people who are willing to state their voting intention. Use of information on past voting and other attitudinal questions to correct for any differential refusal that remains is one technique to be explored further.

The use of secret ballots was adopted by one British pollster shortly after the election, although comparisions over the past year or so show this has nil effect, comparing its finding to the average of the others. Other ways must be explored in which refusal to participate in surveys could be reduced: public awareness of the importance of survey research should be enhanced to assist in reducing refusal rates.

Sample Design and Quotas

In theory, differential refusal to participate by Conservatives ought not to have distorted the polls, because if the quota and weighting systems had been operating perfectly this would have compensated, with other, similar voters who were prepared to disclose their opinions being interviewed instead. The third cause that appears to have contributed to the error is inadequacies in the sampling. This arose partly because the quotas set for interviewers and the weights applied after interviewing did not reflect sufficiently accurately the social profile of the electorate at the time of the election; this should be easy to correct, with care, in future elections, using accurate, up-to-date sources for setting quotas and weighting. It also arose partly because the variables used in setting quotas and weights were not correlated closely enough with voting behaviour to ensure that the polls reflected the distribution of political support among the electorate. We need to try to identify other variables more closely related to voting behaviour, to ensure samples are as representative as possible. This is more of a challenge.

One solution being advocated is to weight surveys by declared past vote, as is routine in some other countries. However, we would be very wary of adopting a technique that in all previous elections – probably even including 1992 – would have made predictions worse rather than better. British voters have a strong tradition of failing to recall that they voted for the Liberal Democrats or their predecessors. Consequently polls usually underestimate the number of ex-Liberals in their samples and the distortion that this would cause on weighting by past vote would far outweigh any corrective effects between the two main parties. Although since 1992 the recalled Liberal vote has, unusually, held up fairly well at a realistic level, it would be rash to bank on this continuing to be the case.

A less contentious approach is to expand the number and variety of demographic variables used in quotas and weighting, particularly by the use of economic variables such as car ownership. So long as reliable baseline data are available, such measures can be implemented without much difficulty and may well improve the political representativeness of samples.

Appendix: Code of Practice of the Association of Professional Opinion Polling Organizations

1 Every substantial published report of the poll findings should give:
    (a) the sampling method used and population represented;
    (b) the sample size and geographical coverage;
    (c) the dates of fieldwork;
    (d) the name of the organization carrying out the survey.
2 Where, in reply to the questions on voting intention, there are sharp changes in the number of those who say they would not vote, or who are undecided, these facts should be published.

3   The polls will, on request, make available to a reasonable number of journalists, academics, students, other polling organizations, political parties and others, the following additional information:
   (a) the number and type of sampling areas;
   (b) other details of sample design, such as stratification, clustering and success rates;
   (c) composition of sample;
   (d) the questions used;
   (e) description of the method used to collect the information (e.g. personal interview, postal questionnaire).
4   Where the polling organization retains the copyright of poll findings which have not been published by their newspaper clients, they will continue to make these findings available through other media, after ascertaining that the sponsoring media does not intend to use them within a reasonable time.
5   No poll of national voting intentions of fewer than 1,000 respondents shall be published.
6   Where data from a private poll are leaked to the media, whether by a client or by a third party, the polling firm will clarify/correct any misleading or incorrect impressions.

Notes

1   *The Opinion Polls and the 1992 General Election: A Report to the Market Research Society*, London: Market Research Society, 1994.
2   *The Opinion Polls and the 1992 General Election: A Report to the Market Research Society: Summary*, London: Market Research Society, 1994.
3   Ivor Crewe, 'A nation of liars? The opinion polls in the 1992 election', *Parliamentary Affairs*, 45(4), October 1992. It is curious that the article's conclusion is to repudiate the suggestion of its title. See also Roger Jowell, Barry Hedges, Peter Lynn, Graham Farrant and Anthony Heath, 'The 1992 British election: the failure of the polls', *Public Opinion Quarterly*, 57 (1993), pp. 238–63.
4   Peter Clifford and Anthony Heath, 'The election campaign', in Anthony Heath, Roger Jowell, John Curtice with Bridget Taylor, *Labour's Last Chance?* Aldershot: Dartmouth Press, 1994, pp. 7–24.
5   Robin Oakley, 'Leadership gap still troubles Labour despite lead in polls', *Times*, 18 March 1992.
6   Ivor Crewe, 'One poll victory does not make Kinnock's summer', *Times*, 18 March 1992.
7   *The Opinion Polls and the 1992 General Election: A Report to the Market Research Society*, London: Market Research Society, 1994.
8   Elisabeth Noelle-Neumann, *The Spiral of Silence*, Chicago: University of Chicago Press, 1984.

Source: Worcester, 1995: 539–49, 551–2

Reading C: Studying Sexual Lifestyles

Julia Field, Anne Johnson, Jane Wadsworth and Kaye Wellings

The amount of speculation and discussion of sexual behaviour stands in stark contrast to the lack of reliable empirical evidence. Despite the apparent trend towards greater openness in sexual matters, this remains one of the most underdeveloped fields in the human sciences. Scholars from many disciplines have contributed to the understanding of sexuality and its expression, but their insights have been limited by the difficulty of investigative work in the area. Research has seldom been conducted without controversy, and researchers who have ventured into the area have rarely avoided suspicion and constraint.

As a result, important questions have gone largely unanswered. What proportion of people have homosexual experience, have exclusive relationships, are celibate, have visited prostitutes? When do men and women first become sexually active? What factors influence the range and regularity of sexual practices? How are attitudes to sex and sexuality changing and how are they associated with behaviour? What evidence is there for generational trends in behaviour and what are the social and demographic correlates of variability in sexual lifestyle?

The emergence in the 1980s of a worldwide epidemic of a predominantly sexually acquired infection, human immunodeficiency virus (HIV), sharply focused these gaps in knowledge, and served to demonstrate the need for research into sexual lifestyles. Efforts to mount effective public health education campaigns, to predict the likely extent and pattern of the spread of HIV, and to plan services for those affected were all hampered by the absence of reliable data on sexual behaviour.

Although the HIV epidemic highlighted the dearth of information on sexual lifestyles, the need for robust research has been recognized for some time. The lack of reliable information on the subject has long handicapped those specializing in the fields of sexual and reproductive health, as well as those in the broader disciplines of education and medicine. Reliable quantitative data are essential for understanding fertility patterns, contraceptive use and the epidemiology of sexually transmitted diseases, and are fundamental to informed debate about the timing and content of sex education.

Information is needed not only about current sexual behaviour but also about the dynamics of change and its possible explanations. The forces that fashion human sexual behaviour are as yet imperfectly understood, but factors that influence change over time include technological and demographic changes, population mobility, advances in control of fertility and sexually transmitted diseases (STDs), the emergence of new diseases, changing theories of sexuality, in addition to changes in the moral climate and the law.

Examples of such forces in the recent past are easily instanced. In the past thirty years, reliable contraception has increasingly separated sex from its procreative function and diminished the fear of unwanted pregnancy. Modern medicine has improved control of venereal diseases such as syphilis and gonorrhoea, reducing further the adverse consequences of sexual expression. Public discussion of studies of sexual satisfaction may have increased expectations of sexual performance and pleasure (Masters and Johnson, 1966; Masters and Johnson, 1970). Successive acts of legislative and statutory reform have liberalized aspects of sexual behaviour: the legalization of homosexuality and abortion, for example, and the provision of contraceptive advice and supplies to single women. More recently, with the emerging HIV epidemic and concerns about other sexually acquired conditions resistant to cure, such as genital herpes and invasive cervical cancer, new forces may be affecting sexual behaviour. The influence of these factors on patterns of behaviour has gone largely uncharted . . .

The Rationale for the Survey

Undeniably the emergence of the HIV epidemic provided the impetus, the legitimation and the funding opportunities for this study. Every aspect of the survey, from the theoretical framework and the measurement objectives to the size of the sample and the content of the questionnaire, necessarily reflects the aims of the survey and the uses to which the data are to be put. The study was conceived in the context of the need for information that would help in assessing and preventing the future spread of HIV. Two of the main purposes of the survey were to provide data that would increase understanding of the transmission patterns of HIV and other sexually transmitted infections, and would aid the selection of appropriate and effective health education strategies for epidemic control.

Both these objectives required information on patterns of sexual behaviour in the population. Epidemiological evidence indicated that the virus behaved like many other sexually acquired infections. Once it was introduced into a community, the likelihood of an individual becoming infected in the early stages of the epidemic increased with the number of sexual partners (homosexual or heterosexual) with whom unprotected intercourse had taken place (Johnson, 1988). Spread outside the populations initially affected was likely to depend on the proportion of the population engaging in high-risk activities, the pattern and frequency of partner change in the population and the extent of mixing between different groups (Johnson, 1992; Anderson et al., 1986; Potts et al., 1991). A series of studies aimed at estimating the potential spread of HIV in the UK were commissioned through the Department of Health (Report of a Working Group, 1989 and 1990), but although attempts were made to assess the prevalence of risk behaviours from available data sources, it became evident that too little was known about key behavioural variables that could determine current prevalence or future transmission.

There were, for example, no estimates of the proportion of men who had homosexual partners. It was not known how representative were clinic-based or volunteer samples of homosexual men (Coxon, 1988; McManus and McEvoy, 1987), how homosexuality should be defined, what was the extent of same-gender contact in the population, nor what proportion engaged in practices that were risky for the transmission of HIV (primarily anal intercourse). Similar concerns arose in relation to the heterosexual population. Little was known about the overall pattern of sexual behaviours, in particular the pattern of heterosexual partner change in the population and the frequency and prevalence of different sexual practices.

A large sample size was required in order to represent and characterize these patterns adequately, and to obtain sufficient representation of more unusual kinds of behaviour. Some high-risk practices, such as injecting drug use and homosexual anal intercourse, involve only a small minority of the population. Similarly, a relatively small proportion of the population has very large numbers of sexual partners, but may contribute disproportionately to the spread of STDs (Hethcote and Yorke, 1984).

Reliable data on sexual behaviour were also essential for those concerned with developing an effective policy for prevention. In particular it was necessary to describe the socio-demographic and attitudinal characteristics of those with different sexual lifestyles. Success in limiting further spread of the virus is currently dependent on the ability of educational and other interventions to establish norms of safer sex. Advice on risk reduction must be presented in a form acceptable to sexually active populations. A sound understanding of patterns of human sexuality is a necessary prerequisite for the design of preventive interventions, since it is difficult to focus interventions or to monitor their impact over time in the absence of such data. This survey sought to collect data that could help to define target populations for specific interventions, to determine those risk-reduction messages that are most likely to meet with acceptance, to identify preferred educational agencies, to identify needs for information, and to provide baseline data for monitoring and evaluating the impact of interventions.

To a considerable extent, the public-health implications of the HIV epidemic have dictated the direction of research. But while such concerns have both stimulated and in some sense limited the scope of the survey, every attempt has been made to extend its relevance to other areas of health and human behaviour. An understanding of sexual experience in the population is of importance to many disciplines: to social historians documenting generational changes in sexual behaviour, to anthropologists concerned with cross-cultural comparisons, to educationalists requiring a more realistic understanding of contemporary teenage sexual experience in order to design effective sex education programmes, to demographers concerned with changing patterns of family formation, and to health workers in many fields. As a result, while the need for data for use in the context of the AIDS epidemic remained high on the research agenda, the questionnaire was designed to be sufficiently durable and broad-based for it to be relevant to a range of disciplines concerned with sexuality, sexual health and reproduction.

The desire to provide data of broad interest had to be balanced against concern to maximize response on the key issues of contemporary importance, and to avoid jeopardizing the acceptability of the survey by widening its scope too far. Future historians may wonder at the absence of information on the psychological and pleasurable nature of sexual relationships. The omissions must remain the responsibility of the researchers, but, in mitigation, the acceptability of detailed inquiry into sexual behaviour in the general population was largely unknown when this work began, and the sensitivities of funding bodies spending government money were made clear at a relatively early stage.

Theoretical Framework for the Study

The rationale for the survey has shaped its theoretical perspective as well as its investigative focus. This perspective is centrally and fairly exclusively social and epidemiological. Certainly the aims of the survey would not have been served by the kind of narrowly biological perspective that has characterized much writing on the subject. The belief that the determinants of sexual expression are to be found in instinct has – as Weeks points out – a long provenance, dating from Plato and Aristotle and reappearing in the Middle Ages in the concept of natural law (Weeks, 1985). The concept of sex as a natural urge is a recurrent theme in the writing of the sexologists of the late nineteenth century; Havelock Ellis, for example, described it as an 'impulse', and Freud as a 'drive' (Freud, 1953). The biological imperative is hinted at in the choice of terms used in the accounts of Kinsey's research, in the term 'outlet' for example (Kinsey et al., 1948; Kinsey et al., 1953) and certainly the attempt to develop a taxonomy of human sexual behaviours, carefully categorized in a manner characteristic of the natural sciences, very much reflected Kinsey's background in biology.

Biological determinants of sexual behaviour cannot be ignored. Any theory of sexuality will have recourse to an understanding of anatomical and biological potential and limits which provide the preconditions for human sexuality (Weeks, 1985). But while the biological human sexual capacity is universal, its expression is influenced by socio-cultural forces (Carballo *et al.*, 1989). Sexuality is defined, regulated, and given meaning through cultural norms. While biological and psychological causes may be central when comparing individuals, they are not of first importance when comparing societies. Biology explains little of the variation between population groups. If sexuality were solely biologically determined, then forms of sexual expression would vary little cross-culturally or historically, and the evidence suggests that they do (Ford and Beach, 1952). Narrowly biological explanations are inadequate when research questions concern social trends and variations between different populations and subgroups.

It is in the potential of sexuality for diversity that the seeds of hope may be found in the selection of sexual health strategies. Human relationships offer an enormous range of choices in terms of sexual expression. We owe a debt to Kinsey for demonstrating this to be so. In the search for a healthy lifestyle, a perspective that sees in sexuality opportunities for choice and diversity is of greater value than one that sees sexual behaviour as immutably fixed by biological forces . . .

The Survey Methodology

Defining the Objectives

The investigative focus of the study needed to reflect its aims, which were, as already stated, to assist in the prevention of further spread of the virus and in the planning and provision of health-care services for those already affected. Since this survey was originally expected to draw extensively on public funds, and since there was no certainty that these funds would be available on a regular basis, the research instrument was designed to provide data that would assist health-care professionals working in many areas of sexual health – psycho-sexual counselling, the prevention of sexually transmitted disease, and family planning, for example. This was the policy-driven objective but, although of most practical urgency, it was not the only one guiding the content of the survey. In addition, the hope was that the survey would stimulate further social inquiry in this field, addressing questions raised by previous research and posing fresh ones by generating new hypotheses.

The measurement objectives of the study were defined as follows:

1   To quantify components of sexual history, such as numbers of partners in particular time intervals and age at first sexual intercourse, in a representative sample of the British population.
2   To measure the prevalence and distribution of different patterns of sexual orientation.
3   To measure the frequency and extent of experience of particular risk practices.
4   To measure attitudes towards sexual behaviour, knowledge of possible associated health risks and to examine their relationship with behaviour.
5   To determine the demographic characteristics of those whose current sexual lifestyle puts them at greatest risk of HIV and other STDs.
6   To assess changes in sexual lifestyles through generational comparisons of sexual histories.

Development Work

The study of sexual behaviour undoubtedly presents certain methodological challenges and a number of methodological issues had to be resolved at the start of the survey. In addition to formulation of the measurement objectives, decisions needed to be taken on the mode of data collection, the size and nature of the sample and the form and content of the questionnaire. To help make these decisions, several stages of fieldwork took place during the course of a two-year development and pilot phase of the research leading to the implementation of the main stage.

Method of Data Collection

Decisions about the method of data collection centred on the breadth and complexity of the information sought, and its sensitive and personal nature. The advantages of face-to-face interviewing in terms of establishing rapport with the respondent and providing opportunities for clarification had to be balanced against the possible greater opportunities for bias due to interviewer effect and reduced anonymity.

The amount of data to be collected favoured a personal interview survey. The length of the interviews planned (on average, just under an hour for a quarter of the sample, and 40–45 minutes for the remainder) is less acceptable for postal or telephone surveys than for face-to-face interviews. The complexity of the data to be sought, and the need for careful definition of terms and extensive filtering and routing instructions also militated against a postal method. The restriction on interview techniques, chiefly the impossibility of using show-cards, militated against a telephone survey. An additional problem with a telephone survey is that the interviewer has little control over whether the interview is conducted in comfort or out of earshot of other household members.

Both postal (Sundet *et al.*, 1988) and telephone surveys (ACSF Investigators, 1992; McQueen *et al.*, 1991) on the subject have been carried out successfully in surveys of sexual behaviour in Britain and in other countries. But the high proportion of individuals without telephones in Britain, particularly young people, and the lack of an efficient sampling method for telephone interviewing, discouraged the use of this method (Collins and Sykes, 1987; Foreman and Collins, 1991). The use of personal interview seemed best suited to the specific objectives and social context of this study.

Qualitative Research to Guide Questionnaire Design

The first phase of fieldwork consisted of a series of 40 in-depth interviews carried out with men and women from a wide age range, all social classes and both urban and rural areas (Spencer *et al.*, 1988). A topic guide was used to control the content of the interviews, which were otherwise unstructured and lasted over an hour. The main aims of these exploratory interviews were to discover the extent of sexual information that members of the public were willing to disclose, the source of any discomfort, the terminology preferred and understood, and the accuracy with which people were able to recall sexual experiences, such as numbers of partners, lengths of relationships and when they occurred.

Designing the Questionnaire

Format   Having decided on a personal interview, a decision was needed on whether to use face-to-face delivery, or self-completion – or both and in what combination. This was guided by a concern to minimize interview bias, to maximize clarity, and to provide a sequence of questions that would lead to reliable responses. In making the choice, the advantages of face-to-face presentation of questions in terms of opportunities for clarification and facilitating a good rapport between respondent and interviewer were obvious. On the other hand, a self-completion component containing the more sensitive questions allowed privacy of reporting, with consequent advantages for validity. The challenge lay in finding a mix that optimally combined the merits of both.

Evidence of greater willingness to report sensitive sexual behaviours on self-administered questionnaires in other surveys was confirmed in the qualitative stage of development work, which revealed some discomfort on the part of both interviewer and respondent at face-to-face disclosure of more intimate information. The decision was taken to combine a face-to-face component with a self-completion booklet. The first part of the schedule, conducted as a face-to-face interview, included questions of a less personal nature – on general health, family circumstances, etc. – moving on to family background and then into memories of sex education and early sexual experiences. Relatively neutral questions led gently on to more intimate and sensitive ones, such as those on first heterosexual experiences and sexual orientation (responses to which were needed in order to decide whether a booklet should be given at all). Answers to the more personal questions asked in the face-to-face part of the interview were elicited through the use of show-cards.

More sensitive questions on, for example, numbers of sexual partners, frequency and nature of different sexual practices, history of contact with prostitutes and injecting drug use were included in a booklet unseen by the interviewer, sealed by the respondent and identified only by a number. Only where problems of literacy or language made self-completion impossible did the interviewer read the questions to the respondent. Respondents aged under 18 with no experience of heterosexual intercourse and those of any age with no sexual experience at all were not asked to complete the booklet.

Questions on attitudes were placed towards the end of the questionnaire, on the basis that it would be easier for respondents to report their own behaviours before making judgement on behaviour in general. The final part of the interview collected information on demographic characteristics. Two versions of the questionnaire were developed. The longer version, containing a full module of attitude questions and more detailed questions on a family background and influences, first intercourse and sex education, was given to a quarter of the sample (a fully representative random subset of the total selected) and a reduced module to the remaining three-quarters.

The use of a combined instrument afforded opportunities to compare responses on items repeated in both self-completion and face-to-face interview (e.g. homosexual experience).

Wording the Questions   Of crucial importance to the acceptability and validity of the survey is the way in which questions are phrased and posed. Misreporting of sensitive personal information is often as much a function of question design as of unwillingness or inability to report (Marquis *et al.*, 1986). Discomfort with, and misunderstanding of, the language used will jeopardize both willingness to respond and the ability to produce accurate responses.

An early decision was needed on whether or not the questionnaire should be fully standardized or whether there should be some flexibility to allow respondents to use their own language. Several surveys have successfully adopted this latter formula (Kinsey *et al.*, 1948; AIMN, 1988) and researchers, including Kinsey, have cautioned against the use of a standardized questionnaire and neutral terminology, counselling instead the use of the vernacular. Our own preparatory work failed to instil confidence that the use of the respondent's own language would provide the required standardization.

Sexual behaviour is rarely spoken about publicly and as a result the language used to describe it is inadequate and inappropriate. Many terms used in the vernacular in the English language double also as terms of abuse and their use in the research setting may cause offence. The use of terms describing sexual experience, their meaning and respondents' preferences for use, were all explored in the course of the qualitative phase of development work. This revealed a wide diversity of language styles used to describe sexual behaviour, ranging from the biblical ('couple', 'copulate', fornicate') to the vernacular ('screw', 'fuck'), from the euphemistic ('doing it', 'having it') to the romantic ('making love'), and from lay terms ('having sex', 'sexual intercourse') to the scientific ('coitus'). Because of the variability, meanings were far from precise enough for research purposes.

The development work also unearthed a problem of misunderstanding. The meaning of many terms – 'vaginal sex', 'oral sex', 'penetrative sex', 'heterosexual' – were unclear to a sizeable enough number of people to threaten substantially the overall validity of response. A starting point for quantitative estimates is to ensure that common definitions are attached to specific acts. Yet there was wide variation in the meaning attached to crucial variables such as 'sexual partner' and 'having sex'. Some respondents discounted their spouse as a 'sexual partner', for example. For heterosexual respondents, the term 'having sex' was generally equated with vaginal intercourse, while homosexual respondents included in the definition a broader repertoire of sexual acts.

In the qualitative, in-depth interviews, respondents were asked to state explicitly their preferences for terms and style of language. A general consensus emerged for use of fairly formal terms ('sexual intercourse', 'penis', 'vagina', etc.) with explanations provided where necessary. There was some evidence of discomfort on the part of respondents and interviewers alike with the use of the vernacular. The decision was therefore to use standard neutral terms throughout the questionnaire, both in the face-to-face interview and the self-completion booklet, with a glossary. Terms were defined not simply according to dictionary definitions, but in concrete practical terms, For example, 'partners' were defined as 'people who have had sex together just once, or a few times, or as regular partners, or as married partners' . . . In the face-to-face section of the interview schedule, interviewers were provided with explanations to offer to respondents.

Questionnaire Piloting

Draft versions of the structured questionnaire were tested in several rounds of small-scale pilots. These pilot stages enabled the questionnaire to be refined in readiness for the feasibility survey and provided valuable experience which was to guide other aspects of the study, such as introducing the survey on the doorstep, wording introductory letters and training interviewers.

Reliability and Validity

Attempts at obtaining quantitative data on sexual behaviour must rely on self-reports and there are few opportunities for checking information obtained against that from other sources. For these reasons the need to ensure reliability (the potential of the research instrument to replicate the results, and the extent to which findings are generalizable to the population as a whole) and validity (whether the question measures what is intended to be measured) were paramount in designing the research instrument.

Two important and related aspects of reliability and validity are the twin problems of veracity and recall. One of the chief concerns voiced over the legitimacy of value of research in this area of behaviour is whether people will give honest responses. Yet the problem is not exclusive to research into sexual behaviour. Problems relating to people's ability to report reliably and accurately beset investigation into many aspects of human behaviour. Topics on which people might be tempted to give less than honest replies include drinking and smoking behaviour, frequency of having a bath or shower, disclosure of earnings, views on racial minorities, etc. (Belson, 1981). Researchers display few reservations about investigating these areas of behaviour on the grounds of doubtful disclosure.

Nevertheless this is an area in which the presence of an interviewer effect could threaten validity of response. Some of the behaviours respondents were asked to reveal are not only socially disapproved, but are actually illegal in this country (anal sex between a man and a woman, for example). A guarantee of confidentiality can also do much to ensure veracity of response. Reassuring respondents of the confidentiality of the survey was of greatest importance in relation to the self-completion booklet which contained the more intimate and personal questions. A non-judgmental approach on the part of the interviewer and a guarantee of confidentiality were also essential. A firm understanding on the part of the respondent of the urgent need for the data and the credentials and integrity of the originators also does much to overcome this problem. In this respect the introduction was made easier by a reference to health and AIDS and the need for the information.

The use of neutral questions, the avoidance of stigmatizing labels and judgmental questions also aided candid disclosure. Finally, the authority of the funding and investigative agencies was significant in motivating honesty. Respondents were asked, at the end of the in-depth interview, whether they had answered truthfully and whether they believed others would do so, and the majority claimed that they themselves had done so because of the urgent need for the data and the credentials of the originators.

The problem of accuracy of recall, in common with that of veracity, is not exclusive to research into sexual behaviour. Social-survey researchers regularly rely for their data on the memories of respondents. The two problems are often related since forgetting may be as much a process of active blocking as passive memory decay, and so the problem responds to the same kinds of methodological devices designed to deal with the problem of honesty.

Large-scale quantitative surveys have, however, particular limitations in eliciting data that is difficult to recall. Recall can be more a process of gradual reminiscence than instant recollection, and techniques involving a slow, careful process of retrieval are more likely to facilitate this. Design features that can facilitate the process of recall included scheduling the question order in such a way that the early section includes a number of life-stage questions ('When did you first . . .?'), providing respondents with a framework in which to locate less easily recalled experiences and triggering associations between life events. The feasibility survey provided the opportunity to experiment with some of these strategies.

Feasibility Study

A feasibility study developed from the qualitative and pilot work was carried out by SCPR [Social and Community Planning Research] to assess the acceptability of the survey, the extent to which it would produce valid and reliable results, and the sample size needed to obtain accurate estimates of minority behaviours. This was a large-scale test of the instrument and sampling strategy, the target being an achieved sample of around 1000 interviews. The design was a multi-stage random sample stratified by socio-economic characteristics of the neighbourhood within the Registrar General's Standard Regions (Acorn groupings). Each address was approached by an interviewer and all members of the household aged 16–59 enumerated. From this, one individual was chosen by a random selection procedure and invited for interview. The target response rate (65%) was achieved and experiments on question wording and order successfully resolved the remaining design dilemmas. The results, which included extensive searches of internal and external consistency, reported in some detail elsewhere (Wellings *et al.*, 1990), formed the basis of the application for funding of the main study.

References

ACSF Investigators (1992) 'AIDS and sexual behaviour in France', *Nature*, 360: 407–9.
AIMN (1988) *AIDS in a Multicultural Neighbourhood.* Bayview-Hunter's Point Foundation for Community Improvement, 6025 Third Street, San Francisco, California.
Anderson, R.M., Medley, G.F., May, R.M. and Johnson, A.M. (1986) 'A preliminary study of the transmission dynamics of the human immunodeficiency virus (HIV), the causative agent of AIDS', *Journal of Maths, Applied Medicine and Biology*, 3: 229–63.
Belson, W.A. (1981) *The Design and Understanding of Survey Questions.* London: Gower.
Carballo, M., Cleland, J., Carael, M. and Albrecht, G. (1989) 'A cross national study of patterns of sexual behaviour', *Journal of Sex Research*, 26(3): 287–99.
Collins, M. and Sykes, W. (1987) 'The problems of non-coverage and unlisted numbers in telephone surveys in Britain', *Journal of the Royal Statistical Society*, series A, 150(3): 241–53.
Coxon, A. (1988). 'The numbers game', in P. Aggleton and H. Homans (eds) *Social Aspects of AIDS.* Lees: Falmer Press.
Ford, C.S. and Beach, F.A.S. (1952) *Patterns of Sexual Behaviour.* London: Eyre and Spottiswoode.
Foreman, J. and Collins, M. (1991) 'The viability of random digit dialling in the UK', *Journal of the Market Research Society*, 33(3): 218–27.
Freud, S. (1953) 'Introductory lectures on psychoanalysis', lecture 12 in James Strachey (ed.) *The Standard Edition of the Complete Psychological Works of Sigmund Freud*, vol. 16, p. 323. London: Hogarth Press and the Institute of Psychoanalysis, 24 vols (1953–74).
Hethcote, H.W. and Yorke, J.A. (1984) 'Gonorrhoea: transmission dynamics and control. Lecture notes', *Biomathematics*, 56: 1–105.
Johnson, A.M. (1988) 'Social and behavioural aspects of the HIV epidemic – a review', *Journal of the Royal Statistical Society*, series A, 151: 99–114.
Johnson, A.M. (1992) 'Epidemiology of HIV infection in women', in D.D. Johnstone (ed.) *Baillière's Clinical Obstetrics and Gynaecology*, 6th edn, pp. 13–31. London: Baillière Tindall.
Kinsey, A.C., Pomeroy, W.B. and Martin, C.E. (1948) *Sexual Behaviour in the Human Male.* Philadelphia: W.B. Saunders.
Kinsey, A.C., Pomeroy, W.B., Martin, C.E. and Gebhard, P.H. (1953) *Sexual Behaviour in the Human Female.* Philadelphia: W.B. Saunders.
McManus, T.J. and McEvoy, M. (1987) 'Some aspects of male homosexual behaviour in the United Kingdom', *British Journal of Sexual Medicine*, 14: 110–20.

McQueen, D.V., Robertson, B.J. and Nisbet, L. (1991) *Data-Update: AIDS-Related Behaviour, Knowledge and Attitudes, Provisional Data*. No. 27, RUHBC, University of Edinburgh.

Marquis, K.H., Marquis, S. and Pollitch, M. (1986) 'Response bias and reliability in sensitive topic surveys', *Journal of the American Statistical Association*, 394: 381–9.

Masters, W. and Johnson, V. (1966) *Human Sexual Response*. London: Churchill.

Masters, W. and Johnson, V. (1970) *Human Sexual Inadequacy*. London: Churchill.

Potts, M., Anderson, R. and Boily, M.-C. (1991) 'Slowing the spread of human immuno-deficiency virus in developing countries', *Lancet*, 338, 608–12.

Report of a Working Group (Chairman D. Cox) (1989) *Shor Term Prediction of HIV Infection and AIDS in England and Wales*. London: HMSO.

Report of a Working Group (Chairman N.E. Dau) (1990) 'AIDS in England and Wales to end 1993. Projections using data to end September 1989', *Communicable Diseases Report*, 1–12.

Spencer, L., Faulkner, A. and Keegan, J. (1988) *Talking about Sex*. London: Social and Community Planning Research.

Sundet, J.M., Kvalem, I.L., Magnus, P. and Bakketeig, L.S. (1988) 'Prevalence of risk-prone behaviour in the general population of Norway', in A.F. Fleming, M. Carballo and D.F. Fitzsimons (eds) *The Global Impact of AIDS*. London: Alan R. Liss.

Weeks, J. (1985) *Sexuality and its Discontents*. London: Routledge and Kegan Paul.

Wellings, K., Field, J., Wadsworth, J., Johnson, A.M., Anderson, R.M. and Bradshaw, S.A. (1990) 'Sexual lifestyles under scrutiny', *Nature*, 348: 276–8.

Source: Field *et al.*, 1994: 1–2, 5–8, 14–22

Reading D: Studying Sexual Lifestyles: Long Questionnaire

Julia Field, Anne Johnson, Jane Wadsworth and Kaye Wellings

ASK ALL

IF INTERVIEWING IN ENGLAND OR WALES, ASK ABOUT 'BRITAIN'

IF INTERVIEWING IN SCOTLAND, ASK ABOUT 'SCOTLAND'

36. Do you think that divorce in (Britain/Scotland) should be . . . **READ OUT**

. . . easier to obtain than it is now . . . 1

or, more difficult . . . 2

or, should things remain as they are? . . . 3

(Don't know) . . . 1

37. CARD N

As I read from this list, please look at the card and tell me how important you think each one is to a successful marriage . . . **READ OUT**

		very important	quite important	not very important	not at all important	(don't know)
a)	. . . Faithfulness?	1	2	3	4	8
b)	An adequate income?	1	2	3	4	8
c)	Mutual respect and appreciation?	1	2	3	4	8
d)	Shared religious beliefs?	1	2	3	4	8
e)	A happy sexual relationship?	1	2	3	4	8
f)	Sharing household chores?	1	2	3	4	8
g)	Having children?	1	2	3	4	8
h)	Tastes and interests in common?	1	2	3	4	8

38.a) In general, what age do you think is a good age for a man to get married:

ENTER AGE _____

Varies/Depends/No particular age . . . 96

Other answer including age range (STATE BELOW)

_____ . . . 97

Don't know . . . 98

b) And for a woman to get married?

ENTER AGE _____

Varies/Depends/No particular age . . . 96

Other answer including age range (STATE BELOW)

_____ . . . 97

Don't know . . . 98

ASK ALL

CARD O

39. From this card, what are your opinions about the following sexual relationships . . . **READ OUT**

	always wrong	mostly wrong	sometimes wrong	rarely wrong	not wrong at all	depends/ don't know
a) ... If a man and a woman have sexual relations before marriage, what would your general opinion be?	1	2	3	4	5	8
b) What about a married person having sexual relations with someone other than his or her partner?	1	2	3	4	5	8
c) What about a person who is living with a partner, not married, having sexual relations with someone other than his or her partner?	1	2	3	4	5	8
d) And a person who has a regular partner they don't live with, having sexual relations with someone else?	1	2	3	4	5	8
e) What about a person having one night stands?	1	2	3	4	5	8

What is your general opinion about:

	always wrong	mostly wrong	sometimes wrong	rarely wrong	not wrong at all	depends/ don't know
f) Sexual relations between two adult men?	1	2	3	4	5	8
g) And sexual relations between two adult women?	1	2	3	4	5	8
h) Lastly, what is your general opinion about abortion?	1	2	3	4	5	8

ASK ALL

CARD P

40. Now please would you say how far you agree or disagree with each of these things ... **READ OUT**

	agree strongly	agree	neither agree nor disagree	disagree	disagree strongly	don't know
a) ... It is natural for people to want sex less often as they get older?	1	2	3	4	5	8
b) Having a sexual relationship outside a regular one doesn't necessarily harm that relationship?	1	2	3	4	5	8

Source: Field *et al.*, 1994: 406–7

Solution to Chapter 3 SAQs

SAQ 3.1

Five types of work, ranked according to best/most to worst/least, could be: 1 company chairman; 2 member of parliament; 3 university lecturer; 4 plumber; 5 domestic worker.

Criteria for selecting work items could have been paid employment (except most domestic work is unpaid) or non-leisure activity (though lecturers often mix leisure activity and work; e.g. reading). Criteria for ranking the work could be 'social status' (though some might argue that MPs have a higher status than company chairmen) or salary levels (though a skilled plumber working overtime might earn as much as or more than a lecturer).

SAQ 3.2

1   The items refer to 'your immediate boss', 'your fellow team-members', etc. No mention is therefore made of a specific structure, though some kind of hierarchy is assumed.
2   The items in the measure refer to 'relationships between management and workers in the organisation', 'the way your department is managed', 'your chance of promotion or progression within the organisation'.
3   The language used reflects the context: terms such as 'boss', 'rate of pay', 'hours of work', even the term 'work' rather than 'employment', all point to a particular type of work and workers. There are of course types of work without 'bosses', for example commune-based work, work without 'team-members', for example home-working, and work with salaries rather than wages and flexible hours, for example most professional work.

As an optional task you could answer and score the measure for yourself in a job you have held.

SAQ 3.3

1   Very unlikely.
2   Though the interviewer was told to select 50% of the households and did so, the selection was biased by a number of factors:
    (a)   First house visited, occupants away on holiday.
    (b)   Second house, first interview, selected due to proximity to first. Interviewer did not have to cross the road.
    (c)   Third house, second interview, selected because it was near the ice-cream van. You could even argue that the weather was a factor here.
    (d)   Fourth house, third interview, selected due to the proximity to the third house.

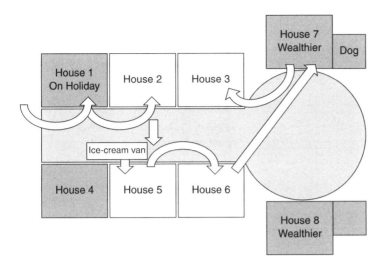

Figure 3.3 *Houses where interview was conducted.*

(e) Fifth house selected as it was on the other side of the street and then rejected because of the dog. Also note that this household was wealthier, probably indicating a different type of occupation for the occupants.

(f) Sixth house selected due to proximity to fifth.

3 The interviewer controlled the sampling process, selecting four houses out of six visited, 66%, on criteria ranging from being next door to each other to the presence of dogs and ice-cream vans. This means that the probability of a house being selected is unknown as we cannot easily measure the chance that the interviewer will select a specific house.

4 A better sampling process would have to take the control out of the hands of the interviewer on the ground. To decide on how to improve the method we need to ask a few questions about the population from which the sample will be taken. From the map we can see that houses 7 and 8 belong to higher income households, or at least they are more expensive houses. We therefore have a structure to our population. In the story so far the interviewer did not select either of these houses. We could then use either a structural or quota method. We could insist that the interviewer select three houses from numbers 1 to 6 and one from numbers 7 and 8. We would then have a sample that reflected the basic structure of the street. We would still be faced with problem of the dog and the ice-cream van. One way to resolve this would be to use a stratified or structured random sample. We would still have a 50% chance of selecting any house and we would randomly select, maybe by rolling a die, which of the first six houses would be surveyed. All we need to do is roll the die a few times until we have four different house numbers. We could then roll the die to select one of the larger houses (numbers 7 and 8) by selecting house 7 if the die came up odd or 8 if it came up even. We would then have a randomly selected set of houses with a structure proportional to the different types of house. Then, if we came up with houses 1, 4, 6 and 8, the interviewer would have to collect data from these households only. This would involve

waiting for house 1 to return from holiday and braving the dog at house 7. The interviewer would have no impact on the sampling procedure. Though a form of random sampling proved best in this case, there are many other contexts where other methods are better, or reasonably reliable, or the only practical option.

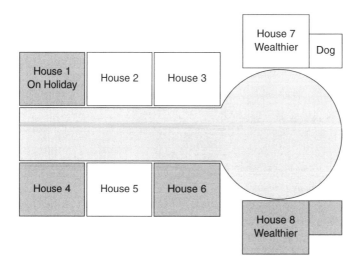

Figure 3.4 *Structured random sample of houses*

SAQ 3.4

1   Random sampling and quota sampling are mentioned. Interestingly, Reading B argues that quota sampling proved more accurate than random sampling, the reason given being the inaccuarcy of the registers of voters and other official lists used for the random selection process. Inaccurate lists may lead to unintentionally biased samples or ones where there is a larger than normal proportion of missing cases. This points out a key weakness of random sampling: its reliance on highly accurate lists from which cases are selected. Quota sampling on the other hand can rely upon accurate information about the number of people in different general demographic categories (income, gender, occupation, etc.) and use these to construct a representative sample. As was argued in the main text, the choice of best method depends upon the information and resources available.

2   Reading B implies that a well constructed sample of between 1,000 and 2,000 people would be as accurate and representative as one of 10,000 people or more. The size of sample required to ensure an accurate and representative result depends upon how varied is the population you are studying. One way of meauring this is to select the most important causes of this variance – income, gender, age, occupation, for example. With knowledge of these categories you can calculate the optimum size of sample you need from the large population to ensure that all the various groups are represented in the

right proportions. The bigger your sample the better, but after a point the increase in accuracy you gain by adding more cases gets smaller and smaller. In the case of the UK population and voting, going beyond 2,000 people does not improve the accuracy enough to warrant bigger surveys.

3   Reading B points out that most of the final poll predictions since 1945 have been within 1 or 2% of the actual result – a reasonably accurate result. Also, the errors in any direction for the main parties has balanced out across most of the elections. The polls for the 1992 general election were far more inaccurate. Reading B gives three reasons for this. First, there was a 'late swing', where voters decided at the last minute to change their minds. Second, there was the problem of dealing with 'missing cases' and the 'don't know' answers. It was found that Conservative voters were more likely to refuse an interview (missing cases) or say 'don't know'. Third, there were various errors in the sample designs. These errors included badly chosen demographics which did not help to build representative quotas.

4   First, to develop means of predicting the actual votes of 'don't knows' as their swing to one party or another after the final opinion polls is a major source of the error, especially given the 'silent' behaviour of Conservative voters. For instance using questions which tap into previous voting behaviour or other indicators of voting preference such as opinions on social cultural topics. Second, important improvements in the design of the samples, based on more accurate demographic data.

SAQ 3.5

1   The several policy aims of the research focused mainly on the need for up-to-date information on sexual lifestyles to help in the fight against AIDS and other sexually transmitted diseases.

2   The researchers have based their methodology on a social rather than a purely biological perspective on sexual behaviour. This is best summed up by the statement that 'Sexuality is defined, regulated and given meaning through cultural norms.'
    This general theory is also tied to their policy objectives. If sexual behaviour is primarily enacted through cultural processes, then there are 'the seeds of hope' that health practitioners armed with good information can help change those behaviours and improve people's health. Specifically, they can help change behaviours to prevent the spread of diseases such as AIDS.

3   (a) Components of sexual histories; (b) prevalence and distribution of patterns of sexual orientation; (c) the frequency and extent of risky behaviours; (d) attitudes to behaviours and knowledge of health risks; (e) the demographics (general social and personal characteristics) of those at risk due to behaviours from HIV infection; (f) changes in sexual behaviour by comparing different generations.

4   Because of the length of time the interview would take and the complexity of the information needed. Face-to-face interviews provide the opportunity for clarification of questions and allow more flexibility in interview techniques. There was also concern that the lack of telephone access, especially amongst

younger people, would limit the representativeness of the sample. Note that this was not the case for the pollsters in Reading B.

5   The researchers conducted in-depth interviews to find out how much information people were likely to be willing to give. This helped them design the questionnaire. Once it was designed, the researchers conducted a pilot study to test its reliability and usability.

6   More sensitive questions were answered through the use of a self-completed, anonymised questionnaire.

7   The preliminary in-depth interviews made apparent the discomfort that both interviewers and subjects felt with the use of vernacular terms. To make sure that the standard terms were understood the interviewers were provided with explanations to offer to subjects in cases of misunderstanding.

SAQ 3.6

1   Question 36 is a two-way question. Two extremes, 'easier' and 'more difficult' are provided, along with the middle ground of 'remain as they are' as well as a 'don't know' option. Question 37 is a combination of a scaled and a multiple-choice question. Question 38 (a + b) is a good example of a direct question with options to deal with vague answers, including generally unsure ('varies/depends/no particular age') and a response that defines a range of ages. Question 39 is a classic set of scaled questions, much like the work satisfaction measure discussed on pp. 22–24.

2   Question 38 clearly requires some interpretation by the interviewers. In truth, all the answers to the questions might need some form of interpretation by the interviewer.

3   One of the problems of closed questions is that the opinions people hold are not fixed facts in their minds. Often we only form an opinion once we are required to, in a conversation say, or when asked in an interview such as this one. This is not to say that the results are 'wrong' or 'untrue'; instead it points to the importance of interpretation and meaning in the construction and presentation of questions. For some critics of survey methods the closed and fixed nature of questions is seen to force the respondents to provide a limited set of responses which may not give insight into the complex ideas, opinions and feelings they have on an issue. Methods that attempt to get access to these more complex aspects of people's ideas and opinions are discussed in Part III. Survey researchers would reply that a well designed questionnaire, using well thought through measures, can provide quite rich and complex results. They might also reply that their intention is to describe the general features of a population and that closed questions are an efficient and practical means of doing this.

4   *Experimental Research*

So far we have looked at the process of survey research. In this chapter we explore the method of experimental research, which differs from survey research in a number of respects. First, in addition to some form of sampling, a major source of control is gained through the design of the experiment. In most cases specially selected groups are compared on some measure. This leads to the second main difference. Experiments often observe/measure the behaviour of participants rather than just ask questions of them.

Conditions

One quick way of thinking about the design of experiments is to keep in mind the question 'compared to what?' Most experiments are about comparing two or more **conditions**. A condition can range from belonging to a particular group (e.g. young people vs. older people), or having experienced a specific event (e.g. seen a film vs. not seen a film), or having a specific skill (e.g. chess masters vs. chess novices) and so on. The actual conditions in an experiment are defined by the hypothesis under examination. The classic two conditions in an experiment are the control condition and the experimental condition. The control condition will often be the 'normal' or 'standard' case. In medical research where a new treatment is being tested this will often be the patients who are receiving a standard treatment. The experimental group will be those receiving the new treatment. By comparing the results from the two groups, how much each group's health improved, the effectiveness of the new treatment can be assessed.

Constructing an Hypothesis

Experimental conditions are related to our hypotheses and that hypotheses are drawn from our general theory. In experimental quantitative research hypotheses need to be quite precise. In order to acheive this, hypotheses use the general claims of the theory to make precise statements about the effect of one variable on another variable. A variable is essentially something that we can measure or quantify in some way: height, weight, exam scores, type of job, status of jobs, voting preferences, for example. They are termed variables as they often differ from case to case and can also change over time.

If we look back over the work satisfaction example (pp. 22–25), the general theory was that:

> The social status of a job would directly affect satisfaction with the job.

From this general theory we could then formulate a precise hypothesis:

> The higher the social status a job has, the higher workers in that job will score on the work satisfaction scale.

The two variables here are work satisfaction and job status. Notice how the hypothesis refers directly to the variables to be measured. We could measure these variables for a sample of workers and see if there was support for such a claim. We would need to ensure that we had a representative sample so as to ensure a generalisable result. In experimental research the main form of control comes from the direct manipulation of one of the variables rather than the sampling process. In the same way that a chemist could add more or less of a chemical to test its effects, so experimental researchers can control one or more of the variables under consideration.

An experimental version of research on job satisfaction would start with the same theory and hypothesis but would be based upon the manipulation of one of the variables. Now we can't make a job more satisfying, but we could let workers try different-status jobs and then measure their satisfaction with each of the jobs they tried. We would gather together a selection of workers, we could even sample them in some way, and then we would set them to work in a number of different jobs of higher or lower social status. After each worker had spent some time in a job they would have to fill in the work satisfaction measure for that job. In this case we are manipulating the work status variable. The variable which you manipulate is known as the independent variable, as you are free to control this as you wish. The independent variable often defines the set of conditions in the experiment. In this case each of the different jobs represents a different condition. The variable which measures the results of the experiment, in this case the work satisfaction measure, is known as the **dependent variable**. The results depend upon the manipulations you made.

Don't worry if these terms are new to you. In a moment you will get the chance to look at an example of an actual experiment which will help you get to grips with the terminology. But before this we need to consider one more issue. Chapter 1 argued that quantitative research attempts to achieve a level of control or closure through three methods: sampling, experimental design and statistics. There are important relationships between both sampling and experimental design and the statistical analysis of the data. In the case of survey research one should ensure that the sample is large and representative enough for you to be confident that your statistical results are generally true for the population surveyed. Experiments can often be complex and time consuming and it is unlikely that you would be able to work with as large a number of cases as you might in a survey. This therefore calls for a different statistical approach. In the case of experiments one tends to work with statistics that compare your results with the results you would have got if only random chance were at work. If there is a difference between your results and random chance this implies that some other process is likely to be at work. Your theory supplies a possible explanation of what that process might be.

The Null Hypothesis

To ensure that experiments are conducted with the issue of random chance kept in mind, every experimental hypothesis has a null hypothesis. The null hypothesis in most cases states:

- the results of the experiment will simply be the product of random chance.

The null hypothesis is *not* the opposite of your hypothesis, *nor* is it an alternative hypothesis. If we can *disprove* the null hypothesis we gain *support* for our hypothesis. It simply states that your results will be due to chance. For example, in a medical experiment 100 patients get a new treatment while 100 patients get the existing treatment. If you then found that 70 patients got better with the new treatment compared to 50 with the old treatment you need to know if this was an effect of the different treatments. The null hypothesis lets you test this. It says that any result you get is simply some other random effect; maybe the 70 patients with the new treatment had happier medical staff and so felt better quicker! If you could prove that the result was not random, or very unlikely to be random, then you could claim that it was the treatment which had the effect. This is what statistical tests do. In Chapter 5 you will work through an example of a statistical calculation, the end result of which will be a measure of how likely it is that a result is due to random chance. Generally, if there is a 5% probability that the result was due to random chance and therefore a 95% probability that it was not, we can be confident that some other process than random chance is at work. In this case we *reject* the null hypothesis and argue that there is *support* for our hypothesis.

SAQ 4.1

Given this hypothesis, which of statements (a) to (d) is the null hypothesis?

Hypothesis: workers with high work satisfaction scores will vote for the current party in government.

(a) Workers with low work satisfaction scores will vote for a different party than the one in power.
(b) Workers with low work satisfaction scores will not vote.
(c) Differences in workers' voting behaviour will be due to random chance.
(d) Workers with high work satisfaction scores will vote for a different party than the one in government.

This discussion of chance and probability is important. When we rely upon sampling for our control we are making the argument: if this is a good sample and we find some result, say that 60% of the people surveyed like product x and 40% do not, then we can be pretty sure this is true for the population overall. In the case of an experiment we make a different argument: if the result we get is statistically significant, in other words it is unlikely to be due to chance, then we can rely upon this result. Therefore, a result of 60 in one condition and 40 in another that is *not* significant – is likely to be the product of chance – can't be relied upon. On the other hand, a result of 51 in one condition and 49 in another that *is* significant – is not likely to be due to chance – can be relied upon. It is not the *size* of the difference that makes it a good result, but whether or not it is likely to be due to chance.

Control in Experiments

SAQ 4.2

In this SAQ you will be making notes on Reading E, 'Age differences in source forgetting: effects on reality monitoring and on eyewitness testimony'. The section of this extract headed 'Results' contains a discussion of the statistical results. Students who already have some knowledge of statistics and feel reasonably comfortable with the terminology should not find this too difficult. Don't worry if you are not comfortable with the terminology and symbols. Once you have worked through the example of a statistical analysis in Chapter 5, and have been introduced to the relevant ideas, you will be asked to look again at these sections of Reading E. As you read them focus upon whether or not the researchers think the results support their hypothesis. Also look at the way in which the statistical results are reported. In particular take note of the way in which a 'significant result' is both discussed and measured – the 'p' values. Overall, you should identify:

1 the hypothesis in this experiment;
2 the variables in this experiment;
3 the independent variables;
4 the dependent variable;
5 the number of different conditions in the experiment. What are they?
6 whether the result is in line with the hypothesis.

To return to the question of control and closure, in Reading E the experimenters gained a level of control in several ways. First, they were able to select two groups by age. To ensure that nothing else might affect the experiment, the groups were matched across a number of factors. These specifically included educational and social backgrounds. This was to prevent one group, say the older group, having been more formally educated and so forth than the other. This form of control was not a form of sampling; rather, as the experimenters assume that the things they are measuring are common to all people, they need to ensure that social differences don't mask the underlying psychological differences due to age.

Second, they were able to control the cases' experiences. All the cases watched a video. After this all cases conducted vocabulary tests. These tests were 'distractor tasks', designed to prevent any of the cases rehearsing events over and over in their minds. One group was then given misleading information and another was given true information. Both groups then worked on the same vocabulary tests again. Having eliminated social factors and controlled the age range and experience of the cases, the only difference between them should be due to their age or the fact that some were given misleading information. Any differences between the groups which cannot be attributed to random chance are likely therefore to be the product of either age and/or their different experiences during the experiment. This was the conclusion reached by the researchers.

In this case the experiment had a 'control group' who took the role of the 'compared to' in the question 'compared to what?' This control group was not subjected to any misinformation and therefore enabled the comparison between the two groups. Not all experiments have such a clearly defined control group. In some experiments only one group is used and the results are compared to random chance. In other cases a number of different groups may be compared with each other. Whatever the specifics of the experimental design, this form of experimental control clearly differs from the statistical control achieved through sampling. Achieving control of some kind allows the researcher to make general claims. The level of control places limits on the range of these general claims. In the case of sampling the researcher who has a representative sample can make claims about the population of which the sample is representative. Experimenters can make claims to have found a general result that holds true for the variables controlled. They cannot comment on the effects of other variables without conducting further experiments. Despite all of this, both survey and experimental research methods draw upon statistical methods to ensure that random/external factors not known or accounted for can be discounted. This aspect of quantitative methods is explored in Chapter 5.

Experiments and Positivism

Of all the material discussed so far, the experimental method most clearly adheres to the assumption of naturalism – that social phenomena and people can be studied using the methods of natural science. One can, though, raise questions about the levels of experimental control that can be gained in the context of human behaviour. One might want to raise questions about the assumption that matching for social factors removes social effects. To truly match cases across all major markers of social and cultural difference might require far more cases than are normally used in such experiments. In many natural science experiments, especially those in the physical sciences, levels of control can in some cases be absolute, and in others near-absolute. Social science experiments cannot claim to match such levels of control. Having said this, many sciences, especially biological and medical sciences, are also faced with complex systems which cannot be controlled to the extent found in the physical sciences. Once again we find that social science methods are drawing upon the 'spirit' of the naturalist argument but not the fine detail. As with the survey method, we can conclude that the experiment provides us with a useful working practical method. The general success of these methods in providing new and useful knowledge raises doubts about the practicality and usefulness of a rigid adherence to the ideas of positivism.

We can also raise questions about the importance of values and subjective experience in experimental contexts. In the experiment in Reading E, though correct and incorrect answers can be directly experienced and easily defined, what one subject means by 'very sure' may not be the same for another subject. As with the questions used in surveys, experimental questions also transgress the assumptions of nominalism and phenomenalism – we can't be sure that all things have the same meanings for each participant, and we are not always collecting results that are from direct experience. These issues are discussed further by Smith (1998: Chapters 2, 6 and 7).

We also need to address a more complex question about experiments, and in part about survey research. How 'normal' or 'natural' is the experiment, and how 'normal' or 'natural' is answering a survey? Experiments and surveys are not day-to-day contexts of social life. We can ask, therefore, how representative such contexts are and how reliable and generalisable are the results from such specific contexts. One response to this criticism is to argue strongly that social context has a minimal impact upon the social and psychological issues under study, and in many cases this is a reasonable claim. In others this is not so clear, and this points to the main overall limitation of these methods. By drawing upon a general model which is informed by positivism, surveys and experiments limit the range of social issues that they can address. Social scientists who wish to address the complex issues of meaning, values, understanding and representation that take place in social interaction may need methods informed by positions other than that of positivism. In Part III you will explore some of these qualitative research methods, but before we move on you need to study the final stage of the research process: analysing data and interpreting results.

Further Reading

Brown, S.R. and Melamed, L.E. (1990) *Experimental Design and Analysis*. London: Sage.
Leik, R.K. (1997) *Experimental Design and the Analysis of Variance*. London: Sage.
Levin, I.P. (1999) *Relating Statistics and Experimental Design: An Introduction*. London: Sage.
Lewis-Beck, M.S. (1993) *Experimental Design and Methods*. London: Sage.

Reading E: Age Differences in Source Forgetting: Effects on Reality Monitoring and on Eyewitness Testimony

Gillian Cohen and Dorothy Faulkner

The ability to remember the source of a memory is an important ingredient in cognitive competence. Memories originate from many different sources, and in order to function efficiently, people need to be able to remember these sources correctly. Some memories have external sources and include events that have been witnessed, actions that have been performed, and words that have been heard or spoken, read or written. Other memories have an internal source originating in imagination, in dreams, or in plans and intentions. To distinguish between the true and the false, the real and the imagined, the enacted and the planned, we need to be able to distinguish between memories with internal sources and memories with external sources. It is also important to be able to remember the precise source of an external memory. In order to make sense of the world in a consistent and coherent fashion and to be able to evaluate the reliability of the information we receive, we need to be able to remember who said what and who did what, and whether information came to us directly through our own sensory experience or only indirectly through hearsay . . .

Experiment 2: Age Differences in Eyewitness Testimony

In a typical eyewitness experiment (e.g. Loftus, Miller and Burns, 1978), subjects view a series of events depicted on film or in a slide sequence. Subsequently, one half of the subjects (the misled group) are exposed to written or spoken false information about some of these events and the other half of the subjects (the control group) are exposed to a true version. In a recognition test, a significant proportion of the misled subjects choose the false version of the original events. In effect, then, they are making a source confusion error, claiming to have watched an event that they had only read or heard about.

The explanation for this kind of error is controversial. Loftus has interpreted the effect (e.g. in Loftus and Loftus, 1980) as showing that the memory of the original event has been changed or distorted to conform with the false information. This interpretation has been challenged by McCloskey and Zaragoza (1985), who claimed that misleading post event information has no effect on the original memory but simply biases the response. They argued that a high proportion of subjects in both control and misled groups will have forgotten the original information. Then, in a two-choice recognition test, one half of the control subjects who have forgotten the original will choose the correct alternative by pure chance. The same proportion of the misled subjects will also have forgotten the original information, but they will have a higher probability of choosing the misleading information alternative in the recognition test because they were exposed to it and remember it. According to this interpretation, the effect of misleading information is not to transform the original memory but to bias the response.

How do these different explanations relate to memory for sources? Loftus and Loftus (1980) claimed that subjects who choose the misleading alternative have forgotten its source. The false information has become integrated with the original memory and is attributed to the original source. In McCloskey and Zaragoza's (1985) view, those who choose the misleading alternative may also have forgotten its source. Although it is conceivable that people might choose the misleading alternative knowing that it came from the wrong source, they would be more likely to do so if they had forgotten its source, so source forgetting would tend to increase the probability of being misled.

There are, therefore, two factors that make a person more susceptible to misleading information, forgetting the source of the false information and forgetting the original event. Yarmey (1984) reported that elderly witnesses remembered fewer details and were less accurate than young witnesses were in recalling an event. Experiment 1 [omitted in this extract] showed that elderly people were more likely than young people to make errors in identifying the source of a memory. In particular, they claimed that actions that had never occurred (new or imagined actions) had been watched. In the eyewitness paradigm, this tendency would make elderly subjects more susceptible to misleading information. They would be more likely to believe that they had actually witnessed events that had not occurred, but had been falsely added or changed in a subsequent misleading account of the event. Thus, both factors would make the elderly more susceptible to misleading information. In addition to the theoretical importance of age differences in source forgetting, this issue is of very considerable practical importance in the assessment of the credibility of witnesses.

Method

Subjects   A total of 64 subjects were tested. They were divided into two age groups, a young group aged 25–45 (*M* age = 34.9 years) and an elderly group aged 62–82 (*M* age = 70.4 years). The subjects were matched for educational and social background.

Materials   A video recording entitled 'The Kidnapping' was made of an extract from a film. It was presented without sound and lasted 3 minutes. The main events in the film were as follows:

> In a busy street a middle aged man greets acquaintances. He then bicycles towards home. At first he is accompanied by a young friend, but his companion is forced to stop because the chain comes off his bicycle. The middle aged man turns back to help him, but then goes on alone. When he reaches his home he is attacked by four youths, and after a fight and a chase, he is abducted.

Two 600 word story versions of these events were prepared. The correct version was an accurate account of all of the events of the film, but the misleading version contained false versions of two critical incidents. In one of these, the middle aged man was described as showing a letter to someone he met in the street when he really showed a book. And in the other incident, when the chain comes off his companion's bicycle, the man is described as cycling on without stopping, when he actually went back to offer help.

Procedure   Within each age group, one half of the subjects were assigned to the misled condition and the other half to the control condition in such a way as to equate the mean age of subjects in each condition. The subjects were tested in small groups of 6 or 8. The experimental procedure was in three phases.

Phase 1. The film: Subjects were told to watch the film carefully because their memory would be tested. After the film there was a 10 minute interval during which they worked through written vocabulary tests.

Phase 2. The story: Subjects in the misled group were given the misleading version of the story. Subjects in the control group were given the true version. Both groups were told 'Here is the story of the film you just saw. Read it through once only at your own pace.' They were given no indication that the story might contain misleading information. After they had read the story, they continued working on the vocabulary tests for a further 10 mins.

Phase 3. The recognition test: A recognition test consisting of 18 multiple choice questions was administered. Before beginning the test, subjects were told, 'Now cast your mind back to the film and choose the alternative which corresponds to what you saw in the film.' Two of the questions tested memory for the critical incidents. For these critical questions, the multiple choice alternatives were (a) the correct answer, (b) the false information from the misleading version of the story (MFI), and (c) another false alternative that had not appeared in either the film or the story (FI). For the 16 noncritical questions, one of the three alternatives was always the correct answer, which had appeared in both film and story and the other two were both FIs that had not appeared in either film or story. In constructing the questionnaire, pilot tests with a different group of subjects were carried out to ensure that false alternatives were equally plausible. The order of the three types of alternative was randomly varied across questions. The questions were presented in the same order as the events they concerned had appeared in the film. Each question was accompanied by a 3-point scale (*very sure, not sure, just guessing*) on which subjects were asked to rate how confident they were that their chosen answer was correct.

Results

Errors Table 1 shows the proportions of errors made by the young and elderly subjects in the misled and control conditions for the critical and noncritical questions. The differences between proportions were tested. In the misled condition, the elderly group made significantly more errors than the young group on the critical questions ($z = 2.1$, $p < 0.02$), but in the control condition, the difference between age groups did not reach significance ($z = 1.4$, *ns*). In the elderly group, the misled subjects made 29% more errors than the control subjects, and this difference was significant ($z = 2.3$, $p < 0.02$). In the young group, misled subjects made 15% more errors than the control subjects, and this difference was just significant ($z = 1.7$, $p < 0.05$).

Table 1 *Proportions of errors made by each age group on critical and noncritical questions*

| | Questions | | | |
| | Critical | | Noncritical | |
Age group	Misled	Control	Misled	Control
Elderly	0.57	0.28	0.23	0.21
Young	0.28	0.13	0.17	0.13
Age difference	0.29	0.15	0.06	0.07

For the noncritical questions, there were no significant differences between the age groups either in the misled condition ($z = 0.05$) or in the control condition ($z = 0.7$), and there was no difference between misled and control conditions either in the elderly group ($z = 0.14$) or in the young group ($z = 0.35$).

Types of Error For the noncritical questions, two of the three alternative answers were false information (FI), and both of these choices were classified as FI errors. For the critical questions, one alternative was an FI error and one alternative consisted of the misleading false information and was classified as an MFI error. Table 2 shows the proportions of each type of error made in response to the critical questions. The elderly misled made significantly more MFI errors than the elderly control subjects ($z = 2.8$, $p < 0.01$); the young misled also made more MFI errors than the young control subjects ($z = 2.3$, $p < 0.02$). The elderly misled made more MFI errors than the young misled ($z = 2.5$, $p < 0.01$) (but this was the only significant age difference).

Table 2 *Proportions of false information (FI) and misleading false information (MFI) errors made by each age group on critical questions*

Age group	Misled		Control	
	MFI	FI	MFI	FI
Elderly	0.57	0.00	0.18	0.06
Young	0.25	0.03	0.06	0.06
Age difference	0.32	−0.03	0.12	0.00

Confidence Ratings Following a procedure outlined by Loftus (1979), a suggestibility resistance score was calculated for each subject. This score combined the accuracy of the responses with the level of confidence as follows. A correct response with the highest confidence rating (*very sure*) received a score of 6; a correct response with a moderate confidence rating (*not sure*) received 5; a correct response with the lowest confidence rating (*just guessing*) received 4; an incorrect response with the lowest confidence rating scored 3; an incorrect response with moderate confidence scored 2; and an incorrect response made with the highest level of confidence received a score of 1. (The best performance is to be right and to be sure that you are right. The worst performance is to be wrong and to be sure that you are right.) These scores were calculated for the critical questions for the misled groups and indicate how strongly the misleading information was resisted. The young misled group had a mean score of 9.06 out of a maximum possible of 12, and the elderly misled had a mean score of 6.4, which was significantly lower, $t(15) = 2.1$, $p < 0.05$.

Of the responses made by the elderly misled group to the critical questions 37.5 per cent were MFI errors made with a confidence rating of *very sure*. In the young misled group, only 9.4 per cent of their responses were of this kind and this difference was significant ($z = 3.4$, $p < 0.01$).

Discussion

Results showed that when they were not exposed to misleading false information, the elderly subjects remembered events they had witnessed in the film and read in the story as well as did the young subjects. However, when they had read an account of these events containing misleading information, they were more likely to be influenced by it. When critical incidents were misrepresented in the written version, elderly subjects were more likely to claim later that these were the correct representations of the events they originally witnessed.

Logically, there are several different explanations for this error. Subjects may choose the misleading alternative if (a) they remember the original event in the film and they also remember the misleading alternative for the story, but they confuse the sources of the two versions. Because no subjects reported noticing discrepancies between film and story, this possibility is unlikely. (b) They have forgotten the original event in the film; they remember the misleading alternative from the story but have forgotten its source, and conclude that it came from the film. (c) They have forgotten the original event; they remember the misleading alternative and remember that it came from the story, but conclude that it must also have been in the film. (d) They have forgotten the original event and have also forgotten the misleading alternative, but may choose this response (with a probability of 0.3) by pure chance. However, only 4.3 per cent of all responses were rated as *just guesses*, so this explanation is unlikely to account for many of the misled errors.

These possibilities illustrate the fact that choosing the misleading alternative may result from either forgetting events, forgetting sources, or some combination of both kinds of forgetting. The age groups did not differ significantly in the control condition or in the number of errors made to noncritical questions, so on this evidence there does not appear to be any marked age deficit in memory for events. It is reasonable, therefore, to conclude that the age deficit in the misled condition originates mainly from an age-related impairment of memory for sources.

When accuracy and confidence measures were combined, it was apparent that the elderly witnesses were not only misled into accepting a false account of what they had seen but that they were often strongly convinced and highly confident that it was correct. This finding is consistent with the results of Experiment 1, in which elderly subjects also made false positive errors with a high level of confidence, and should be taken into account when the credibility of elderly witnesses is being assessed in a legal context. However, as the studies reviewed by Loftus (1979) show, the effects of misleading information are variable and depend on factors such as the salience of the witnessed event, the interval between the original event and the misleading information, and whether the source of the misleading information is authoritative. In some circumstances, subjects are better able to resist the distorting influence of misleading information. The present results were obtained using a procedure whereby the questions in the recognition test preserve the same sequential order as the original events. According to Bekerian and Bowers (1983), this procedure tends to provide cues that reinstate the original memory and minimize the effect of misleading information. The fact that, in the present study, the effect of misleading information was still observed, despite the sequential testing procedure, may be due to the greater number and variety of events in the sequence. Because of this variability in the effect of misleading information, it cannot be assumed that the age-related increase in susceptibility to misleading information observed in the present experiment will be apparent in all circumstances. The factors that make elderly people particularly vulnerable to false information remain to be explored . . .

References

Bekerian, D.A. and Bowers, J.M. (1983) 'Eyewitness testimony: were we misled?' *Journal of Experimental Psychology: Learning, Memory and Cognition*, 9: 139–45.
Loftus, E.F. (1979) *Eyewitness Testimony*. Cambridge, MA: Harvard University Press.

Loftus, E.F. and Loftus, G.R. (1980) 'On the permanence of stored information in the human brain', *American Psychologist*, 35: 409–20.

Loftus, E.F., Miller, D.G. and Burns, H.J. (1978) 'Semantic integration of visual information into a visual memory', *Journal of Experimental Psychology: Human Learning and Memory*, 4: 19–31.

McCloskey, M. and Zaragoza, M. (1985) 'Misleading postevent information and memory for events: arguments and evidence against memory impairment hypotheses', *Journal of Experimental Psychology: General*, 114: 1–16.

Yarmey, A.D. (1984) 'Accuracy and credibility of the elderly witness', *Canadian Journal on Ageing*, 3: 79–90.

Source: Cohen and Faulkner, 1989: 10, 14–17

Solutions to Chapter 4 SAQs

SAQ 4.1

(c) Differences in workers' voting behaviour will be due to random chance.

SAQ 4.2

1 This experiment did not lay out a one-line hypothesis, rather the final paragraph of the introduction lays out the hypothesis through a general argument. If we condense this to a one-sentence version it might look like: Elderly people are likely to be more susceptible to misleading information than young people when remembering eyewitness events.

The reasoning for this was: older people are more likely to forget the source of information; they are also more likely to attribute later information to the original source. In other words, they will be sure that they saw an event which in fact they were told about later.

2 (a) Age: split into two categories – young and old. Note that care was taken when selecting these groups to ensure that their social and educational backgrounds matched. This does not mean that they are a representative sample, but it does mean that the two groups are similar to each other.

(b) Misleading: split into two categories – misled subjects and not-misled subjects (control). You might not have considered this a variable. Remember that variables are things which we can measure or control in an experiment. Here we control the experience of the subjects.

(c) Correctly/incorrectly recalled information. This was measured in a number of ways. First, the proportion of incorrectly remembered information (errors). Second, there are two types of error, false-information (i.e. simply wrong), and misled-false-information (i.e. false information that fits the misleading information given to the misled group). Third, a combined measure of correctness and confidence derived from a measure which asked how confident subjects were with their answer to each question. The measure included questions about the events in the video for which misleading information was supplied (critical questions), as well as questions about other events in the video (non-critical questions).

3   'Age' and 'misleading' are the independent variables as they are the variables controlled by the experimenter.

4   'Correctly/incorrectly recalled information' is the dependent variable.

5   There are four conditions in the experiment. These come from the two independent variables, as there are two levels, or categories, in each variable. This makes 2 × 2, or four, conditions: (a) young, misled subjects; (b) young, control subjects; (c) old, misled subjects; (d) old, control subjects.

6   The results were pretty much in line with the hypothesis. Older subjects made more errors and specifically were more likely to be misled. They were also more likely to be sure of the correctness of their wrong answers than the younger subjects.

5   *Numerical Data Analysis*

In this chapter we look at the calculations of 'statistical tests'. Statistical tests inform us about the relationship between variables. Statistics do not tell us if our theories and hypotheses are 'true' or 'correct'. Rather they inform us of the likelihood that the results we have are simply the product of random chance, or, in contrast, that they are unlikely to be due to chance. A result that fits our hypothesis or theory and which is not likely to be due to chance lends support to the theory or hypothesis. Thinking back to Chapter 4 on experimental methods you will remember that the goal of the experiment is to gain a result that will allow us to reject the null hypothesis – the claim that our results will be due to chance. Statistics are the measure we use to check this. We will look at three examples of statistical tests:

- Correlations – for use with 'continuous' measures
- Chi-squares – for use with 'groups' or 'categories'
- t-tests – for comparing 'averages' across groups

These examples reflect the main types of statistical tests available and each is related to a specific type, or combination of types, of data. We have to choose the right kind of statistical test to go with the type of data we have collected.

Correlation statistics are used where the two variables are measured on essentially 'continuous' scales – in other words where the values can be put in some kind of 'order'. An example of such a scale would be the results from the work satisfaction measure in Chapter 3. However, the other variable in that example, job status, would consist of a set of categories (e.g. manual vs. non-manual), not a continuous scale, so correlation statistics would not be appropriate. For a correlation test we need two 'continuous' scale measurements. Correlation type analyses are performed on both survey and experimental data.

The chi-squared test compares non-continuous data such as groupings (male/female, British/German etc.). The chi-square test evaluates whether the distribution of cases among a set of groups is 'random' or not. If the distribution is not random then the variables that define the groups are likely to relate in some manner. Chi-squared analyses are more likely to be found in survey work where measures are compared across demographic variables, though they can be used in experimental settings. The t-test is used to compare the mean – the 'average' results between two groups. It checks if the difference in 'average' results between the groups is likely to be due to chance or not. The t-test belongs to a family of tests – known as parametric tests – that are often used in experimental settings.

Note on the Use of Statistical Software

In most cases statistics are now done on computer through the use of statistical analysis software such as:

- SPSS
- SAS
- Statistica
- Minitab

So why have I gone to the trouble of explaining the process by which you can calculate these results 'by hand'? There is one important reason. Statistics are not straightforward and there are many issues you need to take into account. By working through these examples you will gain a better understanding of how statistics work and what they can really tell us. To fully utilise the software systems listed above you need to understand what they are doing and what the data you are working with is like.

Types of Data

The choice of statistical test you use is (mainly) determined by the type of data that you have. Now you may design an experiment or survey with the intention of using a certain test or set of tests. If so, you need to ensure that the measures you use and the data you collect are appropriate. On the other hand you may be limited in terms of the data you can collect. In this case your choices will be limited by the data. So what kinds of data are there? Data can be categorised into two main types:

- Categorical data – when cases belong to discrete categories
- 'Continuous' data – where the data can be placed in some kind of order

We will take a quick look at these types of data before moving on to the first example, analysis.

Categorical Data

Data is said to be categorical if you can place the cases into distinct 'categories'. An example might be an equal opportunities form asking information about your 'ethnic group':

- White (British), White (European), Asian, Afro-Caribbean, African, etc.

Now you need to ensure that the cases being categorised are 'discrete', that is, they must be distinct and separate. It must not be possible for a case to be in more than one category of a variable. You therefore need to choose categories carefully when designing a questionnaire or an experiment. The key principle to remember is that every case should belong to one and only one category in any variable – and there should be no doubt as to which one. Some textbooks may refer to categorical data as nominal data.

Continuous Data

There are three types of continuous data. These range from categories that have some inherent order through to truly continuous scales. The three types of continuous data are:

- Ordinal
- Interval
- Ratio

Ordinal scales are those where the data are essentially in categories but the categories are in ascending or descending rank. Good examples of this type of data are the results from the types of measures discussed in Chapter 3 such as Likert scales. The distance between points on the scale is 'meaningless' but the categories can be placed in some kind of order. For example:

- agree/neither agree nor disagree/disagree
- like a lot/like a little/no preference/dislike a little/dislike a lot

Interval scales are those where the values held by cases are points on a scale with a distinct unit 'size'. Importantly the 'interval' between values is the same size throughout the scale. Therefore the difference between 5 and 8 is the same as between 1 and 4. Such measures do not have a true 'zero' value so one value (e.g. 10) cannot be said to be a multiple (e.g. '5 times' bigger than) of some other value (e.g. 2). Many psychological measures produce data that comes into this category. The data from the work satisfaction measure from Chapter 3 would fit here. Another classic example is temperature in degrees Celsius or Fahrenheit. Zero degrees Celsius is not a point of 'no heat' – though it does feel cold!

Ratio scales are like interval scales but they have true zero points. A temperature example is the Kelvin scale as this scale has a true zero point ('absolute zero' as it is called) and this is a true ratio scale. In other words 100 degrees C is not twice as hot as 50 degrees C but 100 degrees Kelvin *is* twice as hot as 50 degrees Kelvin. Other obvious examples are height, length, mass, volume, density, etc. We will start by looking at a statistical test for use when the data you are looking at are continuous.

Analysing Continuous Data: Correlations

The statistical test we will be looking at now is known as a correlation. The basic rationale behind a correlation is to explore the relationship between two 'continuous' variables. The result of a correlation tells us how two variables change with respect to each other. If variable A goes up, does variable B go up or down? For example, does the time taken to read a document rise with the number of new technical terms presented in it? In most cases of social and psychological research ordinal or interval scales are used. The example of a statistical analysis that follows is designed for ordinal data – the test is called a Spearman rank correlation. There are other types of correlation tests – for example for use with interval and ratio data. We will not discuss these here but you can find them discussed in any good statistics textbook. Some suggested further reading on statistical methods is given at the end of this chapter. This section will explore the way in which the test is conducted. In the next section we will explore the idea of 'statistical significance' – the main aspects of which are the same for all statistical tests – and conclude the discussion of correlations.

SAQ 5.1

Correlating reading and spelling

Suppose a researcher has predicted a correlation between children's reading scores and spelling scores.

1 Write down the two variables in this study.
2 Write down the pair of scores each child will produce.

How can a researcher judge whether there is a correlation in the predicted direction? If children who have good spelling scores also have good reading scores, while other children tend to have low scores on both variables, there is likely to be a correlation between the variables of reading and spelling.

Positive Correlations

The next question is how to determine whether there is in fact any correlation between the pairs of scores. First, the researcher would give all the cases two tests, a reading test and a spelling test. From these it would be possible to calculate a spelling score and a reading score for each child. Table 5.1 shows a simplified example of such scores.

Table 5.1 *Spelling scores (out of 20) and reading scores (out of 10)*

Child	Spelling score	Reading score
1	20	10
2	18	9
3	16	8
4	14	7
5	12	6
6	10	5
7	8	4
8	6	3
9	4	2
10	2	1

Look at the scores in Table 5.1. Child 1 is top at both spelling and reading, child 2 is next best at both, and so on down to child 10, who gets the lowest scores on both tests.

In a case like this, it can be claimed that spelling and reading scores are highly correlated. This is known as a **positive correlation** because the variables move in the same direction. High scores on spelling 'go together' with high scores on reading, medium scores go with medium scores, and low scores go with low scores.

SAQ 5.2

Positive correlations

Which of the following are most likely to result in a high positive correlation? Which are not likely to be correlated at all?

1 height/shoe size
2 number of cinema tickets sold/the number of customers in the audience
3 amount of spinach eaten/size of wins on football pools.

It is obvious from the examples in SAQ 5.2 that positive correlations between some pairs of scores are likely to be very high, while others are low or non-existent. How can we measure whether a correlation is high or low?

Correlation Coefficients

Correlations are measured in terms of correlation coefficients, which indicate the size of the correlation between two variables. Correlation coefficients run from 0, that is, no correlation, to 1 for a perfect positive correlation. In Table 5.1 there is a complete one-to-one relationship between the pairs of scores. This represents a perfect positive correlation coefficient of 1 between the variables of spelling scores and reading scores.

Of course in actual social science research, scores would not be so perfectly correlated. There are sure to be some good spellers who are bad at reading and vice versa. Most positive correlations fall somewhere between the two extremes of 0 and 1.

Positive correlation coefficients are expressed as decimal numbers falling between 0 and 1, in the form of 'nought point something', for example 0.1, 0.2, 0.3 and so on, up to 0.9. The nearer a correlation coefficient is to 0, the lower the correlation; the nearer it is to 1, the higher the positive correlation.

SAQ 5.3

1   Which of the three correlation coefficients listed below expresses the lowest and the highest correlations? List them in order from lowest to highest.
    (a) 0.5   (b) 0   (c) 0.9
2   Which of these correlation coefficients is most likely to express the relationship between the number of miles in a journey by train and the cost of a single standard-class ticket for the trip?
3   Which of the correlational coefficients is most likely to express the relationship between the number of pedestrian crossings in a town and average earnings?

Negative Correlations

We have looked at the amount of positive correlation between pairs of scores; that is, the extent to which the two variables vary in the same direction. But what about cases where high scores on one variable might be expected to be linked with low scores on another variable? For instance, children who achieve excellent scores on a quiz about sport may score low on writing essays, and vice versa. In this case there is still a correlation, but it is a negative correlation. This represents the fact that scores are moving in the opposite direction to each other. For instance, a high score on the sports quiz will be associated with a low essay writing score; a low sports quiz score will go with a high essay writing score.

SAQ 5.4

Which of the following are likely to be a positive correlation and which negative?

1 temperatures in winter and size of electricity bills
2 amount of rain and sale of umbrellas.

A perfect negative correlation occurs when high scores on one variable are perfectly associated with low scores on the other. Table 5.2 shows a set of scores that are perfectly negatively correlated: the higher the quiz score, the lower the essay score, and the lower the quiz score, the higher the essay score.

Table 5.2 *Quiz scores and essay writing scores (both out of 10)*

Child	Quiz score	Essay score
1	10	1
2	9	2
3	8	3
4	7	4
5	6	5

Such relationships between variables are expressed by negative correlation coefficients, which run from 0 down to –1. A coefficient of –1 represents a perfect negative correlation. This would represent the relationship between the pairs of scores in Table 5.2. (Note that, although child 5 actually got a higher score for the sports quiz than the essay, it is still true that relatively this child got the lowest of the quiz scores and the highest of the essay scores.)

As with positive correlations, negative correlation coefficients are expressed as decimal numbers, but this time between 0 and –1. In effect, negative correlation coefficients are exactly equivalent to the range of decimal numbers for positive correlations, except that they all have a minus sign, for example, –0.1, –0.5 and –0.9. The size of a negative correlation coefficient is related to whether it is nearer 0 (a low negative correlation) or –1 (a perfect negative correlation). So a negative coefficient of –0.9 represents a very high negative correlation.

To sum up, a correlation coefficient of zero means that there is no relation at all between the variables. A high negative correlation coefficient (say –0.9) represents a large negative correlation, just as +0.9 represents a large positive correlation. It is a general rule that the higher the correlation coefficient, whether positive or negative, the higher the correlation. Smaller correlation coefficients (e.g. 0.2 and –0.2) indicate lower correlations between variables. Figure 5.1 shows the full range of possible correlation coefficients.

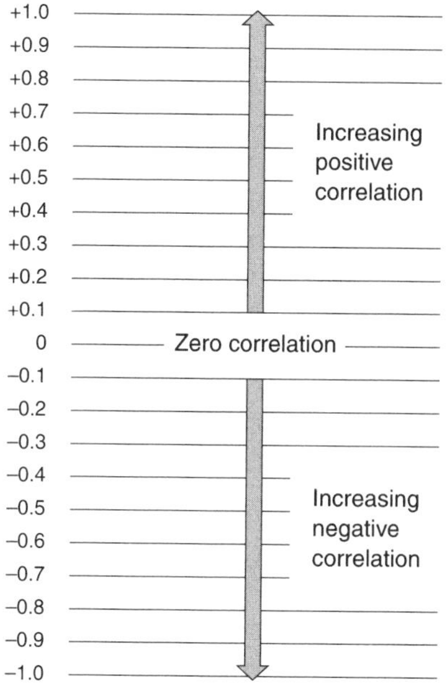

Figure 5.1 *Range of correlation coefficient values*

SAQ 5.5

Which of these coefficients represents the highest correlation? This is similar to SAQ 5.3, but with a negative correlation.

(a) +0.5   (b) 0   (c) −0.65

Summary

- A correlation represents the association between pairs of variables.
- Correlation coefficients measure the size of a correlation between pairs of scores on each variable.
- Positive correlations occur when scores on one variable move in the same direction as scores on the other variable.
- Negative correlations occur when scores on one variable move in the opposite direction to scores on the other variable.
- Correlation coefficients are measured on a scale running from +1 (perfect positive correlation) through 0 (zero correlation) to −1 (perfect negative correlation).

• The nearer a correlation coefficient is to one (+1 or –1), the higher the correlation between two variables.

Statistical Analysis

The next step is to consider how correlation coefficients can be calculated. It may seem pretty clear that the scores in Table 5.1 are perfectly correlated and therefore the value of the correlation coefficient will be +1. Similarly, the scores in Table 5.2 represent a perfect negative correlation of –1. But now take a look at the scores for twelve children in Table 5.3. Here the value of the correlation coefficient is not so obvious. For instance, child 7 got a very low score of 2 out of 10 on spelling but a good score of 4 out of 5 for reading. Is it still possible to claim that spelling scores and reading scores are positively correlated?

Table 5.3 *Spelling scores (out of 10) and reading scores (out of 5)*

Child	Spelling score	Reading score
1	5	2
2	3	2
3	7	4
4	10	5
5	9	4
6	9	5
7	2	4
8	6	3
9	3	1
10	4	1
11	8	4
12	10	5

We need a way of measuring correlations so as to obtain the actual value of the correlation coefficient. The Spearman rank correlation coefficient, described below, is designed to measure the size of correlation between two sets of scores.

Preparing the Data

Before you can start to calculate any statistics you need to prepare the data of your research study in the form of a table showing the pairs of scores for your cases. For correlational research designs this means preparing a table of results which shows the scores obtained by your cases on each of the variables. It is always essential to give tables clear titles and labels indicating what is being measured. Table 5.3 shows the pair of scores for each child case, that is, a spelling score (out of a possible top score of 10) and a reading score (out of a possible top score of 5). This can be analysed so as to calculate an exact correlation coefficient that will indicate the size of the correlation between the variables of spelling and reading.

How to Rank Scores

In order to carry out the data analysis for the Spearman rank correlation coefficient, it is first necessary to rank the scores. This process is quite simple, but it needs to be carried out with care. To rank scores all you have to do is assign ranks of 1, 2, 3, 4, etc. to each score in order of magnitude. In Table 5.4 you will notice that we attribute rank 1 to the smallest score of 3. We shall always stick to this procedure, assigning the smallest rank to the smallest score. So, in Table 5.4 we assign rank 2 to the next smallest score of 4, rank 3 to the next smallest score of 5, and so on.

Table 5.4 *Ranking scores*

Score	Rank
6	4
3	1
12	7
4	2
7	5
5	3
8	6

How to Rank Tied Scores

Look at the scores in Table 5.5. Three cases all produced scores of 1, and two other cases produced scores of 4. These are known as tied scores. The question is how to assign ranks to these scores.

Table 5.5 *Ranking tied scores*

Score	Rank
1	2
2	4
1	2
4	6.5
1	2
3	5
4	6.5
6	9
5	8

The aim is to give the same rank to the tied scores. The procedure used is to give all the tied scores the average of the ranks they would have been entitled to. The three scores of 1 in Table 5.5 would have been assigned ranks 1, 2 and 3 because they are equivalent to the three smallest scores. So all three are given the same rank, which is the average of these ranks:

$$\frac{1 + 2 + 3}{3} = \frac{6}{3} = 2$$

Having assigned the average rank of 2 to the three tied scores of 1, the next smallest score is 2. Since the ranks of 1, 2 and 3 have already been used up, this score is assigned rank 4. The next smallest score of 3 is given the next rank 5. Then we have the two scores of 4, which would have been entitled to ranks 6 and 7. Since the average of ranks 6 and 7 is 6.5, the tied scores of 4 are both assigned this average rank. After using up ranks 6 and 7, the next available rank is 8, which can be assigned to the score of 5. Finally, the highest score of 6 is assigned the highest rank of 9. Note that if the highest scores themselves are tied, the highest ranks will also be tied and so you will end up with the average of the highest ranks. Note also that the number of scores and the number of ranks is always the same. So, in Table 5.5, there are nine scores and nine ranks.

SAQ 5.6

Allocate ranks to the following scores.

Score	Rank
1	
0	
2	
1	
3	

You will probably have realised that assigning ranks to scores gives you information about which are the smallest and largest scores. In fact, ranks exactly reflect the range of scores from lowest to highest. The reason ranks are assigned to scores is essentially a technical one. Correlational statistics are relatively simple, although difficult enough for beginners. This specific statistical test can be calculated only by using ranks.

Spearman Rank Correlation Coefficient

The Spearman rank correlation coefficient (written as the symbol r_s) calculates a statistic called rho. This statistic measures the size of the correlation coefficient for two sets of scores by taking into account the differences between the ranked scores.

We will now use the Spearman rank correlation coefficient to calculate the size of the correlation between the variables of reading and spelling using sample data of spelling and reading scores for twelve children. The first step is to rank the scores for each variable. In Table 5.6, the column headed 'Spelling rank (A)' shows the ranks for the spelling scores, and the one headed 'Reading rank (B)' shows the ranks for the reading scores. Check for yourselves that the ranks have been correctly assigned to each of these sets of scores, allowing for tied scores.

Table 5.6 *Calculating the Spearman rank correlation coefficient*

Case	Spelling score	Spelling rank (A)	Reading score	Reading rank (B)	d (A–B)	d²
1	5	5	2	3.5	+1.5	2.25
2	3	2.5	2	3.5	−1	1
3	7	7	4	7.5	−0.5	0.25
4	10	11.5	5	11	+0.5	0.25
5	9	9.5	4	7.5	+2	4
6	9	9.5	5	11	−1.5	2.25
7	2	1	4	7.5	−6.5	42.25
8	6	6	3		+1	1
9	3	2.5	1	1.5	+1	1
10	4	4	1	1.5	+2.5	6.25
11	8	8	4	7.5	+0.5	0.25
12	10	11.5	5	11	+0.5	0.25
						$\Sigma d^2 = 61$

You may have found it quite difficult to work out the ranks for all the tied scores, especially for the reading scores. This is always a problem when the range of scores on a variable is so limited.

As you can see in Table 5.6, the next step is to work out the differences between the A and B ranks by subtracting rank B from rank A for each of the cases. The resulting plus and minus numbers in the 'd(A–B)' column represent the difference for each individual case between their rank score for spelling and their rank score for reading.

What is really happening is that by ranking each case's pair of scores, it is possible to compare the spelling and reading scores for each child with those of the other children. A particular child's spelling score may come out with a high rank. If one is testing a positive correlation, what one wants to know is whether that same child will also come out with a comparatively highly ranked score on reading. The rationale is that the smaller the differences between the ranks, the more likely it is that the two sets of scores are positively correlated.

Instructions for Calculating Rho (r_s)

The step-by-step instructions in Equation 1 take you through the calculations. Before you start you will need to note the meaning of the following symbols:

d refers to the differences between ranks

d² means that each difference in the 'd' column is squared (multiplied by itself)

N refers to the number of cases whose pairs of scores are being compared

Σ stands for 'total' or 'sum' – that is, add up all the numbers that follow this symbol.

At each stage of the calculation you will have to refer to the data in Table 5.6. You should note that the value of the r_s correlation coefficient does not have to be calculated to more than two decimal points.

Equation 1 *Step-by-step instructions for calculating the value of Spearman's r_s correlation coefficient*

1 Rank the spelling scores, assigning 1 to the smallest score and so on (see pp. 87–88)	'Spelling rank (A)' column in Table 5.6
Do the same for the reading scores	'Reading rank (B) column' in Table 5.6
2 Calculate the difference (d) between each pair of A and B ranks by subtracting each rank B from each rank A	'd(A–B)' column in Table 5.6
3 Square each difference in the d column	'd^2' column in Table 5.6
4 Add up the d^2 column to obtain Σd^2 (the sum total of all the entries in the d^2 column)	$\Sigma d^2 = 61$
5 Count the number of cases (N)	$N = 12$

6 Find the value of r_s using the formula:

$$r_s = 1 - \frac{6\,\Sigma d^2}{N(N^2 - 1)}$$

$$r_s = 1 - \frac{6 \times 61}{12\,(144 - 1)}$$

$$= 1 - \frac{366}{12 \times 143}$$

$$= 1 - \frac{366}{1716}$$

$$= 1 - 0.21$$

$$= 0.79$$

Essentially, the statistic measures differences between the ranks for two sets of scores. If two variables are positively correlated, people who have low ranks on one set of scores should have low ranks on the other, and people who have high ranks on one should have high ranks on the other. From this it follows that, if there is a high positive correlation, there will tend to be small differences between people's ranks on both variables. So the smaller the differences between the ranks for the two variables, the larger the positive correlation.

If you look at the formula in Equation 1 you will see that the final step is to subtract from 1 at the end of the calculation. You will remember that +1 represents a perfect positive correlation. The smaller the number you subtract from 1, the higher the positive correlation. In Equation 1 the result was $1 - 0.21$, giving the relatively high positive correlation of 0.79.

SAQ 5.7

1 Look back to Table 5.1. Assign ranks to each of the two sets of scores separately. Work out the differences between the ranks for each child. Following the step-by-step instructions, calculate the rho (r_s) value of the correlation coefficient. Remember that any figure multiplied by zero is zero, so the square of 0 is $0 \times 0 = 0$.
2 Is there anything special about the value of the correlation coefficient?

Calculating Correlation Coefficients

What happens with negative correlations? Remember that with negative correlations it is high scores on one variable (e.g. a sports quiz) that go with low scores on the other variable (e.g. writing essays). So, in this case, one would expect the differences between the ranked scores to be large. This would result in a large number being subtracted from 1 at the end of the step-by-step instructions, giving a negative value for the correlation coefficient.

SAQ 5.8

1 Look back to Table 5.2. Assign ranks to each set of scores separately. Work out the differences between the ranks for each child. Following the step-by-step instructions, calculate the rho (r_s) value of the correlation coefficient.
2 Is there anything special about the value of the correlation coefficient?

The results of SAQ 5.7 and SAQ 5.8 demonstrate the extreme cases when the correlation coefficient works out at +1 or –1 to represent a perfect positive or negative correlation. The sets of scores in Table 5.6 are much more like the data found in social science experiments. The value of the correlation coefficient works out as somewhere between +1 and –1, indicating a less than perfect positive or negative correlation. The first point to consider is whether the value of rho (r_s) has a high absolute value, indicating that there is a strong association between the two variables being tested. But we also have to ask whether a high correlation is also significant using the statistical test on p. 95.

Summary

- The Spearman rank correlation coefficient is a statistical technique for calculating the rho (r_s) correlation coefficient from pairs of scores on two variables.
- The scores on each variable have to be ranked separately, following rules for assigning ranks to tied scores.
- The Spearman statistical technique calculates the differences between ranks on the two variables, to give a value for a rho (r_s) that indicates the size of a positive or negative correlation.
- The value of rho (r_s) has to be high to demonstrate the strength of a correlation. It also has to be shown to be significant in terms of a statistical test.

Statistical Tests of Significance

Using the Spearman rank correlation method we can calculate correlation coefficients that represent the size of the correlation between sets of scores. These coefficients can range from zero to perfect correlations. Researchers naturally want to find high correlations, as predicted by their hypotheses, for instance that good readers are likely to be good spellers as well. Suppose they find a correlation of 0.79, or 0.2, or 0.6? Does this mean that these correlations are significant? Or might they have occurred by chance? In order to decide this question, we have to carry out a statistical test on each correlation coefficient. This will involve looking up the correlation coefficient in a statistical table.

Random Variability

People are, of course, all unique individuals and so will react to situations in different ways. This will affect the way children perform on spelling tests and reading tests. So there is certain to be quite a lot of unforeseen random variability in people's responses. Because of this, a research hypothesis is always formulated in contrast to a null hypothesis, which states that there are no significant relationships between the variables. A more precise way of formulating the null hypothesis is to say that any results are due to chance fluctuations in people's performance, that is, to random variability.

Let us imagine that you had tested only two children's spelling and reading scores. Child A has a low spelling score and a low reading score. Child B has a high spelling score and a high reading score. So it looks as if spelling and reading are perfectly correlated (i.e. a positive correlation of +1). But could a researcher really be convinced by looking at the scores of only two children that there is a significant positive correlation?

From this example, it is clear that the number of people providing scores is very important. If 100 children were tested and all their spelling and reading scores were correlated, this would be much more convincing evidence. However, with so many children we would be likely to come up against the problem of random variability. Some of the children may have high spelling scores but low reading scores, thus giving a less than perfect correlation. This raises the question: is a perfect correlation of 1 between only two children likely to be more or less significant than a correlation of 0.8 between the scores of 100 children?

Statistical tests can settle this question for you. By taking into account the number of cases taking part in your research, and the differences between their ranked scores on two variables, you can work out whether the research data represent a significant correlation as predicted by your research hypothesis. If so, you are entitled to reject the null hypothesis that any differences are due to random variability in performance. What statistical tests tell you is whether the overall variability in people's scores is likely to be due to the predicted relationship between variables, rather than being due to random variability.

This is the basis of all statistical tests of significance. If a statistical test reveals that the probability of getting the scores found in your experiment by chance is very low, you can reject the null hypothesis that the scores are due to random variability. Instead, you can accept the research hypothesis that your results are significant.

When we talk about whether or not a research result is significant, you should bear in mind that there is always a specific probability that every result is a random result. Suppose, for instance, you tossed a coin a thousand times and got heads every time. You would probably think that the coin was definitely biased towards heads. However, there is a tiny probability that a run of a thousand 'heads' in a row could occur even if the coin was perfectly normal. Even so, because the probability of this happening is exceedingly small, you would be very likely to accept that the coin is biased. It is just the same with the data from social science research. There is always a small probability that the results of your research are due to random variability. The most you can say is that the probability of your data having occurred randomly is so tiny that you are prepared to take the risk of rejecting the null hypothesis and accepting that there is a significant correlation.

Levels of Significance

So, how small must the 'tiny' probability of random variability be when it comes to deciding whether or not to reject the null hypothesis? What risk would you be prepared to accept that the scores resulting from your experiment occurred randomly, as stated by the null hypothesis, and were not significant at all? You would of course like to be certain that the correlation is significant, but unfortunately things are never so clear-cut as this, since there is always a probability that cases' scores are random after all.

Imagine that you were investigating whether a new reading scheme might help children to learn, and you carried out an experiment in which you compared the progress of a group of children using your new scheme with the progress of another group using traditional methods. Suppose you found a difference in reading improvement scores between the two groups in favour of the new scheme. Suppose the probability that this difference could have occurred by chance was 5% (i.e. there was a 5 in 100 probability that there were only random chance differences rather than a significant difference attributable to the reading scheme). Would you accept that the difference was significant and introduce the new reading scheme, and at what cost in materials and teacher training?

Imagine another case where you are testing a powerful drug with severe side effects, and you find a correlation between patients' blood pressures and the occurrence of the side effects. Suppose these results could have occurred by chance 5 in 100 times. Would you accept that the correlation is significant and refrain from giving the drug to patients with high blood pressure? Would you accept the odds if you knew that without the drug most of the patients would die anyway? And how would you feel if an aeroplane you were going to fly in had a 5% probability of developing electrical failure?

These examples bring home the fact that choosing a significance level is always a matter of deciding what odds you are prepared to accept that your data are random. In the case of the reading scheme probably no one would suffer too much if it was all due to chance after all. As long as it was not too expensive, you would probably go ahead and introduce the new scheme. You might, however, feel more doubtful about administering a powerful drug with side effects if there was a 5 in 100 probability that it was doing no good at all, although you might accept these odds if it were the only hope of saving people's lives. I don't think any of us would fly in a plane with a 5% chance of crashing.

In scientific research it is a convention to accept odds of either 1 in 100 (i.e. 1%) or 5 in 100 (i.e. 5%) as grounds for rejecting the null hypothesis and accepting that the research hypothesis has been supported. This is expressed by stating that the probability of a result being random is less than 1% or less than 5%, that is, that findings were significant ($p < 0.01$) or ($p < 0.05$). This means that the probability (p) of a result occurring by chance is less than (expressed as $<$) the appropriate percentage. Thus $p < 0.01$ means a probability of less than 1% and $p < 0.05$ means a probability of less than 5%. Sometimes you will find other probabilities such as $p < 0.02$ or $p < 0.001$ used, that is, a chance result of only 2 times in 100 or 1 in 1000 (2% or 0.1%). These percentages are shown in Table 5.7.

Table 5.7 *p values*

$p < 0.5$	less than 5% (5 percent)	5 in 100
$p < 0.2$	less than 2% (2 percent)	2 in 100
$p < 0.01$	less than 1% (1 percent)	1 in 100
$p < 0.001$	less than 0.1% (0.1 percent)	1 in 1000

SAQ 5.9

Suppose that an experimenter reports that a correlation coefficient between spelling and reading scores is significant ($p < 0.01$).

1   Which, if any, of the following percentages represents $p < 0.01$?
      (a) 1 in 20 (5%)   (b) 1 in 100 (1%)   (c) 1 in 1000 (0.1%)
2   Which of the above percentages would indicate the greatest level of significance? Which indicates the least significance?

3   Which of the conventional levels of significance ($p < 0.05$) and ($p < 0.01$) indicates a lower probability of random variability?

4   Express $p < 0.025$ as a percentage and as a probability out of 100.

Looking up the Significance of Rho (r_s)

Having followed the step-by-step instructions in Equation 1 to calculate the value of Spearman's rho (r_s) correlation coefficient, the next step is to look up its significance in a statistical table. Along the top row of Table 5.23 (see p. 130) you will find the two conventional levels of significance $p < 0.05$ and $p < 0.01$. Down the left-hand column are listed the number of cases (N) being tested. For any N the calculated value of r_s is significant if it is *larger* than or *equal to* the critical values in the table.

The entries in Table 5.23 represent correlation coefficient values shown in each case to two decimal places. For instance, in the $p < 0.01$ column, the coefficient values run from a perfect correlation of 1.00 (1.00 is the same as 1) for $N = 5$ down to a correlation coefficient of 0.43 for $N = 30$. These are the correlation coefficient values which would be significant at the $p < 0.01$ level for different numbers of cases. Remember that this means that there is only a 1% probability that these values might have occurred by chance.

As you can see, whether a correlation coefficient value is significant depends on how many cases there are. If there are only five cases, you would need a perfect correlation coefficient of 1.00 to reach a significance level of $p < 0.01$. If there are more cases, then a lower correlation coefficient value will be significant; for example, for 30 cases a correlation of 0.31 will be significant ($p < 0.05$).

SAQ 5.10

1   What correlation coefficient value would be significant at the $p < 0.05$ level for five cases?

2   What correlation coefficient value would be significant at the $p < 0.01$ level for 24 cases?

Now we are in a position to look up the significance of the correlation coefficient we calculated in Equation 1. If you look back to this equation you will see that the calculated r_s correlation coefficient was 0.79, and the number of cases (N) was twelve. This means that we need to look along the row for $N = 12$ in Table 5.23. The correlation coefficient value listed for $p < 0.05$ is 0.51 and for $p < 0.01$ it is 0.71. In order for a calculated correlation coefficient to be significant, it has to be equal to or larger than the coefficient values given in Table 5.23. As it turns out, the calculated value of r_s = 0.79 is larger than the value of 0.71 for the $p < 0.01$ significance level. This means that a correlation of 0.79 for twelve cases is significant ($p < 0.01$). In other words, the probability that the 0.79 correlation between reading and spelling scores is due to random variability in the children's performance is less than 1%.

You should remember that the null hypothesis states that any results are due to random fluctuations in people's performance. The significance level of $p < 0.01$ indicates that the probability of a random result is 1% (i.e. 1 in 100). Because this represents a low probability of a result due to random variability, the null hypothesis can be rejected. The usual way of expressing the results of a research study is to state that the correlation between reading scores and spelling scores of 0.79 was significant ($p < 0.01$) and that this supports the predictions stated in the research hypothesis. If the calculated value of r_s had been less than the required values in Table 5.23, the correlation would not have been significant.

You will notice that all the coefficient values in Table 5.23 are positive. But suppose your calculated value of r_s had worked out as a negative correlation coefficient of –0.79. This represents the size of a correlation whether it is positive or negative. So you would still have to look along the N = 12 row to see whether a correlation value of 0.79 for twelve cases is significant. You will find that it is larger than the coefficient value of 0.71 for the $p < 0.01$ significance level in Table 5.1, so you can reject the null hypothesis of random variability. However, you would have to interpret the results of your study as confirming a predicted negative relationship between two variables.

SAQ 5.11

Table 5.8 shows the scores obtained from a test for memory of shapes and a test for spelling ability. Both tests were given to the same set of ten cases.

Table 5.8 *Shape memory scores and spelling scores*

Case	Shape memory score	Shape memory rank (A)	Spelling score	Spelling rank (B)	d	d^2
1	7		13			
2	8		19			
3	6		16			
4	9		21			
5	4		10			
6	3		11			
7	9		18			
8	8		18			
9	10		14			
10	11		16			$\Sigma d^2 =$

1 Use the blank columns to calculate the value of the rho (r_s) correlation coefficient.
2 Can the experimental hypothesis that shape memory is associated with spelling ability be supported?

Conclusion

You should by now have a good general grasp of the idea of a correlation and of the idea of statistical significance. Statistics are an important part of the process of quantitative social research. As you will have noted from the discussion of statistical significance, it is not enough to find a correlation. One also needs to know if the correlation is likely to be due to random chance. If it is not and the results are in line with our initial hypothesis, we can reject the null hypothesis. We have not, though, proved our hypothesis to be true. Rather we can claim, within the context of the sample or the experimental design, that our result is unlikely to be a product of random factors. We can therefore be reasonably confident in attributing the findings to the population we sampled from or to the variables we controlled in the experiment. This stage of the process is often referred to as the 'interpretation' of the results. On pp. 112–116 we look at this process in more detail, but before we move on it will be useful to look again at Reading E.

SAQ 5.12

Turn again to Reading E, 'Age differences in source forgetting: effects on reality monitoring and on eyewitness testimony', and re-read the 'Results' section which reports the statistical results. The statistical test used in this case is not a correlation but a z-test, which examines differences between cases rather than correlations between cases. As with a correlation, the z-test produces a single score like the r_s score, in this case a z score. Using this score and information about the number of cases and conditions, the significance can be calculated, the p values, for each comparison made. While you are re-reading this material make notes on:

1 What were the various significance levels for each of the findings?
2 Which was the most statistically significant finding?

Summary

- Because human behaviour is variable, there will be variability in cases' scores.
- Statistical tests are used to calculate the probabilities that differences in scores are due to random variability, as stated by the null hypothesis.
- Conventional levels of significance represent probabilities of less than 5% ($p < 0.05$) or less than 1% ($p < 0.01$) that scores are due to random variability.
- Statistics, such as Spearman's rho (r_s), can be used to calculate correlation coefficients. These values of r_s can be looked up in a statistical table to see whether the calculated value exceeds the correlation coefficient values in Table 5.23.
- Low probabilities of random variability, conventionally $p < 0.05$ and $p < 0.01$, allow researchers to reject the null hypothesis and instead to claim that their findings are significant and support the experimental hypothesis.

Analysing Categorical Data: Chi-square

The chi-square test is just about the only test you can use if all your data are categorical. This is very often the case with 'demographic' data such as gender, age bracket, occupation, wage bracket and so forth. The chi-square test examines if the distribution of membership across a range of categories is likely to be the product of chance. If there is a very low probability that the distribution is a product of chance then it is more likely that the memberships of the various categories influence each other. That is to say does membership (or not) of one category influence membership of another? For each variable you will need at least two mutually exclusive categories. Car ownership is a good example – you either do or don't own a car. A bad example might be to split pet ownership into categories such as dog owner, cat owner, emu owner, etc.! The problem here is that one person could be in all three categories.

Let us consider an example research project. We may wish to examine if party political affiliation and union membership are related. To do this we may send out questionnaires to a representative sample of the population, or we might look at a specific case such as a single workplace. From this we might get the data in Table 5.9 and Table 5.10.

Table 5.9 *Representative national sample*

	Labour	Liberal	Conservative
Trade union members	5125	1055	425
Non-trade union members	1065	895	2555

Table 5.10 *All staff in call centre*

	Labour	Liberal	Conservative
Trade union members	45	10	6
Non-trade union members	638	188	333

In the national case it looks very likely that being a union member is linked to being a Labour party member. And not being in a union is linked to being a Conservative supporter. In the second case it is hard to tell. It looks as if union members are also Labour supporters but there are more Labour supporters in the workforce, and on the whole people are not members of a union. This might imply that the context itself, the call centre, has an impact on union membership. We can, though, check in both cases if the result is likely to be an interaction between the two variables. This is where the chi-square test comes in.

Preparing the Data

Table 5.9 and Table 5.10 are examples of how the data need to be tabulated in the first place. You will have to draw up such tables from lists of actual responses or measures of cases. These are likely to be in some format similar to that in Table 5.11.

Table 5.11 *Party-political affiliation and union membership*

Respondent Number	Union membership 1 = Union, 0 = Non-union	Political party 1 = Labour, 2 = Liberal, 3 = Conservative
1	1	1
2	0	3
3	0	2
4	1	1
5	1	2
6	1	1
7	1	3
8	0	1
9	1	2
10	1	1

To tabulate these data you need to total up the number of cases in each cell of the table. The number of rows in the table is defined by the categories in one variable and the number of columns by the number of categories in the other variable. We therefore have two rows and three columns (or three rows and two columns) – as in Table 5.9 and Table 5.10. Table 5.12 totals the number of cases in each cell. Each occurrence of a case in a cell of the table is marked with 'strikes' or 'ticks'. Ticking off the cases is one way of totalling the number of cases in each cell. That is the number of cases where the person is (or is not) a union member and is a member of the relevant party.

Table 5.12 *Tallies of task and tools counts*

	Labour	Liberal	Conservative
Trade union members	IIII	II	I
Non-trade union members	I	I	I

SAQ 5.13

Try this for yourself. Draw a 2 × 3 table as in Table 5.12 and add up the cases in each cell for the data in Table 5.13.

Table 5.13 *SAQ 5.9 data*

Respondent Number	Area 1 = Union, 0 = Non-union	Political party 1 = Labour, 2 = Liberal, 3 = Conservative
1	0	1
2	0	2
3	0	3
4	1	1
5	1	1
6	1	1
7	1	3
8	1	2
9	1	2
10	1	1

The more data you have, the longer this task takes and most spreadsheet software can sort or tabulate such data for you. But by whatever means you get there this is the first stage of the chi-square calculation done.

Calculating the Chi-square Value (χ^2)

The chi-square test works by comparing the values you have in the actual cells with those you should expect to get if the data were unaffected by the variables. These 'expected values' are calculated by assuming that the overall total distribution of cases between the categories will be mirrored in the actual cells of the table. So, for example, if 25% of all the cases are Labour supporters then we should expect that 25% of the members of union and non-union members will also be Labour supporters. The chi-square calculation generates a measure of the variation from this set of 'expected values'. If this variation is great enough given the number of cases and the number of possibilities implied by the number of cells then it is unlikely that it is a random outcome. Therefore we could assert that the two variables influence one another in some manner. So the next step is to calculate the expected values.

Calculating Expected Values

Before moving on the calculation we need to set up a few symbols:

O   refers to the observed number of cases in a cell
E   refers to the expected number of cases in a cell
N   refers to the number of cases
Σ   stands for 'total' or 'sum' – that is, add up all the numbers that follow this symbol.

We start by adding up the totals cases in each row, column and overall. This has been done in Table 5.14.

Table 5.14 *Calculation of row and column totals*

Row number	Column number	1	2	3	
		Labour	Liberal	Conservative	**Totals rows**
1	Union members	45	10	6	**45+10+6 = 61**
2	Non-union members	638	188	333	**638+188+333 = 1159**
	Totals columns	**45+ 638**	**10+188**	**6+333 = 339**	**61+ 1159 = 1220**
		= 683	**= 198**		
					Or
					683+198+339 = 1220

We can now use the figures to calculate an 'expected value' for each cell. This is done by the following equation:

$$\text{Expected value} = \frac{\text{Total for the row} \times \text{Total for the column}}{i\text{Total number of cases}}$$

So for the Labour supporters who are union members (row 1, column 1) the expected value (E_{11}) is:

$$E_{11} = \frac{61 \times 683}{1200} = 34.15$$

SAQ 5.14

Do this calculation for each of the other cells in the table – you can check these against Table 5.15.

Table 5.15 *Expected values*

Column number	1		2		3		Totals
Row	Labour Observed	Expected	Liberal Observed	Expected	Conservative Observed	Expected	
1 Union members	45	34.15	10	9.9	6	16.95	61
2 Non-union members	638	648.85	188	188.1	333	322.05	1159
Totals columns	683		198		339		1220

Table 5.15 presents the results of the calculations you should have made in 5.14. The chi square is the sum of the squared difference between the observed (O) and expected (E) values divided by the expected value for each cell. So first we need to calculate the difference between the observed and expected values and the square of this value for each cell. The results of this are presented in Table 5.16. Next we divide the square value for each cell by the expected value for that cell. Finally we add up these calculated values from each cell. This is done in Table 5.17.

Table 5.16 *Calculation of observed–expected square values*

Column number	1		2		3	
Row	Labour Difference (O–E)	Square $(O-E)^2$	Liberal Difference (O–E)	Square $(O-E)^2$	Conservative Difference (O–E)	Square $(O-E)^2$
1 Union members	10.85	117.7225	0.1	0.01	−10.95	119.9025
2 Non-union members	−10.85	117.7225	−0.1	0.01	10.95	119.9025

Table 5.17 *Calculation of chi-square value*

Column number	1	2	3
Row	Labour Calculated value $(O-E)^2/E$	Liberal Calculated value $(O-E)^2/E$	Conservative Calculated value $(O-E)^2/E$
1 Union members	3.447218	0.00101	7.073894
2 Non-union members	0.181433	0.0000532	0.37231

Total (chi-square value) = 3.447218+0.00101+7.073894+0.181433+0.0000532+0.37231=11.08

We can now calculate the chi-square value for the whole table. This is given in Equation 2.

Equation 2 *Step-by-step instructions for calculating the value of the chi square*

1 Set up a table with rows and columns equal to the number of categories in each of the two variables then tally up the scores in each cell of the table	See Table 5.12
2 Calculate column, row and overall totals	See Table 5.14
3 Calculate expected values for each cell in the table	See Table 5.15
4 Calculate the difference between the observed (O) the expected (E) each case and square this result	$(O - E)^2$ see Table 5.16
5 Divide this result by the expected value	$\dfrac{(O - E)^2}{E}$ see Table 5.17
6 Sum the result from each cell to give the chi-square value	$\sum \dfrac{(O - E)^2}{E} = 11.08$ (see Table 5.17)

Looking up the Significance of Chi Squared (χ^2)

As with the result from the correlation, this value needs to be checked against a standard table to see if the result is likely to be due to chance or not. In the case of the correlation we needed to check the value against our chosen significance level and the number of subjects. In the case of a chi-square we need to check the value against our chosen significance level and against a value called the 'degrees of freedom'. The degrees of freedom essentially tells how many cells an individual case is free to be in given its value in one of the variables. It is as follows:

$$df = (\text{number of columns} - 1) \times (\text{number of rows} - 1)$$

In our case this is:

$$df = (3 - 1) \times (2 - 1) = 2 \times 1 = 2$$

So we now look up the chi-square value in Table 5.24 (see p. 131) for 2 degrees of freedom and find that the result is significant at the $p < 0.01$ level. From this we can conclude that the distribution of trade union membership and political party membership in the call centre is unlikely to be due to chance.

SAQ 5.15

Repeat the chi-square calculation using the data in Table 5.18 below. This fictional table provides data on the types of newspapers read by political party supporters.

Table 5.18 *SAQ 5.15. data*

	Labour	Liberal	Conservative	Totals
Tabloid	150	30	75	255
Broadsheet	150	60	100	310
No paper	700	210	325	1235
Totals	1000	300	500	1800

Summary

- The chi-squared test is a statistical technique for calculating the chi-square (χ^2) value from the distribution of cases across two categorical variables.
- A table is constructed with the relevant number of columns and rows and the number of cases in each cell of the table is counted.
- The chi-squared technique calculates a chi-square (χ^2) value from the differences between the observed and expected values in each cell.
- The value of chi-square (χ^2) has to be shown to be significant in terms of a statistical test.

Analysing 'Averages': t-test

We now turn to a third type of statistical test. These tests are used when you have variables of two different kinds. On the one hand you have cases sorted by some categorical variable and on the other you have a 'continuous' measure of some variable for each case. So for example you might have on the one hand categories – such as individuals' membership (or not) of a professional organisation – and on the other the hand a continuous measure such as each person's salary. We then need to know if any difference between the two groups – such as more or less pay – is an actual difference or just the product of chance. In fact the t-test we will look at compares the average or mean scores of each group. The t-test is one of a set of tests known as 'parametric' tests. As such it can only be used on truly interval or ratio data – it can't be used on ranks. Parametric tests are very powerful statistical techniques and the complex types (known as ANOVAs, and factor analyses) tell you not only if the result is 'random' or not; they also 'measure' the effects of different variables on the measured result. These types of statistical tests are often used in experimental settings when we have two groups – a control group and an experimental group. More generally these are described as 'conditions' – that is categories into which participants (cases) in the experiment can be placed. Each participant (case) is 'measured' using a continuous scale in one or several of the conditions.

To work properly parametric tests assume that the data you are working on are 'normally distributed'. By this we mean that the data are reasonably distributed about the 'mean'. This can be checked for by plotting a graph and is best illustrated with some examples. Figure 5.2 shows three examples of the distribution of data – you can get most spreadsheets and all statistical software to produce such plots for you. If your data look 'normally distributed' it probably is. But you may not have enough cases to draw a good graph, and it is best to explore the data before using the t-test. We therefore need to look at a few issues before looking at the t-test. First, what do we mean by an average? Second, how can we evaluate the distribution of cases in ways other than drawing a graph?

Normal distribution
Here the data are normally distributed about a mean of 8

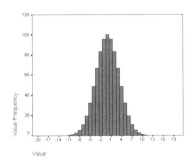

Skewed data – negative
Here the data are skewed towards lower values. In other words there are more values below the mean than above it.

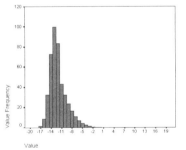

Skewed data – positive
Here the data are skewed towards higher values. In other words there are more values above the mean than below it.

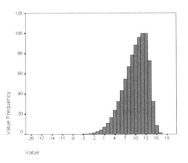

Figure 5.2 *Normal and skewed data*

Averages and Means

We therefore need to briefly discuss what is meant by an 'average' or a 'mean'. There are three ways in which you can calculate an average, and they are called:

- mean
- median
- mode

Mean

The arithmetic mean is what most people talk of as the 'average'. To obtain the mean of a variable, you add together all the values of the variable from each case, and then divide this total by the number of cases in the set. The mean is calculated as follows:

$$\bar{x} = \frac{\sum_{1}^{n} x_n}{N}$$

where x_n is the value of the variable for case n and N is the total number of cases. It is this kind of mean that we will be looking at when we discuss the t-test in a moment. The mean can be affected by individual or small numbers of cases with high or low values. For instance the 'mean' income in many countries is higher than the income 'most' people get – the 'mode' income. This is due to the fact that a small number of people earn far more than most other people. An example of a distribution of data like this is the 'Skewed data – negative' example in Figure 5.2. It is important to note that you can't take a 'meaningful' mean of a categorical data set.

Median

The median is the value between the lowest and highest values of a variable such that below and above it there are an equal number of cases. The median is derived as follows. First, put the data in ascending order. The median is the value 'half way' along this list. In fact it is the value at the position in the list given by:

$$l = \frac{(N + 1)}{2}$$

where N is the number of cases. Now if N is odd then l will be a specific point in the list, the median value. If N is even then p will be not be a whole number, it will be some value 'and a half'. This will fall between two points in the ordered list. You now need to take the mean of these two values to get the median. You can therefore only get a median for a variable that can be ordered into a list – in other words for ordinal, interval or ratio data. The median will differ from the 'mean' and the 'mode' in skewed data.

Mode

The mode is the most frequently occurring value in a set of data. It is mainly used with categorical data – it indicates which category has the most cases. There can be more than one mode if two or more values are equally common. To obtain the mode, count all occurrences of each value in a data set, and then select the value that occurs the greatest number of times. If you have a ratio or interval data, or an ordinal scale with a lot of points along it, then you need to split the data into 'ranges'. For instance you might split heights into 5 cm ranges. You then select the range (or ranges) with the most cases. In the case of incomes the 'mode' income tends to be lower than the mean as there are more people on lower incomes than high ones.

'Variation' around the Mean

There are other ways in which we can look at the distribution of data – to see if it is reasonably 'normally distributed'. First, you may look at the range of the values in the variable. The range is a measure of the spread or the dispersion of the observations. It is very easy to calculate: it is the difference between the largest and the smallest observed values. Two things are worth noting about the range of a data set:

- The range value of a data set is greatly affected by the presence of just one unusually large or small value in the sample.
- As only the largest and the smallest data values are considered, a great deal of information (all the other values) is ignored when calculating the range.

Second, we can consider how the data are spread out through the cases. We can calculate what is known as a 'standard deviation'. Standard deviation (σ) is essentially a measure of 'average' difference between values in the data set and the mean. The more widely the values are spread out, the larger the standard deviation from the mean value. Standard deviation is useful to determine whether results are tightly grouped together or whether they are more widely spread. Standard deviation is calculated by the formula:

$$\sigma = \sqrt{\frac{\sum_{1}^{n} (\bar{x} - x_n)}{N - 1}}$$

where the symbols all have the same meaning as before. The standard deviation tells you how the data is spread out, on 'average' around the mean value. You can't calculate a meaningful standard deviation for categorical data and you should be wary of such a measure of ordinal data.

Third, we can actually test if a distribution is skewed. As noted in the income example, the mean and mode and median are different in a skewed distribution. The 'direction' of skew – whether the cases tend to be high or low – can be judged by the position of the 'mean' in relation to the 'median'. When the mean is higher than the median, the distribution of scores is said to be positively skewed. When the mean is lower than the median it is said to be negatively skewed. There are several measures of skew but the standard one is the Pearson measure that is given by:

$$skew = \frac{3(\bar{x} - median)}{s}$$

where s is the standard deviation. For practical purposes, skews of less than 0.5 (positive or negative) are considered sufficiently symmetrical – that is to say 'normally distributed'.

If you do not think that your data are normally distributed you will need to use a 'non-parametric' test. There are non-parametric statistical tests such as the Mann–Whitney and Wilcoxon tests that do the same kind of analysis as t-tests and ANOVAs. These tests can therefore use ranked data. We will not present these here but you can find explanations of how to use them in any good textbook on statistics.

Preparing the Data

The t-test compares the means from two 'conditions' to see if any difference between the conditions is the product of random chance or not. So for example we might wish to evaluate the usefulness of some education software. We might let one group use the software and compare their performance on a test with another group who did not get to use the software. This could give us the result shown in Table 5.19.

Table 5.19 *Mean scores for groups using (or not using) a training manual*

	Mean for no software group	Mean for software-using group
Mean score for group	3.7	6.4

By 'conditions' we mean a specific context under which the measure is applied to the cases or participants. So in the example above, using and not using the software are our two contexts or 'conditions'. The t-test can be run in two different ways depending on the relationship of our conditions (contexts) to each other. The first is a 'between subjects' design also known as an 'unrelated' design. This is akin to the example above where one group uses the software and one group does not. The second is a 'within subjects' design also known as a 'related' design. Here the same people are in each condition. So for example we might want to test if the use of the software improved people's knowledge. Here we could test them before and after using the software. This would be a 'within subjects' design, as the same people are in each condition. Whether it is a within or between subjects condition affects how you do the t-test calculation. In the example to follow we will use a 'within subjects' or 'related' design.

Let us assume that we want to test the effectiveness of an educational software package designed to improve the knowledge of children in a certain topic. Let us assume that we can 'measure' the knowledge of the children in a ratio manner. We will therefore get a score for each child before and after they have used the software. Table 5.20 shows the results of such an experiment on ten children.

Table 5.20 *Data for example t-test*

Child	SA: Score after using software	SB: Score before using software
1	5	4
2	5	1
3	10	2
4	6	3
5	3	4
6	6	7
7	9	4
8	5	5
9	7	2
10	8	5
Total	64	37
Mean	6.4	3.7

It is clear that the children did better after using the software. But this could be simply due to luck. The t-test tests if the difference in mean scores between the conditions is likely to be due to chance or not. In this case, where the same people are in both conditions, the statistical test can take into account the variation between individuals as well as the group. It therefore tells us if we can rely on this result and claim that the software affected performance. The first thing we need to do is to calculate the difference in scores before and after use of the software. This is done in Table 5.21. From this we calculate the t value. Before moving on to the calculation we need to set up a few symbols:

d refers to the difference between the score before and after
d^2 refers to the square of this value
N refers to the number of cases
Σ stands for 'total' or 'sum' – that is, add up all the numbers that follow this symbol.

Table 5.21 *Calculation of differences and squares of difference*

Worker	SA: Score after using manual	SB: Score before using manual	d: Difference in score (SA–SB)	d^2: Square of difference
1	5	4	1	1
2	5	1	4	16
3	10	2	8	64
4	6	3	3	9
5	3	4	−1	1
6	6	7	−1	1
7	9	4	5	25
8	5	5	0	0
9	7	2	5	25
10	8	5	3	9
Total	64	37		
			$\Sigma d = 27$	$\Sigma d^2 = 151$
Mean	6.4	3.7		

Equation 3 *Step-by-step instructions for calculating the value of the t-test*

1 Tabulate the data from each case and calculate the difference between the two conditions	See Table 5.21
2 Calculate the square of the difference (that is multiply each difference by itself)	See Table 5.21
3 Calculate column totals to give: Total of the differences – Σd Total of the squared differences – Σd^2	See Table 5.21
4 Calculate the square of the total of the differences	$(\Sigma d)^2 = 27 \times 27 = 729$
5 Calculate t using the related t-test equation	

$$t = \frac{\Sigma d}{\sqrt{\dfrac{N\Sigma d^2 - (\Sigma d)^2}{N-1}}}$$

$$t = \frac{27}{\sqrt{\dfrac{10 \times 151 - 729}{10 - 1}}}$$

$$t = \frac{27}{\sqrt{\dfrac{1510 - 729}{9}}}$$

$$t = \frac{27}{\sqrt{86.78}}$$

$$= 2.89$$

Looking up the Significance of t

As with the chi-square test we need to calculate the degrees of freedom. In t case:

$$df = N - 1$$

Therefore the degrees of freedom are 9. Once again we need to look up the t score in a relevant table to check if it is 'significant'. Table 5.25 (see p.132) lists the critical values of t for various degrees of freedom. You will notice there are two rows for the probability or significance level. These are marked one and two tailed. This relates to the nature of our experiment and any hypotheses we made. For instance if we predicted a difference in a certain direction – here we might have expected the software to improve the performance – we use the 'one-tailed' column. If on the other hand we just expected a difference in any direction – the software could have made things worse, not better – then we would use the two-tailed column. Here we can see that our t score of 2.89 is above the value for a significance of 0.05 for a one-tailed hypothesis. Given this small study we would be happy with this as a 'significant' result, and be able to reject our null hypothesis that this is a 'random' result (due to chance). It therefore implies that the software had an effect. In the next section we will discuss how you interpret statistical results.

SAQ 5.16

Repeat the t-test calculation using the data given below. This fictional table provides data on the performance of workers who used an online training manual. The scores reflect their performance on a relevant task.

Worker	SA: Score after using manual	SB: Score before using manual	d: Difference in score (SA–SB)	d²: Square of difference
1	4	3		
2	7	1		
3	8	3		
4	10	4		
5	8	3		
6	8	2		
7	5	7		
8	3	4		
Totals				
Mean				

itistical technique for calculating the t value from the data
'o 'conditions'.
used with either a 'within' subjects (related) design or a
(unrelated) design – but the form of the correct test must

_ parametric test' and therefore requires reasonably 'normally
_..iouted' data.
• The t-test evaluates if the difference in the mean scores of the two conditions
  is due to chance or not.
• The value of t has to be shown to be significant in terms of a statistical test –
  this may be one or two tailed.

Overall Summary

• Because human behaviour is variable, there will be variability in cases'
  scores.
• Statistical tests are used to calculate the probabilities that differences in
  scores are due to random variability, as stated by the null hypothesis.
• Conventional levels of significance represent probabilities of less than 5%
  ($p < 0.05$) or less than 1% ($p < 0.01$) that scores are due to random
  variability.
• Statistics, such as Spearman's rho (r_s), chi-square (χ^2) and the t-test (t) can
  be used to calculate measures of this randomness. These values of r_s, χ^2
  and t can be looked up in a statistical table to see whether the calculated
  value exceeds a predetermined value for a level of significance.
• Low probabilities of random variability, conventionally $p < 0.05$ and $p <$
  0.01, allow researchers to reject the null hypothesis and instead to claim that
  their findings are significant and support the experimental hypothesis.

Interpretation, Causality, Prediction and Falsification

Calculating a statistical result might seem the most difficult and laborious aspect
of quantitative research. In truth researchers use computer-based statistical,
spreadsheet and database software systems. These systems allow for very large
data sets and very complex analyses. Researchers can in most cases simply enter
their data, press a few keys and out come the results. But the real skill, whether you
calculated by hand or by computer, comes in the interpretation. Interpretation
brings in the issues of causality, prediction and falsification. These are concepts that
positivist philosophers have explored, discussed and argued over at length. Smith
(1998) provides a detailed discussion of these issues (see Chapter 2, section 3.3;
Chapter 3, Table 3.1, section 4.1 in Smith, 1998). By causality I mean: how do we
decide what causes what? If you find a correlation between parents' income and
children's school performance you would tend to assume that it was the parents'
income that influenced (caused) the school performance. Such a correlation might
allow you to predict a new set of children's overall school performance. It might

also 'falsify' a theory which predicted that parents' income had no effect. But how reliable are these claims when based on statistical evidence?

Let us look at the interpretation of a specific result. A researcher carries out a study to investigate whether there is a correlation between spelling scores and reading scores. The result of the experiment is shown in the data displayed in Table 5.6 (p. 89). The Spearman rank correlation coefficient is calculated as 0.79 (see Equation 1 (p. 90), which indicates a high degree of association between the two variables of spelling ability and reading ability. When this correlation is looked up in Table 5.23, it is found to be significant at $p < 0.01$. At this level of significance the researcher is able to reject the null hypothesis. The conclusion would be that there is a positive correlation between children's spelling ability and their reading ability, as predicted by the research hypothesis.

The researcher naturally had something in mind when originally planning the research. For instance, the aim may have been to test a theory that good spelling enables children to recognise combinations of letters, and that this helps them to learn to read unfamiliar words. If children are poor spellers, they may be handicapped in recognising combinations of letters. Consequently, the ability to read depends on the ability to spell.

This may sound a plausible interpretation of the significant positive correlation found between spelling and reading scores. It would imply that the ability to spell is a direct cause of reading ability. But is the researcher justified in drawing this conclusion from a significant positive correlation between spelling and reading scores? There has to be an important note of caution here. All that has been shown is that the two sets of scores are associated, demonstrating that there is some association between spelling and reading. But this says nothing about which of the variables is affecting the other.

Some examples should bring home the fact that two events (A and B) can be highly associated with each other, without A necessarily being the direct cause of B, or vice versa (Figure 5.3).

Figure 5.3 *Events associated with each other*

In both cases A and B are associated, and we could conclude that one is causing the other. However, Figure 5.4 shows the possibility that A is not the cause of B, nor B the cause of A, but rather that an underlying factor C is the cause.

Figure 5.4 *Underlying causes*

To return to the association between spelling scores and reading scores, it would be possible to give plausible arguments in favour of three quite different relationships between spelling ability and reading ability, as follows.

1   Spelling aids reading.
2   Being a good reader improves spelling ability.
3   Both good spelling and reading ability are the result of some other factor; for example, parents' positive attitude towards school.

SAQ 5.17

1   Draw diagrams like those in Figures 5.3 and 5.4 to represent each of the three above possibilities.
2   Suppose a significant correlation has been demonstrated between the number of days a child fails to turn up for school and failure at spelling tests. Suggest three possible causal explanations for a correlation between truancy and test failures (like the ones between spelling scores and reading scores).
3   Suppose there is a correlation between the trees in Brighton swaying about and the height of the waves off the pier. Does the swaying of trees cause the waves, or vice versa? What is the most likely explanation for a positive correlation between these two variables?

Because it is not possible to identify cause and effect, researchers interpret correlations as indicating an association between variables, rather than concluding that one variable causes, or is directly responsible for, the other variable.

Correlations are particularly important in psychological research into personality. If people's responses on two personality scales are highly correlated, it is legitimate to assume that the scales may be measuring some underlying personality variable. For instance, if a significant correlation is found between scales measuring authoritarian tendencies and racist attitudes, personality researchers would be encouraged to seek for an underlying personality factor which accounts for both measures. However, it is all too easy to slip into thinking that something 'internal' such as an authoritarian attitude is directly responsible for racist behaviour, or that something such as missing school must be responsible for academic failure. When using a correlational research design, it is important to be clear about the implications of predicted correlations between two aspects of human behaviour.

SAQ 5.18

Now turn to Reading F, 'Causality and research design', which is a continuation of the Bryman and Cramer material from Reading A. As you read this extract make notes on these questions:

1   From which method, according to Bryman and Cramer, is it easier to develop causal explanations?
2   How do experimental designs allow you to interpret possible causes and make predictions?
3   How do survey designs allow you to interpret possible causes and make predictions?

Causality, Interpretation, Prediction and Positivism

One of the key assumptions of positivism (see Chapter 2) we have not yet addressed is the building of scientific laws. Positivists have debated a number of ways in which they claim this is to be done. In general, the appearance of an 'empirical regularity' – the constant appearance (correlation/interaction/difference) of two 'things' together – is seen as providing the basis for a scientific law. Statistical tests provide researchers with a means of assessing whether such correlations, interactions or differences are likely to be due to random chance or to some other factor. In the case of a correlation a significant result indicates that the relationship between two variables is not random. In the memory experiment in Reading F a significant result indicated that the difference between two groups was not random and was therefore likely to be due to another factor. In both cases the significant result does not indicate a causal relationship. Rather, as SAQ 5.18 makes clear, such relationships are interpreted from the results. Statistics essentially point us to an empirical regularity of some kind. The statements we can then make about our results may reflect the role of positivist assumptions in our work.

On another score our results should allow us to make new predictions about social processes which themselves can be researched. If you look back to Figure 2.1 (p. 7) you will note that the model assumes that our results will modify our theories and lead to new predictions, new hypotheses. The process is one where our results either support or refute a truth claim – what philosophers call 'falsification'. Once again the importance of interpretation to the process of quantitative research raises questions about whether we can rely upon these methods to provide falsifying evidence. In many cases this may be possible. People will or will not do x. In other cases, for instance the memory example in Reading E, it is clear that the results are in line with a number of conflicting explanations and interpretations. Though we can probably design a different experiment to explore the different explanations, we then come up against the probabilistic nature of statistics. Even at a 5% level ($p < 0.5$) of significance, 1 in 20 results will actually be random. We can never be 100% sure that our support for, or refutation of, a result is secure. In many cases a non-significant result only forces the researchers, for the first few times, to improve the experiment or the sample, and not to alter their hypothesis. Once again we can conclude that the realities of social research may not come up to the finer measures of positivist philosophy.

Conclusion

I would not want you to finish this journey through quantitative research with the feeling that somehow these methods do not come up to scratch. As Smith (1998) shows, the measure we have been using, positivism, is itself flawed in a number of ways, one of the major flaws being the underlying model of science upon which it is based. In truth, the practical realities of quantitative research have helped inform the debates discussed at length by Smith (1998). The fact that quantitative research has been highly informed by the positivist agenda, and has in one form or another attempted to implement it, provides insights into the agenda itself. One could argue that the methods of quantitative research, which provide the contemporary social world with a great deal of the knowledge it has about itself, have empirically tested positivist philosophy and found it lacking in the context of social research.

A different measure of these methods is their constant use, and misuse. Nearly all of the major social institutions of modern society, from the state to the health services, from major companies to small pressure groups, employ forms of quantitative research to help inform their actions and decisions. In such contexts they are useful and informative methods. Having said this, the reasons why these methods fail to meet positivist criteria reflect a key difference between the objects of study of the social sciences and the natural sciences. At nearly every stage of the research process we have found that quantitative researchers have had to address the problem of meaning and, importantly, the relative nature of meaning. In dealing with this, quantitative researchers have had to transgress the positivist assumptions of nominalism and phenomenalism. A great part of human behaviour is centrally placed within the realm of meaning and therefore requires research methods which deal with the important role of meaning and meaningful activity. Part III, on qualitative research, explores methods that focus specifically on this issue.

Further Reading

Bryman, A. and Burgess, R.G. (eds) (1994) *Analysing Quantitative Data*. London: Routledge.

Bryman, A. and Burgess, R.G. (eds) (1999) *Quantitative Data*. London: Sage.

Bryman, A. and Cramer, D. (1990) *Quantitative Data Analysis for Social Scientists*. London: Routledge.

Coolidge, F.L. (2000) *Statistics: A Gentle Introduction*. London: Sage.

Erickson, B.H. and Nosanchuuk, T.A. (1992) *Understanding Data*, 2nd edn. Buckingham: Open University Press.

Howitt, D. and Cramer, D. (1997) *A Guide to Computing Statistics with SPSS for Windows*. London: Prentice-Hall.

Howitt, D. and Cramer, D. (1997) *An Introduction to Statistics in Psychology: A Complete Guide for Students*. London: Prentice-Hall.

Reading F: Causality and Research Design

Alan Bryman and Duncan Cramer

[O]ne of the chief preoccupations among quantitative researchers is to establish causality. This preoccupation in large part derives from a concern to establish findings similar to those of the natural sciences, which often take a causal form. Moreover, findings which establish cause and effect can have considerable practical importance: if we know that one thing affects another, we can manipulate the cause to produce an effect. In much the same way that our knowledge that smoking may cause a number of illnesses, such as lung cancer and heart disease, the social scientist is able to provide potentially practical information by demonstrating causal relationships in appropriate settings.

To say that something causes something else is not to suggest that the dependent variable (the effect) is totally influenced by the independent variable (the cause). You do not necessarily contract a disease if you smoke and many of the diseases contracted by people who smoke afflict those who never smoke. 'Cause' here should be taken to mean that variation in the dependent variable is affected by variation in the independent variable. Those who smoke a lot are more likely than those who smoke less, who in turn are more likely than those who do not smoke at all, to contract a variety of diseases that are associated with smoking. Similarly, if we find that watching violence on television induces aggressive behaviour, we are not saying that only people who watch televised violence will behave aggressively, nor that only those people who behave aggressively watch violent television programmes. Causal relationships are invariably about the likelihood of an effect occurring in the light of particular levels of the cause: aggressive behaviour may be more likely to occur when a lot of television violence is watched and people who watch relatively little television violence may be less likely to behave aggressively.

Establishing Causality

In order to establish a causal relationship, three criteria have to be fulfilled. First, it is necessary to establish that there is an apparent relationship between two variables. This means that it is necessary to demonstrate that the distribution of values of one variable corresponds to the distribution of values of another variable. Table 5.22 provides information for ten children on the number of aggressive acts they exhibit when they play in two groups of five for two hours per group. The point to note is that there is a relationship between the two variables in that the distribution of values for the number of aggressive acts coincides with the distribution for the amount of televised violence watched – children who watch more violence exhibit more aggression than those who watch little violence. The relationship is not perfect: three pairs of children – 3 and 4, 6 and 7, and 9 and 10 – record the same number of aggressive acts, even though they watch different amounts of television violence. Moreover, 8 exhibits more aggression than 6 or 7, even though the latter watch more violence. None the less, a clear pattern is evident which suggests that there is a relationship between the two variables.

Table 5.22 *Data on television violence and aggression*

Child	Number of hours of violence watched on television per week	Number of aggressive acts recorded
1	9.50	9
2	9.25	8
3	8.75	7
4	8.25	7
5	8.00	6
6	5.50	4
7	5.25	4
8	4.75	5
9	4.50	3
10	4.00	3

Second, it is necessary to demonstrate that the relationship is *non-spurious*. A spurious relationship occurs when there is not a 'true' relationship between two variables that appear to be connected. The variation exhibited by each variable is affected by a common variable. Imagine that the first five children are boys and the second five are girls. This would suggest that gender has a considerable impact on both variables. Boys are more likely than girls both to watch more television violence *and* to exhibit greater aggressiveness. There is still a slight tendency for watching more violence and aggression to be related for both boys and girls, but these tendencies are far less pronounced than for the ten children as a whole. In other words, gender affects each of the two variables. It is because boys are much more likely than girls both to watch more television violence and to behave aggressively that there is a spurious relationship, as illustrated by Figure 5.5.

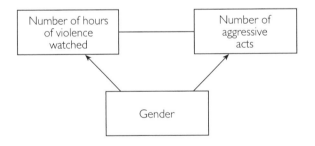

Figure 5.5 *A spurious relationship*

Third, it is necessary to establish that the cause precedes the effect, i.e. the time order of the two related variables. In other words, we must establish that aggression is a consequence of watching televised violence and not the other way around. An effect simply cannot come before a cause. This may seem an extremely obvious criterion that is easy to demonstrate, but as we will see, it constitutes a very considerable problem for non-experimental research designs.

Causality and Experimental Designs

A research design provides the basic structure within which an investigation takes place. While a number of different designs can be found, a basic distinction is that between experimental and non-experimental research designs, of which the survey/correlational is the most prominent. In an experiment, the elucidation of cause and effect is an explicit feature of the framework. The term *internal validity* is often employed as an attribute of research and indicates whether the causal findings deriving from an investigation are relatively unequivocal. An internally valid study is one which provides firm evidence of cause and effect. Experimental designs are especially strong in respect of internal validity; this attribute is scarcely surprising in view of the fact that they have been developed specifically in order to generate findings which indicate cause and effect.

If we wanted to establish that watching violence on television enhances aggression in children, we might conceive of the following study. We bring together a group of ten children. They are allowed to interact and play for two hours, during which the number of aggressive acts committed by each child is recorded by the observers, and the children are then exposed to a television programme with a great deal of violence. Such exposure is often called the experimental treatment. They are then allowed a further two-hour period of play and interaction. Aggressive behaviour is recorded in exactly the same way. What we have here is a sequence which runs

$$Obs_1 \; Exp \; Obs_2$$

where Obs_1 is the initial measurement of aggressive behaviour (often called the *pre-test*), Exp is the experimental treatment which allows the independent variable to be introduced, and Obs_2 is the subsequent measurement of aggression (often called the *post-test*).

Let us say that Obs_2 is 30 per cent higher than Obs_1, suggesting that aggressive behaviour has increased substantially. Does this mean that we can say that the increase in aggression was caused by the violence? We cannot make such an attribution because there are alternative explanations of the presumed causal connection. The children may well have become more aggressive over time simply as a consequence of being together and becoming irritated by each other. The researchers may not have given the children enough food or drink and this may have contributed to their bad humour. There is even the possibility that different observers were used for the pre- and post-tests who used different criteria of aggressiveness. So long as we cannot discount these alternative explanations, a definitive conclusion about causation cannot be proffered.

Anyone familiar with the natural sciences will know that an important facet of a properly conducted experiment is that it is controlled so that potentially contaminating factors are minimized. In order to control the contaminating factors that have been mentioned (and therefore to allow the alternative explanations to be rejected), a *control group* is required. This group has exactly the same cluster of experiences as the group which receives the first treatment – known as the *experimental group* – but it does not receive the experimental treatment. In the context of our imaginary television study, we now have two groups of children who are exposed to exactly the same conditions, except that one group watches the violent films (the experimental group) and the second group has no experimental treatment (the control group). This design is illustrated in Figure 5.6. The two groups' experiences have to be as similar as possible, so that only the experimental group's exposure to the experimental treatment distinguishes them.

It is also necessary to ensure that the members of the two groups are as similar as possible. This is achieved by taking a sample of children and *randomly assigning* them to either the experimental or the control group. If random assignment is not carried out, there is always the possibility that the differences between the two groups can be attributed to divergent personal or other characteristics. There may, for example, be more boys than girls in one group, or differences in the ethnic composition of the two groups. Such differences in personal or background characteristics would mean that the ensuing findings could not be validly attributed to the independent variable, and that factor alone.

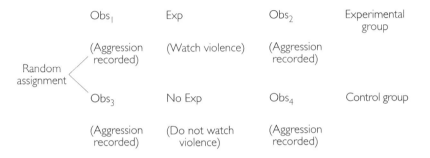

Figure 5.6 *An experiment*

Let us say that the difference between Obs_1 and Obs_2 is 30 per cent and between Obs_3 and Obs_4 is 28 per cent. If this were the case, we would conclude that the difference between the two groups is so small that it appears that the experimental treatment (Exp) has made no difference to the increase in aggression; in other words, aggression in the experimental group would probably have increased anyway. The frustration of being together too long or insufficient food or drink or some other factor probably accounts for the $Obs_2 - Obs_1$ difference. However, if the difference between Obs_3 and Obs_4 were only 3 per cent, we would be much more prepared to say that watching violence has increased aggression in the experimental group. It would suggest that around 27 per cent of the increase in aggressive behaviour in the experimental group (i.e. 30 − 3) can be attributed to the experimental treatment. Differences between experimental and control groups are not usually as clear-cut as in this illustration, since often the difference between the groups is fairly small. Statistical tests are necessary in this context to determine the probability of obtaining such a difference by chance . . .

In this imaginary investigation, the three criteria of causality are met, and therefore if we did find that the increase in the dependent variable were considerably greater for the experimental group than the control group we would have considerable confidence in saying that watching television violence caused greater aggression. First, a relationship is established by demonstrating that subjects watching television violence exhibited greater aggression than those who did not. Second, the combination of a control group and random assignment allows the possibility of the relationship being spurious to be eliminated, since other factors which may impinge on the two variables would apply equally to the two groups. Third, the time order of the variables is demonstrated by the increase in aggressive behaviour succeeding the experimental group's exposure to the television violence. Precisely because the independent variable is manipulated by the researcher, time order can be easily demonstrated, since the effects of the manipulation can be

directly gauged. Thus, we could say confidently that Watching television violence →
Aggressive behaviour, since the investigation exhibits a high degree of internal
validity.

There is a variety of different types of experimental design. These are briefly
summarized in Figure 5.7. In the first design, there is no pre-test, just a comparison
between the experimental and control groups in terms of the dependent variable.
With the second design, there is a number of groups. This is a frequent occurrence
in the social sciences, where one is more likely to be interested in different levels or
types of the independent variable rather than simply its presence or absence. Thus,
in the television–violence context, we could envisage four groups consisting of
different degrees of violence. The third design, a *factorial* design, occurs where the
researcher is interested in the effects of more than one independent variable on the
dependent variable. The researcher might be interested in whether the presence of
adults in close proximity reduces children's propensity to behave aggressively.
We might then have four possible combinations deriving from the manipulation of
each of the two independent variables. Thus, for example, Exp_{1+A} would mean a
combination of watching violence and adults in close proximity; Exp_{1+B} would be
watching violence and no adults in close proximity.

1	Random assignment	Exp	Obs_1	
		No Exp	Obs_2	
2	Random assignment	Obs_1	Exp_1	Obs_2
		Obs_3	Exp_2	Obs_4
		Obs_5	Exp_3	Obs_6
		Obs_7	No Exp	Obs_8
3	Random assignment	Obs_1	Exp_{1+A}	Obs_2
		Obs_3	Exp_{1+B}	Obs_4
		Obs_5	Exp_{2+A}	Obs_6
		Obs_7	Exp_{2+B}	Obs_8

Figure 5.7 *Three types of experimental design*

Survey Design and Causality

When a social survey is carried out, the nature of the research design is very different
from the experiment. The survey usually entails the collection of data on a number
of variables at a single juncture. The researcher might be interested in the
relationship between people's political attitudes and behaviour on the one hand, and
a number of other variables such as each respondent's occupation, social
background, race, gender, age, and various non-political attitudes. However, none
of these variables is manipulated as in the experiment. Indeed, many variables
cannot be manipulated and their relationships with other variables can only be
examined through a social survey. We cannot make some people old, others young,

and still others middle-aged and then observe the effects of age on political attitudes. Moreover, not only are variables not manipulated in a social-survey study, data on variables are simultaneously collected so that it is not possible to establish a time order to the variables in question. In an experiment, a time order can be discerned in that the effect of the manipulated independent variable on the dependent variable is directly observed. The characteristics of surveys are not solely associated with research using interviews or questionnaires. Many studies using archival statistics, such as those collected by governments and organizations, exhibit the same characteristics, since data are often available in relation to a number of variables for a particular year.

Survey designs are often called *correlational* designs to denote the tendency for such research to be able to reveal relationships between variables and to draw attention to their limited capacity in connection with the elucidation of causal processes. Precisely because in survey research variables are not manipulated (and often are not capable of manipulation), the ability of the researcher to impute cause and effect is limited. Let us say that we collect data on manual workers' levels of job satisfaction and productivity in a firm. We may find . . . that there is a strong relationship between the two, suggesting that workers who exhibit high levels of job satisfaction also have high levels of productivity. We can say that there is a relationship between the two variables (see Figure 5.8), but as we have seen, this is only a first step in the demonstration of causality. It is also necessary to confirm that the relationship is non-spurious. Could it be, for example, that workers who have been with the firm a long time are both more satisfied and more productive (see Figure 5.9)? . . .

Figure 5.8 *A relationship between two variables*

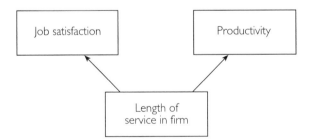

Figure 5.9 *Is the relationship spurious?*

However, the third hurdle – establishing that the putative cause precedes the putative effect – is extremely difficult. The problem is that either of the two possibilities depicted in Figure 5.10 may be true. Job satisfaction may cause greater productivity, but it has long been recognized that the causal connection may work the other way around (i.e. if you are good at your job you often enjoy it more). Because data relating to each of the two variables have been simultaneously collected, it is not possible to arbitrate between the two versions of causality presented in Figure 5.10. One way of dealing with this problem is through a reconstruction of the likely causal order of the variables involved. Sometimes this process of inference can be fairly uncontroversial. If, for example, we find a relationship between race and number of years spent in formal schooling, we can say that the former affects the latter. However, this modelling of likely causal connections is more fraught when it is not obvious which variable precedes the other, as with the relationship between job satisfaction and productivity. When such difficulties arise, it may be necessary to include a second wave of data collection in relation to the same respondents in order to see, for example, whether the impact of job satisfaction on subsequent productivity is greater than the impact of productivity on subsequent job satisfaction. Such a design is known as a *panel design* (Cramer, 1988), but is not very common in the social sciences.

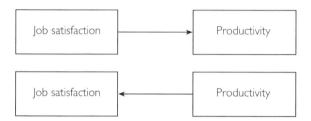

Figure 5.10 *Two possible causal interpretations of a relationship*

. . .The chief point to be gleaned from the preceding discussion is that the extraction of causal connections among variables can be undertaken with greater facility in the context of experimental research than when survey data are being analysed.

Reference

Cramer, D. (1988) 'Self-esteem and facilitative close relationships: a cross-lagged panel correlation analysis', *British Journal of Social Psychology*, 27: 115–26.

Source: Bryman and Cramer, 1990: 7–15

Solutions to Chapter 5 SAQs

SAQ 5.1

1   Reading ability and spelling ability.
2   A reading score and a spelling score.

SAQ 5.2

1   There is usually a high positive correlation, though this is not a perfect correlation, since some tall people have very small feet.
2   There should be a perfect positive correlation.

3   There is most unlikely to be any correlation.

SAQ 5.3

1   0, 0.5, 0.9 (0 – no correlation at all; 0.5 – exactly halfway between 0 and 1; 0.9 – only slightly less than a perfect correlation of 1).
2   0.9. There is a high positive correlation between number of miles in a journey and the cost of a railway ticket, but this will not be a perfect correlation because on some lines tickets can cost more for slightly shorter journeys.
3   Probably 0.

SAQ 5.4

1   In winter, the lower the temperature, the higher electrical bills are likely to be. This is a negative correlation because low temperatures go with high electricity bills. The variables of temperature and the amounts charged for electricity are moving in opposite directions.
2   There is likely to be a positive correlation between the amount of rain falling and the number of umbrella sales.

SAQ 5.5

–0.65 represents the highest correlation because it is nearest to +1 or –1. The positive correlation of +0.5 is quite high, but not as high as –0.65.

SAQ 5.6

Score	Rank
1	2.5
0	1
2	4
1	2.5
3	5

The lowest score is 0, so this is assigned the lowest rank of 1. The two tied scores of 1 are assigned the average of the next two ranks of 2 and 3, i.e. 2.5. The next highest score of 2 is assigned the next available rank of 4 and the highest score of 3 is assigned the highest rank of 5. Note that five ranks have been assigned to five scores.

SAQ 5.7

Child	Spelling score	Spelling rank (A)	Reading score	Reading rank (B)	d(A – B)	d²
1	20	10	10	10	0	0
2	18	9	9	9	0	0
3	16	8	8	8	0	0
4	14	7	7	7	0	0
5	12	6	6	6	0	0
6	10	5	5	5	0	0
7	8	4	4	4	0	0
8	6	3	3	3	0	0
9	4	2	2	2	0	0
10	2	1	1	1	0	0
						$\Sigma d^2 = 0$

$$r_s = 1 - \frac{6 \times 0}{10(100 - 1)} \quad (N = 10 \text{ because there are 10 subjects})$$

$$= 1 - \frac{0}{10 \times 99}$$

$$= 1 - 0$$

$$= 1$$

2   It is not surprising that the value of the correlation coefficient works out at +1. The scores in Table 5.1 were specially selected to give a perfect positive correlation.

SAQ 5.8

1

Child	Quiz score	Quiz rank (A)	Essay score	Essay rank (B)	d(A–B)	d²
1	10	5	1	1	4	16
2	9	4	2	2	2	4
3	8	3	3	3	0	0
4	7	2	4	4	-2	4
5	6	1		5		16
						$\Sigma d^2 = 40$

$$r_s = 1 - \frac{6 \times 40}{5(25 - 1)}$$

$$= 1 - \frac{240}{5 \times 24}$$

$$= 1 - \frac{240}{120}$$

$$= 1 - 2$$

$$= -1$$

2   The data in Table 5.2 represent a perfect negative correlation. In this case, the differences between the ranked scores were large, giving a correlation co-efficient of –1 as a result of the subtraction from 1 at the end of the calculation.

SAQ 5.9

1   Less than 1%, i.e. 1 in 100 probability.
2   $p < 0.001$ (equivalent to 1 in 1000) is the greatest level of significance. This is because it expresses the smallest probability of only 0.1% that the results are due to random variability. $p < 0.05$ (equivalent to 1 in 20) represents the least significant result because the probability of a random result is as high as 5%.
3   $p < 0.01$ indicates a lower probability of a random result than $p < 0.05$ and therefore indicates a more significant result.
4   2.5%, i.e. 2.5 in a 100 probability.

SAQ 5.10

1   0.90 would be significant ($p < 0.05$).
2   0.49 would be significant ($p < 0.01$).

SAQ 5.11

1

Subject	Shape memory	Rank A	Spelling	Rank B	d	d²
1	7	4	13	3	1	1
2	8	5.5	19	9	–3.5	12.25
3	6	3	16	5.5	–2.5	6.25
4	9	7.5	21	10	–2.5	6.25
5	4		10	1	1	1
6	3	1	11	2	–1	1
7	9	7.5	18	7.5	0	0
8	8	5.5	18	7.5	–2	4
9	10	9	14	4	5	25
10	11	10	16	5.5	4.5	20.25
						$\Sigma d^2 = 77$

$$r_s = 1 - \frac{6 \times 77}{10 \times 99}$$

$$= 1 - 0.467$$

$$= 0.533$$

$$= 0.53$$

Note that the intermediate answer of 0.46666 etc. is rounded to 0.467 and the final answer of 0.533 is rounded to 0.53.

2 For ten subjects, the correlation coefficient values in Table 5.23 are 0.56 for $p < 0.05$ and 0.75 for $p < 0.01$. Remember that, for a correlation coefficient to be significant, it has to be equal to or larger than the values in Table 5.23 (see p. 130). Since the calculated coefficient of 0.53 is not larger than either of these values, this means that the correlation of 0.53 is not significant. There is too high a probability that the results are due to random variability (more than 5%; since the correlation is not significant at less then 5%, i.e. $p < 0.05$). So the null hypothesis cannot be rejected.

SAQ 5.12

1 Reading E has eight statistical results. The significance levels are: $p < 0.01$ is quoted three times; $p < 0.02$ is quoted three times; $p < 0.05$ is quoted twice;
2 $p < 0.01$ is the most statistically significant finding (0.01 = 1 in 100, whereas 0.05 = 5 in 100 and 0.02 = 2 in 100).

SAQ 5.13

Tallies from the data in Table 5.13.

	Labour	Liberal	Conservative
Trade union members	I	I	I
Non-trade union members	IIII	II	I

SAQ 5.14

Table 5.15 provides the results of this calculation.

SAQ 5.15

The following table presents the results of each calculation.

	Labour	Liberal	Conservative	Totals
Observed values: O				
Tabloid	150	30	75	255
Broadsheet	150	60	100	310
No paper	700	210	325	1235
Totals	1000	300	500	1800
Expected values: E				
Tabloid	141.67	42.50	70.83	
Broadsheet	172.22	51.67	86.11	
No paper	686.11	205.83	343.06	
Difference (O – E)				
Tabloid	8.33	–12.50	4.17	
Broadsheet	–22.22	8.33	13.89	
No paper	13.89	4.17	–18.06	
Chi values				
Tabloid	0.49	3.68	0.25	
Broadsheet	2.87	1.34	2.24	
No paper	0.28	0.08	0.95	

Total: = 12.18
$df = (3 – 1) \times (3 – 1) = 4$

Looking up this result in Table 5.24 (on p. 131) we find that the result is significant at the $p < 0.05$ level. You might have noted that it is not significant at the $p < 0.01$ or 0.001 levels. Whether or not you accept this result as being significant – i.e. you are confident to reject the null hypothesis – depends on the value of p you are prepared to accept. In this case I would be happy with this result. If this were a medical experiment I might not be!

SAQ 5.16

The following table and calculation present the results of the t-test.

Worker	SA: Score after using manual	SB: Score before using manual	d: Difference in score (SA–SB)	d^2: Square of difference
1	4	3	1	1
2	7	1	6	36
3	8	3	5	25
4	10	4	6	36
5	8	3	5	25
6	8	2	6	36
7	5	7	–2	4
8	3	4	–1	1
Total			Total = 26	Total = 164
Mean				

$$t = \frac{\Sigma\,d}{\sqrt{\dfrac{N\,\Sigma\,d^2 - (\Sigma\,d)^2}{N-1}}}$$

$$t = \frac{26}{\sqrt{\dfrac{8 \times 164 - 676}{8 - 1}}}$$

$$= 2.73$$

$$df = 8{-}1 = 7$$

Looking up this result in Table 5.25 we ignore the 'negative' value of t and just compare the size (2.73). The negative sign simply indicates the direction of the difference between the results. Looking up the result we see it is significant at the $p < 0.05$ (one tail). The test is a one-tailed test as we predicted that using the manual would improve.

SAQ 5.17

1

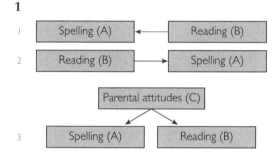

Figure 5.11 *Possible relationships between reading and spelling*

2 Possible explanations are: (a) missing days at school is the cause of failing tests; (b) failing tests causes a child to avoid school; (c) parental attitudes are the underlying cause of both truancy and academic failure.

3 In this case, there seems no doubt that it is an underlying factor, strong winds, which is the cause of both the swaying of the trees and the high waves.

SAQ 5.18

1 Experimental designs.

2 Experimental designs allow you to make interpretations about causes and effects because you have controlled a number of variables (the independent variables) and can therefore claim that it is these variables which have caused the effects in the dependent variable.

3 A well constructed sample allows you to explore the relationship between different variables for the population you have sampled from. This permits

you to interpret the possible causal variables and affected variables through the use of statistical techniques such as correlations.

Critical Values for Statistical Tests

Table 5.23 *Critical values for r_s for the various levels of significance (Spearman rank order correlation coefficient)*

N (number of cases)	Levels of significance	
	$p < 0.05$	$p < 0.01$
5	0.90	1.00
6	0.83	0.94
7	0.71	0.89
8	0.64	0.83
9	0.60	0.78
10	0.56	0.75
12	0.51	0.71
14	0.46	0.65
16	0.43	0.60
18	0.40	0.56
20	0.38	0.53
22	0.36	0.51
24	0.34	0.49
26	0.33	0.47
28	0.32	0.45
30	0.31	0.43

Table 5.24 *Chi-square significance look-up table*

Result is significant at the desired significance level if the chi-square value is greater than that indicated in the table

df	Significance level 0.050	0.010	0.001	df	Significance level 0.050	0.010	0.001
1	3.841	6.635	10.827	26	38.885	45.642	54.051
2	5.991	9.210	13.815	27	40.113	46.963	55.475
3	7.815	11.345	16.266	28	41.337	48.278	56.892
4	9.488	13.277	18.466	29	42.557	49.588	58.301
5	11.070	15.086	20.515	30	43.773	50.892	59.702
6	12.592	16.812	22.457	31	44.985	52.191	61.098
7	14.067	18.475	24.321	32	46.194	53.486	62.487
8	15.507	20.090	26.124	33	47.400	54.775	63.869
9	16.919	21.666	27.877	34	48.602	56.061	65.247
10	18.307	23.209	29.588	35	49.802	57.342	66.619
11	19.675	24.725	31.264	36	50.998	58.619	67.985
12	21.026	26.217	32.909	37	52.192	59.893	69.348
13	22.362	27.688	34.527	38	53.384	61.162	70.704
14	23.685	29.141	36.124	39	54.572	62.428	72.055
15	24.996	30.578	37.698	40	55.758	63.691	73.403
16	26.296	32.000	39.252	41	56.942	64.950	74.744
17	27.587	33.409	40.791	42	58.124	66.206	76.084
18	28.869	34.805	42.312	43	59.304	67.459	77.418
19	30.144	36.191	43.819	44	60.481	68.710	78.749
20	31.410	37.566	45.314	45	61.656	69.957	80.078
21	32.671	38.932	46.796	46	62.830	71.201	81.400
22	33.924	40.289	48.268	47	64.001	72.443	82.720
23	35.172	41.638	49.728	48	65.171	73.683	84.037
24	36.415	42.980	51.179	49	66.339	74.919	85.350
25	37.652	44.314	52.619	50	67.505	76.154	86.660

Table 5.25 *Critical values of t for one- and two-tailed tests*

Degrees of freedom	Probability, *p*			
One tailed	**0.1**	**0.05**	**0.01**	**0.001**
Two tailed	*0.05*	*0.025*	*0.005*	*0.0005*
1	6.31	12.71	63.66	636.62
2	2.92	4.30	9.93	31.60
3	2.35	3.18	5.84	12.92
4	2.13	2.78	4.60	8.61
5	2.02	2.57	4.03	6.87
6	1.94	2.45	3.71	5.96
7	1.89	2.37	3.50	5.41
8	1.86	2.31	3.36	5.04
9	1.83	2.26	3.25	4.78
10	1.81	2.23	3.17	4.59
11	1.80	2.20	3.11	4.44
12	1.78	2.18	3.06	4.32
13	1.77	2.16	3.01	4.22
14	1.76	2.14	2.98	4.14
15	1.75	2.13	2.95	4.07
16	1.75	2.12	2.92	4.02
17	1.74	2.11	2.90	3.97
18	1.73	2.10	2.88	3.92
19	1.73	2.09	2.86	3.88
20	1.72	2.09	2.85	3.85
21	1.72	2.08	2.83	3.82
22	1.72	2.07	2.82	3.79
23	1.71	2.07	2.82	3.77
24	1.71	2.06	2.80	3.75
25	1.71	2.06	2.79	3.73
26	1.71	2.06	2.78	3.71
27	1.70	2.05	2.77	3.69
28	1.70	2.05	2.76	3.67
29	1.70	2.05	2.76	3.66
30	1.70	2.04	2.75	3.65
40	1.68	2.02	2.70	3.55
60	1.67	2.00	2.66	3.46
120	1.66	1.98	2.62	3.37

PART III
QUALITATIVE RESEARCH METHODS

Introduction

In this part we explore the collection and analysis of qualitative and textual data. Part III deals with qualitative data analysis, focusing mainly upon examples from social anthropology and sociology. Within these examples you will be briefly introduced to a range of data collection methods that exist under the general heading of 'ethnography', including:

- in-depth interviews – semi-structured and unstructured interactions with participants that explore issues in greater depth than questionnaires;
- focus group interviews – in which social researchers conduct an interview/discussion focused upon a specific topic with a group of people;
- participant observation – in which social scientists take part in the social activity under study, sometimes actually living as part of a specific community;
- non-participant observation – in which social scientists observe but do not take part in the social activity under study.

Part III also examines the ways in which social scientists have tended to analyse the data collected by such methods. You may have noted in Part II that the examples of quantitative and numerical methods tended to fall into areas such as sociology, psychology and politics. This reflects the fact that quantitative methods have been strongly associated with these disciplines. In this part you will find that the examples tend to fall into the areas of sociology, social anthropology, social psychology and cultural studies, reflecting the greater use of qualitative and textual methods in these disciplines. Having said that, you must not assume that each discipline uses only one of the methods presented here. Researchers from all disciplines make use of one or more of all these methods.

Part III considers two general topics. First, it examines methods of data collection in qualitative work. It covers in-depth interviewing and focus groups as well as broader ethnographic practices. Second, it considers qualitative data analysis and looks at one method, termed 'grounded theory'. It then discusses the ideas and practices linked to discourse analysis, another area in which a wide range of methods is used, beginning by considering what 'discourse' and 'discourse analysis' are. After pointing out that qualitative data analysis and discourse analysis share very similar types of data, some of the key differences between these two research methods, both at a philosophical and a methodological level, are highlighted. A psychological and a socio-linguistic approach to discourse analysis are then compared.

We could conclude from our discussions in Part II that social scientists who wish to address the complex issues of meaning, values, understanding and representation in social interaction may need methods informed by positions other than that of positivism. In many respects this is what the qualitative and textual research methods discussed here do: they explore the 'rich texture' of 'everyday social life'. In the readings for Part III you will find that the researchers tend to focus on the 'meanings' inherent in social life. This contrasts with the ideas in Part II, which are primarily focused upon 'measuring' social life. Both qualitative data analysis and discourse analysis can be seen as ways of researching the meanings embedded in the actions and products of individuals and societies. In many respects these methods developed out of criticisms regarding the limitations of quantitative research, and they mark a shift from 'measuring' to 'understanding' the social world.

Unlike Part II where we could view most quantitative and numerical methods as being influenced by positivist ideas, a wide range of related and often competing philosophical positions informs qualitative and 'textual' methods. Why do I describe these methods as 'textual'? In the main this reflects the fact that most of the methods discussed here involve the study and analysis of 'cultural artefacts' as well as things spoken and written by participants – things that are now broadly called 'texts' in social science (see Smith, 1998: Chapters 6 and 7). It also reflects the practical reality that these methods tend to produce a lot of material that is written and that needs to be read over numerous times and written on (coded) and described. This is in contrast to the numerical and mathematical methods of analysis described in Part II.

6   *Positioning Qualitative Work*

What are the philosophical positions that inform qualitative work? I see these as falling into three types of work – but in many cases qualitative work crosses these boundaries:

- Phenomenological positions
- Hermeneutic positions
- Relativist positions

Overall these positions can be described as 'idealist' – that is to say they are philosophical positions that prioritise or focus upon the ways in which 'ideas' are made and used. This position contrasts with the positivists who focus upon the observation of 'empirical' events and in turn describe most types of other activity as 'metaphysical'. Smith (1998) points out how the eighteenth-century philosopher Kant tried to make some links between these positions by asking, 'What are conditions needed for knowledge and knowing?' Kant's position and that of many who have followed his ideas is one which tries to develop a compromise between

- 'rationalism' – ideas and thoughts guide us to the truth; and
- 'empiricism' – observed empirical facts guide us to the truth.

Importantly such approaches embrace the complexity – 'open system-ness' – of social life. Open and closed systems were discussed in Chapter 2. Holders of this position argue, unlike positivists, that there may be different approaches to creating valid knowledge depending on your *object* of study. Broadly speaking they identify two types of approach:

- nomothetic – the goal of which is the constructing generalised laws; and
- idiographic – whose goal is the detailed description of particular circumstances.

Most quantitative work – but not all – falls into the first approach. Most qualitative work – but not all – falls into the second. There are of course methods that span both approaches. We will briefly look at one of these before moving on to quickly explore some specific 'idealist' philosophical positions and to consider what we mean by 'qualitative' or 'textual' data.

Study Comment
As in Part II, you will gain a much better understanding of the issues if you engage with the self-assessment questions (SAQs). Please ensure that you attempt each of the self-assessment questions as a large part of the teaching takes place in these tasks. If you leave out the SAQs you will limit your learning and understanding of the material.

SAQ 6.1

Turn to Reading G, 'The visual life history interview'. As you read these research results, make notes on the following:

1   What variables does this method allow you to measure?
2   Is this a quantitative method? Think about how much interpretation is needed to analyse the data when answering this question.

Approaches to Qualitative Work

I argued above that I see three broad philosophical influences on qualitative research. So how do these affect the way this research is done. My first category was 'phenomenological positions'. Some qualitative work is specifically described by its practitioners as 'phenomenological'. **Phenomenology** as philosophy is based on the work of Husserl and Heidegger and was later developed into a social science theory by Alfred Schutz. It stresses the 'inter-subjective' nature of human interaction – we constantly work with models of the minds of others – good, bad, complex, simple but never complete models. Social science therefore has to account for the motives, means, ends, shared relationships, plans and expectations of human beings. One area of qualitative research that can be seen as an offshoot of these ideas is that of **ethnomethodology** and **conversation analysis** (a form of discourse analysis). Ethnomethodology and conversation analysis focus on the organised and planned actions of people, but try to do so from 'within' the action. For example they look at the plans, methods and rules we employ individually in making a 'queue', crossing the road or conversation – not general 'macro' models of crowd behaviour or language use.

A **hermeneutic** approach to qualitative research focuses on the meanings that objects and actions have for participants. Hermeneutics is an old term derived from the study of the text of the Bible in order to uncover its 'true meaning'. Today it is used to describe a philosophical position that stresses the need for a focus on meaning and human beings as meaning-making and meaning-using creatures. It has many parallels with the phenomenological position. Much qualitative research is a mix of these positions, leading to a focus on the planned actions and interactions with objects that human beings find 'meaningful'.

Relativist positions are quite varied and run through a spectrum of ideas that are too wide and complex to discuss here. Put very simply, relativists raise questions about the existence of a single 'reality' or 'truth' out there to be 'found'. This position provides the strongest rejection of positivist or empiricist models. It argues that there is no 'one' way of evaluating the 'truthfulness' or factualness of people's claims or accounts – unlike the view of positivists, who see this in the 'scientific method'. Though relativists vary in the form and extent of their claims they broadly argue that no one account is 'better' in some sense (scientifically, ethically, morally, linguistically, etc.) than any others. The question then becomes one of 'interpreting' between the cultures and contexts that provide accounts of events. For example an ethnographer might not claim to describe the practices of people in another culture 'scientifically'. Rather such ethnographers act as an interpreter communicating meanings between their own culture and that understudy – reflecting on both cultures and their position within both cultures.

Whatever the philosophy that informs qualitative work, researchers are still faced with the practical task of doing research. In the rest of this chapter we will consider what counts as 'qualitative data'. In Chapter 7 we will consider how you can collect qualitative data. Chapter 8 will examine two approaches to 'qualitative data analysis' and Chapter 9 will look at three types of discourse analysis. As with the coverage of statistical analyses, these chapters are only introductions to the main ideas. As such they should provide you with the basic ideas needed to get started in your study and use of the methods.

What is Qualitative Data?

This section looks at the ways in which social researchers approach the collection and analysis of qualitative data. But what is 'qualitative data'? One direct answer to this question is: 'not quantitative data'. In many respects this answer fits the way in which quantitative data and methods have been contrasted with qualitative data and methods. This sets up the two types of data as opposites – if it is not quantitative it is qualitative, and vice versa.

This is, of course, too simple a distinction. In both cases the types of data collected and the methods of analysis are, rightly or wrongly, also associated with a range of philosophical positions. Those working with quantitative data will bring forward arguments based on positivist ideas which stress the need for such things as 'objectivity' – the separation of the object of study from the observer – and 'reliability' – the ability to repeat results. Those working with qualitative methods, on the other hand, will use arguments derived from philosophical traditions such as idealism, often associated with relativism, or post-structuralism. They therefore stress the importance of such things as the subjective experiences of the researcher and the participants, the central importance of meaning to social life, and the importance of social and cultural context in situating different meanings and interpretations. In many respects the uptake of qualitative methods can be viewed in part as a reaction against positivism and empiricism as the philosophical basis for social research, though methods such as participant observation have their roots in some of the earliest forms of social research (see Smith, 1998: Chapters 3, 4 and 6). As you will see, some of those working with qualitative data reject positivism and the survey and experimental methods that have become associated with it. Others argue for a combination of such methods as are needed, while others deploy qualitative analysis, with its focus on the subjective and on meaning, within a framework similar to that outlined in Figure 2.1 (see p. 7).

If we can distinguish qualitative researchers by their reference to non-positivist methodological traditions, we have not yet said what qualitative data is. Part of an answer to this question is given above, when both qualitative data analysis and discourse analysis were described as ways of researching the meanings embedded in the actions and products of individuals and societies. Qualitative data consists of things that we find in the world which hold meaning for ourselves or for others. So, what things can hold meaning? And what can we gain from examining such data? We can start to answer these questions by noting the types of goals the rich variety of qualitative research tends to have. For example qualitative work often attempts to do one or more of the following:

- achieve an in-depth understanding and detailed description of a particular aspect of an individual, a case history or a group's experience(s);
- explore how individuals or group members give meaning to and express their understanding of themselves, their experiences and/or their worlds;
- find out and describe in detail social events and to explore *why* they are happening, rather than how often;
- explore the complexity, ambiguity and specific detailed processes taking place in a social context.

SAQ 6.2

Let's think about 'things that carry meaning'. Think about the place where you live, or another place where you spend a good deal of time. Now think about this question: what is it like to live in your country today?

To help answer this question, write down up to ten sources of information that can be found in the place where you live or spend your time. These sources can be anything that carries information or meaning about the world around you. Don't spend more than 15 minutes on this task.

From SAQ 6.2 we can conclude that nearly everything you find in a home or similar context could count as carrying meaning and therefore be seen as qualitative data. But why would we wish to view these as sources of qualitative rather than quantitative data? We could just count the number and type of each item or develop some form of specific measure to quantify these things and then we would have quantitative data. To begin to answer this question, let's look at a methodological discussion of the question: what is qualitative data?

SAQ 6.3

Turn to Reading H, 'What is qualitative data?'. As you read this extract make notes on the following questions:

1   What does Dey claim that quantitative data deals with?
2   What does Dey claim that qualitative data deals with?
3   Where does meaning 'reside', according to Dey?
4   List the sources of qualitative data that Dey mentions.
5   What do these sources have in common, according to Dey?
6   According to Dey, what has the term 'qualitative research' come to refer to in the social sciences?
7   Does Dey think you can neatly split research into qualitative and quantitative methods?

It is clear from Reading H that those working with qualitative data believe that it provides a 'richer' and 'more valid' basis for social research than simply dealing with numbers and measures. The data is seen as being 'richer' for a number of reasons. First, the data collection methods do not place as many constraints on the form and content of the data as a measure or experiment would. Second, the range of data sources is far wider: all meaningful human actions or artefacts and all social practices are legitimate sources. One upshot of this is that we don't have an everyday word or clear concept which encompasses all of these types of data.

In the case of quantitative methods we tend to refer to 'numerical' data. Contemporary social scientists often refer to the wide range of qualitative data types, from TV and film through books and newspapers to CDs and even computer games, and the social contexts in which they exist, as 'texts' (see Smith, 1998: Chapters 6 and 7). For the moment, you can consider a *text* to be 'any socially and contextually complete unit of meaning or meaningful activity', for example a film, a book, a TV programme, a telephone conversation, a trip to the cinema.

That said, this use of the term *text* can and should be challenged on a number of grounds. Importantly, it does not distinguish between 'practices' – what people do – and 'texts' – the objects which they produce or consume through practices. In the case of going to the cinema, the 'going' is a set of 'practices' and the 'film' is the 'text'. The data collected by the social researcher will be some record of this event (a video, field notes, etc.), and is therefore also a 'text'.

The argument that qualitative data is in some sense 'more valid' derives from the idealist position within the philosophy of social science. One of the major arguments made against quantitative methods, especially surveys and experiments, is that data is collected in 'artificial' situations, that is, situations which differ from everyday social activity. As such, they can be described as artificial ways of exploring social life. You will remember from Part II that one of the intentions of the experimental method is to create as 'closed' a system as possible by controlling and excluding many aspects of the situation. Qualitative researchers often argue that surveys with closed questions (see Chapter 3) impose the researcher's models and theories on the respondents by providing only limited responses to what can be quite complex questions. They also argue that survey questionnaires create an artificial setting in which people's responses to questions may vary quite considerably from the wide range of complex behaviour they engage in when in 'real' social settings. This claim also holds for experiments, since they are deliberately constructed artificial settings. Because of this some social researchers question how general and complete are results gained from such an approach. In contrast, those working with qualitative data claim that they have access to a far more extensive range of material that gives deeper and richer insights into the finer detail of people, social contexts and social practices.

In the case of quantitative methods we looked at a number of ways of collecting data, the two main ones being surveys and experiments, both of which make use of measures. Given the wide range of things that can count as qualitative data, there are many methods of data collection. In Reading H (p. 147) Dey lists four types:

- participant and non-participant observation – watching or being part of a social context;
- semi-structured and unstructured in-depth interviews – using open questions rather than closed questions, either covering a selected set of topics or allowing a free development of the interview;
- group discussions and interviews – often called focus groups;
- collecting documentary materials – anything from letters or memos to novels or reports.

There are more possibilities than just these four, and, in fact, the range of identifiable methods for qualitative data collection is broad. The four methods described above are those traditionally associated with a particular type of data collection method: ethnography. More recently social scientists have tended to describe these as qualitative methods and use one or more of these methods separately within the context of any study. So for example a study might only use in-depth interviews or it may only use focus groups. There is a long tradition in media and marketing research of using focus groups. The term 'ethnography' tends to be used for studies that involve 'fieldwork' – that is where researchers use all of the above methods in combination to study and observe a specific context or group. There are of course numerous debates about the nature and form of ethnographic work. For the purposes of the next sections I am going to focus on two practical methods of qualitative data collection that I will term 'in-depth' interviews and 'ethnographic fieldwork'. I am not claiming that these are the only methods, or that my representation of them is the 'best' or 'sole' approach. Rather I am presenting them as practical ways into this type of work. We will begin first with in-depth interviews. There are some important reasons for starting with interviews. First, most ethnographic work involves some form of interviewing or interaction with participants. Second, many of the practical and interpersonal skills required for interviewing are required for ethnographic work. Third, most qualitative researchers use in-depth interviewing. This includes discourse analysts (see Chapter 9), and you will need to understand this approach in order to evaluate their work.

Further Reading

Flick, U. (1998) *An Introduction to Qualitative Research*. London: Sage.
Ritchie, J. and Lewis, J. (2003) *Qualitative Research Practice: A Guide for Social Science Students and Researchers*. London: Sage.
Silverman, D. (ed.) (1997) *Qualitative Research: Theory, Method and Practice*. London: Sage.

Reading G: The Visual Life History Interview

Annabel Tomas

This paper describes the use of the visual life history interview in on-going research concerned with the experience of housing and the meaning of home for homeless women in Brighton, South East England. Whilst preliminary findings on the pathways into homelessness for women are reported elsewhere (Tomas and Dittmar, 1995), this paper will briefly describe the development of the visual protocol before making explicit the first of three stages undertaken in that research.

The development of the visual life history interview   The visual life history interview was originally developed as a way of understanding the responses which homeless women gave me when I asked them about the meaning of home. For example, what did the homeless woman mean when she said, 'I don't have a home and I live there all the time'? On the basis of what experience and with what understanding did she come to such a paradoxical conclusion? The interview schedule was designed to accommodate the complexity of her housing experience as well as its diversity, and to help me engage with, and come to, a shared understanding of what home means *in its absence* – the paradox of home for homeless women.

The structure of the interview   We are all 'housed' in history, culture and language, and we all experience people, places and events – these are the universal features of experience which provide the structure of the schedule and the basis for a shared understanding. The visual protocol, with its symbols and colour codes, was designed to help 'house' the homeless experience by putting it in its right time and space *(stage one)*, as well as providing a framework for reflection – a way of looking down on the pattern of this experience in order to come to an understanding of it *(stages two and three)*.

The step by step guide to stage one, *'drawing out experience'*, is presented below for use by anyone interested in drawing up a rough guide to their own lives. Here the concern is with mapping out, in a chronological time, where people, places and events converge. Experiences are drawn out along a time-line using symbols and colour-codes making it easier to see.

To begin with you should not be looking for absolute precision in timing, nor be concerned with an interpretation beyond the recall. The questions at this stage are straightforward (e.g. what school, where, when, what age, for how long). The concern is with establishing, as accurately as possible, the time when people, places and events were experienced. The meaning of this experience is not enquired into at this stage.

Recall of experience is always selective and there will be many absences or gaps. People forget things or choose not to tell things or are not aware of things – for all sorts of reasons. I assume that what is not recalled, is not recalled for a reason. I therefore do not try to purposefully fill in gaps by 'digging' for more information (as if they were not reasonable), rather the gaps will close themselves up as you go along or they will remain as gaps. This is both protective of the individual and also allows for the recording of experiences which, for whatever reasons, are not talked about or cannot be articulated. Many such gaps or absences may be based on traumatic experiences for which there are no words – only silence . . . Such gaps are often easier to symbolise in a drawing than to talk about, and in this way the meaning of home for homeless women – home *in its absence* – can at least be seen.

Before you begin, keep in mind the audience. The first version should be for yourself only. Later versions can be edited for different audiences, for example you can draw up an educational history or a work history without having to show your whole life. For any audience you need to be careful about 'naming' people. Once you have drawn out the major dimensions of your life (people, places, events) you are then in a position to draw in as many details of this experience as you wish. You can use the visual format to look at one experience across a whole life, or to look at a number of experiences in a part of a life.

Step by Step Guide

The Time-line

The Lifescape sheet is divided into twenty-five units. Depending on your age you can divide this by two to reach fifty years, by three for seventy-five years, or halve it for younger ages. Starting with your year of birth, put in both the years and your age (at approximately the point within a year) to the year 2000. For example, if you were born in 1981 then you would turn one year old in 1982. Most mistakes are made at this stage so take care.

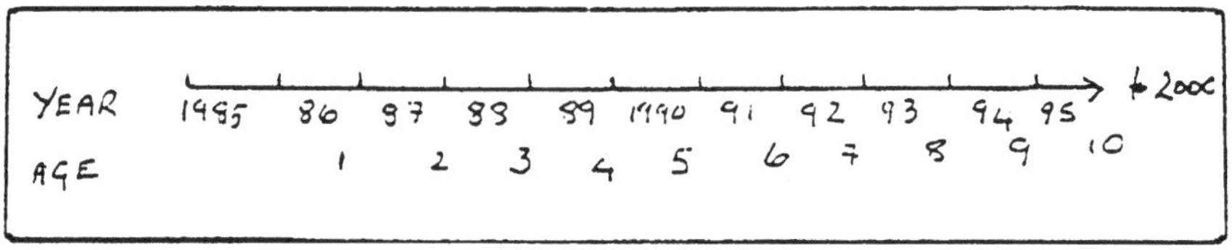

Figure 6.1 *Time-line*

Housing

Draw in all the places you have lived along the time-line, being as accurate as you can. Use memory markers such as birthdays, celebrations, first day at school, etc., to jog memory. Move backwards or forwards until you are fairly certain. If dates are uncertain move on and leave gaps till later.

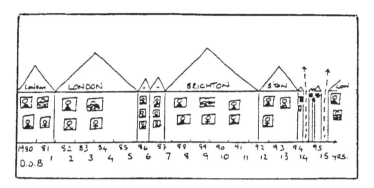

Figure 6.2 *Houses with place names*

Housing can mean a flat, a tent, a boat, or wherever you regularly slept. If there was no regular house then leave as a gap, marked by an arrow. If the duration of stay was short, or you moved very often in a short space of time, then mark the beginning and end of this episode with an approximate number of moves. Where you can, in each of the places you stayed, draw a window with you looking out of it. Colour yourself in red.

Draw in the people associated with where you lived

Draw windows in the houses and put in the faces of people who lived with you there. Using the colour code printed on the Lifescape sheet colour these people in. In the space above the houses draw in all the people you want to remember who you first met either in your housing or in your neighbourhood (for example, friends of parents, milkman, neighbour, etc.).

General rules for drawing in people

- Draw people in at the first time of meeting only.
- Put a dot by any person that you still know and have contact with.
- Draw a blue dot next to the person considered by you to be a close friend *at the time*.
- If that person is no longer considered a close friend cross over the blue dot.
- If the person is 'not a friend' then you can show this by marking with your own code.

Schooling

Put in all the schools and colleges which you have attended. Include evening classes or any educational course, however brief. Draw in yourself and the people who you met there and want to remember, either in a window or in the space above. Colour yourself red and these people orange. Cross-check with housing.

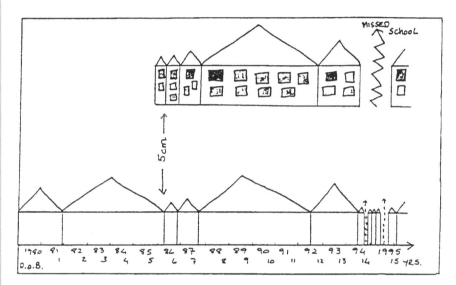

Figure 6.3 *Houses/schools*

Work

Draw in all the places of work, whether paid or not. If more than one workplace at the same time (i.e. two part-time jobs) then show as shown below. Where there is no workplace and no day-time schooling, then write in the space what you were doing during the day. If work is not done in a place, e.g. paper round, then write in paper round. Colour work mates who you want to remember yellow and put yourself in red. Cross-check with schooling and housing.

Other Places and Other People

Draw in the other places (not housing, school or workplace) that have been significant to you. For example, the park, the pub, the church, grandparents' house, friends' houses. Besides these places draw in the people associated with them. Cross-check to keep dates and places tallied. Remember to colour code those who were considered close friends and to mark with a dot those who you still have contact with.

Significant Events and Experiences

In this section you record any event or experience which has been, or is, important to you. Cross-check dates with place. You can mark this experience with a plus or minus symbol depending on how positive or negative you consider this experience to have been.

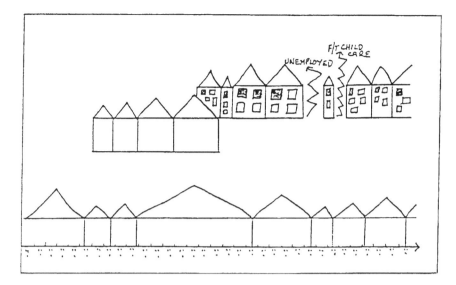

Figure 6.4 *Workplaces*

Psychological Weather Map

You can create your own psychological weather map and apply this to individual events, people, places, or across a whole period of time.

Family Trees

At the top of the Lifescape sheet draw in your family trees. One can be 'family of origin', giving names of parents, uncles, aunts, cousins and grandparents, and the other a 'family of friends', showing those people who you have chosen.

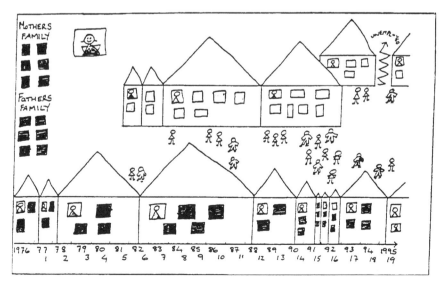

Figure 6.5 *Family/people*

Drawing to a Conclusion

You should now have a 'rough guide' to the people, places and events of your life in their right time and space. This is the data-base upon which you can reflect and analyse.

Conclusion

The first stage of the visual life history interview is concerned with documenting, in a chronological time, where people, places, ages, and events, converge. Subsequent steps in the life history interview with homeless women continue to fill in details of this history. This becomes the data-base, upon which we later reflect and discuss the experience of housing and the meaning of home for them.

Notes

The lack of colour seriously compromises the visual impact of the data.

Reference

Tomas, A. and Dittmar, H. (1995) 'The experience of homeless women: an exploration of housing histories and the meaning of home', *Housing Studies*, 10(4).

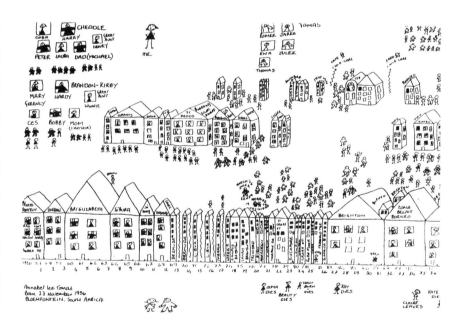

Figure 6.6 *Complete map*

Source: Tomas, 1997.

Reading H: What Is Qualitative Data?

Ian Dey

Compare the following reports of a game of soccer (Winter 1991).

Wimbledon 0 Liverpool 0

There was more excitement in the Selhurst car park than on the pitch . . .

Here we have both a quantitative result, and a qualitative assessment of the same game. Which do we care more about – the result, or the game? The points, or the passion? Which we find more important or illuminating will depend on what we are interested in. If we are team managers or fanatical fans, we may care more about the result than about how it was achieved. If we are neutral spectators, then we may care more about the quality of the game than about the result – in which case the match report confirms our worst fears of a no scoring draw! In social research as in everyday life, our assessment of quantitative and qualitative data is likely to reflect the interests we bring to it and the use we want to make of it.

We use quantitative data in a whole range of everyday activities, such as shopping, cooking, travelling, watching the time or assessing the Government's economic performance. How long? How often? How much? How many? We often ask and answer questions such as these using quantitative data.

Suppose I take 30 minutes to jog 5 miles to a shop and spend £5 on a litre of Chilean wine and 100 grams of Kenyan green beans. My behaviour may seem somewhat eccentric, but the terms in which it is expressed – minutes, miles, pounds, litres and grams – are entirely familiar. Each of these is a unit of measurement, in terms of which we can measure quantity. How do we measure quantities? We can count the coins or notes. We use a watch to tell the time. We weigh the beans on a weighing machine. We can use a milometer to check on distance and a measuring jug for volume. In each case, we have a measuring device which can express variations in quantity in terms of an established scale of standard units. But what is it that varies? We use minutes to measure time, miles to measure distance, pounds to measure expenditure, litres to measure volume and grams to measure weight. Time, distance, expenditure, volume and weight can be thought of as variables which can take on a range of different values. We don't always agree on how to measure our variables – we could have used kilometres, dollars, pints and ounces. But the important point is that for each of these variables we can confidently measure numerical differences in the values they can adopt. This is possible because we can establish a unit of measurement agreed upon as a common standard which is replicable, i.e. it can be applied again and again with the same results (Blalock 1960).

While 'quantities' permeate our everyday life, they are most likely to be used in a physical or physiological context, where measurement in terms of standard units is well established. We readily accept conventional measures of time, space and weight. Even in a physical context, though, we make qualitative as well as quantitative assessments. Is the bus dirty? Is the meal appetizing? Is the view breathtaking? These involve assessments for which we either cannot or do not use concepts which can be measured in quantitative terms. In a psychological or social context, we are much more likely to rely on qualitative assessment. Is this person sympathetic? Is this city exciting? Is this book interesting? These are areas where we tend to rely on qualitative assessment rather than on some quantitative measure.

By comparison with quantities, qualities seem elusive and ethereal. We often use 'quality' as a measure of relative worth, as when referring to a 'quality performance' or 'a person of quality', or asking whether something is of good or poor quality. Suppose I have just watched a film and I am asked what I thought of it. What was the film like? My evaluation will refer to the qualities of the film. Was it entertaining, or profound? Did it make me laugh or cry? Was the plot plausible? Were the characters convincing? Was the acting good? Was the script well crafted? These questions are all concerned with what I made of the film. But my evaluation of the film cannot be separated from how I understood and interpreted it. Quality is a measure of relative value, but based on an evaluation of the general character or intrinsic nature of what we are assessing. What was the story? What was the point of the film? What values did it express? Did the film achieve what it set out to do? In short, what did the film mean to me?

Whereas quantitative data deals with numbers, qualitative data deals with meanings. Meanings are mediated mainly through language and action. Language is not a matter of subjective opinion. Concepts are constructed in terms of an inter-subjective language which allows us to communicate intelligibly and interact effectively (cf. Sayer 1992: 32). Take the very idea of a film. The word derives from the Old English word 'filmen' meaning a membrane, and in modern usage has been extended to include a thin coating of light-sensitive emulsion, used in photography, and hence to the cinema where it refers rather to what is recorded on film. The meanings which constitute the concept 'film' are embodied in changing social practices such as the drive-in movie or the home video. What it may mean to make or see a film has changed considerably over the past twenty years. My somewhat dated dictionary defines films in terms of cinema-going and has not yet caught up with TV movies, never mind the video recorder. Because concepts are subject to such continual shifts in meaning, we have to treat them with caution.

Meaning is essentially a matter of making distinctions. When I describe a film as 'boring', for example, I am making one or more distinctions: this situation is 'boring' and not 'exciting' or 'stimulating' or 'interesting' or 'amusing'. Meaning is bound up with the contrast between what is asserted and what is implied not to be the case. To understand the assertion that a film is 'boring', I have to understand the distinction being drawn between what is and what might have been the case.

Meanings reside in social practice, and not just in the heads of individuals. Going to the movies expresses meaning, just as much as does reviewing them. The 'social construction' of a night out at the cinema is a complex accomplishment in terms of meaningful action. The cinema itself is not just a building, but one designed and constructed for a particular purpose. Showing a film in the cinema is the culmination of a complex sequence of meaningful actions, including the whole process of producing, making, distributing and advertising the film. My 'night out' at the cinema is a comparable accomplishment, predicated upon social practices in the form of transportation (I have to get to the cinema), economic exchange (I have to buy a ticket) and audience behaviour (silence please!).

Such social phenomena are, in Sayer's words, 'concept-dependent': unlike natural phenomena they are not impervious to the meanings we ascribe to them (1992: 30). The film industry, the entertainment business, the transport system and the 'night out' are social practices which can only be understood in terms of the meanings we invest in them. To vary a stock example, when one billiard ball 'kisses' another, the physical reaction that takes place is not affected by any meaningful behaviour on the part of the billiard balls. But when one person kisses another, the reaction can only be understood as meaningful behaviour. The natural scientist may worry about what it means when one billiard ball kisses another, but only about what it means to the scientist (e.g. in terms of force, inertia, momentum). The social scientist also has to worry about what the kiss means for the persons involved.

As my example of the film suggests, in dealing with meanings we by no means need to confine our attention to text. On the contrary, we should note the richness and diversity of qualitative data, since it encompasses virtually any kind of data: sounds, pictures, videos, music, songs, prose, poetry or whatever. Text is by no means the only, nor is it always the most effective, means of communicating qualitative information; in an electronic age, art and design have become powerful media tools. The importance of image as well as text is not merely an aspect of contemporary culture; the art historian Michael Baxandall (1974) comments that 'a painting is the deposit of a social relationship'. Qualitative data embraces an enormously rich spectrum of cultural and social artefacts.

What do these different kinds of data have in common? They all convey meaningful information in a form other than numbers. However, note that numbers too sometimes convey only meanings, as, for example, when we refer to the numbers on football jerseys, car number plates, or the box numbers in personal ads. It would be absurd to treat these numbers as numerical data, to be added, subtracted or otherwise subject to mathematical manipulation. But it is not always so easy to distinguish between the use of number as a descriptor of quality and its use as a measure of quantity. This is particularly true where, for convenience in manipulating data, we use numbers as names. It is then all too easy to forget that the numbers are only names, and proceed as if they 'meant' more than they do. Often, for example, response categories in an interview are coded by number. This may be convenient for the analysis. But if we forget that these numbers are really just names, we may analyse them as though they conveyed more information than they actually do. In distinguishing between quantitative and qualitative data in terms of numbers and meanings, we have to avoid the fallacy of treating numbers as numbers where they are used only to convey meaning.

By comparison with numbers, meanings may seem shifty and unreliable. But often they may also be more important, more illuminating and more fun. If I am a boringly meticulous jogger, I may use a pedometer to measure the distance I jog, a watch to measure my time, and the scales afterwards to measure my weight. For each concept – distance, time, weight – we can measure behaviour in terms of standard units – yards, minutes and pounds: 'I jog 3,476 yards every day, in 20 minutes on average, and I hope to lose 5lb after a month'. However, I happen to know that with jogging this obsession with quantitative measurement is counter-productive: it adds stress and reduces enjoyment. I also know that by replacing fat with muscle, I am liable to gain rather than lose weight! Therefore, I prefer to measure my jogging in qualitative terms: 'I jog until I am tired out. By the end of the month I hope I'll feel fitter.' Short of conducting some medical tests, there are no quantitative measures in terms of which to quantify my exhaustion, or my fitness. But I can describe my exhaustion, and I can compare how much fitter I feel now than before I began to jog. Although I could use quantitative measures (e.g. my pulse rate) as a way of assessing my fitness, these may not provide a very meaningful assessment of how fit I felt.

It would be wrong to assume that quantitative data must take precedence over qualitative data simply because it involves numbers. Take the ever topical question of weight watching. There are various ways we can weight watch. We might use the scales and measure how many kilos or pounds we weigh. This is a quantitative measure, but it doesn't tell us how the weight is distributed, nor how a particular point in the scale translates into overall appearance. We might prefer to rely on how we look, whether 'fat' or 'thin' or maybe 'just right'. These are qualitative judgements, but in a social context these may be the judgements that count. If we do not measure data in quantitative terms, it may be that (at least for the moment) we lack the tools necessary to do the job. Or it may be that we simply prefer qualitative assessments because they are more meaningful, if less precise, than any quantitative measures.

Take colour as an example. For most purposes we are content to use a fairly crude classification based on a very limited colour range. If we are buying (or selling) paint, though, we may want a more sophisticated classification. And if we are using colour in an industrial or scientific context, we may want more precision: a spectrophotometer measures the amount of light reflected or transmitted across the visible spectrum, allowing colours to be measured precisely in terms of their wavelengths. However, the mathematical specification of a colour does not reveal how it will look to different observers in variable light conditions; although measurement is more accurate, it is less useful for everyday purposes than cruder methods which rely on visual classification (Varley 1983: 134–5).

Because qualitative assessments are less standardized and less precise than quantitative measures, there are areas of social life where we do attempt to establish the latter. Money is the medium through which we measure equivalence in market transactions, though in contrast to physical measures, confidence in currencies can collapse completely. Qualifications are another medium used to measure educational achievement, though here also 'inflation' can undermine confidence in established standards. Attempts to measure educational performance, intelligence, health status, social adjustment, quality of life and so on in quantitative terms are dogged by suspicion that these do not capture the 'quality' of psychological or social aspects of life. For example, compare the following statements on educational achievement:

'Only 5% of British employees in commercial and clerical work have educational qualifications above A-level standard.'	'Education is what survives when what has been learnt has been forgotten.'

In reducing educational achievement to a quantitative measure, do we neglect or overlook altogether what is important about education – its quality?

This tension between quantitative measures and qualitative assessment is also apparent in social research. On the one hand, qualitative data is often presented as 'richer' and 'more valid' than quantitative data. On the other hand, it is often dismissed as 'too subjective' because assessments are not made in terms of established standards. In practice, this implies an unnecessary polarization between the different types of data. We have to consider the reliability and validity of whatever measures we choose. But as is often the case, the existence of a dichotomy has tended to polarize not only thinking but people (Galtung 1967: 23). Qualitative data has become narrowly associated with research approaches emphasizing unstructured methods of obtaining data.

Qualitative research has become a fashionable term to use for any method other than the survey: participant (and non-participant) observation, unstructured interviewing, group interviews, the collection of documentary materials and the like. Data produced from such sources may include fieldnotes, interview transcripts, documents, photographs, sketches, video or tape recordings, and so on. What these various forms of research often have in common is a rejection of the supposedly positivist 'sins' associated with survey methods of investigation, most particularly where data are elicited through closed questions using researcher-defined categories. A grudging exception may be allowed for open questions in a questionnaire survey, but in practice – for the sake of purity, perhaps – data from this source are often ignored. The hallmark of qualitative data from this perspective is that it should be a product of 'unstructured' methods of social research.

However, it is not very helpful to see qualitative data simply as the output of qualitative research. Distinctions between different methods are as hard to draw as distinctions between types of data! For example, we might contrast the survey as a method involving the collection and comparison of data across a range of cases, with the single case study approach more commonly associated with qualitative methods. However, in recent years there has been an upsurge of interest in 'multi-case' (or 'multi-site') fieldwork methods, eroding the force of the case study/survey distinction. Moreover, the survey itself can be used as a data collection instrument within the context of a case study; for example, we might survey teacher opinion as part of a case study of a particular school.

Another distinction sometimes drawn between qualitative and quantitative methods is that the former produce data which are freely defined by the subject rather than structured in advance by the researcher (Patton 1980). 'Pre-structured' data are taken to involve selection from a limited range of researcher-defined alternatives, for example in an observation schedule or multiple choice questionnaire. With subject-defined data, the length, detail, content and relevance of the data are not determined by the researcher, but recorded 'as spoken' or 'as it happens', usually in the form of notes or tape recordings.

However, it is difficult to draw such a sharp divide between these methods. Observations may be more or less 'structured' without falling clearly into one type or another. Similarly, between the 'structured' and 'unstructured' interview are a variety of interviewing forms which resist such ready classification. Take open and closed questions in interviewing as an obvious example. With the closed question, the respondent must choose from the options specified by the researcher. With an open question, respondents are free to respond as they like. But these alternatives are not really so clear-cut. For example, questions which indicate a range of response categories may still include the option: 'Other – please specify'. And even the most non-directive interviewer must implicitly 'direct' an interview to some extent if it is to cover certain topics within the time available. It would be naive to discount the role played by the researcher as participant observer or unstructured interviewer in eliciting and shaping the data they obtain.

The point is that any 'data', regardless of method, are in fact 'produced' by the researcher. In this respect, the idea that we 'collect' data is a bit misleading. Data are not 'out there' waiting collection, like so many rubbish bags on the pavement. For a start, they have to be noticed by the researcher, and treated as data for the purposes of his or her research. 'Collecting' data always involves selecting data, and the techniques of data collection and transcription (through notes, tape recordings or whatever) will affect what finally constitutes 'data' for the purposes of research.

A method of data collection may in any case produce various types of data. The most obvious example is the questionnaire survey, where we can design a wide range of questions, more or less 'open' or 'closed', to elicit various types of data. The same holds true of fieldwork methods, such as document searches or observation; while the data produced through these methods may be predominantly qualitative in character, there is no reason to presume that it will be exclusively so. Sometimes of course we simply do not get the kind of data we expected.

What's the main difference between students of the 1960s and the 1990s?	What result would you get if you laid a class of 30 students, average height 5'5", end to end?
Thirty years.	They'd all fall asleep.

In practice, research often involves a range of methods producing a variety of data. We would do better to focus on the data which has been produced, rather than implying rigid distinctions between styles of research and methods of data collection.

If qualitative research is equated with the use of unstructured methods, it follows that qualitative data is therefore seen as 'unstructured'. The difference between 'structured' and 'unstructured' data turns on whether or not the data has been classified. Take the following example of structured and unstructured responses to a question about the use of closed questions in an interview.

Structured and unstuctured responses to the question 'What are the main advantages and disadvantages of closed questions in an interview?'

Structured response	Unstructured response
Closed questions expedite the interview for both interviewer and respondent Closed questions expedite later processing of data Closed questions convey more exact meaning by defining the range of appropriate responses Closed questions improve reliability	Well, it can put people off, not being able to answer in their own words. But the important thing is that people may not be able to answer as they'd like. Answers to open questions are more likely to reflect a person's own thinking – to be more valid. It's much better to analyse the data afterwards, even if it's more time-consuming. Of course time is of the essence, especially when you've had the kind of medical problems I've had over the last year, I had that operation in January, etc. etc.

The structured response has been classified, for the data is divided into separate statements denoting distinctive advantages of closed questions, relating to the conduct of the interview, the ease of data processing and the communication of meaning. By contrast, the unstructured response is descriptive but unclassified: the response covers a range of points – not all of them relevant – which are not organized and presented as distinctive elements.

Lack of structure is evident in the characteristic volume and complexity of much research data: in those apparently endless pages upon pages of fieldnotes; in the varied mass of documentary materials; in those lengthy and lavish interview transcripts. Such data may often lack structure, but this can be a problem as much as a virtue. The idea that qualitative data is mainly 'unstructured' is useful, if this is taken not as a definition but rather as an imperative for analysis. Although unstructured data may not be classified, it can be classified and indeed one of the main aims of qualitative analysis is often to do just that. While a lot of qualitative data may be unstructured, it is misleading to define qualitative data as 'unstructured' data. Is a response less 'qualitative' because I classify my observations? Suppose I am asked to describe the colour of my hair. Is my response less 'qualitative' if I (sadly but honestly) select 'grey' from a list of alternatives, than if I write 'grey' in the space provided?

Ironically, in defining qualitative data in terms of unstructured data or a particular family of research methods, qualitative analysts underestimate the significance of qualitative data across the whole research spectrum. They also underestimate the concern amongst other research traditions with problems of meaning and conceptualizaion (Fielding and Fielding 1986; Bryman 1988). Rather than counter-posing qualitative and quantitative data in this way, it makes more sense to consider how these can complement each other in social research (Giarelli 1988).

References

Baxandall, Michael (1974) *Painting's Experience in 15th Century Italy*. Oxford: Oxford University Press.
Blalock, Hubert M. (1960) *Social Statistics*. London: McGraw-Hill.
Bryman, Alan (1988) *Quantity and Quality in Social Research*. London: Unwin Hyman.
Fielding, Nigel and Fielding, Jane (1986) *Linking Data*. London: Sage.
Galtung, Johan (1967) *Theory and Methods of Social Research*. London: Allen and Unwin.
Giarelli, James M. (1988) 'Qualitative inquiry in philosophy and education: notes on the pragmatic tradition', in Robert R. Sherman, and Rodman B. Webb (eds) *Qualitative Research for Education: Focus and Methods*. London: The Falmer Press.
Patton, Michael Quinn (1980) *Qualitative Evaluation Methods*. London: Sage.
Sayer, Andrew (1992) *Method in Social Science: A Realist Approach*. London and New York: Routledge.
Varley, Helen (1983) *Colour*. London: Marshall Editions.
Winter, Henry (1991) 'Liverpool requires a new forward plan', *The Independent*, 25 November.

Source: Dey, 1993: 9–17

Solution to Chapter 6 SAQs

SAQ 6.1

1   This method lets you measure a range of variables including: time in any one place; key relationships; places and types of schooling and education; places and types of work and employment.
2   This is a hard question to answer. On one level it provides specific numerical results, such as the time spent in different locations. On the other hand, the method requires a lot of interpretation, a feature more common to qualitative methods.

SAQ 6.2

If I think about my home there is a huge amount of material that could provide information to help answer the question: what is social life in the UK like today? As an academic I have a lot of books, about 300 in fact, ranging from novels to academic texts, on a wide range of subjects. Though they might tell a lot about me, they might also help someone address various aspects of the question. I also tend to have newspapers and magazines around as I take them for recycling, about 20 newspapers and 10 magazines. Newspapers and magazines are an obvious choice if one wishes to know about life in a specific country. I like collecting films on video and DVD: I have about 60 videos/DVDs. Again, films can tell us a great deal about the society that made or watched them. I also have a large music collection on tape and CD, about 360 albums, which would form another possible source of information. Other possessions such as electrical equipment, bicycles, furniture, etc. could also provide information.

One might want to examine the decoration of the house, or my choice of clothes, for information about current fashions. In fact nearly everything in my home could help answer this question, as my home and I are part of UK society and the things in my home reflect social processes in the UK, my position within that society and so forth. They also reflect how I have interacted with the social world around me and the types of choices I have made or been able to make. All these things hold meanings, in themselves, as part of my home and as part of UK society at large. If qualitative data are about exploring the meanings and meaningful objects found in the social world, then all of these things could be sources of qualitative data.

SAQ 6.3

1   In the main Dey sees quantitative data as being about numbers.
2   Dey sees qualitative data as being mainly about meanings. Interestingly, numbers can have meanings over and above their role as markers of amount. The number 7 might mean a great deal to fans of a specific football club; the number 17 might be meaningful to people born on the 17th of a month; 6:45 might mean 'get up early for the train to work'. Importantly, the 'numbers' that are the result of quantitative research also carry meaning as they are markers or measures of meaningful aspects of social and psychological life.
3   Dey claims that meanings reside in social practices: not only does a film have meaning for the audience, or a book for the reader, but the act of going to the pictures is enmeshed in a plethora of meanings, as is the act of reading a book (see Smith, 1998: Chapters 6 and 7). In this argument human life is about the meanings which reside in everything we do, make or consume.
4   Dey mentions the following throughout the extract: sounds, pictures, videos, music, songs, prose, poetry, games (billiards), painting, interviews, transcripts, numbers (see above).
5   All of these types of data carry meaningful information in a non-numerical way.
6   According to Dey qualitative research has come to denote those types of research methods that don't make use of surveys (and we could add experiments) as a form of data collection. These include: observation (participant or not), unstructured interviewing, (focus) group interviewing, collecting documentary sources, etc. Dey notes that the proponents of such methods tend to reject the positivist basis upon which they claim survey methods are built.
7   Dey argues that the distinction between qualitative and quantitative data and methods is not so clear-cut as some would claim. Dey argues that rather than be seen as competing alternatives, both methods should learn from each other and are best used to complement each other.

7   Collecting Qualitative Data

This chapter explores the ways in which qualitative data can be collected. Like Chapters 3 and 4 it will focus on the more practical aspects of data collection – but with reference to broader philosophical issues. The chapter covers three topics:

- in-depth interviews – semi-structured and unstructured interactions with participants;
- focus group interviews – essentially group versions of in-depth interviews;
- ethnographic fieldwork – the collection of qualitative data from a range of contexts.

In essence the chapter 'builds up' from one-to-one data collection to larger projects that cover a range of data collection methods.

Issues in In-depth Research Interviewing

In this and the following two sections we will consider one of the main methods used in conducting qualitative research – the in-depth interview. To start with we will address such questions as:

- What is an in-depth research interview?
- Why might you want to do an in-depth interview?
- What kinds of research questions can you explore using in-depth interviews?
- What ethical and practical issues will you need to address?

Later sections will cover aspects of four broad topics:

- *Designing an interview.* This includes constructing an interview schedule, considering the themes in the interview discussion, and how to generate themes and questions.
- *Fieldwork.* This includes how one gets access to participants, where one conducts the interviews and managing yourself and your data.
- *Interview skills.* Interviews are hard work and require a set of key skills.

These include: managing the interview interaction, establishing rapport, eliciting 'thick description', openings and closings and reinforcement and listening skills.

- *Group interviews.* We will also explore how you move up from one-to-one to group interviewing (focus groups) and how this draws on similar and additional skills.

Positioning In-depth Interviews

As argued earlier in this book, there are a variety of links between epistemological positions – theories of knowledge construction – and the methods used to gain that knowledge. I have argued that most 'idealist' and 'relativist' approaches to social research emphasise the search for 'meanings' rather than attempt to 'measure' aspects of the social world. In order to explore, analyse and understand the meanings people use in everyday life we need to get access to these in some manner. Some approaches such as content analysis and varieties of discourse analysis (see Chapter 9) make use of existing materials such a newspapers, novels, or even music and Internet media. More often though, qualitative researchers make use of in-depth interviews. As when finding information out about people – the best way is to ask them!

The reason for this is found in the meaning of the word 'interview' itself. 'Interview' literally means to develop a shared perspective and understanding (a view) between (inter) two or more people. In other words the researcher and the participant(s) develop a shared understanding of the topic under discussion. The extent to which this understanding is viewed as that of the participant, jointly that of the researcher and participant or as a context-bound product of jointly interactional work, all depends on your theoretical or epistemological position. These issues will be explored further when we consider how to analyse qualitative data (see Chapter 8).

So what do we mean by 'in-depth' interviews? There is a whole range of interviewing techniques. Many quantitative surveys are conducted through the use of a face-to-face interview. There are also semi-structured interviews, where a pre-set agenda is used to define the flow of the interview. There are unstructured interviews with no pre-set agenda. There are of course many other social contexts where interviews are used that are not about social research. These include: job candidate appraisal, police investigations, TV news, etc. In this section we are concerned with the set of interviews that involves a lengthy and involved interaction with the participant. These interviews may be semi-structured or unstructured but they are focused on getting a 'rich' and detailed account of the subjects' understandings, feelings, knowledge, etc. on the research topic.

Speakers' Perspectives

In most cases qualitative work is concerned with the perspective of the participants – it is how they understand the social world and the meanings things have for them that is under study. The central concern is therefore the 'speaker's perspective'. This represents a commitment to understanding events, actions, values etc. from the perspective of the person being studied. It is an attempt to 'see through the eyes of the person being studied'. How we do this and the role of our social theories in helping us do this forms a major debating point for qualitative workers. From this position the key question is: what is the participant's 'life-world' like for them? This perspective is sometimes termed a *phenomenological* perspective, in which: 'The constructs that people use in order to render the world meaningful and intelligible to them [should be] the key focus of a phenomenologically grounded social science' (Schutz, 1967). In general such a position argues that:

- human behaviour is a product of the way people interpret their world – that is to say that the meanings we give to things in the world are also those by which we explain it to ourselves;
- there is a multiplicity of worldviews and not everyone shares the same worldview.

As was argued in Chapter 7 we can try to summarise some of the goals of research in these areas as follows:

- to achieve an in-depth understanding and detailed description of a particular aspect of an individual, a case history or a group's experience(s);
- to explore how individuals or group members give meaning to and express their understanding of themselves, their experiences and/or their worlds;
- to find out and describe in detail social events and to explore why they are happening, rather than how often;
- to explore the complexity, ambiguity and specific detailed processes taking place in a social context.

Researchers often rely upon in-depth interviews to provide them with the type of data needed to achieve these goals. Having said all this, as with all social research there are many who use in-depth interviews who do not subscribe to these goals or who do not remain within a broadly qualitative epistemology when conducting the analysis of the data.

SAQ 7.1

Look at the following questions which are taken from a survey about attitudes to violence on TV. Write down five advantages of using survey methods like these. Write down five disadvantages of survey methods.

For each of the following statements mark if you agree, disagree with the statement:

	Agree	Disagree	Don't know
TV programmes containing violence should be broadcast late at night			
There are too many programmes on television that contain violence			
We would be better off without violence on television; there is already enough in real life			
I sometimes wish that violence in programmes (like *The Sweeney*) was more realistic			
People who say that television is harmful to people don't know what they're talking about			
Sometimes I can feel quite violent after watching crime programmes			

Next write a 100–200-word answer to the following question:

- How do you feel violence on TV affects you as a viewer?

Can you provide a clear definition of how these two types of data differ? What are the advantages or disadvantages of each? In what way is the 100–200-word answer 'richer'?

Research Topics and Research Questions

Why and when should in-depth interviews be used? There is no hard and fast answer to this question. As with all selection of methods a mix of practicality, theory and epistemology will come into play. I would argue that any research with similar goals to those outlined above and in Chapter 6 should consider the use of in-depth interviews as a data collection method. The method is useful when you need to gain detailed understandings that are best communicated through detailed examples and narratives. In particular it allows the exploration or detailing of the subjective understandings of the social world that people use and that make up their social life. Some examples of topics that might be best approached from a qualitative perspective where in-depth interviews are appropriate are 'life changes' such as motherhood, pregnancy, marriage, divorce, unemployment, new job, starting university, new friendships, etc. For example we might use in-depth interviews to examine:

- the experience of starting a new job;
- the experience of mature students starting out on a distance education course;

- how a woman's sense of her identity changes during her first pregnancy and the transition to motherhood.

SAQ 7.2

For each of the following areas select a group or focus and try to think up a research question that would be best served by the use of in-depth interviews.

Area	Group/focus
Occupational experiences	policemen, doctors, company directors, teachers
Sport	climbing, athletics, aerobics, football, swimming
Political beliefs	animal rights, feminism, anti-capitalism, Conservative party membership
Cultural phenomena	club culture, graffiti art, body-piercing, ballroom dancing

Consider why you might want to study these topics and what policy or practical impact the research might have.

Ethical and Practical Concerns

This short section is on the issues surrounding researchers' social and moral conduct in relation to in-depth interviewing. Much of what is discussed here is also of relevance in ethnographic and discourse work. We cannot explore all of the major issues and debates on the ethics and practicalities of gaining access to participants in the space here. What I am going to point out are a number of the main issues and an important practical way of dealing with these issues. The debate can be summarised broadly in the following terms: Which is more important: the protection of research participants' rights or the 'value' of the research? Over the last few decades the emphasis on the former (participants' rights) has grown over the latter ('value' of the research). As Bulmer (1982) argues, 'The rights of subjects override the rights of science.' But what does this mean in practice?

As you may have noted in SAQ 7.2 many of the topics where in-depth interviews are appropriate involve exploring quite personal or emotive aspects of people's lives. One thing we wish to ensure is that participants feel comfortable about speaking on these topics. This can be for two reasons. For some researchers it is a question of ensuring that participants feel they can speak 'honestly' or 'truthfully'; for others it is the ethical issue of creating a context in which the participant can express opinions without feeling uncomfortable or exploited. Very often the baseline method of achieving this is that of employing some method to mask the identity of the participants or make the contributions anonymous when reporting the results.

But is this protecting their rights? In some cases it may even be illegal to anonymously quote participants! For example in cases of research into or using on-line electronic communication participants' messages are copyright to them under UK law! In other cases it may be in the interest of the participants to be named. A second method is that of involving the participants by allowing them to comment on the outputs of the research (e.g. drafts of papers and books) and the manners in which they are represented in these. Again this could be problematic as researchers may feel that their representations are fair but the participants do not. For example if one had interviewed members of an extreme political party and carefully detailed how their political discourse was racist or extreme in some other manner, it may be that they would not want to be represented in this way. What the researcher needs to consider are the specific moral and ethical issues they face in any real case.

Seven Key Ethical Issues

I would argue that the following issues are the main ones faced by qualitative researchers making use of in-depth interviews, or when conducing detailed ethnographic work:

1 *Gaining access to participants: what is your route in?* By this I mean how do you gain access to the participants? This can have a major influence on how they respond to you and how you will be able to construct an 'inter-view' – a rapport or relationship with them. For example if you wish to study a group of workers – say call centre staff – do you approach the management? Or the union (if they have one)? Or the personnel department? Or were you approached by the workers themselves? Or are you a worker?

2 *Getting past 'gatekeepers': who controls access?* By this I am referring to those people who may control or have power within the research context you are proposing to explore. This is probably part and parcel of point 1 above but may have specific features. For example do you gain access to workers via the managing director, personnel or the union? This may all affect how you appear to participants (see point 7 below).

3 *Informed consent: how much do you tell the participants?* How much do you tell the participants about the research project? In many cases researchers do not wish to overly inform participants in case this knowledge will impact on how they respond in an interview. For example if you wish to know about stress in call centre work do you tell the workers this? If so, might they not focus on stress as a topic – as they think that is what you want to know about? The subsequent analysis of the data may imply that all call centre staff are very concerned about stress. Or do you say something more general – such as 'call centre work experiences' and see if stress is something that is addressed by staff? The question is again one of giving participants rights and also ensuring the usefulness of the data collected.

4 *Deception: are there grounds for deceiving the participants?* In nearly all cases the answer to this question is 'no' on principled moral and ethical grounds. But . . . there may be cases where this is justified. There are a number of examples from the history of ethnographic and qualitative research where useful and

interesting results would not have been obtained without some form of covert observation or deception. I would personally argue that unless there is a clear-cut case that the research results will help to protect or prevent harm to others that there are few if any examples where completely covert research is justified. But the grey area is implied in point 3 above – that being 100% open may have a detrimental impact on the research itself.

5   *Right to privacy: how private are the things being discussed?* This issue was discussed at the start of the section. To what extent do the participants wish to be identified as the individuals involved in the research? For example the call centre workers may wish to remain anonymous so as to be able to make critical comments without fear of a response from management. On the other hand if you are interviewing experts on best ethical practice in qualitative research they may wish to be publicly linked to their comments.

6   *Right to withdraw: how do participants get out of research?* There are few if any cases where the participants would not have a right to withdraw. It should be part and parcel of how the interview or research is set up to allow participants a clearly defined means of withdrawing from the research at any stage.

7   *Self-presentation: how do you present yourself in the interview/research context?* Lastly how do you present yourself? In the case of the call centre workers are you: management, personnel staff, union representative, 'detached scientist', colleague, friend? This may be one of the hardest parts of doing qualitative and in-depth interviewing – the building and maintenance of a 'face' – doing what Goffman (1959) calls 'face-work'. It may also be very dependent on how you have dealt with the issues in points 1 to 6!

SAQ 7.3

Use the seven issues above to consider the following three cases. What might the issues and problems be in each case?

- Interviewing women about their use of computer games
- Interviewing women about sexism at work
- Interviewing staff in a company about the implementation of new technology

Research Contract and Copies of Data

One means of resolving many of the above issues is the use of a 'research contract.' Research contracts lay out the rights and responsibilities of all parties. In the research contract you will explain the following:

- what the research is about;

- how the interview will work/be structured;
- what topics you may wish to discuss;
- how the data will be used;
- how and if you will involve the participant in the analysis or allow feedback on results;
- how and if the data will be anonymous;
- how the participant can withdraw.

Depending on the research topic and those involved, you may need to include more information. The contract can be a document that you and the participants sign. Where such formal methods may be inappropriate – they may be intimidating or participants may not have the requisite literacy skills – another method is to read out the above, or include it in the start of the interview. One can then ask the participant to confirm that they have understood the information. In these cases it may be doubly important that you provide participants with copies of tape recordings, transcripts or notes so that they too have an accessible copy of the contract. In general it is good practice to allow participants some formal copy of their own words. This allows them the chance to withdraw if they feel the need or to evaluate your analysis of their words.

To be read at the start of the interview
Vary the 'patter' as required but ensure that all the key points are clearly made
Thanks for being here to take part in this interview. Just before we start I'd like to make a few things clear about what we are doing.

You have been invited to take part in an interview about 'why you play computer games'. This interview is part of research being undertaken at the University of 'X'.

The interview will look at the reasons why people play computer games, what they enjoy about playing computer games and which computer games they like etc.

The interview will be recorded. The recording of the interview may be typed up and used as part of research or teaching work in the Department of 'Y' at the University of 'X'.

Your name will not be used in the typed copy – it will be replaced by a 'fictional' name. Your name will also not be used in any teaching or research work.

If you wish, we will provide you with a copy of the recording, the transcript (typed copy) and any research or teaching documents that make use of the interview.

You can withdraw from the research at any time, both during the interview and afterwards by letting the interviewer know. If this is after the interview you can let us know you wish to withdraw in person or by letter.

We hope that you will find the interview interesting and thanks for agreeing to take part. If you have some further questions about the interview or the research we will make time at the end of the discussion to answer your questions.

Example 1 *Research interview research contract*

Constructing an Interview Schedule

This section considers how you construct an interview schedule – a conversational guide – with which to manage your interview. This will involve generating a set of questions organised under a series of themes. Two things will determine the themes: your research question; and the information you think that the participants can provide. Why do you do this? There are a number of reasons for constructing an interview schedule. The following four are probably most important:

- It helps to articulate starting assumptions – by this I mean that developing a schedule allows you to think about and clarify research goals.
- It makes you think explicitly about what you hope the interview will cover – in other words you will have to think through the key issues that you want the interview to address.
- It allows you to anticipate difficulties – for example the wording of sensitive questions or the discussion of complex ideas.
- Most importantly it makes you prepared for the interview and therefore helps you to concentrate more fully on what the interviewee is saying on the day.

Content Themes

Once you have decided upon the overall issue to be tackled in your interview, you need to start thinking about the questions you will ask. To begin with you need to identify the possible range of themes that you think you might want to cover. What aspects of the topic do you need to explore for your research project?

There are ranges of resources you can go to, for example:

- personal involvement/knowledge – you may already know a lot about the issue;
- observation – you may have already observed or need to observe the participants or the context of study;
- literature – there may be existing academic, professional or lay literature on the topic; this material may also be qualitative data in itself;
- informal pilots – running informal pilots with participants or even with friends or colleagues 'role playing' can help raise issues;
- colleagues – discussions with colleagues can also be a good way to think through the issues.

Importantly – don't assume that the set of themes that you think up at your desk or on the train on the first day of the research design will be right. They may change a lot and they may even change during the interviews!

SAQ 7.4

Try to think up some themes or issues that the following questions might raise:

- The role of an office manager
- Students' use of support systems when learning through distance education

Keep a note of the themes you develop, as they will be used in following SAQ tasks.

Once you have defined the themes you wish to explore in your interview, consider some additional issues. First, what is the logical order of the themes – you need to ensure a smooth transition from topic to topic. This helps you to manage the interview, it may help the participant in structuring their responses, and it may even help later when reviewing and analysing the data. Second, where to place sensitive topics? In most cases they will be best placed towards the middle or end of the interview. You don't want to jump in at the start with issues that may be difficult or sensitive before you have built a rapport with the participant. Third, in most cases you want the interview to be relaxed and therefore you might want to follow a 'conversational pattern' that is more informal. A possible basic outline for an interview would be as follows:

Casual chat: talk about the 'weather', why you are interested in the research topic; any points of familiarity, or common ground with the participant. This will help relax the participant and 'open up' the channels of communication. You may need, if appropriate, to give them confidence about themselves by referring to their expertise/competence. You might use this as a chance to introduce the 'research contract' issues.

Start the interview proper with questions that collect basic descriptive information – you may have some of this already but again it helps to set up a rapport if the first questions are straightforward. You may, or may not, wish to state formally that the interview has started. If not, these types of questions are generally seen as marking the start of the 'interview' as opposed to opening chat.

You can now move on to emotionally sensitive, conceptually difficult or provocative questions. You need to think about the logical order of the questions and may want to move the more difficult ones to later in the interview. This allows more time for rapport to develop and it gives you and the participant time to develop the conversational resources and existing referents (the ideas, themes, people, places, etc. that have already been mentioned) often needed to deal with more complex issues.

Wind down with some descriptive questions or follow-up questions that fill in details or catch up on any points that have been left unclear. Very often it is inappropriate to ask for more detail or description when the participant is in 'full flow'. You should take notes at this point and come back to the issue at a later stage. Asking a set of these short clarification questions can be a good way to indicate that the interview is coming to an end.

Formally close the interview. This will involve thanking the participant – never forget to do this! It may also involve some forms of administration such as setting up further interviews or going over the research contract issues again. Finish with some casual chat.

As we noted at the start of this section, in-depth interviews differ in the extent to which the interviewer is 'allowed' to vary the content and order of the questions that are asked. There is a spectrum of interview formats, though three main approaches can be defined:

- *Structured*: short specific questions; read questions exactly as on the schedule; ask the questions in order specified by the schedule. Respondent is therefore constrained in their replies – it deliberately limits what can be talked about. These are just slightly more in-depth than quantitative surveys.
- *Semi-structured*: interviewer is merely guided by the schedule – attempt to establish rapport; ordering of questions is less important; interviewer free to probe areas of interest; can follow participant's interests and concerns.
- *Unstructured*: the interviews have no real overall structure, maybe a number of possible topics. In this respect they are slightly less than a free flowing conversation with the participant.

Most in-depth interviews are a form of semi-structured interview. As such they take advantage of the following features of semi-structured interviews:

- Flexibility – good way of exploring participants' subjective meanings. Can tailor questions to the ongoing concerns and questions of the participant – can talk about things you might not have thought of yourself at the outset of the project.
- Allows exploration of complexity, ambiguity, contradictions and process. Can consider subtlety of social situations – impossible within a restricted structured interview or questionnaire.
- Can explore and negotiate potential meanings of questions and answers as you explore the perspective of the respondent.

Designing Questions

In order to design your interview schedule you will need to consider the main types of 'questions' you can ask. There are three types: initiating questions, probes, and follow-up questions. We will look at each of these in turn.

Initiating Questions

These are the main questions relating to interview themes you have defined and are used to direct the conversation. We have already looked at some of the issues in question design in Chapter 3, where we considered quantitative measures.

There are a few points to reiterate and to specifically consider when designing initiating questions for qualitative interviews. These include the following:

- Questions should be neutral, not leading (i.e. directing the respondent towards an expected answer) or value-laden. For example: 'Do you agree that the prime minister is doing a bad job?' is a leading question. 'What do you think of the prime minister's record in office so far?' is a more open and neutral question.
- Avoid jargon – think about the language that the participant(s) is/are familiar with and stick to those terms.
- *Don't* assume shared definitions – explore what your interviewee understands about concepts/terminology. This contrasts with quantitative questions, where shared understanding has to be assumed. Exploring what people understand by ideas, terms, phrases, etc. is key to qualitative research work.
- Use open questions/avoid closed questions. Open questions can be answered in a number of ways by a participant – the questions should encourage them to 'open up' about attitudes, thoughts or feelings. As indicated earlier (see Chapter 3), closed questions have a single answer or can be answered with just a short response (e.g. yes–no). Some examples are:
  Closed version: Should 'political party X' continue to be excluded from peace talks?
  Open version: In your opinion who should be invited to the current peace talks?
  Closed version: When buying a car, is the colour of the car important to you?
  Open version: When buying a car, what factors are important to you?
- Ask one question at a time. (This issue was also addressed in Chapter 3.)
- Overall use a 'directing' or 'funnelling' technique. Start by asking general 'initiating' questions that open up a topic, then ask specific follow-up or probing questions on specific details or issues.

SAQ 7.5

Pick one of the following topics and design three questions based on the themes you worked out earlier in SAQ 7.4.

- The role of an office manager
- Students' use of support systems when learning through distance education

Probes

Very often it is necessary, or interesting, to ask the participant for more information or to elaborate on points. This may be more necessary with some participants (either individuals or groups). I found that interviewing journalists was easy as they are good interviewers and understand the structure of interviews. They therefore provide good detail and anticipate many questions and probes or ask for clarification. But this is the exception rather than the rule!

Probes are used to encourage participants to expand on their initial responses and to develop points without changing topic or asking a new initiating question. Some examples are:

- *Clarifications*: What exactly do you mean by x?
- *Justifications*: Why did you say that?
- *Relevance to discussion*: Does this relate to what you were telling me earlier about x?
- *Examples to make things 'real'*: Could you give me an example of that? Can you think of a specific instance when you felt like that?
- *Extension*: Can you tell me a little bit more about that? Can you remember anything else about that? What happened then?
- *Affective probes*: How did that make you feel?
- *Echoes* (don't use very often):
  Response: It was very exciting she said she was stunned by it all.
  Echo/Probe: She said she was stunned by it all?

Follow-up Questions

Questions that pursue themes during the course of the interview are follow-up questions. These may already have been planned for. In the call centre case, you may decide to ask a participant about the availability or quality of stress counselling if they bring up the topic when discussing stress in general. On the other hand follow-up questions develop spontaneously as the interview develops. These questions make the process flexible and continuous. They allow ideas to develop and change. They may arise as you work on the schedule and as you start to pilot the schedule and interview your first participants. In longer term projects, for example, you might expect to be regularly reviewing your questions in the light of how the last participant has responded and making some follow-up questions part of the schedule.

SAQ 7.6

Look at the following example interview schedule and comment on its structure and format.

Example interview schedule

What follows is a guide. You will wish to vary the presentation and interaction, you will find that some themes emerge spontaneously and may wish to vary the order of the questions as the interview develops. Probe and ask for elaborations and examples as time permits.

Preface: Set the interviewee at rest: explain purpose of interviews; anticipated outcomes for us and the payback for the informant; rules of confidentiality, etc.

1 What sort of meaning does the word 'professional' have for you?
Probe answer for examples, elaboration etc.
2 Using what you have said in (1), is journalism professional work?
3 Could we turn to your work as a correspondent/subject specialist? Could you help me to see what is professional about your work as a correspondent/subject specialist?
Probe to see how far categories used in (1) and (2) apply.
4 Could we turn to another aspect of your work, the use of Information and Communication Techologies (ICTs)? Could you help me to see how this supports your professional role?
Probe to see how far categories used in (1) and (2) apply.
5 Can you call to mind a recent episode or incident that has involved you using ICTs as a professional journalist and tell me about it, please?
Probe: What is there about that incident that shows you acting as a professional?
6 Can you describe any ways in which using ICTs has made your work easier?
7 Have there been any changes in the professional standing of journalists over the past ten years?
8 (If not answered in (7)) Have ICTs changed the professional standing of journalists?

Close by asking whether there is anything the informant wants to add about the professional nature of journalism. Promise copy of transcript and a summary of overall findings. Ask whether they would be prepared to participate in a follow-up interview (in 6–12 months' time).

SAQ 7.7

Develop a schedule for the topic, themes and questions you have developed in SAQ 7.4 and SAQ 7.5.

Conducting and Managing an Interview

In-depth interviews are hard work. I have found out the hard way that doing too many in a day leaves you very tired! This is because they require you to engage in a lot of different activities at once. These include: following the schedule, asking the questions, keeping a track of the flow of the conversation, taking notes, listening and, importantly, maintaining the required 'face'. It's useful to think of an interview as a 'socially skilled performance'. We can analyse the skills required to conduct a successful interview so that you can practise and therefore improve your technique. First and foremost we need the types of social skills that are central to good face-to-face interaction. Second, we need to use these skills to achieve the goal of conducting an 'effective' interview. In other words interviews draw upon all of our existing conversational skills, but interviews are different from ordinary conversations. In most cases they are a 'research context' rather than a day-to-day conversational context. We as interviewers are expecting the participant to engage in often quite in-depth reflection on life and events with a stranger. You therefore need to develop and practise those social skills that will help you achieve the specific goals of the interview situation: in particular how to establish rapport, how to encourage the interviewee to participate and to talk freely and how to get the participant to elaborate on points, examples, clarification, explanations, stories, details, etc. Use your 'notebook' to help manage the process: it is good practice to make notes at all stages to help with the interview, as well as for future reference. As in-depth interviews are hard work, give yourself enough time! This includes time to set up, organise and to have some rest and refreshment between interviews.

Opening, Reinforcing, Listening and Closing

Interviews require that you manage a range of things. Beyond simply asking the questions you will need to address the social process that is an interview. There are four key areas you must address: managing the opening of the interview; supporting the participant through reinforcement; listening to the participant to provide support, to ensure you are collecting the data you need, and to guide the interview through the schedule; and closing the interview. We have already discussed some practical aspects of opening and closing interviews when discussing the designing of a schedule. Here we will address some of the more general social interaction issues.

Openings

The initial stages of the interview are important because here you will establish a frame of reference – guidelines – for what is to follow. This is not just the information about the interview, or possibly laying out the research contract, but setting up expectations. Initial interactions will define the reasonable objectives for the interview ahead. These need to be negotiated rather than imposed. You must also start the process of building rapport in order to make the participant as comfortable as possible.

You also need to set up a good social context. In most cases you need to establish an amicable relationship with the participant. You should engage in polite welcoming behaviour – remember that interviewees are not 'servants' or 'data points' but people to be welcomed into a participatory process. As was discussed earlier, don't jump into the interview immediately. You should use non-task comments to break the ice. You as the interviewer also need to feel comfortable. You are neither a computer nor a tape recorder! Some conversational contact with the world outside the interview or (if inappropriate) old-fashioned trivial chat can be used to make a connection and set all parties at ease. Last but not least, provide some 'creature comforts' – drinks, biscuits, comfortable chairs, etc. for the participant and yourself.

How you present yourself is crucial. This is not just about how you dress or carry yourself, but the whole interview context. A room that is set up to look like a job interview is not going to relax the participants! You may be limited in what you can use but think through carefully how you set up the interview context. I have had to use a whole range of places – from empty white 'clinical' rooms, through noisy offices to participants' own front rooms at home.

Prepare the participant 'mentally' for the task to follow. Choose an easy starting point such as checking basic or background information. Also allow interviewees to express what they think they will get out of or how they see the interview. Importantly, let the interviewee know where you see the interview going by outlining your goals for the interview.

Rapport and Reinforcement

Positive reinforcement is central to making an interview work. You need to make the participant feel that they are making a positive contribution and that you want to know what they are telling you. One key aspect of this is 'listening', which we will discuss in a moment. In addition you need to ensure that you are appropriately making use of verbal and non-verbal 'reinforces'. Verbal reinforces include such things as acknowledgements and confirmations. They are often short and take the form of 'discourse markers' such as 'OK', 'yes', 'right', 'fine', 'I see', 'that's it', etc. Also appropriately provide support or 'praise' by saying 'good', 'excellent', 'well done', etc. Such things imply that you find what is said worthwhile. You should also respond to developments. Ideas or topics suggested by the participant should be explored and become part of the on-going discourse. Non-verbal reinforces in the form of smiles and eye contact, nodding and other indications of support and interest imply attention and involvement. They can also increase the amount of talking by the participant.

Listening

Listening is different from just hearing. Listening is a mental process that enables you to do a range of things. These include focusing specifically upon and understanding accurately and fully what the participant is communicating to you. Without this you cannot manage the interview effectively. Indicating that you are listening fully is the main means by which you provide the participant with support. You can demonstrate that you are listening by making reference to past statements and making sure that you make related comments and ask related follow-up or probing questions. Try to avoid interruption as this can indicate that you are not interested in what is being said by the participant. Listening is a hard task. You can support yourself by making appropriate notes about issues, topics or points that you want to return to, thus allowing the participant to speak and allowing you to keep track. Notes provide a basis for good probes, follow-ups and supporting comments. The whole interview process is hard work and listening well is impossible if you are tired, or the environment is unhelpful (e.g. noisy, hot or uncomfortable).

Ending the Interview: Closings

Closure involves signalling that the interaction is about to end, discussing what will happen in the future and breaking interpersonal contact in a positive way. As was noted earlier, you should plan to cover relevant 'closing' topics at the end of the interview. This might involve inviting questions or comments from the participant, a discussion of follow-up contacts or a review of the 'research contract' issues. Most importantly, you need to express thanks and indicate that you've enjoyed the discussion.

Group Interviewing: Focus Groups

Focus groups can be seen as a form of 'group in-depth interviewing'. As such all the advice in the preceding section is also true for focus groups. There are a few key differences. First, they are a group rather than one-to-one interaction! Getting the participants to talk, discuss and debate amongst themselves is part of the reasoning behind focus groups. Second, focus groups are used by a range of social researchers but historically have become associated with such things as market research and political opinion research. Very often they are used as the 'qualitative element' within a larger 'quantitative' study such as a survey. Third, as with in-depth interviews focus groups should have a topic, an object, a text or some other 'focus'. They are not simply a general discussion. Unlike in interviews, focus groups have one or more 'moderators' or 'facilitators' rather than an 'interviewer'. It is their job to ensure that the discussion addresses the topics in the schedule for the focus group.

There is a long history of using focus groups in a range of social research and traditions have developed in each area of work. Rather than attempt to discuss these varieties I will point out a number of advantages and weaknesses of focus groups. Reading O, which is explored in Chapter 8, provides an example of the use of a focus group for qualitative research work.

Focus groups are often described as being a fast and easy way to collect qualitative data ('quick and dirty' is the less charitable description). It is true that focus groups take less time and 'effort' to generate a similar amount of qualitative data to that of in-depth interviews. By including a range of participants a range of views can be collected in less time than would be needed for individual interviews. Focus groups also generate discussion that can bring a variety of issues to the fore and are possibly less influenced by the 'interviewer/moderator' than one-to-one interviews. At the same time, by being fast and easy they also have disadvantages. They may not provide as in-depth and personal information as interviews. Also group interactions have to be well managed or some participants dominate discussion. Group interactions produce *different* data than individual interviews. If you are to make use of focus groups you will need to think through these issues. Focus groups should not be a cheap replacement for individual in-depth interviewing! They should be used where the group aspect is useful or important to the research question at hand.

Ethnographic Fieldwork

Ethnography, like surveys and experiments, covers a wide range of actual practices. In the main, though, ethnography often involves some form of direct observation of a social situation or group. This can be an 'external' or 'non-participant' observation, where the social scientist is not part of the context being observed. For example, a sociologist interested in the production of TV news might observe the work of a TV newsroom without being involved in the process itself. On the other hand, one can conduct 'internal' or 'participant' observation, where the researcher is involved to some extent or another in the thing being observed. This is the classic method of social anthropology, where the researcher lives with the group under study. Observation can come in a wide range of forms but often involves the taking of field notes and audio or video recordings. Ethnography usually involves the collection of as many types of data as possible. This can and does cover all of the types of material discussed in SAQs 6.2 and 6.3 and very often involves in-depth interviews. Once the data has been collected, the ethnographer engages in some form of qualitative data analysis. The period of an ethnographic study when data is being collected is often called 'fieldwork'.

SAQ 7.8

Turn to Reading I, 'Thinking through fieldwork (1)', in which Judith Okely describes her experience of the fieldwork process. In this account Okely points out a number of key methodological differences between quantitative and qualitative methods. As you read make notes on the following questions:

1   What does Okely see as being the main historical difference between sociology and social anthropology?
2   Which philosophical position does Okely attribute to survey methods?
3   Why, according to Okely, were early social anthropologists able to ignore methods based in positivist or empiricist ideas?
4   List three aspects of modern UK society that Okely notes have been studied by social anthropologists.
5   Why does Okely argue that ethnography tends to be conducted by individual researchers rather than by research teams?
6   What does Okely mean by the 'funnel approach'?
7   How does Okely view the role of hypotheses in her research?

From Reading I we can see that ethnography and fieldwork are very different from surveys and experiments. Okely points out how ethnography requires researchers to be open to all the various data sources around them and at the outset not to assume what is or is not important. This makes the process of data collection extensive and difficult. One way in which ethnographers collect data is through the taking of field notes.

SAQ 7.9

Now turn to Reading J, 'Thinking through fieldwork (2)', another extract from Okely, and make notes on the following questions:

1   How did Okely's data collection method change once she spoke to Malcolm Mcleod?
2   Why could Okely not easily ask direct questions of the Gypsies?
3   What data sources did Okely use?

In the two extracts you have read for SAQs 7.8 and 7.9 Okely discusses the difference between her methods of subject selection as compared to survey methods. In particular she notes how she was not required, 'like a pollster', 'to find select individuals and then hurry on after each interview'. This does not mean she was not making selection choices; quite the opposite, she 'always grabbed the opportunity to meet new individuals or families'. At the same time she tried to balance meeting new people 'with the benefits of increasing rapport with core clusters of families in camps where I lived and in the locality as a whole'. It is clear from this argument that Okely was making selection choices based upon her knowledge and understanding of the people themselves, but also partly upon the opportunities presented to her. If we apply the language of sampling (see Part II, p. 25ff.), Okely was purposively sampling. Indeed, case selection is a very important aspect of ethnographic work.

As with survey work, selection of a case is most often driven by a current theory, idea or question that you wish to address. Having said this, many ethnographic studies arise from the opportunity to study a social group or practice that has not previously been explored in depth. In ethnographic research, especially participant observation work, 'opportunities' only arise where it is possible to gain the co-operation of the people under study. Even when cases have been selected because they are believed to shed light on a specific issue, experience in the field will often require changes, possibly radical ones, in the ethnographer's initial ideas. This is a point that is made clear in the Okely material you have read. Okely notes that though specific policy issues initially drove the research, field experience provided information that continually altered aspects of her research ideas and goals.

Ethnographic work such as that of Okely tends to focus intensively on one case. This arises for a number of reasons. First, as ethnography tends to be conducted by a single person, or at most by two or three people, and requires considerable time, few research projects can deal with more than one or two cases. Second, as the intention of the research is not to produce broad general results but to detail the specific rich texture of a case, exploring many cases would be counter-productive. Selecting a 'useful' case is therefore important.

SAQ 7.10

This SAQ should take about 20 minutes.

Turn to Reading K, 'Selecting a case', and compare Simeon Yates's model with that described by Okely. Make some notes to answer the following questions:

1   How did previous theories, current issues, ideas or questions affect the choice of case in each of the examples?
2   What types of comparison were the projects able to make?
3   Were there any key stages in the development of the cases over time?
4   Which group/individuals within the case(s) did the two researchers focus upon?
5   Are there different physical settings where specific types of activity take place?
6   What were the 'back-stage areas', away from the main activity, where people could relax their 'public faces'?

Managing Ethnography – Fieldwork Journals/Notebooks

Keeping a track of everything is central to good research practice. This is doubly the case in qualitative work, where you need to keep track of many documents, tape recordings, participants, interview appointments, etc. Many issues may come up in in-depth interviews that impact on either the flow or management of that interview or of the whole project. A notebook and/or diary is a good means of keeping track. This may take the form of a loose-leaf folder of papers, or a hard-backed notebook of some kind: whatever you find is best (or appropriate for the setting) make full use of it. The things I put in a notebook are as follows:

> *Diary entries* – including dates and times of interviews, dates of phone calls made or received, letters sent or received;
> *Thoughts and comments* – any and all thoughts and comments that come to mind about the research, whether this be when reading papers, doing interviews or eating breakfast;

Notes on actual interviews – these include notes taken during the interview, details of the tapes and other materials collected during the interview, details about the context of the interview, even some notes on how I felt both in general (was I tired after a long day of interviews) or specifically about how I felt during the interview (was I embarrassed or upset or cheered up by anything said);

Index/contents list and coding – an index at the back of the notebook so that I can find information quickly, a method or scheme of codes for linking points in the notebook to tape recordings, documents and the like filed elsewhere, and possibly some kind of colour coding of my notes to differentiate things (e.g. black ink for interview notes, red ink for comments and thoughts, green ink for cross-references).

All the above are just examples, and if you do many qualitative interviews or research projects you will develop your own method of managing the materials.

Further Reading

Arskey, H. and Knight, P. (1999) *Interviewing for Social Scientists*. London: Sage.
Bloor, M., Frankland, J., Tomas, M. and Robson, K. (2001) *Focus Groups in Social Research*. London: Sage.
Denzin, N.K. (1997) *Interpretative Ethnography: Ethnographic Practice for the 21st Century*. London: Sage.
Hammersley, M. (1992) *What's Wrong with Ethnography*? London: Routledge.
Hammersley, M. and Atkinson, P. (eds) (1983) *Ethnography: Principles in Practice*. London: Routledge.
Kvale, S. (1996) *Interviews: An Introduction to Qualitative Research Interviewing*. London: Sage.
Rubin, H.J. and Rubin, I.S. (1995) *Qualitative Interviewing: The Art of Hearing Data*. London: Sage.
Taylor, S. (ed.) (2001) *Ethnographic Research: A Reader*. London: Sage.

Reading I: Thinking through Fieldwork (1)

Judith Okely

[Here] I describe the way in which I interpreted and wrote up my material from an intensive fieldwork study of Gypsies and aspects of government policy. The approach and methods which informed this work were those of social anthropology. I give details of how I recorded my material and how I made use of it along with the totality of my field experience for the ensuing publications. Since the term 'qualitative' has been applied to a range of different methodologies within the social sciences, it is important to outline the distinctive characteristics of social anthropological research. 'Qualitative' can refer to research using only a small sample of interviews, whether structured or unstructured. In either case the qualitative material is bounded by the cultural conventions of the interview. Paradoxically, the interview format is associated first and foremost with quantitative surveys whose positivistic conventions have set the agenda (cf. Oakley 1981). 'Qualitative' has also come to be used to describe the research . . . which emerges from participant observation.

There are significant contrasts between anthropological and sociological empirical research, with implications for analysis. The two disciplines came from different contexts. Social anthropology was formerly associated with the study of non-western societies, mainly by westerners. Sociology's empirical work was concerned mainly with western societies of which the sociologist was a member. Unlike the sociologist, the anthropologist could not take much as given, he or she could not isolate one theme extracted from a wider context, since the society as a whole was largely unknown to the researcher, and undocumented. Rigidly formulated questionnaires were inappropriate. These and the interview mode are culture bound. The sociologist could be more presumptuous in knowledge of the wider social context. Whereas Durkheim (1897) could claim to identify and sub-classify suicide in France, Malinowski (1926) had first to discover and then redefine such a practice among the Trobrianders. He had no statistics to play with.

The way in which the anthropologist carries out fieldwork affects the sort of material produced, then analysed and presented in the final texts. The anthropologist rarely commences research with an hypothesis to test. There are few pre-set, neatly honed questions, although there are multiple questions in the fieldworker's head. There are theories, themes, ideas and ethnographic details to discover, examine or dismiss. The anthropologist, despite months of literature reviews, possibly years of theoretical and comparative reading, will have to eject hypotheses like so much ballast. The people may not live as recorded, there could be famine, strife or civil war. Rituals may be missionized, nomads dispersed, leaders imprisoned, documentation a distortion or deflection from the outsider's gaze. The ethnographer must, like a surrealist, be *disponible* (cf. Breton 1937), and open to *objets trouvés*, after arriving in the field. This approach inevitably affects the subsequent interpretation and analysis.

Although early field anthropologists made claims for the scientific status of their work, they have been less vulnerable than empirical sociologists to demands for positivist legitimacy in methods. Formerly, it was considered sufficiently impressive that anthropologists actually uprooted themselves and went to live elsewhere for extended periods. Social scientists who stayed at home were not in a position to challenge the techniques of pioneers in the unknown fields of exotica. There has been greater freedom in the analysis of fieldwork research. A great deal is taken on trust about the way material is written up. There can be no easily replicable formulae. The notion of techniques to be applied uniformly across the globe is inappropriate. Granted, social anthropologists of the earlier school have been too cavalier in both preparing students for the field and in conveying advice about how to write up. The lacunae are best filled by detailed autobiographical accounts of fieldwork and the ways in which interpretations are arrived at. These are relatively rare and split off from what are seen as the core concerns of the discipline (Okely 1991). The increasing bureaucratic and pedagogic demand for explicit methods 'training' has sometimes meant that social anthropologists have half-heartedly and inappropriately fallen back on textbooks devised for sociologists and others.

The historically divisive association of sociology with western societies and anthropology with non-western societies is no longer appropriate. Each discipline has strayed into the other's territory. While retaining its traditional methods, social anthropology can be used in the study of *any* group or society. I have, for example, applied it in the study of transport, the elderly and planning in East Anglia (Okely 1991), in addition to the study of Gypsies and government policy in England. Others have adopted an anthropological approach in Britain for scrutinizing the police (Young 1991) and views of death (Hockey 1990). These studies show that the kind of qualitative material which anthropology's methods and theories generate is different from other disciplines within the social sciences.

Each discipline retains its different historical approaches to methodology. Within sociology there appears to be a widespread association of participant observation with the theoretical perspective of symbolic interactionism (Hammersley and Atkinson 1983, Silverman 1985). By contrast, the research material gathered by anthropologists can be placed in as many of the theoretical perspectives as there exist in both the social sciences and, if relevant, the humanities.

It is the custom for the anthropologist to be both fieldworker and analyst-author. Division of research labour into discrete tasks, or between individuals, is at a minimum. The anthropologist fieldworker records, interprets and writes up his or her own material. For the anthropologist, the stages of knowledge of the research progresses are not sectioned between persons. So there is no need to formulate mechanical procedures and managerial-type instructions to ensure uniformity of perspective along some chain of command. The anthropologist does not have to check and double-check whether numerous assistants and interviewers have understood or even faked the collection of data. He or she has instead to look to his or her specific relationship with the people who are the subject of study. The anthropologist becomes the collector and a walking archive, with ever unfolding resources for interpretation. By contrast, a social scientist in a prestigious research centre asserted that in order to follow the correct social science procedure and to attain 'objectivity', ideally someone other than I, the fieldworker, should write up the final report with the aid of my field notes. The fact that I completed the task myself was seen uneasily as a form of intellectual cheating rather than a scientific necessity and standard anthropological practice. Such a division between collection and analysis might be possible in a research tradition where the researcher delegates the former to a reserve army of interviewers with pre-ordained questionnaire and clone-like application. The pre-selected choice of answers gives material which can be mechanically classified as part of the analysis.

Agar, the anthropologist, has offered an alternative descriptive term for research and fieldwork which is not hypothesis bound. A somewhat mechanistic metaphor, which doubtless allays the worries of those wanting proof of 'tools' of research, is what he names the 'funnel approach' (1980: 13). From the outset of fieldwork, the anthropologist adopts an open-ended approach to the full range of information and to all manner of people. This is the essence of the holistic approach. The material and ethnographic concerns are not cut to size at the start. The people who are the subject of study are themselves free to volunteer their concerns in their own voice and context. All this has implications for the kind of material and field notes which the anthropologist is faced with when it comes to writing up.

Both during the fieldwork and after, themes gradually emerge. Patterns and priorities impose themselves upon the ethnographer. Voices and ideas are neither muffled nor dismissed. To the professional positivist this seems like chaos. The voices and material lead the researcher in unpredictable, uncontrollable directions. This is indeed not a controlled experiment. The fieldworker cannot separate the act of gathering material from that of its continuing interpretation. Ideas and hunches emerge during the encounter and are explored or eventually discarded as fieldwork progresses. Writing up involves a similar experience. The ensuing analysis is creative, demanding and all consuming. It cannot be fully comprehended at the early writing-up stages by someone other than the fieldworker.

Long-term participant experience helps to make sense of even the most detached survey data. Leach, in a critique (1967) of an extensive survey of landownership in Ceylon (Sarkar and Tambiah 1957), was able to draw on his fieldwork in just one village to counter some interpretations of the statistics for 57 villages. The survey had concluded that 335 households were landless. However, from his detailed first-hand observation of inheritance practice in the region, Leach was able to point out that over time, a considerable number of the younger informants would inherit land. The same applied to many sharecroppers who were in fact heirs of owners. He also suggested that some of the interpretation of the apparently unproblematic survey data was convincing only because the main researchers, already familiar with the region, arrived inadvertently 'at their conclusions by intuitive methods . . . The numerical apparatus in which these conclusions are embedded seems to me to be very largely a complicated piece of self deception' (1967: 76).

After fieldwork, the material found in notebooks, in transcripts and even in contemporary written sources is only a guide and trigger. The anthropologist-writer draws also on the totality of the experience, parts of which may not, cannot, be cerebrally written down at the time. It is recorded in memory, body and all the senses. Ideas and themes have worked through the whole being throughout the experience of fieldwork. They have gestated in dreams and the subconscious in both sleep and in waking hours, away from the field, at the anthropologist's desk, in libraries and in dialogue with the people on return visits. Photographs point to details hitherto unnoticed by the fieldworker in the midst of the action. They may also revive hidden memories. The anthropologist may notice ethnographic detail which photographers do not perceive. The photograph on the cover of my 1983 book shows the interior of a Gypsy trailer-caravan. The professional who provided it failed to notice both before and after the event that the kitchen area had no sink. This is a crucial clue to Gypsies' pollution taboos. Other sources have also to be carefully scrutinized. Snatches of music may conjure up images and forgotten or half-submerged insights. The act of interpretation and writing from past fieldwork may be as evocative and sensory as Proust's description of the tasting of the madeleine cake in *A la recherche du temps perdu* (1954).

The understanding and ways of making sense of the material and of writing cannot be routinized and streamlined as instructions for methodology textbooks. Nor can it be fully assessed at this stage by a non-participant. Instead, to admit to the vastness, unpredictability and creative turbulence in which the ethnographic writer is immersed can be a reassurance that positivism is no guide. The methods in which many social scientists have been instructed have been an intellectual carapace. The puzzled novice researcher may be contaminated by positivistic notions of 'contamination', 'detachment', 'prediction', 'operationalization' or 'typicality'. Since ethnographic openness or *disponibilité* has defied hypotheses, the material cannot be subjected to strict formulae. The problem is how to convince researchers from other traditions or those who are schooled in positivistic formulae.

References

Agar, M. (1980) *The Professional Stranger*. London: Academic Press.
Breton, A. (1937) *L'Amour fou*. Paris: Gallimard.
Durkheim, E. (1897) *Le Suicide*. Paris: Alcan.
Hammersley, M. and Atkinson, P. (1983) *Ethnography: Principles in Practice*. London: Tavistock.
Hockey, J. (1990) *Experiencing Death: An Anthropological Account*. Edinburgh: Edinburgh University Press.
Leach, E.R. (1967) 'An anthropologist's reflections on a social survey', in D. Jongmans and P. Gutkind (eds) *Anthropologists in the Field*. Assen: Van Gorcum.
Malinowski, B. (1926) *Crime and Custom in Primitive Society*. London: Routlege and Kegan Paul.
Oakley, A. (1981) 'Interviewing women: a contradiction in terms', in H. Roberts (ed.) *Doing Feminist Research*. London: Routledge.
Okely, J. (1983) *The Traveller-Gypsies*. Cambridge: Cambridge University Press.
Okely, J. (1991) 'The ethnographic method applied to rural transport, the elderly and planning', report to the Economic and Social Research Council.

Proust, M. (1954) *A la recherche du temps perdu*. Paris: Gallimard.
Sarkar, N.K. and Tambiah, S.J. (1957) *The Disintegrating Village*. Colombo.
Silverman, D. (1985) *Qualitative Methodology and Sociology*. Aldershot: Gower.
Young, M. (1991) *An Inside Job*. Oxford: Oxford University Press.

Source: Okely, 1994: 18–22

Reading J: Thinking through Fieldwork (2)

Judith Okely

It is standard practice for an anthropologist to live alongside a group of people for at least a year. I lived in a trailer-caravan on Gypsy encampments and went out to work with them: calling for scrap metal and joining a potato-picking gang. Research entailed periods amounting to about two years, including return visits, as well as participant observation among government officials and others in regular contact with Gypsies. Nothing approximating to an interview was used in the research for which I was responsible. Accordingly, the material which informs my writing is very different from that gleaned from one-to-one interviews with individuals divorced from daily practice and context. When I conducted research among government officials and non-Gypsies or 'Gorgios', as Gypsies call them, in the area, free-flowing conversations and dialogue occurred as I accompanied them about their business and at their leisure. All together, the number of people, whether Gypsy or Gorgio, whom I encountered and from whom I gained information amounted to several hundred, but my approach still places me behind what is considered to be the qualitative divide. The number of 'informants' is not an adequate guide to the distinction between very different research approaches.

Some of the themes and subsequent chapters in my early publication on Gypsies were explicitly affected by the demands and brief of the policy-oriented centre. The aim was to examine the Gypsies' position and preferences in the light of recent legislation which presumed long-term sedentarization and assimilation of this ethnic group. The needs of this travelling people and their conflict with the dominant society were unavoidably a key focus in the sort of questions addressed by the ethnographer at all stages of the research. Thus the political context and funding proposal influenced the way fieldwork was conducted, the themes selected in analysis and the projected readership (Adams *et al.* 1975). Even without the policy subtext, however, it still would have been impossible to write of a 'self-contained community' (Okely 1983). The non-Gypsy or Gorgio made an appearance every day on the Gypsy camps in body or spirit. Thus the Gorgio appeared in field notes and published text.

With minimal success, I had combed the anthropological monographs and other literature for guidance and for reassurance in the face of increasing scepticism among my employers about non-questionnaire research. Then a chance meeting with the Africanist anthropologist, Malcolm Mcleod, afforded me the best and only detailed methodological advice I was to find at the outset of fieldwork. From his experience, he suggested, 'write down everything you hear, smell and see; even the colour of the carpets . . . Ideally you should fill an exercise book for each day.' So I jettisoned my earlier, increasingly unsatisfactory attempts at writing notes under prescribed headings. I had been prematurely deciding what was relevant and in the process omitting other details, possibly for ever. My notes took the form of a chronological journal. The only marker was the date on each page. Events were written up as soon as possible. The record for some days did indeed, when time allowed, stretch to exercise-book length. Ideas, tentative interpretations and dominant themes were also written into the text, as the field experience developed. However crude or speculative the ideas at that early stage, it did not matter. As both fieldworker and future author, I was free to allow the ideas to germinate in their own time and through my own thinking, not by proxy. Subsequent participant observation and extended contemplation would sift out the wheat from the chaff.

Given the Gypsies' resistance to direct questioning, especially by outsiders, the material was acquired through daily, informal communication, which I recorded in detail. Thus the seemingly trivial descriptions of domestic objects, trailer interiors, and stray remarks volunteered in conversation, all meticulously noted, assumed massive significance when scrutinized and sifted, months and sometimes years later. Often the description, if properly open-ended, can seem innocent of deeper meaning when it is first recorded. Later, it is up to the anthropologist to read for the meaning.

References

Adams, B., Okely, J., Morgan, D. and Smith, D. (1975) *Gypsies and Government Policy in England*. London: Heinemann Educational.
Okely, J. (1983) *The Traveller-Gypsies*. Cambridge: Cambridge University Press.

Source: Okely, 1994: 22–4

Reading K: Selecting a Case

Simeon J. Yates

The study used four cases. The overall intention was to explore the relationship between new technology and the production of TV news. Later the focus changed to look specifically at new digital technologies, especially the World Wide Web, new digital editing and production technologies and shared production environments. The project has involved myself as the main researcher and two colleagues at different stages, both with backgrounds in journalism, one an ex-TV news producer, the other a trainee journalist. We hoped to show that there was a relationship between the technologies used and the organizational structure but also to show, following previous research, that technology did not determine the organizational structures and practices. The study began somewhat serendipitously when I was talking through these ideas with a colleague who was also a senior TV news presenter. She was then able to provide the contact with the first case where the initial design for the study began. In some respects the opportunities and the restrictions placed upon us during the first study (e.g. we could not video tape the newsroom) helped to define the methods used and data collected in all four studies. The data for three of the cases were collected using ethnographic methods (video was used in the next cases) and involved observing the newsroom during the production of two days of news material. All of the four case studies made use of the same standard shared electronic newsroom system (BASYS). The cases were:

1   a 'standard' analogue broadcast television newsroom
2   a small 'standard' analogue satellite broadcast television news desk
3   a satellite broadcast news desk using digital editing/production equipment
4   a small WWW news service based in a broadcast television newsroom

The studies gathered information on a number of factors:

- the organization of the newsroom personnel
- the main roles of newsroom personnel
- the main information sources for news stories
- the main communications systems and channels within the newsroom

In each case data were collected from/on the following key staff:

- news presenter
- news editor
- programme editor
- sampled reporters in the newsroom and in the field

As far as possible these staff were interviewed and observed in their various places of work, from the news desk itself, to editing suites and meeting rooms. As the project developed it became clear that several of these spaces functioned as 'back-stage' areas where people could work away from the gaze of specific colleagues – especially the editing suites where they were able to work alone. Another social back-stage area was the electronic mail/messaging system which allowed people to interact informally without being publicly visible. The content of these interactions were both practically and ethically unavailable to us. The use of the four cases, each using the same underlying management and communications tools, whilst using different production technologies allowed us to separate out the impacts of the technology from organizational issues. This was further helped by the fact that cases 2 and 3 represented the same news desk before and after the introduction of new digital production technologies.

Solutions to Chapter 7 SAQs

SAQ 7.1

Some advantages of using a survey/questionnaire method are:

- standardised format
- easily coded data
- quantifiable data
- quick and simple to use
- ability to numerically or statistically compare cases/groups

Some disadvantages are:

- it assumes all respondents have a similar understanding of the terms (e.g. 'violence')
- it assumes that all respondents understand the question in the same way
- it can't ask respondents for clarifications or examples
- it does not allow respondents to explain subtleties or contradictions
- it imposes a set of ideas or way of thinking about the issue on the respondents

The data will differ in their form: one result will essentially be 'numerical' the other 'textual'. The open question is likely to provide data on the respondents' perspective and is less likely to be influenced by or constrained by the ideas of the researcher. The questionnaire on the other hand is designed around the researcher's assumptions as to what is or is not important. It is this access to the respondents' perspective – the speakers' perspective – that makes some researchers view qualitative and textual data as 'richer' than quantitative data.

SAQ 7.2

Some example research questions for the occupational groups might be:

- How do they view their work as 'professional'?
- What was the experience of moving into their current job like?
- What do they enjoy most about their jobs?

Some example research questions for the sports might be:

- Why do people engage in the sport?
- What role does the sport play in their social lives?
- Do they link sport, fitness and 'body image'?

SAQ 7.3

Interviewing Women about their Use of Computer Games

There may not be many ethical issues that spring to mind here. It all depends upon what the line of questioning becomes. For instance, women may play games at work, something they might not want their boss to know. More subtly game-playing might be part of their relationship with partners and friends. You are then exploring issues to do with their relationships that will be quite personal. Getting access will probably depend on personal knowledge of people who are games players. If not, you might need to go through some kind of gatekeeper such as the organiser of a 'club', or maybe through a games shop or even a games manufacturer. It is likely in this case that you will be able to articulate clearly and fully the reasons for your research. Depending on some of the issues above, you may not need to make respondents 'anonymous' – having said this it may be best (e.g. in relation to gaming at work) to do this. It is a best, clear and simple option. As far as self-presentation goes, this may depend upon your means of access. It also may depend upon your own knowledge of and interaction with computer games. You may suddenly find yourself in a maze of 'sub-cultural' terms and ideas. Not being able to use these correctly may alienate your respondents!

Interviewing Women about Sexism at Work

The obvious ethical concern here is that they will be discussing issues that relate to their day-to-day work. It is very likely that they may not wish their points and ideas to be communicated to colleagues, managers or employers. They may also be discussing events that are upsetting to them. There is of course the possibility that they may discuss physical sexual harassment of various kinds that is likely to be distressing to both the respondent and to the interviewer. The interviewer might even need to think about the possibility that, in raising these issues, the respondent may then need assistance, say counselling or even legal advice, in relation to the events described. There are therefore huge issues of access: no point going through the boss or employer – they may be the people that the women view as sexist or even be engaged in overt sexist behaviour. You will also need to assure women of both the 'privacy' (anonymity) of their comments and provide them with a well-defined means to withdraw from the research. There are also huge issues of self-presentation. One must seriously ask if a man could do this kind of interview work.

Interviewing Staff in a Company about the Implementation of New Technology

Though this might seem fairly innocuous, there are a number of issues you could think about. First, implementing new technologies usually means changes to people's jobs or even the loss of jobs. If you gain access via the management, might you not be seen as part of this process of change (even redundancies)? If so, you might become alienated from your respondents. On the other hand, if your access was through the union, management might view you suspiciously. As with the previous cases, it would be best to keep interviewees anonymous.

SAQ 7.4

If you were researching the role of an office manager, themes might include:

- the role managers feel they should have in the overall company;
- the relationship of managers and staff – both professional and practical;
- the ways in which managers feel they can help in development of staff.

If you were researching students' use of support systems when learning through distance education, themes might include:

- how and when they use the support system;
- how the various elements and people of the support systems relate;
- how and why they do (or do not) use elements of the system.

SAQ 7.5

To find out more about the role of an office manager, questions might be:

- How do you see the office manger's role in the overall running of the company?
- In what ways do you interact with staff in your day-to-day work?
- What do you see as the key stages of staff development process?
- How can office managers contribute to each of the stages of the staff development process?

To find out more about students' use of a support system, questions might be:

- Can you describe an occasion when you had to use the support system?
- Can you describe for me the main types of support available?
- You stated before that you found aspect X [use previous answer] a problem. Can you describe how to get support if you are having problems of this kind with your study?

SAQ 7.6

The interview schedule has a number of key elements.

- It reminds the interviewer that this is a guide, not an absolute rigid format.
- It reminds the interviewer to engage with the respondent and sets them at ease at the start.
- It reminds the interviewer that they should go over the 'research contract' issues at the start.

The questions are then structured to develop in a logical manner. Each main 'initiating' question is followed by notes on topics to 'probe' for specific further information. The schedule finishes with notes on how to wrap up the interview.

All the notes and questions provide the interviewer with support and reminders that help get the interview done.

SAQ 7.7

There is no one answer to this question! A range of schedules would address these issues from a spectrum of positions. You can evaluate your schedule by considering the following questions.

- Are the main initiating questions clear and open? Look at the example schedule and the section on question design in Chapter 3 (pp. 31–36).
- Are the questions structured in a logical order? Look at the example schedule.
- Have you got reminders to yourself about the overall process – especially setting up and winding down the interview?

- Have you thought through issues and topics to probe for if respondents do not initially address them?

If you can answer yes to these questions, then the schedule is probably ready to be used. You may then find that it needs some tweaking after the first few interviews.

SAQ 7.8

1   Okely notes that, historically, sociology focused upon western societies and social anthropology focused upon non-western societies.
2   Okely associates surveys with a positivist position.
3   Okely argues that early anthropologists were able to use non-quantitative methods as they often worked in difficult social, cultural and geographical conditions. This led to a greater freedom in their choice and application of methods. Having said this, Okely notes that more contemporary training of social anthropologists has fallen back on more standard 'sociological' methods.
4   Okely lists the following examples: her own work on transport and the elderly, and on Gypsies; Young's work on the police; and Hockey's work on death.
5   Okely makes a strong argument for the importance of conducting participant observation. She claims that a deep immersion in the experience and the data and a long personal reflection on the data form part of the ethnographic process for social anthropologists. She contrasts this with survey work where the researcher is often managing a larger team and then brings data collected by the team together in the final analysis.
6   Okely takes the term 'funnel approach' from Agar, arguing that ethnography/social anthropology involves an initial openness to large amounts of data and experience which is then funnelled down through time and analysis into the final presented results.
7   Hypotheses in the formal sense presented in Part II do not form part of Okely's approach. Okely makes clear the importance of being open to many types of data and exploring the many possible interpretations. In fact, Okely argues that the model of the research process laid out in Chapter 2, with its logical steps from theory to hypothesis through to data collection and analysis and back to theory, may not be a good guide for the ethnographer at all.

SAQ 7.9

1   Okely shifted from writing field notes under 'prescribed headings' and began to make extensive notes about all aspects of the Gypsies' world, her experiences of it and the analytical ideas that were forming throughout her study.
2   Okely noted that the Gypsies were resistant to direct questioning.
3   Okely recorded information from daily informal conversation, descriptions and stray remarks.

SAQ 7.10

1   Okely's research was driven initially by the need to collect information to help with public policy in relation to Gypsy communities. Though the work later took on other important questions, this remained a key element. It would therefore have been of little use to study truck drivers, another category of people who often travel from place to place. Less obviously, selecting cases which will provide the most insight is tricky. In the case of Yates's research, though this began through an opportunity, it developed a much broader set of goals. These broader goals included the understanding of the relationship between the organisation, the type of news output and the technology in use. Within these wider parameters it became necessary to think about selecting cases both over time and across contexts. This situation was made more complex as the opportunities for access and observation were limited.

2   In some situations you may need to explore one or two cases in order to be able to evaluate the different effects and roles of practices, structures or ideas present in a range of related cases. In the case of Okely's work, though selections were made within the case (see below) the work was an intensive study of one case over an extended period of time. In the main Okely could compare the Gypsies' and Gorgios'/non-Gypsies' perceptions of and reactions to events and issues. In the case of Yates's work, the development of a wider question required that several cases be selected in order to separate out the effects of organisational factors and those arising from the use of the new technology. The differences in technology use could be related to three different factors: organisational structure; type of news output; and technology in use.

3   You might also need to think about the time-scale of your research: will you need to return to the case at a later date in order to evaluate changes over time? Answers to questions like this define a 'temporal sample'. Okely stayed with her case for an extended period and could constantly react to changes as they happened. Yates, on the other hand, could make a limited number of observations only. Being able to observe the same case before and after the introduction of a new production technology allowed Yates to 'control' or 'bracket out' some of the effects of organisational structure and the type of news production.

4   In one way or another both researchers were drawing samples based on social factors with their case studies. Okely had to contact both Gypsies and the 'officials' dealing with the Gypsies. We have already mentioned the way in which Okely had to balance contact with new people with gaining deeper insights into the lives of the people with whom she had already been interacting. Part and parcel of this selection process is coming to understand the relevant and meaningful categories used by those under study themselves. Categories of groups or individuals defined by theories or initial ideas can often come radically unstuck out in the field. In Yates's case the selection was based on existing knowledge of the workings of a TV newsroom both from previous academic study and from information derived from the industry and the staff under study themselves.

5   The locations, both physical and social, in which activity takes place also need

to be considered. This is not so evident in the Okely example, but in the case of Yates's research there were a number of important places: first, the news desk itself; second, the meeting rooms where 'morning meetings' occurred; third, the editing suites where media production actually took place; fourth, the studio gallery and studio itself where the programme was broadcast or recorded.

6   In the case of Okely's work it is clear that a good part of her research took place in both 'public' and private as she was living with the Gypsies. In the case of Yates's work there were a number of 'back-stage areas' away from the main news desk. These included the editing suites that were not easily observed in most cases. There were also other 'back-stage areas' such as the electronic messaging system that allowed people to engage privately in communication that they would not normally have conducted publicly – 'a virtual back-stage' of which the researchers got only a small glimpse.

8   Analysing Qualitative Data

At the end of the data collection activities the qualitative researcher is faced with a large body of text. This collection, consisting of everything from field notes to video recordings to historical documents, is often called a corpus. Analysing this corpus can seem a daunting task. As you will have seen from your reading of the Okely extracts, how to deal with the collected data is a constant concern of the ethnographer. In fact, there is no well-defined consensus on how to approach the analysis of qualitative data. Okely used her personal experience of living with the Gypsies to make sense of the data.

This contrasts greatly with the statistical methods used in quantitative research. In quantitative research the types of analysis available are limited to a specific set of mathematical procedures in the form of specific statistical tests. The choice of test and the types of possible interpretation are set by such factors as the type of measure, the nature of the sample, the structure of the experiment and the number of variables in play. Though you may have got the feeling from Chapter 7 that there are no fixed or absolute 'rules' to guide qualitative data analysis, there are a number of 'traditions' that are often employed. We shall now examine one such tradition – that of 'grounded theorising' – and contrast it with the method used by Okely.

Two Models of Qualitative Data Analysis

SAQ 8.1

1   Turn to Reading L, 'Thinking through fieldwork (3)', which is a continuation of the Okely paper. Read this extract and also look back over Readings B and C and your notes on them. Write notes on the following questions:
    (a)   What major classifications does Okely derive from her data?
    (b)   Did Okely produce any numerical results?
    (c)   How did Okely go about practically sorting all of her corpus of data?
2   Turn to Reading M, 'Qualitative analysis for social scientists', by Anselm Strauss. Along with Glaser, Strauss put forward a model of qualitative data

analysis in 1967 in *The Discovery of Grounded Theory* (Glaser and Strauss, 1968). In this extract Strauss gives a basic introduction to their ideas. Make some notes on the following questions:

(a)   What are the similarities and differences between the method proposed by Strauss and that of Okely?

(b)   What are the three types of coding proposed by Strauss?

(c)   Can you think of some criticisms that Okely might make of Strauss?

In SAQ 8.1 you considered two competing models of qualitative data analysis. Though there are a number of important similarities, there are clear differences in their underlying assumptions and the types of results they provide. The similarities are based on a number of things. First, both approaches use texts as their main data source. Second, both approaches employ similar practical methods when it comes to dealing with a corpus – both mark up sections of texts with codes. Third, both use the codes as the basis for their analysis and interpretation. The differences lie in their relationship to philosophical models of the research process. In many respects the grounded theory approach takes on board the model of the research process presented in Figure 2.1 (see p. 7) which we associated with positivist ideas. Having said this, it would be difficult to describe a method so reliant upon subjective assessments and interpretations, which form an important part of the grounded theory method, as 'positivist'. In contrast, Okely's work rejects this model of conducting social research. It draws upon, though not overtly, idealist and relativist philosophical positions. Once again we have a situation where the relationship of actual practical research methods to the philosophical models of the social research process is quite complex.

SAQ 8.2

Below is a sample of data, part of a transcript from an interview with a TV journalist. First, look over the Okely and Strauss extracts (Readings J, K, L and M) and your notes on them. Then read through the 'Example transcript' a few times. Try to put yourself in the role of a researcher interested in the work of journalists, in how they see that work and how they actually gather and produce the news. Now, spend about one hour 'coding' this data. Okely marked up, copied and cut and stapled her data. Read over the 'open coding' section of the Strauss paper (Reading M) before starting this task.

There is no 'right' answer to this task. If you are not clear about how to go about it, one way of starting is to read the transcript and then 'brainstorm' all the words and ideas that the transcript brings to mind, as you might when revising a course or preparing an essay. Write all these words and ideas down and then see if they help you to generate a list of related terms and ideas. You can then code or categorise parts of the data by marking the text where the terms and ideas appear.

Remember that you can code the same section of text in more than one way. As Strauss notes, starting coding can be the hardest part for people new to qualitative data analysis, so here are a few suggestions:

I am **community affairs correspondent** *[1][1.1]*, as such I am one of seven correspondents – regionally, therefore I am one of the **bi-media reporters** *[1.2]*.	**Code 1: Correspondent** **Code 1.1: Correspondent: community affairs** **Code 1.2: Correspondent: bi-media**
My particular **remit** *[2]* is mainly, but not exclusively, **inner city** *[2.1]* reporting and within that the **main remit** *[2]*, about 85% is reporting on issues affecting the **ethnic minorities** *[2.2]*.	**Code 2: Remit** **Code 2.1: Remit: inner city** **Code 2.2: Remit: ethnic minorities**

If you are still unsure of what to do, read the first half of Reading O, ' "Becoming a mother" – developing a new theory of early motherhood' and consider the types of coding used in the research it describes.

Example transcript

Interviewer: Could you describe your role – what you do – within the newsroom?

Correspondent 1: I am community affairs correspondent, as such I am one of seven correspondents – regionally, therefore I am one of the bi-media reporters. I am producing materials not only for *Look North* but as all the other correspondents will tell you for BBC local radio stations in the region – Leeds, Yorkshire, Sheffield and Humberside. My particular remit is mainly, but not exclusively, inner city reporting and within that the main remit, about 85% is reporting on issues affecting the ethnic minorities, therefore the bulk of the stories I do will be in the larger urban areas, namely Leeds, Bradford in particular and Sheffield, but I do across the region, it's not all ethnic minorities and it's not all inner city.

Interviewer: Thinking about that role – can you identify or describe in more detail some of the things you see as your key, practical day-to-day tasks which you undertake in order to do that – whether in or out of the newsroom?

Correspondent 1: The correspondents obviously operate, I think, quite distinctively differently from the reporters. The reporters will come in and by and large they will be fed a story which they are there to do that day and they will be given a researcher to back them and they will go out and hot-tail it around the region and come back with the goods. That can be the system for the correspondents some days, some days we are doing on the day stories but the main *raison d'être* of the job is basically to dig out your own material, wherever possible exclusive material, within your remit, research it yourself, this may involve spending a day outside researching not actually producing something, there's a lot of phone bashing goes on but eventually you will arrive at a story or a series of stories which you want to do and that type of story will mainly be free-shot rather than shot on the day, it's a mixture of on-the-day stuff mainly, on any given day I might be doing a lot of phone bashing, I might be going out to see contacts, going out to research a story or going out and pre-shooting or shooting on the day as I was on Friday – all shot and researched on the day.

If we followed through the analysis in SAQ 8.2 with more data and developed our codes, following Okely's or Strauss's methods, we would end up with a coded corpus of text. We can then use this coded corpus in a number of ways. First, we can use the codes to sort the marked sections of text into categories based on our codes. This will bring sections on similar topics or dealing with similar issues together. Using the example from SAQ 8.2, this might bring all statements by newsroom staff about their work roles together. Second, we can cross-reference codes by splitting our sorted texts according to two or more codes or categories. We might then find that correspondents think very differently about their role than do newsroom journalists. Third, we could look at the relationships between our codes. These relationships might start to inform us of systems of thought, practice or meaning in the data, or they might form the basis of a theory about the process under study. If you did a 'brainstorming' exercise before starting SAQ 8.2 you might have drawn a 'spider diagram' that relates the ideas you had. Fourth, we could even use our codes to produce numerical results by counting up the numbers of times and amount of text coded in different ways.

From this coding and sorting we can tell some kind of story, a narrative. If we followed Okely's route this narrative would be a meaningful description of journalists at work. In the case of Strauss and grounded theory we would have developed a complex social theory about journalists' work practices. We then need to present these results to some kind of audience – most likely other social scientists.

Presenting Qualitative Data

We can split the question of how to present qualitative data analysis results into two. First, we can present our results as either a description or a theory of the phenomena upon which we collected data. Second, within that description or theory we can make a number of choices about how to represent our various findings. SAQ 8.3 and SAQ 8.4 look at these two issues and how they relate to the chosen method.

SAQ 8.3

Look over your notes on the Okely article (Readings I, J and L), and then turn to Reading N, 'Thinking through fieldwork (4)', which is the final section of the Okely paper. As you read this extract make notes on the following:

1   What aspects of Gypsy life does Okely provide information about?

2 Where did Okely go for her theoretical models?
3 What role did personal experience play in Okely's final presentation of the results?
4 How did Okely represent the different types of information she collected?

SAQ 8.4

Turn to Reading O, ' "Becoming a mother" '. This is an extract from a study that used a grounded theory approach to develop a 'new theory of early motherhood'. While reading the extract make notes on the following:

1 How were the data collected?
2 What was the core category of the analysis?
3 What were the five related categories?
4 List the ways in which the researchers presented their codings and results.
5 How does this study differ in its form of presentation from the way Okely describes her own publications?

From SAQ 8.3 and SAQ 8.4 you will have seen that qualitative data analysis can be used in very different ways. This is in spite of the similarities in how the data are collected and in the nature of the data themselves. This is also in spite of the basic similarities in the practical approach – coding – to data analysis. In many respects it is up to the researcher to decide which line to follow. Such a decision has to be made not only in the light of basic data collection questions (e.g. should I do participant or non-participant research?), but also through the researcher's own assessment of the philosophical and epistemological issues.

From your reading of the extracts presented here you will have noticed that, despite the rejection of overtly positivist models of research, qualitative data analysis does follow an overall pattern, even if this is not so fixed as that for survey and experimental research. In most cases the research begins with a specific research idea, or the opportunity to observe some social activity or gain access to relevant texts, or a combination of related factors. This is then followed by a period of data collection, which often overlaps with a period of data coding. The coding of the data often overlaps with a period of data analysis, followed by the interpretation that has probably been developing over the whole project. Finally, the analyses and interpretations are written up in some form.

It is by addressing the relationship between texts, languages and society that social researchers have, since the early 1970s, started to consider different qualitative approaches to texts. These approaches, based on a range of social theories that link knowledge, power, language, communication and social practice, come under the broad heading of discourse analysis. Discourse analysis can be seen as a competing or complementary approach to dealing with qualitative, that is, textual, data (see Smith, 1998: Chapters 5, 6 and 7).

Further Reading

Bryman, A. and Burgess, R.G. (eds) (1994) *Analysing Qualitative Data.* London: Routledge.
Dey, I. (1993) *Qualitative Data Analysis: A User Friendly Guide for Social Scientists.* London: Routledge.
Ezzy, D. (2002) *Qualitative Analysis.* London: Routledge.
Glaser, B.G. and Strauss, A.L. (1967) *The Discovery of Grounded Theory: Strategies for Qualitative Research.* Chicago: Aldine.
Miles, M.B. and Huberman, A.M. (1994) *Qualitative Data Analysis.* London: Sage.

Reading L: Thinking through Fieldwork (3)

Judith Okely

At the end of fieldwork, I was faced with thousands of words: the experience written in chronological form. How to analyze? How to write up? First, the notes were typed up with wide margins, but single spaced, each page with the date on top. The final amount filled over eight box files of foolscap paper. Already, themes had emerged and I made a provisional list of topics, with subheadings. The broad headings were consistent with the holistic traditions of classical anthropology. The fieldworker aims for the total context, which includes kinship, the economy, politics and religion. Nothing can be taken for granted nor rigidly prearranged. So the classification is made after, not before, fieldwork. Major examples include:

(1) *Gypsy–Gorgio relations* with (i) council officials, (ii) customers, (iii) the police;
(2) *Work* (i) occupations, e.g. scrap metal, tarmac, antiques, (ii) ideology of self-employment, (iii) links with geographical mobility;
(3) *Gypsy identity* (i) Gorgio categories, (ii) self-ascription;
(4) *Kinship and the family* (i) choice of spouse, (ii) weddings, (iii) child care, (iv) shared residence, (v) alliances;
(5) *Education and socialization;*
(6) *Finance* (i) earnings, (ii) visible assets, (iii) budgeting;
(7) *Gorgio law* (i) courts, (ii) evictions, (iii) violence;
(8) *Gypsy law and community* (i) exchange and reciprocity, (ii) disputes, (iii) alliances;
(9) *Travelling* (i) ideology, (ii) case-studies, (iii) housing;
(10) *Sites* (i) official, (ii) official and temporary, (iii) illegal, (iv) rented, (v) Gypsy owned;
(11) *Religious beliefs.*

As I re-read through the notes, I added to the subheadings and categories. Paragraph by paragraph was bracketed. In many instances there was overlap. For example, a passage on kinship alliances could also be relevant to work partnerships. A case-study of a move from a camp could overlap with the topic of a police eviction. Details of a group discussion would involve individuals from several family or domestic units. The entire piece would be relevant to each unit. This overlap was no technical problem, since twelve photocopies were made of each page and the paragraphs were cut up according to each heading, stapled chronologically, and placed into the relevant named file. Each extract was marked with its original date in order to locate and cross-reference it in the chronology. Today, all this can be done by computer, without the labour-intensive cutting and pasting. Nevertheless, no computer can stand in for the ethnographer's discovery of emergent themes as fieldwork progresses, nor the final thinking and analysis. No computer can think through the fieldwork.

Without a fixed ideal number, I had always grabbed the opportunity to meet new individuals or families. It was a matter of balancing this with the benefits of increasing rapport with core clusters of families in the camps where I lived and in the locality as a whole. I was not under pressure as is a pollster interviewer to find select individuals and then hurry on after each interview. In working through my notes, I found that I had been able to obtain detailed, quantifiable information on seventy-five Gypsy families or domestic units, covering, for example, occupations, shelter, motor vehicles, visible assets, relative wealth or poverty, offspring, past and current marriages, kinship connections, literacy, housing experience and travelling patterns. All this was obtained without clip-board, and its accuracy was assured by the multiple contexts in which it emerged. This information was collated in anonymized family folders and quantified, along with the information on fifty families collected by my three colleagues. Numerical tables were presented in the first publication (Adams *et al.* 1975). The material was satisfactorily interpreted with the aid of knowledge which comes from long-term participant observation. The representative of the computer company which prepared the numerical print-out was intrigued by the fact that this relatively poor group showed, in the 1970s, such an 'atypically' high percentage of motor vehicle ownership. He advised us to make something of this extraordinary fact. Of course this qualitative aspect was unsurprising for a semi-nomadic Traveller-Gypsy group. But such detail was unlikely to have become apparent in a mass survey with quantitative priorities.

The numerical material may have given apparent credibility for policy-makers, but it was only a clue to systematic patterns. Since anthropology has delighted in the specific counter-example to ethnocentric universalisms, the presentation of its research does not rest on numerical majorities. It may require only one remark, one individual's example to unravel the elusive intelligibility of the group or context. People's beliefs, values and actions are not necessarily revealed by head counting. Instead, these crucial revelations are much more likely to emerge from chance incidents, extended comments, and both informal and ceremonial gatherings. All this is the stuff found in field notes or the fieldworker's selective memory. It is worked and thought through from event to text.

Having identified themes with many sub-classifications, and having stapled them sequentially in category folders, I would read and re-read the minutiae of this material. The detail and specificity were material to think with, a starting-point for an elaborated interpretation. The resultant chapters were in no way a collage of these bits and pieces. The folders provided confirmation of hunches, or unravelled false leads. The germs of ideas jotted down in the field offered organizing principles which had continued to simmer away since they first surfaced in crude and tentative form. The newly classified notes contained extended examples. There were first-hand statements whose words had often been forgotten long after the event, now preserved in aspic on paper. These voices were appropriately reproduced in the final text.

Preliminary outlines and drafts of chapters drew also on a wealth of other material. For dominant themes and proposed chapters I made card indexes with references and quotations from wider anthropological reading, from historical and folklore writing on Gypsies and from detailed notes on available contemporary records. Contrary to a still popular stereotyped view of participant observation and the discipline as a whole, anthropology does not ignore other sources. Archival, historical and current written records such as official reports, newspapers and the usual media are all grist to the writer's mill. Before ever encountering Gypsies and local agencies, I was steeped in non-Gypsy writing about this non-literate group who had few of their own records. Outsiders' typologies of 'real' and 'counterfeit' Gypsies offered an important perspective for understanding how the dominant majority rationalizes its repression of an ethnic minority. The racist and sometimes sentimental typology pointed to the constraints or opportunities available to the group in its relations with outsiders. Later, I looked at the use of stereotypes by Gypsies in economic relations with non-Gypsies (Okely 1979). I suggested that the ethnicity of the Gypsy could be exoticized (+), or concealed (0), or degraded (–), or neutralized (+ –). I was not concerned with how many times and how many Gypsies adopted the different strategies. My analysis was intended to demonstrate the underlying principles, rather than any quantitative information.

Given social anthropology's fundamental concern with a people's self-perceptions and view of the world, I was inevitably concerned with how the group defined its own members, Here, first-hand quotes and both ambiguous and unambiguous examples of individuals accepted as authentic members indicated the Gypsies' priorities and significant criteria. A key chapter in the 1975 publication (Okely 1975a) and a more theoretically exploratory chapter in the subsequent monograph (Okely 1983: 66–76) were devoted to questions of Gypsy identity and outsiders' interlocking or contrasting classifications. The theoretical perspective of Barth (1969), who posited the notion of self-ascription for ethnic groups, was an illuminating organizing principle.

Not only is the question of the construction of identity a continuing intellectual concern of anthropology, it is also used as a political weapon by non-Gypsies. The rejection of visible local Gypsies as 'counterfeit' in contrast to a mythically 'real Romany' legitimates a policy of harassment and oppression. So the selection of this theme in writing up was grounded in the historical and political context of the minority. The larger society has itself generated the question about real or counterfeit Gypsies, and invented, beyond the academy, answers to which the academic has to respond. Received views on the 'other' become even more sensitive when the anthropologist is writing about people who inhabit both his or her own geographical territory, and that of the reader. Readers both within and outside the academy have ready-made stereotypes about the 'real' Gypsy. I was never allowed to escape the matter in everyday encounters outside the field. Once my research interests were identified, outsiders invariably offered pronouncements on the popular typology, before seeking my comments.

Written documentation provided the major source for chapters on the history of local policy (Okely 1975b) and an extended overview (Okely 1983: 105–24) of local and national planning. However, its reading and interpretation depended heavily on participant observation both among non-Gypsy officials and voluntary groups. Intensive fieldwork in only a limited locality helped to make sense of wider patterns, just as Leach had once found (1967 . . .). I had, like Agar (1980), approached the material with an open mind. The local authority where I completed the bulk of fieldwork had been represented as one of the most liberal. Temporary sites had been established in the teeth of ferocious opposition. I was, until a subsequent incident outlined below, allowed completely free access to all the county council records and the photocopying machine. I filled two box files with copies of what I deemed to be essential documents: committee minutes and reports, correspondence, ministry directives, an informal census, residents' complaining letters and the odd petition. In the midst of the numerous and bulging filing cabinets was just one intervention from a Gypsy; a non-literate man on one of the camps where I had lived. He must have asked a literate acquaintance to write the letter, in its neat old-fashioned style. It requested the installation of a tap on his temporary council site, something which temporary army camps always regarded as a minimum requirement. The request remained unheeded throughout the three years of the site run by the authority which collected a weekly 'service charge' for the Elsans and rubbish skip. Officially, Gypsies had no political voice except for that one request in the council files. The interpretation and writing must therefore also confront the absences in the material.

Other absences may occur in the published text, not for want of material and analysis but because of powerful controls on information. The investigation of elites and those with power, which Nader has called 'studying up' (1974), is more precarious. As unexpected as the Gypsy's letter was the discovery of correspondence which revealed secret, illegal plans by senior county officials to set up an emergency committee and action group to chase specified Gypsies out of the county. The plan explicitly invited the police to collaborate with council officials. Their proposed task was to identify 'non-local' Gypsies (a contradiction in terms when considering travelling groups, who can rarely be fixed within a single county), and arrange for their deportation. The documentation belied the council's public protestations that the police acted as an independent and impartial body and that only legal methods were used to evict Gypsies from public or private land. The police chief's written response in fact rejected the emergency proposal. He argued that his force had already devised perfectly adequate screening methods. This correspondence could not be published. When my interest in these newly found documents was realized, my access to files was curtailed. The quality and amount of data to be scrutinized and interpreted was thereby diminished. Although I could not publish the evidence, it none the less informed my overall analysis (Okely 1975b), and especially that in my subsequent single-authored publication (Okely 1983: ch. 7).

References

Adams, B., Okely, J., Morgan, D. and Smith, D. (1975) *Gypsies and Government Policy in England*. London: Heinemann Educational.

Agar, M. (1980) *The Professional Stranger*. London: Academic Press.

Barth, F. (1969) 'Introduction', in F. Barth (ed.) *Ethnic Groups and Boundaries*. London: Allen and Unwin.

Leach, E.R. (1967) 'An anthropologist's reflections on a social survey', in D. Jongmans and P. Gutkind (eds) *Anthropologists in the Field*. Assen: Van Gorcum.

Nader, L. (1974) 'Up the anthropologists: perspectives gained from studying up', in D. Hymes (ed.) *Reinventing Anthropology*. New York: Vintage.

Okely, J. (1975a) 'Gypsy identity', in B. Adams, J. Okely, D. Morgan and D. Smith, *Gypsies and Government Policy in England*. London: Heinemann Educational.

Okely, J. (1975b) 'Conflict and accommodation', in B. Adams, J. Okely, D. Morgan and D. Smith, *Gypsies and Government Policy in England*. London: Heinemann Educational.

Okely, J. (1979) 'Trading stereotypes', in S. Wallman (ed.) *Ethnicity at Work*. London: Macmillan.

Okely, J. (1983) *The Traveller-Gypsies*. Cambridge: Cambridge University Press.

Source: Okely, 1994: 24–8

Reading M: Qualitative Analysis for Social Scientists

Anselm Strauss

Part 1

Some Assumptions

A set of assumptions lies behind this approach to qualitative analysis, which first will be listed and then briefly discussed.

1   Very diverse materials (interviews, transcripts of meetings, court proceedings; field observations; other documents, like diaries and letters; questionnaire answers; census statistics; etc.) provide indispensable data for social research.

2   As compared with both the quantitative analysis of data and the actual collection of data by qualitative analysts, the methods for qualitatively *analyzing* materials are rudimentary. They need to be developed and transmitted widely and explicitly throughout the social science community.

3   There is need for effective theory – at various levels of generality – based on the qualitative analysis of data.

4   Without grounding in data, that theory will be speculative, hence ineffective.

5   Social phenomena are complex: Thus, they require complex grounded theory. This means conceptually dense theory that accounts for a great deal of variation in the phenomena studied.

6   While there can be no hard and fast rules governing qualitative analysis – given the diversity of social settings, research projects, individual research styles, and unexpected contingencies that affect the research – it is possible to lay out general guidelines and rules of thumb to effective analysis.

7   Such guidelines can be useful to researchers across a broad spectrum of disciplines (sociology, anthropology, political science, psychology, public health, nursing, and education) and, regardless of 'tradition' or 'theoretical approach,' just as long as they believe their work can be furthered by the qualitative examination of materials. Also, such analytic methods can be useful whether researchers are wedded to the idea of social science per se or to more humanistic versions of social research ('understanding,' 'enlightenment').

8   Finally, research is basically work – a set of tasks, both physical and conceptual – carried out by researchers. Development, use, and teaching of qualitative analysis can be enhanced by thinking specifically of analysis in terms of the organization and conduct of that work. Thus, what we know about work (from research on that phenomenon) can be applied to the improvement of research methods.

Qualitative Analysis of Data: An Introduction

Besides those general assumptions that lie behind our approach to the qualitative analysis of materials, some additional remarks will be useful before the more technical details of grounded theory analysis are discussed.

Complexity   The basic question facing us is how to capture the complexity of reality (phenomena) we study, and how to make convincing sense of it. Part of the capturing of course is through extensive data collection. But making sense of complex data means three things. First, it means that both the complex interpretations and the data collection are guided by successively evolving interpretations made during the course of the study. (The final products are analyses done at a relatively high level of abstraction: that is, *theories*.) The second point is that a theory, to avoid simplistic rendering of the phenomena under study, must be conceptually dense – there are many concepts, and many linkages among them. (Even the best monographs often are rather thin in their conceptual treatment, as betrayed by the monograph's index, which lists few if any new concepts.) The third point: It is necessary to do detailed, intensive, microscopic examination of the data in order to bring out the amazing complexity of what lies in, behind, and beyond those data. (Later, we shall say much more about complexity and capturing it through analysis.)

Experiential Data   To that analysis, as will be seen, analysts bring experiences of various kinds. If not new to the research game, then they bring research skills and savvy to their analyses. What is in their heads also in the way of social science literature also affects their analyses. This is true, whether in the form of specific hypotheses and concepts or, more diffusely, an informed theoretical sensitivity (ways of thinking about data in theoretical terms) – to nuances in their data that less well-read researchers may lack in some degree. Equally important is the utilization of experiential data, which consists not only of analysts' technical knowledge and experience derived from research, but also their personal experiences (see also the next section, Induction, Deduction, and Verification). These experiential data should not be ignored because of the usual canons governing research (which regard personal experience and data as likely to bias the research), for those canons lead to the squashing of valuable experiential data. We say, rather, 'Mine your experience, there is potential gold there!' . . .

Induction, Deduction, and Verification   The grounded theory of analysis involves – as does all scientific theory which is not purely speculative – a grounding in data. Scientific theories require first of all that they be conceived, then elaborated, then checked out. Everyone agrees on that. What they do not always agree on are the exact terms with which to refer to those three aspects of inquiry. The terms which we prefer are induction, deduction, and verification. Induction refers to the actions that lead to discovery of an hypothesis – that is, having a hunch or an idea, then converting it into an hypothesis and assessing whether it might provisionally work as at least a partial condition for a type of event, act, relationship, strategy, etc. Hypotheses are both provisional and conditional. Deduction consists of the drawing of implications from hypotheses or larger systems of them for purposes of verification. The latter term refers to the procedures of verifying, whether that turns out to be total or a partial qualification or negation. All three processes go on throughout the life of the research project. Probably few working scientists would make the mistake of believing these stood in a simple sequential relationship . . .

In fact, it is important to understand that various kinds of experience are central to all these modes of activity – induction, deduction, and verification – that enter into inquiry. Consider induction first: Where do the insights, hunches, generative questions which constitute it come from? Answer: They come from experience with this kind of phenomenon before – whether the experience is personal, or derives more 'professionally' from actual exploratory research into the phenomenon or from a previous research program, or from theoretical sensitivity because of the researcher's knowledge of technical literature. As for deduction: Success at it rests not merely on the ability to think logically but with experience in thinking about the particular kind of data under scrutiny. The researcher is able to think effectively – and propositionally – because he or she has experiences to draw upon in thinking about those data, including the making of comparisons that help measurably in furthering the lines of deduction. Further, a special kind of preparation underlies this deductive ability: experience not only with deductive procedures but with those used specifically in research endeavours. And verification: Quite clearly, this is not primarily a matter of activity or ability. It involves knowledge about sites, events, actions, actors, also procedures and techniques (and learned skills in thinking about them). Again that knowledge is based on personal and professional experience . . .

We should add that in the event an extant grounded theory is used at the beginning or early in the research project, then deductions are made from it in the form of theoretical questions, hypotheses, suggested theoretical sampling, possible categories, and so on. They lead directly into the initial phase of collecting and analyzing data. Thus the role of deduction is the same as if the researcher began without using such a grounded theory . . . This is in marked contrast to a very frequent mode of using previous theory – usually drawn from a well-known theorist, like Goffman, whose theory may be well grounded – but this theory is misused because it is not really checked out in the further inquiry. It is only applied like a label to one's data. This practice almost totally relieves the researcher of three very important responsibilities: of (1) genuinely checking or qualifying the original data; (2) interacting deeply with his or her own data; and (3) developing new theory on the basis of a true transaction between the previous and newly evolving theory. While this practice and its citations may flatter the theorist, and may give the illusion of adding to 'knowledge,' it really does not advance the collective scientific enterprise. In this regard, effective social science research must follow the example of physical science research in its intertwining of the formulating of provisional hypotheses, making deductions, and checking them out – all with the use of data . . .

Several Points about Work Processes   Next, several things are especially worth noting about the basic research work processes – thinking, going to the field, observing, interviewing, note taking, analyzing. *First*, the raising of *generative questions* is essential to making distinctions and comparisons; thinking about possible hypotheses, concepts, and their relationships; sampling, and the like. These come from examination and thinking about the data, often in conjunction with experiential data. The original generative question may come from insight, which actually sparks interest in an aspect of some phenomenon and thus challenges the researcher to study 'it.' But these insights occur along the course of a study (although perhaps especially in the earlier phases), and open up questions about other phenomena or other aspects of the same phenomena.

Second, the researcher will be making a number of interesting, if at first quite provisional, linkages among the 'discovered' (created) concepts. The coding is beginning to yield *conceptually dense theory* which will of course become much more dense as additional linkages are suggested and formulated.

Third, the theory is not just discovered but *verified*, because the provisional character of the linkages – of answers and hypotheses concerning them – gets checked out during the succeeding phases of inquiry, with new data and new coding.

Fourth, the relevance of the coding to the real world of data is a central issue. Of course, 'there is no end to the logical elaboration of dimensions, the drawing of distinctions, the making of linkages, but to run riot with logical elaboration is dangerous – if fun. This thought process *must* be linked with, tied in tightly with, the examination and collection of new data' in order to be of service to the research itself . . .

Fifth, there is the issue of *integration*: Which dimensions, distinctions, categories, linkages are 'most important,' most salient – which, in short, are the *core* of the evolving theory? This issue becomes solved during the course of the inquiry. Conveying how integration happens is not easy, and we shall discuss and illustrate this work later. Suffice it here to say that integration actually begins primitively and provisionally with the first linking up of dimensions, categories, etc. Integration becomes increasingly more certain and 'tighter' as the research continues. The *core category* or *categories* that will best hold together (link up with) all the other categories – as they related to it and to each other – will take hard work and perhaps special techniques to put together in a convincing fashion; convincing both to the researcher and to those who will read his or her resultant publications.

Sixth, theoretical ideas are kept track of, and continuously linked and built up by means of *theoretical memos*. From time to time they are taken out of the file and examined and sorted, which results in new ideas, thus new memos. As research proceeds to later phases, memo writing becomes more intense, more focused, and memos are even more frequently sparked by previous memos or sum up and add to previous ones. *Sorting* of memos (and codes) may occur at any phase of the research. Both examination and sorting produce memos of greater scope and conceptual density. The systematic operation of sorting is especially important in later phases, as the analyst moves into planning the writing up of materials for publication.

Seventh, it is vitally important to recognize the *temporal* as well as *relational* aspect of the triad of analytic operation: data collecting, coding, memoing. Grounded theory practitioners need to understand how very different their perspective on that triad is from that of most other styles of analysis. Figure 1, a simplified diagram of a coding paradigm will illustrate some of the main features of this triad. Note that data collecting leads quickly to coding, which in turn may lead equally quickly – or at least soon – to memoing. Either will then guide the searches for new data. *Or* – and this is important to understand – they may lead to inspecting and coding of *already* gathered (and perhaps already analyzed) data. The *return to the old data* can occur at any phase of the research, right down to writing the last page of the final report of the theory. Furthermore, as the diagram indicates, at any phase of the research coding can lead to more coding; or memoing, directly to further and more integrated memos, helped out of course by the sorting of codes and memos.

This re-examination of all data throughout the life of the research project is a procedure probably engaged in by most qualitative researchers. But they do not usually double back-and-forth between collecting data, coding them, memoing in terms of data collection, coding, and memoing. The more positivistic research traditions proscribe the use of old data for verifying hypotheses, and so drive the researcher forward in a more linear direction, thereby cutting out the potential dividends of this recommended doubling back-and-forth procedure.

Eighth, during the *writing*, need for additional integration will often be

Phases of research

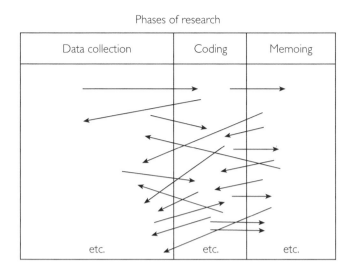

Figure 1 *Coding paradigm*

recognized, the researcher sometimes then going back to the data, collecting some new data, or thinking through the sorted memos and codes, to 'fill in,' thus achieving the necessary integration. However, there is much variation concerning how much those operations will be relied upon during the writing period. How much depends on the degree of thoroughness with which the coding and memoing has been carried out; also on what the researcher realizes ought to be emphasized for particular audiences for who he or she is writing; also on the writer's previous research/writing experience. Also, in team research it happens that so much data will accumulate, so fast, that although much coding is done and many theoretical memos are written, when the researchers sit down to write their various papers and monographs, they discover substantial holes in the previous analyses. This is especially so when some decisions about what to write, and for whom, evolve fairly late in the study . . .

Part 2

Grounded Theory Analysis: Main Elements

In this portion . . . a number of essential research operations are presented. Some of the discussion cannot be completely understood, at least in detail, until the illustrative materials in later pages help to provide visualization for the points made here. So, you might wish to read this . . . quickly to get an overview, then return to it, or parts of it, for reading or study later.

Our approach to the qualitative analysis of data is termed grounded theory 'because of its emphasis on the generation of theory and the data in which that theory is *grounded*.'[1]

Grounded theory 'is a *detailed* grounding by systematically' and intensively 'analyzing data, often sentence by sentence, or phrase by phrase of the field note, interview, or other document; by "constant comparison," data are extensively collected and coded,' using the operations touched on in the previous section, thus producing a well-constructed theory. The focus of analysis is *not* merely on collecting or ordering 'a mass of data, but on *organizing many ideas* which have emerged from analysis of the data.'

We have already seen the basic ingredients in producing complex, conceptually woven, integrated theory; theory which is discovered and formulated developmentally in close conjunction with intensive analysis of data. These procedures vary during the course of a research project. So, that issue will be discussed first, then we shall turn to a more detailed discussion of elements of the main procedures touched on previously. They are:

1   the concept-indicator model which directs the coding
2   data collection
3   coding
4   core categories
5   theoretical sampling
6   comparisons
7   theoretical saturation
8   integration of the theory
9   theoretical memos
10   theoretical sorting

Research Phases and the Operations

We shall now discuss the essential procedures for discovering, verifying, and formulating a ground theory. These are in operation all through the research project and . . . go on in close relationship to each other, in quick sequence and often simultaneously. But what about their relations to different phases of the entire research project? . . .

As we shall see, the earliest phases of the research are more 'open' than later ones are. There is no attempt to foreclose quickly on one or more categories. Many months may pass before the researcher is more or less certain of them and very many more before those core categories are saturated, and linked in a multiplicity of ways with other categories. In the earliest phases, a number of categories probably will be generated which later will be dropped as not very useful, or as unrelated to the core categories. Likewise a number of hypotheses will fall by the wayside, but are freely if provisionally generated by the enthusiastic researcher. Yet, from the earliest days, theoretical sampling directs the data collection and comparative analysis is done from the word go. The first memos are far less integrative than later they will be, and they too may poke up blind alleys or be focused very closely on the early microscopic analysis of data.

Once the core category or categories have been committed to, then the researcher will be seeking to relate other categories to them, thereby gradually densifying the theory. Also, more confidence will be placed in any new categories that 'emerge' from further coding. Further highly directed theoretical sampling will function to generate additional relevant categories and properties. There is likely to be some sorting too, both of codes and memos, during this later phase (presumably by the middle of the project). Memos are likely to become increasingly elaborate, summarizing the previous ones; or focused closely on closing gaps in the theory. Earlier integrative diagrams will be made more elaborate, covering both more concepts and more connections among them. All of that continues until the last phases of the project.

Near the end, achieving integration will be a major focus. Also, considerable thought will be directed at which audiences to write for or speak to, and about what topics; also, what published papers to begin aiming for. Finally, there is the task of pulling the entire theory together for its presentation in a monograph. If a team is involved in this research, then there will be conferencing over who will write which papers, give which talks, write which chapters of the monograph. Or if they decide to publish more than one monograph, there is the question of: Who will write which monographs or portions of them?

Having said all that, we should emphasize that no sequential ministeps can firmly be laid out in advance of the evolving phases of a given research project. Each enterprise will have its own detailed sequences, depending on: the circumstances of what kind of data are available, accessible and required; the nature of the data and the interpretations that the researcher will make of them; the experience of the researcher or researchers; the many contingencies that affect both the researcher personally (and interactionally, if a team also); the character of the audiences for whom they decide to write their publications; and the scope and generality of the theory for which the researchers aim. Only the general lineaments of the unfolding project can be anticipated in advance. The major differences between the grounded style of qualitative analysis and other qualitative analysis modes, however, is not in the relative unpredictability of project phases, but the differences per stage in the combinations and permutations of the operations (theoretical sampling, comparative analysis, theoretical saturation, memo sorting, and so forth). These operations are essential to the development of densely woven and tightly integrated theory.

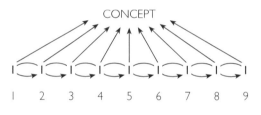

Figure 2 *Indicator-concept model*

Basic Operations

Concepts and Indications   'Grounded theory is based on a *concept-indicator* model, which directs the *conceptual* coding of a set of *empirical indicators*. The latter are actual data, such as behavioral actions and events, observed or described in documents and in the words of interviewees and informants. These data are indicators of a concept the analyst derives from them at first provisionally but later with more certainty.' . . .

The concept-indicator model in Figure 2 is based first of all on the constant comparison of indicator to indicator. That is: Many indicators (behavioral actions/events) are examined comparatively by the analyst who then 'codes' them, naming them as indicators of a class of events/behavioral actions. He or she may give this class a name, thinking of it then as a coded category. By making 'comparisons of indicator to indicator the analyst is forced into confronting similarities, differences, and degrees of consistency of meaning among indicators. This generates an underlying uniformity, which in turn results in a coded' *category*. A second procedural step is that after 'a conceptual code is generated, then indicators are compared to the emergent concept . . . From the comparisons of additional indicators to the conceptual codes, the codes are sharpened to achieve their best fits to data.' Meanwhile 'further properties of categories are generated, until the codes are verified and saturated,' yielding nothing much new. . . .

Data Collection   There is some ambiguity associated with the term *data collection*. Many social scientists do generate their data, through field observation, interviewing, producing videotapes, taping proceedings of meetings, and so on. But, as noted earlier, there are other sources of data: published documents of all kinds and private documents like letters and diaries. Use of those latter sources involves work too – searching for the data, getting access to them, taking notes on them, and nowadays xeroxing those data. In some kinds of library research, the researcher will even use the library much like an ethnographer, deciding upon which shelves to find the data sources (books, periodicals) . . . and like the ethnographer happily coming upon fortuitously useful data, too (see Glaser and Strauss 1967).

The initial data collected may seem confusing, the researcher flooded by their richness and their often puzzling and challenging nature. It should not remain *that* confusing (only challenging) for very long because the analysis of these data begins (in our style of research) with the very first, second, or third interview or after the first day or two of fieldwork if at all feasible. It follows also that the next interviews and observations become informed by analytic questions and hypotheses about categories and their relationships. This guidance becomes increasingly explicit as the analysis of new data continues.

Data collection never entirely ceases because coding and memoing continue to raise fresh questions that can only be addressed by the gathering of new data or the examining of previous data. Theory-guided data collection often leads to the search for – or quick recognition of – valuable additional sources of data: for example a series of directed interviews to supplement the more casual interviews done during the daily fieldwork; or the use of published biographies to supplement a series of interviews. We call these 'slices of data,' for different kinds of data give different views or vantage points, allowing for further coding, including the discovery of relationships among the various categories that are entering into the emergent theory.

Coding   Coding . . . is an essential procedure. Any researcher who wishes to become proficient at doing qualitative analysis must learn to code well and easily. The excellence of the research rests in large part on the excellence of the coding . . .

Coding paradigm.   One important point about coding that is sometimes misunderstood is this: While coding involves the discovery and naming of categories, it must *also* tell the researcher much more than that. It is not enough, for instance, to code an event qua indicator as an instance of a category – say, as 'machine breakdown' – by writing the name of the category in the margins of the page next to the indicating lines of print. Also, the researcher needs to code the associated subcategories which are reflected either in the same lines or which will be reflected in other lines within the same or different interview, fieldnote, or document . . .

So we suggest the following *coding paradigm.* It is central to the coding procedures. Although especially helpful to beginning analysts, in a shorter time this paradigm quite literally becomes part and parcel of the analyst's thought processes. Whether explicit or implicit, it functions as a reminder to code data for relevance to whatever phenomena are referenced by a given category, for the following:

conditions
interaction among the actors

strategies and tactics
consequences

Because beginning researchers sometimes seem to experience difficulty in discovering 'conditions' when inspecting their data, we shall note the following. Conditions are often easy to discover – indeed sometimes the interviewees or actors will point to them specifically – but if not, then look for cues like the use of words such as 'because,' 'since,' 'as,' or phrases like 'on account of.' Likewise, consequences of actions can be pointed to by phrases like 'as a result,' 'because of that,' 'the result was,' 'the consequence was,' and 'in consequence.' Strategies and the more specific tactics associated with strategies seem to present no difficulties for inexperienced analysts. *Interactions* are also easy to discover: They are those interactions occurring between and among actors, other than their straightforward use of tactics and strategies. Remember that without inclusion of the paradigm items, coding is not coding.

Open coding. The *initial* type of coding done during a research project is termed open coding. This is unrestricted coding of the data. This open coding is done by scrutinizing the fieldnote, interview, or other document very closely: line by line, or even word by word. The aim is to produce concepts that seem to fit the data. These concepts and their dimensions are as yet entirely provisional; but thinking about these results in a host of questions and equally provisional answers, which immediately leads to further issues pertaining to conditions, strategies, interactions, and consequences. As the analyst moves to the next words, next lines, the process snowballs, with the quick surfacing of information bearing on the questions and hypotheses, and sometimes even possible crosscutting of dimensions. A single session with a single document can often astonish even the experienced researcher, especially when the document at first glance seemed not to promise much in the way of leads. The point is really that the potential is not so much in the document as in the relationship between it and the inquiring mind and training of a researcher who vigorously and imaginatively engages in the open coding.

Novices at this type of coding characteristically get hung up, will argue intensely, about the 'true' meaning of a line – or about the 'real' motives of the interviewee lying behind the scrutinized line. In terms of open coding, their concern is entirely irrelevant. Why? Because the aim of the coding is to *open up* the inquiry. Every interpretation at this point is tentative. In a genuine sense, the analyst is not primarily concerned with this particular document, but for what it can do to further the next steps of the inquiry. Whatever is wrong in interpreting those lines and words will eventually be cancelled out through later steps of the inquiry. Concepts will then work or not work, distinctions will be useful or not useful – or modified, and so forth. So the experienced analyst learns to play the game of believing everything and believing nothing – at this point – leaving himself or herself as open as the coding itself. For all that, the coding is grounded in data on the page as well as on the conjunctive experiential data, including the knowledge of technical literature which the analyst brings into the inquiry.

This grounding in both sources of data gets researchers away from too literal an immersion in the materials (documents, fieldnotes, interviews, etc.) and quickly gets them to thinking in terms of explicit concepts and their relationships. This stepping away into conceptualization is especially difficult for even experienced researchers who may, in a particular study, either have gone a bit native through personally participating in the field of study, or who know too much experientially and descriptively about the phenomena they are studying and so are literally flooded with their materials. Yet the conceptual stepping back must occur if one is to develop theoretical understanding and theories about the phenomena reflected in the materials . . .

In our teaching experience, the most difficult step (other than integrating the total analysis) for beginners at this style of analysis is actually to get off the ground with genuine coding. Until they have learned this, they are frustrated. Yet it is essential that they learn this skill, since everything that follows rests on it. Other than the general guidelines given directly below . . . we find in teaching students that the following *rules of thumb* are useful:

1   Look for in-vivo codes, terms used by the people who are being studied. The nurse's 'tried to keep my composure' is an instance.
2   Give a provisional name to each code, in-vivo or constructed. Do not be concerned initially abut the aptness of the term – just be sure to name the code.
3   Ask a whole battery of specific questions about words, phrases, sentences, actions in your line-by-line analysis.
4   Move quickly to dimensions that seem relevant to given words, phrases, etc.
5   These dimensions should quickly call up comparative cases, if not then concentrate on finding them.
6   Pay attention to the items in the coding paradigm, as previously listed.

There are several additional guidelines for open coding that tend to ensure its proper use and success. 'The *first* is to ask of the data a set of questions. These must be kept in mind from the very beginning. The most general question is, *What study are these data pertinent to?* This question keeps reminding the researcher that an original idea of what the study was may not turn out to be that at all – in our experience often it is not . . . Another question to ask continually when studying the data is, *What category does this incident indicate?* This is the short form. The long form is, What category or property of a category, or what part of the emerging theory, does this incident indicate? As the theory becomes increasingly well formulated this question becomes easier to answer. The continual asking of this question helps to keep the analyst from getting lost in the rich data her/himself, by forcing the generation of codes that relate to other codes. Lastly, the analyst continually asks: *What is actually happening in the data?* What is the basic problem(s) faced by the participants? What accounts for their basic problem or problems? [Another way to phrase all of this is, What's the main story here, and why?] All of these questions tend to force the generation of a core category of categories which will be at the center of the theory and its eventual write-up.'

The *second* guideline for open coding – remember, this is primarily an initial coding procedure – is to *analyze the data minutely*. As noted several times earlier, this means frequently coding minutely. This effort is entirely necessary 'for achieving an extensive theoretical coverage which is also thoroughly grounded.' A contrasting 'approach to open coding (the *overview approach*) is to read the data over rather quickly, which yields then an impressionistic cluster of categories. We do not recommend this approach by itself because it yields only a few ideas and does not force the evolution of conceptual density. It does not, either, give any idea of what has been missed. To continue in that vein gives conceptually thin and often poorly integrated theory.'

A *third* important guideline for open coding is: 'frequently, to interrupt the coding in order to write a theoretical memo. This leads quickly to accumulated memos as well as moves the analyst further from the data and into a more analytic realm.' A *fourth* guideline is: 'The analyst should not assume the analytic relevance of any "face sheet" or traditional variable such as age, sex, social class, race, until it emerges as relevant. Those, too, must earn their way into the grounded theory.' . . .

It is important to understand that 'open coding both verifies and saturates individual codes.' Initially they are likely to be crude, so they will need much modification. Anyhow they are provisional so will end up considerably modified, elaborated, and so on. Hence, the analyst must not become too committed to the first codes, must not become 'selective too quickly, tempting as that is, since initial codes can seem highly relevant when they are actually not. Open coding proliferates codes quickly, but the process later begins to slow down through the continual verifying that each code really does fit . . . Eventually the code gets saturated and is placed in relationship to other codes, including its relation to the core category or categories – if, indeed, they or it are not actually the core.'

Axial coding. Axial coding is an essential aspect of the open coding. It consists of intense analysis done around one category at a time, in terms of the paradigm items (conditions, consequences, and so forth). This results in cumulative knowledge about relationships between that category and other categories and subcategories. A convenient term for this is *axial coding*, because the analyzing revolves around the 'axis' of one category at a time. It is unlikely to take place during the early days or even weeks when the initial data are collected and analyzed. However, axial coding becomes increasingly prominent during the normally lengthy period of open coding, before the analyst becomes committed to a core category or categories and so moves determinedly into selective coding (to be discussed next). During the open-coding period, however, the very directed axial coding alternates with looser kinds of open coding, especially as the analyst examines new aspects of the phenomena under study. It also runs parallel to the increasing number of relationships becoming specified among the many categories, whether this part of the coding is done as intensively as the axial coding or not. Of course, within this increasingly dense texture of conceptualization, linkages are also being made with the category, or categories, that eventually will be chosen as 'core.'

Selective coding. Selective coding pertains to coding systematically and concertedly for the core category. 'The other codes become subservient to the key code under focus. To code selectively, then, means that the analyst delimits coding to only those codes that relate to the core codes in sufficiently significant ways as to be used in a parsimonious theory.' The core code becomes a guide to further theoretical sampling and data collection. The analyst looks for the conditions, consequences, and so forth, that relate to the core category, coding for them. Selective coding then, is different from open coding but occurs within the context developed while doing open coding. During selective coding, understandably, the analytic memos become more focused and aid in achieving the theory's integration. Selective coding can begin relatively early, but becomes increasingly dominant, since it is more self-consciously systematic than is open coding . . .

Core Categories   'The goal of grounded theory is to generate a theory that accounts for a pattern of behavior which is relevant and problematic for those involved. The generation of theory occurs around a *core* category (and sometimes more).' 'Since a core category accounts for most of the variation in a pattern of behavior,' its different kinds of appearances under different conditions, 'the core category has several important functions for generating theory. It is relevant and works. Most other categories and their properties are related to it, which makes it subject to much qualification and modification. In addition, through these relations among categories and their properties, it has the prime function of integrating the theory and rendering it *dense* and *saturated* as the relationships are discovered. These functions then lead to theoretical *completeness* – accounting for as much variation in a pattern of behavior with as few concepts as possible, thereby maximizing parsimony and scope.'

'The analyst should consciously look for a core variable when coding data. While constantly comparing incidents and concepts, he or she will generate many codes, being alert to the one or two that might be the core. The analyst constantly looks for the "main theme," for what appears to be the main concern of or problem for the people in the setting, for what sums up in a pattern of behavior the substance of what is going on in the data, for what is the essence of relevance reflected in the data.' (As noted earlier, What's the main story here? is a kind of motto-question that the analyst asks repeatedly, to remind himself or herself to keep trying to answer the above questions.)

'As the analyst asks those questions, while analyzing, he or she becomes sensitized to their potential answers.' 'Possible core categories should be given a "best fit" label as soon as possible, so that there is a handle for thinking about them. The researcher may have a feel for what is the core, but be unable to formulate it to his or her satisfaction, so must use a provisional label until a better one can be formulated.'

'After several workable coded categories develop, the analyst attempts to *theoretically saturate* as much as possible those which seem to have explanatory power.' Thus, relations among categories and their properties become apparent and conceptually dense. Theoretical sampling is done to further the saturation of categories because they are related to many others and recur often in the data. With qualitative analysis, 'these relationships must be kept track of in memos, which get spread out or filed until sorted,' and get built into integrative memos. 'The core category must be proven over and over again by its prevalent relationship to other categories.'

'The more data, the more certain one can become of the eventually chosen core category. Time and data can be expensive; in smaller studies the researcher often has to take a chance: and certainly deciding on a core category can test skill and ability. If the analyst decides too rapidly, using a relatively small amount of data, there is a risk that he or she might end up with an undeveloped theory which has little integration and little explanatory power.'

There are several criteria for judging which category should serve as the core category.

1   'It must be *central*, that is, related to as many other categories and their properties as is possible, and more than other candidates for the position of core category. This criterion of centrality is a necessary condition for putting a category at the heart of the analysis: It indicates that the category accounts for a large portion of the variation in a pattern of behavior.'

2   'The core category must appear *frequently* in the data. (More precisely: The indicators pointing to the phenomena represented by the core category must appear frequently.) By frequent recurrence it comes to be seen as a stable pattern, and consequently becomes increasingly related by the analyst to other categories. If it does not appear frequently, that does not mean that it is uninteresting, only that it is not the core category.'

3   'The core category *relates easily* to other categories. These connections need not be forced; rather they come quickly and abundantly. But because the core category is related to many other categories and recurs frequently, it takes more time to saturate the core categories than the others.'

4   'A core category in a substantive study has *clear implications for a more general theory* . . . Thus, an analyst looking at hospital shifts sooner or later may realize the implications of shifts as a basic structural condition for any twenty-four hours a day work operation, and begin to conceive of generating a theory about work shifts in organizations. The various analytic operations which follow,

however, have to utilize data bearing on work shifts from many different substantive areas. Intensive scrutiny of these data is necessary, of course, before the core category or categories for this general theory can be determined.'

5   'As the details of a core category are worked out analytically, the theory moves forward appreciably.'

6   'The core category allows for building in the *maximum variation* to the analysis, since the researcher is coding in terms of its dimensions, properties, conditions, consequences, strategies and so on.' All of these are related to different subpatterns of the phenomenon referenced by the core category. Such variation (also called variance) is, as a colleague once expressed to us, emphasized more usually in quantitative analysis than in discussions of qualitative analysis. He spoke accurately, since many qualitative analysts do not seek for variance, but for very general patterns. It is one of the hallmarks of the grounded theory mode, however, to seek variation.

Who Should Code?   When it is a matter of an individual researcher embarked on his or her project, the answer to that question is obvious. But what if a team is working together on a project? Should all its members code, or only the most experienced, the most efficient, the most brilliant coders; or the professor rather than student assistant; or, on a large project, the top echelon and not the mere data collectors? Some years ago, a qualitative researcher, Julius Roth (1963) severely criticized the principal investigators of survey researchers for their exploitation of the 'hired hands,' who did nothing but the dirty work of data collecting – contrasting this situation with the deep commitment and involvement of the typical fieldworker, who of course did all the research work, including the brainy-work of coding. Those are the two extreme answers to the issue of who should do the coding.

However, the reasonable answer to this issue takes its cues from structural and organizational conditions bearing on the project, on its aims and its audiences. For instance, a large cross-site qualitative project with, say, two professors back home directing it, and concerned with producing 'good results,' and fast results (for career reasons), might handle the who-should-code issue quite differently than might – and probably do – smaller and more collaborative teams consisting of peers or virtual peers (cf. Miles and Huberman 1983: esp. 131–2). In these terms, then, think of organizational conditions like amount of funding, numbers of data sites, amount of data to be collected, number of team participants, the degree of homogeneity of team composition. The team structures can correspondingly look different: some are hierarchical, some quite collaborative, and so on. But also, the aims of the project might include – in their various combinations of salience – reaching fast results, or the 'best' results, or the most effective results for a given expected audience. Or they might include furthering the creativity of each team member, or of the total team which is expected to do further research together. And the product of all this productive research activity can take various forms during a given project: a collectively written monograph, or two or more monographs written by different members or combinations of members, individual or joint or collective papers – or all of these.

So the answer to the coding issue is going to be inevitably and profoundly affected by such considerations. Each person on a team may code his or her materials, because of greater familiarity with the data – and because there is *so* much of it cumulating for the total project. But, at a team meeting, they may together begin coding someone's presented material, or throwing in individually collected data during the analytic discussion . . .

Anyhow, to summarize with these *guidelines* pertaining to non-solo projects devoted to doing really creative research – I believe:

1   Each data collector should code much of his or her own data, but
2   code some of the others' data, separately as well as jointly and as a total team,
3   and this should be done from the onset of the initial data collecting to the very end of the project;
4   meanwhile, all should be engaged in theoretical sampling, making comparative analyses, conceptually densifying, integrating, etc.

I should add that there sometimes is one especially difficult problem encountered by students taught in our research seminars. When they attempt to code their own materials alone, without the support of the seminar's analytic discussion, then they may find this not nearly as easy or 'deep' and may not have sufficient self-confidence in their coding. For this reason they are urged to meet occasionally without the instructor, as well as to work jointly with another student, between the only occasional opportunities to present their materials in class or to confer individually with the instructor.

Theoretical Sampling   Theoretical sampling is a means 'whereby the analyst decides on *analytic grounds* what data to collect next and where to find them.' 'The basic question in theoretical sampling is: *What* groups or subgroups of populations, events, activities (to find varying dimensions, strategies, etc.)' does one turn to *next* in data collection. And for *what* theoretical purpose? 'So, this process of data collection is *controlled* by the emerging theory.' It involves, of course, much calculation and imagination on the part of the analyst. When done well, this analytic operation pays very high dividends because it moves the theory along quickly and efficiently. This type of sampling, so essential to the grounded theory mode of analysis, is of course neither the same as is utilized in quantitative research nor subject to the same canons (see Glaser and Strauss 1967).

Neither is it what Leonard Schatzman has aptly termed *selective sampling* (Schatzman and Strauss 1973), a frequently used sampling method in qualitative analysis. 'Selective sampling refers to the calculated decision to sample a specific locale or type of interviewee according to a preconceived but reasonable initial set of dimensions (such as time, space, identity) which are worked out in advance for a study.

Note

1   . . . this part of Chapter 1 is reproduced almost wholly from Barney Glaser's *Theoretical Sensitivity*, 1978, with some editing and supplementation. The quoted sentences and paragraphs are identifiable by the relevant quotation marks. For more detailed statement of these technical aspects of the grounded theory mode of analysis, readers are advised to consult *Theoretical Sensitivity*.

References

Glaser, B. (1978) *Theoretical Sensitivity*. Mill Valley, CA: Sociology Press.
Glaser, B. and Strauss, A. (1967) *The Discovery of Grounded Theory*. Chicago: Aldine.
Miles, M. and Huberman, M. (1983) *Qualitative Data Analysis*. Beverly Hills, CA: Sage.
Roth, J. (1963) *Timetables*. Indianapolis, IN: Bobbs-Merrill.
Schatzman, L. and Strauss, A. (1973) *Field Research*. Englewood Cliffs, NJ: Prentice-Hall.

Source: Strauss, 1987: 1, 10–14, 17–20, 22–5, 26–9, 30–1, 32–3, 35–7, 38–9

Reading N: Thinking through fieldwork (4)

Judith Okely

In some instances, there were no comparable studies and traditions within anthropology to inform the analysis. This is another feature of such research, whose material can produce new theoretical paradigms and insights. The open-ended approach allows space for the previously unimagined. I had the opportunity to challenge classical concepts and typologies in both economics and kinship. For example, the classical typology of nomads in economic anthropology includes only hunter-gatherers and pastoralists. There was nothing on the specific nomadic formation found among Gypsies, and which, taking off from the articles of Cotton (1954, 1955), I helped to formulate (Okely 1975a, 1983). Gypsies, I suggested, are a unique type of nomad whose economy is directly dependent on a wider, usually sedentary economy. They can never claim to have or approximate to self-sufficiency, as has been said of other nomads. Hitherto, writers about Gypsies had tended to identify their economic activity by a description of the content of their occupations; e.g. horse dealer, tinsmith, knife-grinder, fortune-teller, scrap-dealer, hop-picker. No one except Cotton had attempted to look for a common form or structure. My notes gave me the huge variety of Gypsy occupations. They could be fitted into a common schema which I identified as the 'occasional supply of goods, services and labour where demand and supply are irregular in time and place' (1975a: 114 and expanded 1983: 50–1). My fieldwork confirmed again and again the Gypsies' conscious rejection of wage labour, which they spoke of with contempt. Thus, the popular argument that Gypsies were excluded from wage labour employment solely because of prejudice was untenable. It also explained the failure of well-meaning attempts to 'train' them for 'ordinary' employment.

Similarly, there seemed to be no available categories for the kind of marriage exchanges found in my field material (1983: 175–80). Some anthropologists inaccurately labelled them sister exchange. Segalen, Zonobend (and others) have, I discovered much later, offered the term 'chaining or renewal of alliance' (1987: 114–15) for marriage patterns in the French peasantry which are to some extent similar to those found among British Gypsies. My analysis was here again intimately bound up with the manner in which the material was acquired. Contrary to standard advice in anthropology, dating back at least to Malinowski, the collection of genealogical information was not a way into the group and a means of establishing rapport. Bits and pieces were conveyed in the most unexpected circumstances. Any information on relationships, even names, was considered explosive. My genealogy file was composed of scribbles on cigarette packets, paper hankies and food packaging. I could not ask Gypsies about rules and choices of marriage partners, as I was not supposed to know about, let alone systematize any such matters. My completed diagrams (all anonymized), and perhaps banal to other anthropologists, represented a triumph over all adversity (1983: 175–80). Only other Gypsiologists would understand this.

The opening chapter to *The Traveller-Gypsies* (1983) includes some avowed speculation on the history of Gypsies. The circumstances of contemporary Gypsies derived from my intensive fieldwork, and placed alongside scattered historical data, is used to question the popular diffusionist theories which postulate that the Gypsies' presence in Europe from about the fifteenth century is to be explained only by migration from India. My alternative and still controversial suggestion is that, after the collapse of feudalism, groups of travelling people were formed from landless serfs and indigenous people, as well as from individuals from along the oriental trade routes. Fieldwork had shown how over time Gypsies used consanguines and affinal relations for internal solidarity. Simultaneously, they could incorporate isolated individuals through marriage. They banded together to exploit occupations which required flexibility in space and time and which were outside the fixed wage labour system. More detailed investigation is required by historians.

Meanwhile, the use of the present to analyze the past should be permitted to anthropologists as much as it is to others. Historians such as Thomas (1971) and Ladurie (1981) have made creative use of anthropological insights from living societies to explain rituals, witchcraft and animal symbolism in cultures which flourished centuries ago. Others may do it less explicitly. Mayall (1988) for example, uses the anthropologists' conceptual description of the Gypsy economy, formulated from accumulative participant observation and economic anthropology, of the kind outlined above (Okely 1975a, 1983), to make sense of his nineteenth-century data on Gypsies. Whereas an historian is expected to footnote the written source of every *fact*, he may project *concepts* backwards, without always fully acknowledging their source in recent anthropological analysis and fieldwork (Mayall 1988: 46–54). The use of qualitative anthropological research by historians should discredit a still popular belief in sociology that findings from participant observation are only applicable to the fieldworker's single locality in both time and space.[1]

... priorities emerge through the experiencing, thinking and rethinking. For example, at the outset I had no preconceived notion, let alone hypothesis, that pollution beliefs and animal classification among the Gypsies would turn out to be as significant as I realized they were at the time of the later publication (Okely 1983: Chs 6 and 12). Nor indeed did my policy-oriented research employers, who saw these aspects of Gypsy life as mere 'superstitions', that could only be of interest to denigrated folklorists. Beliefs were not seen then as relevant to the prioritized and pre-defined issues of sedentarization and settlement. The Gypsies' use of pollution beliefs to construct ethnic boundaries became clearer to me through the repeated evidence in field notes of distinct practices; for example, the rejection of sinks in caravans, the use of multiple bowls, and explicit statements or just casual asides by Gypsies about the apparently dirty habits of non-Gypsies.

While unburdened by hypotheses, the anthropologist is of necessity steeped in the broader theoretical and ethnographic concerns of his or her time. A theoretical sensitivity to the subject of pollution or animal symbolism had also been formed from reading Douglas (1966), Leach (1972), Lévi-Strauss (1966) and Tambiah (1973). Once the groundwork has been done, chance plays its part with the open mind.

It was while I was browsing again through *The Journal of the Gypsy Lore Society* that signals I had been alerted to in the field and in anthropological studies were consolidated. A stray example in an article by Thompson, a 'gentleman scholar', gave a clue to the system of the Gypsies' animal classification, evidence of which I could see scattered throughout the field notes. Until then I had not found a pattern in the Gypsies' random comments in identifying one animal as clean and another as polluting. Thompson (1922: 23, cited in Okely 1983: 92) recorded a direct quote, without further investigation, from a Gypsy who denigrated cats and dogs as polluted because they licked themselves, whereas horses were considered clean because they did not have the same habit. Eureka! I saw the demarcation between the inside and outside of the body reflected in the Gypsies' selective focus on animal behaviour, and as consistent with their own view of the body. Ingestation of the 'outer body' broke the rules which governed the Gypsies' washing and eating practices. The bits and pieces, recorded in field notes and in the folklore literature, on dogs, cats, ponies and hedgehogs suddenly fell into a classification grid. In contrast to the work of Lévi-Strauss (1966) and Tambiah (1973), this classification also depended on a relationship with the perceived or actual classification of another, that of non-Gypsies. The analysis, while drawing on structuralists' codes, yet grounded the beliefs in the historical and materialist context of the Gypsies' relations with outsiders. Pollution beliefs among Gypsies elsewhere were to be found in studies carried out by anthropologists working contemporaneously (Kaminski 1980, Miller 1975 . . .). None of these studies had, however, cracked the animal code. As is sometimes the case, the material may be there, but not necessarily interpreted. Jane Dick Zatta (1989) has followed up my analysis of British Gypsy animal classification in a comparison with Italian Gypsies and with intriguing innovation. Qualitative research of this kind has implications beyond territorial boundaries.

Interpretations are attained not only through a combination of anthropological knowledge and textual scrutiny, but also through the memory of field experience, unwritten yet inscribed in the fieldworker's being. The ethnographer, as former participant observer, judges the authenticity of his or her conclusions and interpretations in terms of that total experience. Others cannot so easily do it for her. Anthropologists have not begun to articulate the way in which ideas and interpretations are arrived at. The self and its autobiographical experience are used to relive and rework the material, although many anthropologists are coy about explicitly discussing that self and its history (Okely 1992). The interpretation is intuitive (. . .), yet the intuition is a newly acquired one which has been formed from months of living in the different culture.

Ideas may emerge from only the most intangible link with recorded notes. They arise in part as a response to other theories and ideas, long after fieldwork. For example, when the first book had been sent to press, and I was no longer employed by the policy-oriented research centre but instead registered for a doctorate in the very different atmosphere of a university anthropology department, new ways of thinking about my fieldwork and the Gypsies took shape. Again, the political as well as academic context had implications for the ensuing texts. An all-women seminar of anthropologists took place weekly. Banished by the professor from departmental buildings because men were discouraged, if not excluded,[2] it pursued its creative and co-operative course away from the usual academic cockfights. Suddenly I could see how my political feminism could link up with academic anthropological work and the rethinking of my field material. I had not previously placed women in a separate category when classifying and chopping up field notes. Gender was not consciously highlighted, except to analyze the division of labour. Although I was without a relevant file to think through, I nevertheless found ideas tumbling out. Perhaps the very absence of a file permitted lateral thinking. All the exotic and erotic images of the Gypsy woman in literature, opera and art assailed me. The ideas crystallized after a chance viewing of an old Hollywood movie on Gypsy Rose Lee, the stripper, who had no ethnic connections with the minority group. Key images pointed to the contradictions between the projected fantasy among Gorgios of the Gypsy woman which contrasted with the behaviour I had learned was required of the Gypsies I had encountered.

As a woman researcher, I learned also through personal experience about non-Gypsy projections. To outsiders learning of my research, I was sometimes seen as a 'Gypsy woman', with all the fantastic stereotypes. Vivid and contrasting examples of actual Gypsy women from my fieldwork were recalled. I pursued the contrast in a paper for the women's seminar. Thoughts came at unexpected times; on a walk, in the night, not necessarily when seated with pen and paper at a desk. After the broad schema of ideas was set down, I could look back for some exact details, incidents and statements in the chronological field notes. That is, the ideas and theories, having fermented in the subconscious, emerged by free association from unspecified experience. Only then was empirical evidence instrumentally sought as confirmation or elucidation. This form of analysis was the opposite to how I had worked on some of the other chapters; I now responded entirely to intuition and elusive memory before grounding myself in the recorded notes. There was a moment of relief and freedom when, after a discussion with Shirley Ardener, I felt it was right to trust my new intuitions, while being unable in any empiricist way to point to exact 'proof' in field notes that the ideas were sound. Since I had not and could not have predicted the paradoxes in Gypsy women's position either before or during fieldwork, it was logical that this would not be traceable in the notes. It was a matter of piecing together passing clues and seemingly neutral descriptions, while allowing an imagination, grounded in experience, its proper freedom. My approach rested absolutely on the initial fieldwork which itself helped to form the theories, in a mysterious and uncontrolled way.

In my text (Okely 1975b) I presented stereotypes from literature and opera as icons or as an epiphany to demonstrate the full range of possibilities in stereotypes, not as some numerically calculated evidence. This was misunderstood by some empiricists who complained that my 'proof' rested on just one opera (*Carmen*) and two or three quotes from novels or poems. Since these were labelled as 'only fiction', or 'numerically insignificant', they were not counted (literally) as sufficient evidence. These readers were inappropriately demanding a media content-analysis which entails mechanically counting the number of times a stereotype appears, for example, in newspapers.

To conclude, the interpretation of anthropological materials is, like fieldwork, a continuing and creative experience. The research has combined action and contemplation. Scrutiny of the notes offers both empirical certainty and intuitive reminders. Insights emerge also from the subconscious and from bodily memories, never penned on paper. There are serendipitous connections to be made, if the writer is open to them. Writing and analysis comprise a movement between the tangible and intangible, between the cerebral and sensual, between the visible and invisible. Interpretation moves from evidence to ideas and theory, then back again. There can be no set formulae, only broad guidelines, sensitive to specific cases. The researcher is freed from a division of labour which splits fieldwork from analysis. The author is not alienated from the experience of participant observation, but draws upon it both precisely and amorphously for the resolution of the completed text.[3]

Notes

1   Sociology undergraduates are routinely asked to write essays on the 'limitations' of participant observation. Textbooks inform them that its results may be 'valid', but 'unreliable' anywhere beyond the locality. In this positivistic exercise, quantitative criteria for generalizations predominate.

2   He did not see the inconsistency in being a member of All Souls, one of the richest Oxford colleges, which then excluded women.

3   The construction of anthropological texts has recently been scrutinized. My insertion of some reflexivity (see also Okely 1992), multiple quotations as voices and cultural references as ideology anticipated this. Simultaneously, my intention was to demonstrate that aspects of the classic monograph could be transposed to a western context.

References

Cotton, R.M. (1954) 'An anthropologist looks at gypsiology', *Journal of the Gypsy Lore Society* 3rd series 33(3–4): 107–20.

Cotton, R.M. (1955) 'An anthropologist looks at gypsiology', *Journal of the Gypsy Lore Society* 3rd series, 34(1–2): 20–37.

Dick Zatta, J. (1989) '"The has tre mule!", tabous alimentaires et frontières ethniques', in P. Williams (ed.) *Tsiganes: Identité, évolution.* Paris: Syros Alternatives.

Douglas, M. (1966) *Purity and Danger.* London: Routledge and Kegan Paul.

Kaminski, I.M. (1980) *The State of Ambiguity: Studies of Gypsy Refugees.* Gothenberg: Anthropological Research.

Ladurie, E. Le Roy (1981) *Carnival in Romans.* Harmondsworth: Penguin Books.

Leach, E.R. (1972) 'Anthropological aspects of language: animal categories and verbal abuse', in P. Maranda (ed.) *Mythology.* Harmondsworth: Penguin Books.

Lévi-Stauss, C. (1966) *The Savage Mind*, trans. anon. London: Weidenfeld and Nicolson.

Mayall, D. (1988) *The Gypsy-Travellers in Nineteenth Century Society.* Cambridge: Cambridge University Press.

Miller, C. (1975) 'American Rom and the ideology of defilement', in F. Rehfisch (ed.) *Gypsies, Tinkers and Other Travellers.* London: Academic Press.

Okely, J. (1975a) 'Work and travel', in B. Adams, J. Okely, D. Morgan and D. Smith, *Gypsies and Government Policy in England.* London: Heinemann Educational.

Okely, J. (1975b) 'Gypsy women: models in conflict', in S. Ardener (ed.) *Perceiving Women.* London: Malaby/Dent (part reproduced in Okely 1983).

Okely, J. (1983) *The Traveller-Gypsies.* Cambridge: Cambridge University Press.

Okely, J. (1992) 'Anthropology and autobiography: participant experience and embodied knowledge', in J. Okely and H. Callaway (eds) *Anthropology and Autobiography.* London: Routledge.

Segalen, M. and Zonabend, F. (1987) 'Social anthropology and the ethnology of France: the field of kinship and the family', in A. Jackson (ed.) *Anthropology at Home.* London: Routledge.

Tambiah, S.J. (1973) 'Classification of animals in Thailand', in M. Douglas (ed.) *Rules and Meanings.* Harmondsworth: Penguin Books.

Thomas, K. (1971) *Religion and the Decline of Magic.* London: Weidenfeld and Nicolson.

Thompson, T.W. (1922) 'The uncleanness of women among English Gypsies', *Journal of Gypsy Lore Society* 3rd series, 2(3): 113–39.

Source: Okely, 1994: 28–32

Reading O: 'Becoming a Mother' — Developing a New Theory of Early Motherhood

Frances Rogan, Virginia Shmied, Lesley Barclay, Louise Everitt and Aileen Wyllie

Becoming a mother is increasingly recognised as challenging for women in contemporary western society. The previous paper in this set of two (Barclay *et al.* 1997) describes the magnitude of change that women experience as they become mothers for the first time. New motherhood is characterised by profound change, a strong sense of loss, isolation and fatigue. Using a grounded theory approach (Strauss and Corbin 1990, Glaser and Strauss 1967, Glaser 1978), six categories and a core category have been produced. The categories [of] realising, readiness, drained, aloneness, loss and working it out are integrated through the core category becoming a mother.

This core category encapsulates the process of change experienced by women. Three factors were found to influence or mediate the actions and processes of becoming a mother: previous experience of infants; social support; and the baby's behaviour. This paper unravels the details of the analysis undertaken to reach these conclusions to make explicit both the processes and rigour involved in using this research methodology.

Literature Review

Research and practice in the post-partum and early motherhood period is most commonly underpinned by one of three broad theoretical frameworks. These frameworks emphasise either the cognitive aspects of role attainment (Rubin 1967a, 1967b, 1984), the behavioural and psychosocial aspects of transition (Rossi 1968, Burr 1972) or the emotional ties between a mother and her infant (Klaus and Kennel 1976, 1982, Ainsworth 1962, Gottlieb 1978). Some nursing researchers such as Mercer (1981, 1985), have applied a combination of approaches but most tend to focus on one or another of these areas.

Theories of maternal role attainment based on the work of Reva Rubin emphasise the cognitive and to some extent the subjective experience of mothers. She articulates two fundamental phenomena: (a) the acquisition of the maternal role (role taking) and (b) the identification of the infant (Rubin 1967a, 1967b). Her early work identified behaviour, operations, and processes that women undertake and the models and referents that women utilise (Rubin 1961a, 1961b, 1963, 1967a, 1967b). In later work Rubin describes the enormity of change involved in becoming a mother. She states that 'from onset to its destination, childbearing requires an exchange of a known self in a known world for an unknown self in an unknown world' (Rubin 1984: 52). Rubin's work has had considerable influence on the investigation and provision of post-partum care. A large body of descriptive work has been based on her concepts (for example, puerperal change in Martell et al. 1989, Ament 1990).

Theories of transition (Rossi 1968, Burr 1972) are based on sociological work from the 1950s and 1960s and are commonly employed in nursing/midwifery research (Mercer 1981, 1985, Pridham and Chang 1992). Works based on transition theories emphasise the behavioural and psychosocial aspects of new parenthood and identify factors that expedite or hinder the transition to motherhood. Studies indicate that there is a decline in marital satisfaction (Tomlinson 1987, Mercer et al. 1993) and deterioration in lifestyle, particularly for women (Doober 1980, Majewski 1986, Lenz et al. 1985). Women report the responsibility for child care far exceeds expectations (Hummenick and Bugen 1987, Gennaro et al. 1992). Roberts (1983) demonstrated the significance of infant behaviour in influencing the transition to parenthood. Nursing research, however, rarely moves beyond description (Walker 1992) and infrequently attempts explanation of the transition to parenthood.

Mother–Infant Attachment

A substantial amount of nursing literature has examined the nature of mother–infant attachment. Some of this work is based on original studies of attachment and separation by Bowlby (1951, 1969) and Ainsworth (1962). Most influential, however, is the work on bonding by Klaus *et al.* (1972) and Klaus and Kennel 1976, 1982). Theories of maternal-infant bonding and related maternal behaviours have become central to the assessments that nurses and midwives make of women in the postnatal period. Research has attempted to identify, measure, and predict maternal-infant attachment, using observation and self-report (Walker 1992). Despite many years of criticism of bonding research (Tulmann 1981, Lamb 1982, Goldberg 1983, Eyre 1992) nurses and midwives persist in using these concepts.

Theories of transition and maternal-infant attachment emphasise the ways in which individual women attain a prescribed maternal role. These frameworks identify cognitive processes, behaviours, and emotional responses that are said to represent enactment of the maternal role. They pay little attention to the social context in which new motherhood occurs and pay cursory attention to sociopolitical and cultural variations at an individual level. In this regard, nursing research has been heavily influenced by medical psychological approaches to understanding motherhood. The emphasis is upon individual pathology of women who fail to adjust to motherhood or are unsuccessful in bonding with their baby from a scientific observer's point of view. In contrast, sociological and feminist work focuses on the experience from the mother's perspective.

Early feminist critiques of motherhood held little appeal or currency for family health professionals caring for mothers and their infants. This work located the source of women's oppression within their reproductive ability (Firestone 1970). It was believed that only with the recognition of women's right to safe and effective contraception and abortion (Gordon 1976) and the advent of women-centred reproductive technology would women be freed from the 'tyranny of their biology' (Firestone 1970). During the 1970s and 1980s, frameworks were further developed to explain women's willingness to mother and thereby participate in their own oppression (Millett 1970, Mitchell 1971, Treblicot 1984).

Potential of Motherhood

Rich (1976) was one of the first to undertake a feminist analysis of motherhood that emphasised the potential of motherhood as a source of creativity and joy. She distinguished two meanings of motherhood: the experience – the potential relationship of any woman to her powers of reproduction and to children and the institution – which aims to ensure women remain under male control (Rich 1976).

Renewed interest in the importance of motherhood to women prompted a number of sociologists and feminists to describe motherhood from the point of view of women. In-depth interviews were used in order to allow women to speak freely of their experience of childbirth and motherhood (Oakley 1979, 1980, 1986, Richards 1985, Nicholson 1990, Frydman 1987, Crouch and Manderson 1993). The work of Oakley has been particularly significant. She describes a woman's response to childbirth, particularly first childbirth, as akin to the response to other major life events. Women tell of enormous disruptions to lifestyles, routines, and identities (Oakley 1980). Oakley concludes that easy adaptation to first-time motherhood is unusual. Australians Crouch and Manderson (1993) seek to identify the major themes of women's experience of pregnancy, childbirth, and the early months of mothering. They also conclude that the attainment of motherhood appears almost uniformly problematic for women.

Nursing, sociological, and feminist works lack theory that (a) draws together women's experience of early motherhood, (b) conceptualises the magnitude of change involved and (c) provides strategies to help women negotiate this challenge. The research and the continuing analysis of the experience of 55 Australian women presented in this paper attempts to develop such theory.

Methodology

Sample

The participants were 55 first-time mothers attending Early Childhood Centres (ECHCs) in Southern Sydney in 1992 and 1993. Mothers ranged from two to 26 weeks post-partum with a mean of 11.8 weeks. Mothers who attend these groups are generally healthy. Some modification to theoretical sampling, an important component of grounded theory method, occurred at this point. Data was collected only from mothers attending their ECHC and participating in focus group discussions.

Data Collection

Nine focus groups were conducted at ECHCs. The sessions were audio-taped and transcribed. Open-ended questions were used to provide a focus for each of the discussions, which allowed the mothers to talk about their experiences as they wished. Consistent with theoretical sampling (Strauss and Corbin 1990), some alterations to the focus group questions were made as the analysis emerged.

Data Analysis

An abbreviated version of the results is included to illustrate the process of data analysis. Clarification of the method of analysis is crucial to understanding how the results were derived. The analysis is presented in an orderly sequence but the process was not linear. The analysis moved backwards and forwards from one level of abstraction to another.

The constant comparative method – fundamental to a grounded theory analysis (Glaser and Strauss 1967, Glaser 1978, Strauss and Corbin 1990) – was used to analyse the transcribed focus groups. The data was coded and each piece of data compared so that similarities and difference in phenomena were distinguished (Strauss and Corbin 1990). This method was applied at three different levels of analysis (open, axial, and selective coding) and resulted in increasing levels of interpretation and abstraction of the analysis (Strauss and Corbin 1990). Concepts were categorised according to their characteristics or properties, and relationships between categories were identified. This achieved a dense but parsimonious explanatory theory accounting for as much variation in the mothers' experiences as possible (Strauss and Corbin 1990).

Constant comparative analysis is both inductive and deductive. As concepts, categories, and relationships between them emerged from the data, they were returned to the data for further substantiation and verification. This continued until no new data emerged and theoretical saturation was reached (Strauss and Corbin 1990). Theoretical saturation was evident after examining five transcripts. The remaining four transcripts confirmed and refined the analysis but did not contribute new insights. Analysis was undertaken by five midwife researchers simultaneously. The coding involved much discussion and negotiation which added to the depth and richness of the theory developed (Glaser and Strauss 1967, Stern 1985). The findings were returned to the relevant literature to add theoretical depth, help authenticate the results of the analysis, and place the findings in the context of current knowledge.

Open Coding

Open coding involved examining words, phrases, lines, and paragraphs of the transcripts to discover and name the concepts expressed by mothers in the study. Concepts and categories were labelled with words used by the mothers to ensure the mothers' meanings were captured as closely as possible (Glaser 1978, . . . Strauss and Corbin 1990). Concepts were examined and compared to distinguish their characteristics (properties) and their location on a dimensional range (dimensions). This enabled similar concepts to be grouped and abstract categories to be developed. Open coding resulted in the identification of properties and dimensions of six categories: realising, unready, loss, aloneness, drained, and working it out. A core category, becoming a mother, resulted from further abstraction of the data. The core category integrated and encapsulated all other categories and concepts.

Axial Coding

Axial coding developed the categories further (that is, beyond their properties and dimensions) by specifying the relationships between each category and its subcategories. This level of analysis was achieved through the use of a coding framework called a 'paradigm model' (Strauss and Corbin 1990). The application of this technique is currently contentious (Glaser 1992) but it was found to be helpful in assisting the analysis to 'emerge' rather than being 'forced'.

The paradigm model technique specified: (a) causal conditions, (b) the context, (c) the actions and interactions taken in response to the phenomenon, (d) the intervening conditions that assisted or hindered the actions and interactions taken, and (e) the consequences of the actions and interactions taken (Strauss and Corbin 1990). Application of the model to two of the categories is demonstrated in Figures 1 and 2.

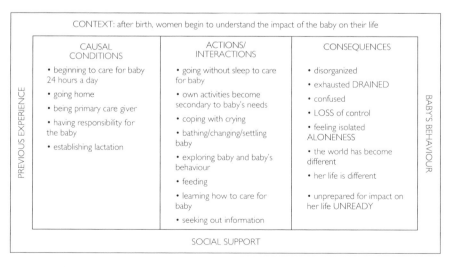

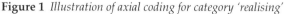

Figure 1 *Illustration of axial coding for category 'realising'*

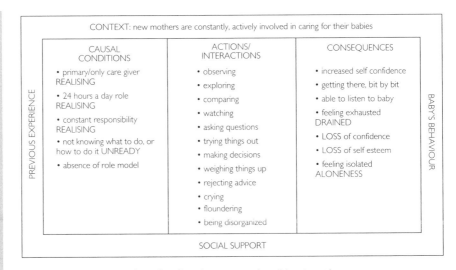

Figure 2 *Illustration of axial coding for category 'working it out'*

The use of the paradigm model (Strauss and Corbin 1990) was a complex process that required further analysis and synthesis of the data than had been undertaken previously. It uncovered complexity and density inherent in the relationship of subcategories and categories not previously evident, and revealed how categories were linked to each other.

Realising was, for example, found to be a causal condition for working it out; being unready made the magnitude of realising monumental for many mothers. As a consequence of realising, particularly when feeling unready, many mothers felt simultaneously drained and a sense of aloneness and loss. In this context mothers started working it out. Working it out further amplified feelings of loss, aloneness, and being drained.

Deeper examination of the data revealed that the same mediating conditions (called 'intervening variables' in Strauss and Corbin 1990) influenced each categorised experience. These were: (a) previous experience, (b) social support, and (c) the baby's behaviour. These conditions appeared to account for variations in women's experiences of motherhood.

Selective Coding

Selective coding enabled integration of the categories through confirmation of the core category and formulation of the grounded theory of the study. This was the step that changed the analysis from mere description of concepts and themes to the development of theory (Becker 1993, Strauss and Corbin 1990).

Through this level of analysis the core category – becoming a mother – was found to meet the characteristics of a Basic Social Process (BSP) (Glaser 1978). A BSP involves at least two clear phases and is the evolution that occurs as people respond to given phenomena and move from one phase to the other (Strauss and Corbin 1990). Variations in people's experiences can be accounted for by identifying factors that influence movement from one phase to the next. Discovery of a BSP strengthens the explanatory power of the theory (Strauss and Corbin 1990, Glaser 1978).

The integration of the categories within the core category and in relation to each other was made explicit in a storyline (Strauss and Corbin 1990) (see Figure 3 for how each category is related to the core category and the others). This storyline was then checked by first time mothers and early childhood health professionals, who indicated areas that needed clarification and modification. These suggestions were then incorporated into a second storyline.

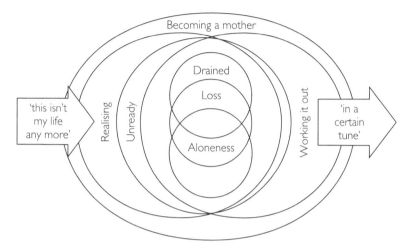

Figure 3 *The relationship of categories and core category*

Storyline

In becoming a mother women progressed from an initial phase, often described as 'this isn't my life any more', to a state identified by women as being 'in a certain tune' with their baby. This process of change was characterised by overwhelming change, constant learning, alteration and development of relationships, and a profound reconstruction of self. The entry point to the BSP occurred as women began realising the impact the birth of their baby has on their life, inherent in which was a recognition that 'this is my baby and I have to care for it'. Many women were overwhelmed by realising the impact of giving birth. This appeared to be related to how unready women felt for the experience.

Whilst feeling [at] least a little unready may be inevitable in the new and unique experience of motherhood, many women felt very unready. One mother felt disconnected from her known self: 'it's like I'm watching a film – this isn't my life any more – it's somebody else's'. This sense of overwhelming change occurred repeatedly, particularly in the early weeks of motherhood as new and unexpected challenges arose. Realising and unready were, therefore, closely linked and contributed to feelings of upheaval and disturbed sense of self.

Feeling overwhelmed and uncertain of their identity created conditions that left many women feeling drained of physical and emotional energy. Depletion of energy meant that many women were less able to interact with others, seek assistance, have time out for themselves, or resume former interests so that they felt alone and mourned the loss of their previous life. Each of these phenomena appeared to be closely linked in creating conditions and consequences that compounded their effect on each other. Feeling loss made women feel more alone and more drained. Women's sense of overwhelming change in themselves and their lives and of altering relationships, particularly with their partners, was exacerbated through the compound effects of these phenomena.

Challenges of Motherhood

In this context women met the challenges of motherhood and started working (it) out how to care for their baby and make the adjustments necessary to incorporate their baby into their life. The hurdles were monumental for many women and consequently contributed to feeling drained, alone, and a sense of loss. Women in the study were exhausted by the all consuming nature of mothering, particularly the need to be constantly learning. They were bombarded with advice and criticism so felt confused and uncertain and lost self esteem. Many felt they struggled along on their own with a keen sense of isolation. 'Bit by bit' women got beyond the difficulty and distress and became organised, slowly gaining confidence in their ability to care for their baby and perceiving gains in interactions with their baby. By working it out women eventually described themselves as 'being in a certain tune' with their baby. This phase was characterised by developing a sense of synchronicity with the baby and sense of self as a mother. Women recognised when they had progressed to this phase. As one woman said: 'I really like being a mum now'. Nevertheless, the sense of change engendered by the experience was irremediable for many women 'it's a big change . . . it really is'.

Women's progression through this process was not linear. Whilst ultimately developmental progression was characterised by irregular, uneven vacillation from one phase to the next. Factors which affected a mother's progression from one phase to the next were the mediating factors or intervening conditions identified in axial coding. That is, previous experience, social support, and behaviour of the baby (see Figures 1 and 2).

Conditional Matrix

In the final stage the analysis was fitted into a conditional matrix (Strauss and Corbin 1990). A conditional matrix is a complex set of interacted conditions (actions/interactions and consequences) influencing a phenomenon, from broad to specific (Strauss and Corbin 1990). The matrix was not fully developed in this work but suggested the relationship of the mediating factors with the core category at the first level of the matrix. The first level of the matrix is: '... people doing things together or with respect to one another in regards to a phenomenon . . .' (Strauss and Corbin 1990). For example, responding to and learning to settle a crying baby is influenced by (a) whether the mother knows from prior experience that this is common, (b) whether she has seen/learned settling strategies before, (c) whether the baby is always or rarely unsettled, and (d) whether she has help dealing with the situation.

At this stage of the analysis it became apparent the mediating factors were 'broad and general conditions bearing upon action/interactional strategies' (Strauss and Corbin 1990). These factors affected the 'broader structural context' of their experience (Strauss and Corbin 1990) (see Figures 1 and 2). They provide a basis for health care strategies to make the experience of becoming a mother less distressing and more positive.

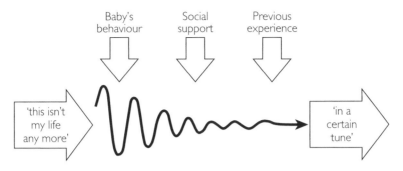

Figure 4 *Factors that mediate the process of becoming a mother*

Verification

The results of the analysis were returned to a group of new mothers and to midwives practising in the postnatal area. Both mothers and health workers confirmed that the theory explained the experience of new mothers. It was then shared with experienced early childhood health care workers across Australia during an International Year of the Family national conference tour. It was not only confirmed that the research explained the experience of mothers but also that it provided a framework for intervention. Factors which alleviated distressing experiences in becoming a mother were agreed to form a sound basis for strategies of family health care.

Discussion

This paper presents theory for explaining experiences of new motherhood in contemporary Australian society. It seems inevitable, perhaps necessary, that in the early post-partum period women enter the initial phase of becoming a mother by realising that 'this baby is mine and I have to care for it'. The recognition of the impact a baby has on one's life, not well documented in nursing and midwifery literature, is prominent in sociological and feminist work (Oakley 1980, Crouch and Manderson 1993, Brown *et al.* 1994). Oakley (1980) relates women's feelings of 'shock' and 'numbness'. Women in Crouch and Manderson's (1993) study spoke of feeling 'overcome', as though they were 'not living in the real world' and were distressed by 'the realisation of the impact that the baby was having on their lives' (Crouch and Manderson 1993). One significant aspect of realising is recognising that reality differs from expectations and this appears to be closely related to how unready women feel. Oakley (1980) found evidence of a lack of preparation in the expectations women held about birth and motherhood. She concluded that if the reality experienced is different from what was expected there is a marked impact upon self esteem. The disparity between the expected and the real is described in Rubin (1984). Rubin highlights self depreciation by the mother resulting in depression; usually in the second and third week post-partum.

   In this paper's analysis realising is closely related to how unready women feel for motherhood. Women who felt very unready were often overwhelmed by realising, particularly when it dawned how much learning is required. Nursing literature demonstrates a positive relationship between attendance at preparation for parenthood classes and the degree of confidence in one's capacity to care for infant and self (Pridham *et al.* 1991). There is also work citing evidence to the contrary

(Brown *et al.* 1994). Although the majority of women in this study attended antenatal classes, and many found this to have helped with the birth, they did not feel prepared for motherhood. Many suggested parenting issues should be included in antenatal classes.

Misery and Suffering

When feeling overwhelmed, unprepared, and unsure of their identity, women become drained and experience strong senses of loss and aloneness. These three categories are closely related, each acting both as a cause and effect of the others. The vivid descriptions used by the women in this study highlight the magnitude of change experienced and describe the misery and suffering experienced by many women during early motherhood. Women questioned their ability to 'mother', lacked confidence, and experienced a lowering of self esteem. Rubin (1984) describes something similar to 'drained' from data collected in the 1960s and 1970s: 'superordinate . . . fatigue dominates the three or four weeks following delivery'. Rubin believes the nuclear household reduces women's contact with the real world in the early post-partum weeks resulting in 'disorientation, depression and despair' (Rubin 1984: 97).

Rubin's description of women's experience parallels some of the feminist and sociological accounts. The women in Oakley's study spoke of feeling anxious, depressed, and found little satisfaction in their new role. The strain of meeting everyone's demands left women exhausted and frustrated. Women spoke of loss, in particular, loss of personal identity (Oakley 1980). For the Australian women in Crouch and Manderson's study caring for a new baby was demanding and unpredictable; women felt a loss of control and a loss of freedom (Crouch and Manderson 1993).

Following Rubin's work on maternal role attainment and the application of transition theories, nursing and midwifery research suggests that adjustment to motherhood takes much longer than a defined six week postnatal period (Mercer 1985, Tulman and Fawcett 1988, 1991). Nursing studies have often asserted that fatigue hinders successful adaptation to the maternal role (Rubin 1984, Tulman and Fawcett 1988, Lee and DeJoseph 1992). they describe the dissatisfaction among mothers noting the costs of their new role (Pickens 1982, Tulman and Fawcett 1991). These works identify areas of desired change, particularly help with housework (Pridham *et al.* 1987, Tulman and Fawcett 1991).

Working It Out

Realising the impact a baby has on one's life, the enormous and unrelenting responsibility and the considerable learning required, the women in this study embarked upon a process of working it out. The characteristics of the category 'working it out' parallel much of the nursing work on maternal role attainment (Rubin 1967a, 1967b, 1984, Mercer 1981, 1985) and work on active problem solving and women's self appraisal (Pridham *et al.* 1987, Pridham and Chang 1992). Women's descriptions of being 'in touch' with their baby and the related increase in self confidence reflects Rubin's (1984) recognition of a mother's identification with her child to the point [that] she knows the child and what to expect of him/her. She becomes able to read the child's appearance and behaviour. In Mercer's model the final and personal stage of maternal role attainment – where mother 'experiences a sense of harmony, confidence, and competence in how she performs (her) role' – is identified (Mercer 1981: 74).

Based on this work nursing/midwifery research has examined the many factors that may hinder or enhance maternal role attainment (Mercer 1985, Walker *et al*. 1986a, 1986b, Pridham *et al*. 1991) and the transition to motherhood (Majewski 1986, Hummenick and Bugen 1987, Mercer *et al*. 1993). This paper's analysis shows that most women draw heavily on their own resources while working it out. They feel depleted and isolated and their social context provides little support or nurturing. There is little discussion in either the nursing or sociological literature of the huge personal strength and resourcefulness these women exhibit in working it out alone, and little exploration of possibilities for providing more support.

Strengths and Limitations of the Study

The application of this theory is limited by a number of factors. Firstly, this analysis of women's experience of new motherhood is based upon data collected in focus groups with new mothers; the analysis was only tested within the one context. The theory could be tested with a wider spatial and sociodemographic sample of first-time mothers over a longer period of time.

Secondly, this study is based upon data collected in the early mothering period. This theory proposes a post-partum entry point to the process of becoming a mother but it is clear that the process of becoming a mother commences during pregnancy and that there is a relationship between women's experience of pregnancy and the post-partum period (Rubin 1984, Mercer 1985). In addition, it is evident that mothers are challenged by many new stages during the first year of an infant's life (Mercer 1985). As children develop, and the demands of motherhood therefore change, there may be more than one entry and exit to the process of becoming a mother.

The theoretical framework does not account for why the experience of becoming a mother in contemporary Western society is so difficult. It is necessary to better identify the sociopolitical and cultural factors that influence motherhood and incorporate other explanatory perspectives into the theoretical model.

Conclusion

Nursing and midwifery research has rarely studied the experience of first time motherhood from the vantage point of women themselves (Everitt *et al*. 1993). Such research has been concerned with the identification and measurement of adaptation or 'maladaptation' to the maternal role and women's experiences have been fragmented. The theoretical frameworks that have been commonly employed to explain women's experience of early motherhood proved inadequate to account for the experience that women described in this research.

Paradoxically, literature on postnatal depression relates more closely to the experience described by women in this study (the women who participate in this research were not diagnosed as depressed, nor would they describe themselves as depressed). Mothers were found to undergo a profound reconstruction of self and significant losses were felt before gains became apparent. This suffering interferes with a new mother's social networks and relationships. The research provides insights into women's isolation during this time in their lives and suggests some strategies for assisting them.

The paper has attempted a cross-disciplinary synthesis by informing and deepening nursing and midwifery research with insights from sociology. It demonstrates how a modified grounded theory analysis is conducted. The theoretical framework that emerged from the data analysis enables predictions of the way individual women are likely to react to early motherhood. Initiatives could be developed on the basis of this research to provide health workers with indications that women and their families are distressed and [that] intervention may be required.

By increasing the understanding of problems suffered by mothers the research also highlights what kinds of intervention are most likely to be effective. An important example of this is the demonstrated importance of social and relationship issues for new mothers. The analysis suggests that preoccupation with individual women rather than their social context prevents full comprehension of their problems and limits the assistance provided to women in adjusting to new motherhood.

References

Ainsworth M. (1962) The effects of maternal deprivation: a review of findings and controversy in the context of research strategy. In *Deprivation of Maternal Care*. Schocken, New York, pp. 287–357.

Ament L.A. (1990) Maternal tasks of the puerperium reidentified. *Journal of Obstetric, Gynaecological, and Neonatal Nursing* **19**(4), 330–5.

Barclay L.B., Everitt L., Rogan F., Schmied V. and Wyllie A. (1997) 'Becoming a mother' – an analysis of women's experience of early motherhood. *Journal of Advanced Nursing* **25**, 719–28.

Becker P. (1993) Pitfalls in grounded theory research. *Qualitative Health Research* **3**(2), 254–60.

Bowlby J. (1951) *Maternal Care and Mental Health*. Schocken, New York.

Bowlby J. (1969) *Attachment and Loss* vol. 1. Basic Books, New York.

Brown S., Lumley J., Small R., and Astbury J. (1994) *Missing Voices: The Experience of Motherhood*. Oxford University Press, Melbourne.

Burr W.R. (1972) Role transition: A reformulation of theory. *Journal of Marriage and the Family* **34**, 407–16.

Crouch M. and Manderson L. (1993) *New Motherhood. Cultural and Personal Transitions*. Gordon and Breach, Australia.

Doober M.E. (1980) Lamaze method of childbirth. *Nursing Research* **29**, 220–4.

Everitt L., Shmied V., Rogan F., Wyllie A., and Barclay L. (1993) The post natal experience of new mothers. Paper presented at the International Confederation of Midwives, 23rd International Congress, Vancouver.

Eyre D.E. (1992) *Mother Infant Bonding: A Scientific Fiction*. Yale University Press, New Haven.

Firestone S. (1970) *The Dialectic of Sex: The Case for Feminist Revolution*. Bantam Books, New York.

Frydman G. (1987) *Mature-Age Mothers*. Penguin, Ringwood, Victoria.

Gennaro S., Greisner A., and Musci R. (1992) Expected versus actual life-style changes in mothers of preterm low birth weight infants. *Neonatal Network* **11**(3), 39–45.

Glaser B. (1978) *Theoretical Sensitivity*. Sociology Press, Mill Valley, California.

Glaser B. (1992) *Basics of Grounded Theory Analysis*. Sociology Press, Mill Valley, California.

Glaser B. and Strauss B. (1967) *The Discovery of Grounded Theory*. Aldine Publishing, New York.

Goldberg S. (1983) Parent–infant bonding: Another look. *Child Development* **54**, 1355–82.

Gordon L. (1976) *Women's Body, Women's Rights: A Social History of Birth Control in America*. Penguin, Harmondsworth.

Gottlieb L. (1978) Maternal attachment in primiparas. *Journal of Obstetrical, Gynaecological and Neonatal Nursing* **7**, 39–44.

Hummenick S.S. and Bugen L.A. (1987) Parenting roles: Expectations versus reality. *American Journal of Maternal Child Nursing* **12**, 36–9.

Klaus M.H. and Kennell J.H. (1976) *Maternal-Infant Bonding*. Mosby, St Louis.

Klaus M.H. and Kennell J.H. (1982) *Parent–Infant Bonding* 2nd edn. Mosby, St Louis.

Klaus M.H., Jerauld R., Kreger M.C., McAlpine W., Steffa M., and Kennell J.H. (1972) Maternal attachment: Importance of the first post-partum days. *New England Journal of Medicine* **286**, 460–3.

Lamb M.E. (1982) The bonding phenomenon: Misinterpretations and their implications. *Journal of Paediatrics* **101**, 555–7.

Lee K.A. and DeJoseph J.F. (1992) Sleep disturbances, vitality and fatigue among a select group of employed childbearing women. *Birth* **19**, 208–13.

Lenz E.R., Soeken K.L., Ranking E.A. and Fischman S.H. (1985) Sex-role attributes, gender and postpartal perceptions of the marital relationship. *Advances in Nursing Science* **7**(3), 49–62.

Majewski J.L. (1986) Conflicts, satisfactions and attitudes during transition to the maternal role. *Nursing Research* **35**, 10–14.

Martell L., Imle M., Horwitz S., and Wheeler L. (1989) Information priorities of new mothers in a short stay program. *Western Journal of Nursing Research* **11**(2), 320–9.

Mercer R.T. (1981) A theoretical framework for studying factors that impact on the maternal role. *Nursing Research* **30**, 73–7.

Mercer R.T. (1985) The process of maternal role attainment at one year. *Nursing Research* **34**, 198–204.

Mercer R.T., Ferkeitch S.L., and DeJoseph J.F. (1993) Predictors of partner relationships during pregnancy and infancy. *Research in Nursing and Health* **16**, 45–56.

Millett K. (1970) *Sexual Politics*. Avon Books, New York.

Mitchell J. (1971) *Women's Estate*. Vintage Books, New York.

Nicholson P. (1990) Understanding postnatal depression: A mother-centred approach. *Journal of Advanced Nursing* **15**, 689–95.

Oakley A. (1979) *Becoming a Mother*. Martin Robertson, Oxford.

Oakley A. (1980) *Women Confined. Towards a Sociology of Childbirth*. Martin Robertson, Oxford.

Oakley A. (1986) *From Here to Maternity. Becoming a Mother*. Penguin, Harmondsworth.

Pickens D.S. (1982) The cognitive processes of career-oriented primiparas in identity reformulation. *Maternal-Child Nursing Journal* **11**, 135–64.

Pridham K.F. and Chang A.S. (1992) Transition to being the mother of a new infant in the first 3 months: Maternal problem solving and self-appraisals. *Journal of Advanced Nursing* **17**, 204–16.

Pridham K.F., Chang A.S., and Hansen M.F. (1987) Mothers' problem-solving skill and use of help with infant-related issues: The role of importance and need for action. *Research in Nursing and Health* **10**, 263–75.

Pridham K.F., Lytton D., Chang A.S., and Rutledge D. (1991) Early post-partum transition: Progress in maternal identity and role attainment. *Research in Nursing and Health* **14**, 21–31.

Rich A. (1976) *Of Woman Born*. Bantam Books, New York.

Richards L. (1985) *Having Families*. Penguin, Ringwood, Victoria.

Roberts F.B. (1983) Infant behaviour and the transition to parenthood. *Nursing Research* **32**, 213–17.

Rossi A.S. (1968) Transition to parenthood. *Journal of Marriage and the Family* **30**(1), 26–39.

Rubin R. (1961a) Basic maternal behaviour. *Nursing Outlook* **9**, 683–6.

Rubin R. (1961b) Puerperal change. *Nursing Outlook* **9**, 753–5.

Rubin R. (1963) Maternal touch. *Nursing Outlook* **11**, 828–31.

Rubin R. (1967a) Attainment of the maternal role – 1 – processes. *Nursing Research* **16**, 237–45.

Rubin R. (1967b) Attainment of the maternal role – 2 – models and referrants. *Nursing Research* **16**, 342–6.

Rubin R. (1984) *Maternal Identity and the Maternal Experience*. Springer, New York.

Stern P. (1985) Using grounded theory method in nursing research. In *Qualitative Research Methods in Nursing* (Leininger M. ed.), Grune and Stratton, Orlando, Florida, pp. 140–59.

Strauss A. and Corbin J. (1990) *Basics of Qualitative Research*. Sage Publications, Newbury Park, California.

Tomlinson P.S. (1987) Spousal differences in marital satisfaction during transition to parenthood. *Nursing Research* **26**, 239–43.

Treblicot J. (1984) *Mothering: Essays in Feminist Theory*. Rowman and Allanheld, Totowa, NJ.

Tulman L.J. (1981) Theories of maternal attachment. *Advances in Nursing Science* **3**(4), 7–14.

Tulman L. and Fawcett J. (1988) Return of functional ability after childbirth. *Nursing Research* **37**, 77–81.

Tulman L. and Fawcett J. (1991) Recovery from childbirth: Looking back 6 months after delivery. *Health Care for Women International* **12**, 341–50.

Walker L.O. (1992) *Parent–Infant Nursing Science: Paradigms, Phenomena, Methods*. F.A. Davis, Philadelphia.

Walker *et al.* (1986a) Maternal role attainment and identity in the post-partum period: Stability and change. *Nursing Research* **35**(2), 68–71.

Walker *et al.* (1986b) Mothering behaviour and maternal role during the post-partum period. *Nursing Research* **35**(6), 352–5.

Source: Rogan *et al.*, 1997: 877–85

Solutions to Chapter 8 SAQs

SAQ 8.1

1 (a) Okely came up with a number of major categories and listed the following as examples: Gypsy–Gorgio relations, work, Gypsy identity, kinship and the family, education and socialisation, finance, Gorgio law, Gypsy law and community, travelling, sites, religious beliefs. Some of these categorisations were then subdivided.

(b) Yes, Okely produced various numerical results. In fact, tables of numerical results that represent basic initial analyses of the data are often produced by qualitative data analysts. One of the hallmarks of qualitative data analysis is the range of ways in which the results can be presented – from tables and graphs, through transcripts and copies of original text, to actual video and audio material.

(c) Okely dealt with her data by marking the actual field notes and documents. These were then cut up and stapled together in files relating to relevant codes and categories. Cut-up items were cross-referenced using dates and index cards. This type of method works well in the case of written/printed notes and documents or photographs. It is not so helpful in the case of audio and video materials. In many cases transcripts of these, possibly including descriptions of non-verbal content and action, have been used. Today digital recordings allow people to make use of computer technologies to help with these types of data. As Okely notes, all aspects of the qualitative data analysis process can now be done on computer and there are specialised programs to help with this task. That said, the computers do not do the thinking for you. As with the example of a statistical analysis, the results must be interpreted by the researcher. Though a computer can calculate your statistical result, or help to organise and sort and even code your field notes, it cannot interpret the meaning of the final result.

2 (a) At one level these two approaches have a number of features in common. First, both use categorical coding of the data, with levels of sub-coding. Second, they also both stress the importance of 'experiential' data – information gained from directly experiencing the phenomena under study, or from others' descriptions of their experiences. Third, both methods stress the importance of collecting a wide range of data. Fourth, both methods stress the importance of being 'open' in the initial stages of the analysis. On the other hand, there are a number of key differences. First, Okely makes clear her opposition to 'textbook' methods, arguing that they constrain and limit the researcher and are often embedded in some form of 'positivist' agenda. The Strauss text is taken from a textbook on qualitative data analysis. Second, Strauss emphasises 'theory building', whereas much of Okely's work is concerned with 'understanding' Gypsies' lives and experiences. Third, Strauss acknowledges the advantages of researchers coding their own data but also argues for more team-based approaches. Fourth, Strauss's method is intended for a range of data collection techniques and not solely focused upon participant observation.

(b) Open coding; axial coding; selective coding. Open coding is the initial part of the 'grounded theory' approach to coding data. This type of coding is 'unrestricted' and consists of 'asking the data' as many questions as you can think of 'imaginatively'. Strauss argues that this should be an intensive and 'minute' form of coding. This coding can change as the researcher gains a more detailed understanding of the data. Part of the purpose of open coding is to allow 'core categories' to 'emerge' or be 'discovered' in the data. Axial coding is part of open coding, but involves focusing upon developing categories and the detailed coding of material relevant to that category and its sub-categories, at the same time keeping the coding system open to new codes. Axial coding also involves exploring the relationships between categories. This helps the researcher decide what are 'core categories'. The selective coding phase occurs when the researcher focuses upon selected core categories as key to building a theoretical model. Any further coding is then kept within the framework of the core categories.

(c) You may have noticed that Strauss makes use of a range of terminology more akin to the quantitative methods described in Part II. These include: hypothesis, variable, dimensions, categories, sampling, phenomena, 'collective scientific enterprise', induction, deduction, verification. In fact one can find many elements of Strauss's argument that fit well with the model of social science research described in Part II and in Smith, (1998: Chapters 1 to 3). One could, therefore, possibly see Okely making the argument that Strauss and the 'grounded theory' approach are tied into the positivist agenda of quantitative social science. The formalised textbook methods of 'grounded theory' might then come in for criticism as placing limits upon the interpretation of ethnographic data. Having said this, Strauss puts a great deal of emphasis on terms such as 'experience' and 'imagination'. Thinking about social science in these terms fits much more with the idealist arguments described in Chapter 4 of Smith (1998).

SAQ 8.2

As noted earlier, there are no 'right' answers to this SAQ. Below is a possible first run through the coding of the first part of the transcript. This is of course far 'cleaner' than would be gained from a 'pencil and paper' attempt of the kind conducted by Okely, or possibly by yourself. If you look through this coding you will find that underlined sections of text have been given codes. A description of these codes is given on the right. Where these are 'sub-codes' the higher level or 'super-ordinate' codes are also given. You will also notice that I have included codes for things not in the transcript but known to me as the researcher who conducted the interview. Before moving on, think about a few questions:

- Is this similar to your coding scheme?
- Do you have codes and sub-codes?
- How did you mark up your version of the text?
- How did you indicate which parts were coded?

Transcript with **marked** and [coded sections]	Descriptions of codes and sub-codes
INTERVIEWER: [I1.1,I2.1]	**I1: Interviewer**
	I1.11: Interviewer: Yates
	I2: Location
Could you describe your role – what you do within the newsroom?	**I2.11: Location: Private office**
Correspondent 1: [0.1,0.2,0.3]	**0: Basic data**
I am **community affairs correspondent, [1.1]** as such I am one of seven correspondents regionally, therefore I am one of the **bi-media reporters [1.2].**	**0.1: Basic data: Male**
	0.2: Basic data: Age 50
I am producing materials not only for *Look North* but as all the other correspondents will tell you for **BBC local radio stations [1.2]** in the region – **Leeds, Yorkshire, Sheffield and Humberside [3.1].**	**0.3: Basic data: UK Regional TV**
	1: Correspondent
	1.1: Correspondent: community affairs
My particular remit is mainly, but not exclusively, **inner city reporting [2.1]** and within that the main remit, about 85% is reporting on issues affecting the **ethnic minorities, [2.2]**	**1.2: Correspondent: Bi-media**
	2: Remit
	2.1: Remit: Inner city
therefore the bulk of the stories I do will be in the larger urban areas, namely **Leeds, Bradford in particular and Sheffield, [3.1]** but I do across the **region, [31] it's not all ethnic minorities [2.2]** and it's not all **inner city** [2.1].	**2.2: Remit: Ethnic minorities**
	3: Region
	3.11: Region: Cities
INTERVIEWER:	**1.3: Correspondent: Role**
Thinking about that role – can you identify or describe in more detail some of the things you see as your key, practical day-to-day tasks which you undertake in order to do that – whether in or out of the newsroom?	**1.3.1: Correspondent: Role:**
	Different from Reporters [4]
	4: Reporters
Correspondent 1:	**4.3: Reporters: Role**
The **correspondents obviously operate, I think, quite distinctively differently from** the **reporters [1.3.1, 4].**	**4.3.1: Reporters: Role: Day to day**
	4.4: Reporters: Activities
The **reporters [4] will come in and by and large they will be fed [4.3. 1] a story [5. 1. 1]** which they are there to do that day and they will be given a **researcher [4.4. 1]** to back them and they will go out and hot-tail it around the **region** [3] and come back with the **goods [5.1.2].**	**4.4.1: Reporters: Activities: Research**
	5: News
	5.1: News: Descriptions
	5.1.1: News: Descriptions: Story
	5.1.2: News: Descriptions: Goods

This is only one possible coding scheme; there are many others. In developing your codes you may have come across a number of problems. The first may have been the problem that you were not the person who collected the data. This could make interpretation of some of the terms, such as bi-media, difficult. Second, you may have felt that the task itself was a little unfocused and unclear. As Strauss notes, this is often the problem faced by people who have not attempted this kind of work before. You might have got out of this problem by trying the 'brainstorming' idea suggested. Third, you may have felt the need to change your codes as you worked through the transcript. This is fine and fairly normal for most forms of qualitative data analysis. Last, you may have felt the need to talk your ideas through with someone else. Looking at both the Okely and Strauss extracts, it is clear that discussing coding ideas can be a useful aid to the process.

SAQ 8.3

1 Okely's research provided information on the eleven areas listed in SAQ 8.2. In the material you have read, Okely discusses publications in which she described such things as occupations, shelter, vehicles, marriages, kinship, literacy, housing and travelling (see Reading L). In Reading N Okely describes in more detail her analysis of Gypsy occupations, concluding that they can best be defined as the 'occasional supply of goods, services and labour, where demand and supply are irregular in time and place'. She also details the difficulty she had in obtaining data on relationships and genealogies. She describes an alternative model of how Gypsy populations developed over European history, and she built a model and description of the pollution taboos and animal and ethnic boundaries that informed Gypsy culture.

2 Okely notes that, on some occasions, existing anthropological literature was of little help to her in interpreting her data. In the case of the pollution taboos Okely was theoretically informed by reading a number of anthropological texts from Douglas, Leach, Lévi-Strauss and Tambiah. Okely notes how using these models, with some modification, she was able to provide a description of the Gypsies' 'classification grid'.

3 Okely uses the first person and links her interpretations and analyses to her experiences of living with the Gypsies. She combines this experiential knowledge with existing anthropological ideas, an 'open mind', textual scrutiny, memories and intuitions in order to develop her interpretations and descriptions of Gypsy life. Also, Okely was able to bring her own personal experiences as a woman academic, combined with feminist theory, to the interpretation of Gypsy women's lives.

4 At various points in the extracts Okely describes how she represented her data. Overall, she used printed texts (books, reports and journal articles). Within these she used tables of numerical data, diagrams, quotes and references to historical and anthropological texts, as well as texts gathered in the field and descriptions developed from her field notes. All of this provided Okely with the ability to provide a rich or 'thick' description of Gypsy life and to comment on various aspects of Gypsy and Gorgio culture. As she notes herself, 'empiricist' critics of her work have argued that such evidence did not count

as 'proof' as it was not 'numerically significant' and contained material that was 'only fiction' (i.e. extracts from plays with Gypsy characters).

SAQ 8.4

1   The data were collected through 'focus group' interviews – group interviews on a 'focused' topic led by a moderator (usually one of the researchers). The discussion is often recorded (on video or audio) and then transcribed. Open questions are used in focus group interviews. These allow free-ranging discussion, and it is the job of the moderator to ensure that the required topics are covered during the session. This method contrasts with the participant methods used by Okely (Readings I, J, L, N) and the non-participant methods used by Yates (Reading K).
2   The core category was 'becoming a mother'.
3   The related categories were: realising, readiness, drained, aloneness, loss, working it out.
4   The range of methods to present their results and codings included: diagrams, a 'storyline', direct quotes, explanations of the elements of the theory.
5   Reading O is structured and presented in the same manner as an experimental or survey report. As such it is clearly making a statement that the information within it is 'scientific'. Not only do the researchers describe in detail how they implemented 'grounded theory', but they also sought to 'validate' or 'verify' their results in a number of ways. This included asking new mothers and health professionals if the theory adequately described the process of becoming a new mother. The researchers also pointed out that the theory could help health care professionals plan 'interventions' to aid new mothers. This contrasts greatly with Okely's work as she notes that it was only after leaving the employment of a policy-orientated organisation that she was able to develop her analysis fully. Similar methods are used in both cases to present information, texts, numbers, diagrams, descriptions, quotes, etc. The main difference lies in the overall goal of the research. In Okely's case this is to provide a complex, rich description of a range of social and cultural aspects of both Gypsy life and representations of Gypsies. In the case of the motherhood research the goal is to build a testable theory of how women become new mothers. This theory is then to be used in the development of nursing and medical practices in relation to new mothers.

9   *Discourse Analysis*

What Is Discourse Analysis?

The term *discourse analysis* covers a great number of different social science practices and ideas. Smith (1998: Chapter 6) points out two different but related approaches to discourse analysis: discursive psychology and post-structuralism. Both of these explore the connections between language, communication, knowledge, social practices and systems of power. In fact there are many contemporary theoretical and empirical research practices that are given the name 'discourse analysis'. Wetherell, Taylor and Yates (2001a, 2001b) argue that these can be placed into three broad areas of work that are described as 'discourse analysis'. These are the study of:

- social interaction
- minds, selves and sense making
- culture and social relations

Tied to these three approaches are two different but related conceptions of a 'discourse'. In the first a discourse consists of 'real' things such as words spoken in a conversation or letters exchanged between people. It is a set of actual examples of language use as part of one or more acts of communication. On the other hand there is a conception of a 'discourse' as a set of ideas, concepts and rules about how one thinks and talks about a topic as well as the knowledge a group, institution, society or culture has about that topic. In other words a discourse can be seen as a socially or culturally defined system of knowledge. One way of thinking about this is to think of 'discourses' (small 'd') that are interactions between people and also of 'Discourses' (big 'D') that are systems of knowledge. So for example we can view a transcript of an interview – of the kind we explored in Chapter 7 (see p. 190) – as small 'd' discourse. Examples of big 'D' discourses might be:

- the discourses of 'racism' – the ways in which people talk about, think about and represent 'race';
- the discourses of 'genetic science' – how all the different individuals, groups, institutions and governments talk about, think about and represent issues around genetics.

In order to explore these discourses you might need to collect a large number of texts – examples of small 'd' discourse – such as press and media coverage, official documents, popular films and novels, and even interviews with individuals. In the following sections we will explore how different approaches to 'discourse analysis' focus on different aspects of 'small' and 'big' 'd' discourses and make use of various types of data.

All three of the types of analysis listed above have something to say about big 'D' and small 'd' discourses, though they may focus upon one more than the other. In studying 'social interaction' discourse analysts explore the ways in which human interaction is ordered and structured. In particular they examine the ways in which language, context and behaviours are linked together. The main focus is therefore on small 'd' discourse. This research might be based in the disciplines of linguistics, sociology or psychology, or some mix of the three. One of the major approaches to discourse in this tradition is that of 'Conversation Analysis', also known as 'CA' (see Sacks, 1992). In Chapter 6 I associated CA with the development of phenomenological approaches to social research.

'Minds, selves and sense making' refers to broadly psychological approaches to discourse – which are therefore termed 'discursive psychology'. These approaches explore two sometimes related issues. First, the ways in which language, social interaction and cognition (the processing of knowledge in the mind) are linked. Second, the ways in which identity and self-knowledge are the products of interactions – especially the ways in which identity is produced in context through interactions. This work often tries to actively link the specific practices of small 'd' discourse with explorations of how big 'D' discourses are made and maintained.

'Culture and social relations' refers to a wide body of work that has been strongly influenced by post-structuralism, especially the work of Foucault as well as work that has been informed by 'critical linguistics'. Critical linguistics is an approach to the study of language that is concerned with the relationship between language and society – especially the functioning of power in society. Overall the concern here is with big 'D' discourses, though many analyses focus on specific texts or examples of small 'd' discourse to demonstrate the 'functioning' of big 'D' discourses.

In the rest of this section we will examine work from these three areas. The first example we will look at introduces some ideas from CA. This will focus on an analysis of a specific interaction. We will work through a more extended example of 'discursive psychology' before examining an example of 'media discourse' research that studies the role of language in the construction of ideological positions.

Discourse Analysis and Context

Before discussing our three examples we need to consider an issue that is key to all discourse analysis work. This is the idea of context. All discourse work starts from an assumption that language use can only be understood in context. That is, one needs to evaluate the data (whatever that might be) in relation to the contexts in which it was both created and (perhaps) later used. This is also important to most qualitative research work and is central to most ethnography. In discourse work it takes on a central importance and we will examine in each of our three cases how context is taken into account. What context means is dependent upon the type of work being undertaken. In some cases it refers to the immediate environment of an interaction – where it is taking place, who is involved, what the roles are, etc. In other cases it might mean the overall cultural or historical situation in which the texts under study were created or used.

Discourse as Social Interaction

What do we mean by studying discourse as 'social interaction'? In many respects what we mean by this is the everyday understanding of the word 'discourse' – that is 'to discourse' – to interact through language, for example how people interact in everyday conversation. Some specific examples of what we might study are:

- how doctors interact with patients;
- how teachers interact with pupils;
- differences and similarities in how men and women interact with each other;
- how people from different cultures interact.

These interactions are likely to be face-to-face but we might also look at telephone, e-mail or written interactions. There are a number of traditions of discourse work that focus on issues of interaction but we can split such work into two basic categories, though much of it links these two areas:

- linguistic research – for example work based in the disciplines of 'socio-linguistics' and the 'ethnography of speaking';
- sociological research – for example conversation analysis.

Both of these approaches focus on the details of individual interactions, mainly through the use and analysis of transcripts – written/printed representations of speech. Linguistic research has a tendency to focus on the structures and forms of the language used. Sociological work tends to focus on the structure of the interaction and the ways in which people 'do things' through interaction. In both cases researchers are often concerned with how people create or in fact re-create social relations and social structures through interactions. At the same time they are interested in demonstrating how we make use of ideas and assumptions about social relations and structures in our everyday interactions. The focus is therefore on 'small' 'd' discourse – upon texts produced by interactions. However, there may be a concern with how these interactions create and are brought into being by 'big' 'D' discourses.

We will now turn to an example of this kind of work called 'conversation analysis' or CA for short. CA developed out of the work of ethnomethodologists such as Harold Garfinkel and ethnographers and symbolic interactionists such as Ervin Goffman. Both of these traditions fit within the phenomenological and hermeneutic approaches to social science described in Chapter 6. CA was first formalised by Harvey Sacks (see Sacks, 1992). CA's goal is to try to make clear the unstated ways of thinking, methods and skills that underlie the ways in which people produce and interpret conversational talk. Most importantly CA is concerned with how the people in the interaction 'orientate to' both the content and the structure of the interaction. In other words we not only deal with the meaning of things said in a conversation but also keep track of and try to guide the way the conversation is 'going'. It can be a complex process if several people are all trying to do all of this at the same time. In other contexts – such as doctor and patient or teacher and pupil – some participants have more control over the flow of the conversation and CA researchers can explore how they exert this control.

What does all this mean in practice? CA provides a method for understanding and describing not just the content but also the structure of an interaction. CA is to some extent also a data-driven form of analysis. It is not what the analyst thinks the data 'means' which is important. Instead the analyst looks for the evidence present in each stage of the interaction about how each turn interprets the previous turn. This is what CA researchers call the 'next-turn proof procedure'.

SAQ 9.1

Look at the following transcript of an interaction. What did the first speaker 'really mean'? What did the second speaker 'hear'? How do we know this?

> S1: Do you know who is going to the party?
> S2: Who?
> S1: I don't know!
> S2: Oh, probably Pete. Jane said Phil and some of the lads might too.

SAQ 9.1 might seem a trivial example. But think back to Chapter 8 on qualitative data analysis. In that case we coded data according to our interpretation of its meaning. Here in this CA analysis the evidence from the transcript itself defines the 'meaning' of a turn. This is an important difference in the approach to qualitative data taken by many (but not all) discourse analysts.

We can also see another aspect of CA work in this transcript. CA does not view turns or 'utterances' as 'containers' that 'transfer' meanings or ideas from one person to another. Rather, CA views all turns as objects which the participants use to accomplish particular things in their interaction with each other. Importantly they argue that they represent examples of specific 'methods' people use to do things in talk. This doing might be things like persuading or informing, but there are also methods to 'gain the floor', 'repair' problems in conversations, to maintain the structure and sometimes to explain and account for the relevance of turns or structures in the conversation. In the above case it is clear to S1 that his/her first turn was misinterpreted and they have to do the work of 'repairing' the conversation in their second turn.

Another key concept in CA is that conversations consist of 'adjacency pairs'.

That is, most turns in an interaction require a response. Classic examples would be questions and answers or invitations and responses. We often have to do 'work' in conversations to get from one to the other. For example:

S1:	Can I have a bottle of beer?	[Adjacency pair 1 – Turn 1]
S2:	Are you over 18?	[Adjacency pair 2 – Turn 1]
S1:	No	[Adjacency pair 2 – Turn 2]
S2:	No	[Adjacency pair 1 – Turn 2]

Here the first question cannot be answered until the second question has been answered. This leads on to another concept in CA, that of 'preference'. Not only do most turns expect some form of 'reply' – they demand or make a 'slot' for a next turn – they also tend to imply a preferred type or preferred content to this next turn. This also implies that certain responses might be 'dispreferred'. For example:

A preferred response

S1: This is a wonderful restaurant, isn't it?
S2: Yeah it's just gorgeous.

A dispreferred response

A: Are you coming to the climbing club tonight?
B: Well, I got a lot of things to do before the meeting tomorrow. If I do it w (.) probably won't be too early.

You may have noticed that the dispreferred response is longer and contains an explanation of 'why not'. It also contains a 'pause' (indicated by the (.)) that breaks up a sentence. Yet in the preferred case no explanation of why S2 thought the restaurant was 'gorgeous' is provided. CA researchers argue that providing such an 'account' often accompanies a dispreferred response. CA analyses often look for occasions where repairs or accounts are present, as they indicate 'troublesome' moments in the interaction. These are points where those interacting have to do 'work' – make use of 'methods' – to keep the interaction going.

We now have some basic CA ideas that we can work with such as the 'next-turn proof procedure', adjacency pairs, repair, preference and accounts. We can use these to do a small amount of analysis.

SAQ 9.2

The following is a transcript of an interview between Martin Bashir (a BBC TV journalist) and Princess Diana. In the transcript are a number of features that can be analysed using the CA concepts we have just outlined. In the transcript (.) denotes a pause of less than 1 second, (2) indicates a 2 second pause, etc.

Using the ideas above, have a go at marking up the adjacency pairs, the repairs, accounts and so forth and make some notes on the things you find.

Next write some notes on the differences between the analysis you did here and that which you did in Chapter 8 (see p. 189).

Diana the ambassador

  1 Bashir: what role do you see for yourself in the future?
  2 Diana: I'd like to be an ambassador for this country (.) I'd like to represent
             this country abroad.
  3   (.) .hhh as I have all this media interest let's not just sit in this country
             (.) and be
  4   battered by it let's take them (.) these people (.) out (.) and (.) to
             represent this country
  5   and the good qualities of it abroad (1) when I go abroad (.) we've got
             sixty to ninety (.)
  6   photographers (.) just from this country with me (.) so let's (.) use it in
             a-a productive
  7   way, to help this country.
  8 Bashir: you say you feel that your future is as some form of ambassador
  9 Diana: mmm
 10 Bashir: at whose behest is that?
 11   (2)
 12 Bashir: on what grounds do you feel that you have the right to think of
             yourself as an ambassador?
 13 Diana: I've been in a (.) privileged position for fifteen years (.) and I've got (.)
             tremendous
 14   knowledge (.) about people and how to communicate (.) I've learnt
             that (.) I've got it (.)
 15   and I want to use it (1) and when I look at people in (.) public life (1)
             hhh I'm not a
 16   political animal (.) but (.) I think the biggest disease this world (.)
             suffers from (.) in this
 17   day and age (.) is the disease of people feeling unloved (.) and I know
             that (.) I can give
 18   (.) love for a minute (.) for half an hour for a day for a month but I can
             give (.) I'm very
 19   happy to do that (.) and I want to do that
 20 Bashir: do you think that the British people are happy with you (.) in your role?
 21 Diana: I think the British people (.) need someone (.) in public life to give
             affection (.) to make
 22   them feel important (.) to support them (.) to give them light (.) in their
             dark tunnels (.)
 23   I see it as a possibly unique role (1) and (1) yes I've had difficulties (.)
             erm a-as
 24   everybody (.) has witnessed over the years (.) but let's now use the
             knowledge I've
 25   gathered (.) to help other people in distress

(*Source*: Abell and Stokoe, 2001)

From SAQ 9.2 you will have seen that CA analyses are considerably different from the qualitative analyses that you undertook in Chapter 8. CA is based on a close reading of the data and uses a set of key concepts that form part of a general theory about the manner in which conversations and interactions are structured. There are of course many more aspects to the theory and method of CA than the few concepts presented here. Also, CA is not the only manner in which such data can be analysed. Other approaches that also focus on interaction and small 'd' discourse include: the ethnography of speaking, interactional socio-linguistics, and certain forms of 'critical discourse analysis'.

CA Context and Epistemology

So what about context? Having said that context is important to all discourse analysis work I have not mentioned context in any of the above examples. CA has a very specific take on the role of context. In the same way that it only views the 'meaning' or 'relevance' of a turn in relation to the evidence from the transcript of the ways it was interpreted in the interaction, it also views context this way. So a conversation might take place between two people in a crowd at a football match. The conversation might be about ballet! If there were no evidence in the data of the fact that the conversation was conducted in a football crowd then CA researchers would argue that this aspect of the context was not relevant to the conversation. On the other hand if there is evidence in the transcript that the conversation was affected by the context they would take this into account: for example if one of the speakers sought to change the topic on the grounds that they viewed it as inappropriate for the context.

Where does CA fit into the types of epistemological position we have been discussing throughout this book? One might argue that there are positivist elements to CA as it insists on the use of evidence from the data. This 'empiricism' is only part of the method. Importantly, CA uses a set of theoretical constructs and theoretically defined methods in order to do the analysis. These include such things as the 'next-turn proof procedure' and the ideas of repair and accounting. CA is clearly then a method that links, in an almost Kantian manner, empirical and theoretical elements. It can be viewed as an idealist method. CA also has strong theoretical links, via ethnomethodology, to phenomenology.

Discourse as Minds, Self and Sense Making

This type of discourse work concerns the ways in which people understand both the world around them and themselves through language use, interaction and language practices. Much of this research has a psychological basis or focus and is sometimes referred to as 'discursive psychology'. There is great variety in this type of work and we will explore one example in detail. This type of research tries to engage with both the small 'd' and big 'D' models of 'discourse'. It tends to focus on the manner in which we generate our conceptions of ourselves, the world around us and systems of knowledge through our day-to-day interactions with each other and various types of 'text'. Let us therefore look at a discussion of this kind of work. The following SAQs provide a structured reading and discussion of an example of 'discursive psychology'.

SAQ 9.3

Turn to Reading P, 'Analyzing discourse (1)'. As you read this extract make notes on the following questions. You may find that the answers to the questions differ slightly from the points made in this section so far – you may want to note these differences.

1   What, according to Potter and Wetherell, are the four types of work that have been labelled discourse analysis?
2   On what three key features do Potter and Wetherell focus?
3   What two main emphases do Potter and Wetherell note are 'largely comp-lementary to each other'?

We can draw a number of conclusions from SAQ 9.3. First, Potter and Wetherell note that discourse analysis, as a research method, focuses upon acts of communication in context. Second, there is a constant awareness of the importance of language and communication as social activities. Language and communication therefore have forms and structures that need to be explored and described. Third, discourse analysis is directly concerned with how people use social and communicative resources in order to generate discourses and to act socially.

What, then, is a discourse for Potter and Wetherell? Potter and Wetherell note that they were mostly concerned with those types of discourse analysis that focus on discourse as a system of knowledge, or as broadly outlined in the works of Foucault. This contrasts with the types of discourse analysis that are concerned with the organisation of conversations (such as CA) and with the psychological processing, understanding and recall of larger texts – another type of 'discursive psychology'. If Potter and Wetherell view their work as differing from CA we need to consider the ways in which it differs from other forms of qualitative research and data analysis. SAQ 9.4 asks you to consider the data used in the Potter and Wetherell study.

SAQ 9.4

Turn to Reading Q, 'Analyzing discourse (2)', a further extract from Potter and Wetherell. As you read this extract answer the following questions:

1   What types of data source did they use?
2   What were the aims of the study?
3   Which of the studies you looked at in Part III had similar aims and collected similar types of data?

If, then, *texts* are the objects of study, what makes discourse analysis different from the types of qualitative data analysis described in Chapter 8? We can give a number of answers to this question. First, as with the CA example, there is a clear focus on texts in context. Second, the analysis is focused upon language, communication and knowledge. Models and theories of linguistic and communicative practices are at the foreground of the analysis. In the case of CA this is a set of theories and models (derived from analyses of interactions) that are deployed in the analysis of new data. In the case of 'discursive psychology' the analyses start with the use of CA-type methods but additional theories and models of the relationship between language practices, interactional structures and psychological states and/or processes are also brought to bear. As we noted about the CA example, it is the role given to ideas and theories about language use that distinguishes discourse analysis from more general qualitative data analysis. The next question to ask is: how does one go about a 'discursive psychological analysis'?

SAQ 9.5

Turn to Reading R, 'Analyzing discourse (3)', which continues the Potter and Wetherell article. As you read this extract make notes on the following questions:

1 What do Potter and Wetherell see as being the five main types of analytical consideration in their work?
2 Are there any parallels with Okely's description of her methods of analysis?
3 Are there any parallels with the grounded theory approach to analysis?

From SAQ 9.5 it is clear that discourse analysis as conducted by Potter and Wetherell has some similarities to qualitative data analysis. One way in which discourse analysis differs greatly from the types of qualitative data analysis you met in Chapters 6 to 8, however, is in its research focus. If we look at the Okely analysis from the perspective of discourse analysis, the research focus could be very different. With the two types of discourse analysis we have mentioned, a number of possible studies of the Gypsy community could have been conducted, including analyses of: Gypsy conversations; Gypsy discourse about Gorgios; Gorgio discourse about Gypsies; government discourse about Gypsies; representations of Gypsies in mass media; social anthropological discourse on Gypsies.

In fact, some of these analyses were part of Okely's work, but they were not central and her analyses were not informed directly by the models of language, communication, knowledge and power which lie behind discourse analysis. The last of the alternative analyses above demonstrates the 'reflexivity' of discourse analysis approaches. All systems of knowledge and communication can be explored by discourse analysis, even the discourses of social sciences and science such as social anthropology.

SAQ 9.6

Look over Reading O, ' "Becoming a mother" ', again and try to make a list of the types of discourse analysis studies that could have been done using the data collected in this study.

'Discursive Psychology' Context and Epistemology

One of the key aspects of discursive psychology is its critique of standard – positivist – approaches to psychology. In particular discursive psychologists raise questions about the 'generalisability' of many psychological results. They also seriously question the way in which many aspects of human psychology are treated as 'internal' states and not as things that come into being through our interaction with the world and with each other. Discursive psychologists see this interaction as being heavily influenced by our ways of talking about the world and each other. The context in which interactions take place is therefore key to any analysis. Rather than assume that data collected in one context can be generalised beyond the context, discursive psychological analyses focus on the ways in which people make sense of the interaction, of themselves or their own mental states in that context. They explore how the ways in which we come to talk about and account for our own mental states (e.g. being worried, having preferences) actually provide the resources for managing and experiencing the world and our own mental states! Discursive psychology is therefore very often described as a 'social constructivist' approach to social science. As such it may also be described as relativist, though there is argument around this point within discursive psychology.

Discourse as Culture and Social Relations

When we refer to discourse as 'culture and social relations' we are in the main referring to work that focuses on big 'D' discourse. That is, work that seeks to analyse the ways in which language practices and texts form part of systems of knowledge; in particular the ways in which such big 'D' discourses form the basis of ideological positions and are linked to, formed by and support systems of power in societies. This type of work has more recently gained the name 'Critical Discourse Analysis' (CDA) and is linked to two main approaches, those based in 'critical linguistics' and those based in 'cultural studies', though there is considerable overlap. CDA is rooted in a range of theoretical traditions. These include:

- philosophy – such as ideas from Wittgenstein;
- sociology – including the works of Gramsci, Althusser, the Frankfurt School, and Foucault;
- linguistics – such as the work of Halliday.

This looks like, and is, a very 'heavy' list of theories and writings! In fact many CDA books provide a good introduction to the key ideas they are going to take from these traditions. Needless to say there is not space here to discuss the specific ways in which the various CDA theorists and analysts combine these ideas. We can, though, consider one or two key aspects and look at a specific example of such an analysis.

CDA tends in the main to focus on 'material' texts rather than interactions – though it is applied to data from interactions. Very often it focuses on written materials, TV programmes, films, books, historical and contemporary documents. The analysis seeks to highlight the ways in which specific representations of people, events or concepts within the texts are linked to systems of power and to the systems of knowledge that support them. CDA is particularly interested in the ways in which the texts are at the same time products of these systems, contain language forms and practices defined by these systems, and also by existing re-create and support the system. One way in which this is done is through the construction of specific interpretations and specific understandings of concepts. SAQ 9.7 looks at linguistically informed CDA examination of a TV programme. In particular it looks at the ways in which the concept of 'poverty' is constructed in and used in the programme.

SAQ 9.7

Turn to Reading S, 'From the street to the screen: *Breadline Britain* and the semiotics of poverty', by Ulrike Meinhof, an extract from a book in which five social researchers working in the area of critical socio-linguistics explore representations of poverty in various media. These representations include newspaper coverage, TV documentaries and the systems of representation expressed by readers and viewers of media coverage. This extract considers a TV documentary series based on a social science survey that developed a 'relative' measure of poverty. Not only does the extract explore the construction of the TV documentary, but it also considers a critical review of the series in another TV programme. As you read, make notes on the following questions. (Points made in the endnotes to this reading will help you to answer these questions.)

1 How does Meinhof describe her methodological position?
2 How does Meinhof see this as differing from a semiotic and a post-modern position?

3   What is the 'thesis' which Meinhof claims forms the basis for the narrative in the *Breadline Britain* documentary? What documentary technique is used to develop this narrative?

4   How does Meinhof describe the role of the people presented?

5   What are the three semiotic layers that Meinhof sees within the text of *Breadline Britain*?

6   What does Meinhof see as the problems with the underlying assumptions of *The Media Show*'s critique of *Breadline Britain*?

7   What does Meinhof see as being the three key aspects of the *Breadline Britain* series that made it necessary to assess the series in relation to the wider social and political discourses of the time, rather than just those of documentary film making?

8   What does Meinhof claim her social-semiotic analysis of the *Breadline Britain* documentary involved? Do you think that her analytical process was clear?

SAQ 9.7 highlights the extent to which the version of CDA in Reading S is reliant upon ideas from linguistics. These ideas are themselves then connected to ideas about knowledge, power, communication and the social activities they support. As with CA and 'discursive psychology', it is the use of a set of theoretical ideas about the nature of texts or interactions, in this case from linguistics, that underpins the analysis.

Discourse analysis marks a substantial shift away from the underlying model of social science that was derived from positivism. Positivism argued that social research methods should be modelled on the practices and ideas of natural science and its approach to its objects of study. Discourse analysis acknowledges and embraces the very different objects of study to be found in social science, namely meaning-creating and meaning-using human beings. To do this discourse analysis draws heavily upon the insights gained from the discipline of linguistics, which is itself founded upon positivist assumptions that language as a system could be (and is) studied using the same methods as natural science.

The relationships between research methods, their philosophical and social theoretical underpinnings and the practical realities of their actual use are complicated and, on the surface, contradictory. This makes selecting and applying research methods a task that should not be taken lightly. In Part IV we briefly address how you might go about selecting methods that are appropriate to the research question you have in mind.

Conclusion

It is not possible, and perhaps even against the philosophical positions of discourse analysts, to summarise their work into a number of individual points but we can make a few key observations:

- There are two main areas of focus in discourse research – big 'D' discourses (ideologies and systems of thought) and small 'd' discourses (actual texts and interactions).

- Many discourse researchers are concerned with the connections between these two areas.
- The analysis of small 'd' discourses tends to examine the structures and forms of texts and interactions and the systems or rules that underlie their production.
- The analysis of big 'D' discourses tends to examine the ways in which social systems of knowledge and power are created and maintained though texts and interactions.
- We can broadly argue that some approaches focus on the fine detail of small 'd' discourses – such as CA – others focus on the big 'D' issues of ideology and power – such as CDA – whereas others seek to find links between the two.
- Overall though most forms of discourse analysis pay some attention to both small 'd' and big 'D' issues.
- Unlike grounded theory, discourse analyses are directly informed by theoretical models of the nature of texts, interactions, ideologies, systems of power, cultural practice, etc. – whatever is their main focus. Some forms of discourse analysis rely upon the theories to provide explanation – especially CDA. Others appeal more to the data itself – for example CA.

What can we conclude from this discussion? You may be feeling that discourse analysis looks 'very hard' – and you would be right if by this you mean that it is not a straightforward thing to simply 'do' discourse-based research! You may also have felt this about the methods in Chapter 8, such as grounded theorising. Very often people assume that 'qualitative' methods are 'simpler' than quantitative ones as they don't require statistics! As with the examples of statistical tests, the qualitative methods presented here are intended to give you a flavour and a basic understanding of the methods used in actual research. In fact I myself feel that qualitative and discourse research can be much harder work, as it requires you to engage with a lot of complex ideas and data. Having said this, such methods provide important results that cannot be achieved using quantitative approaches. We have come a long way from the 'positivist' model of social research presented in Chapter 2, but in all our examples we have continued to engage with 'empirical data' – materials gathered from actual social practices and contexts.

Further Reading

Fairclough, N. (2001) *Language and Power*. London: Longman.

Jaworski, A. and Coupland, N. (eds) (1999) *The Discourse Reader*. London: Routledge.

Potter, J. and Wetherell, M. (1987) *Discourse and Social Psychology: Beyond Attitudes and Behaviour*. London: Sage.

Sacks, H. (1992) *Lectures on Conversation*, ed. G. Jefferson; Introduction by E. Schlegloff Oxford: Blackwell.

Schiffrin, D., Tannen, D. and Hamilton, H.E. (eds) (2001) *Handbook of Discourse Analysis*. Oxford: Blackwell.

Van Dijk, T.A. (1997), *Discourse as Structure and Process*. London: Sage.

Wetherell, M., Taylor, S. and Yates, S.J. (eds) (2001a) *Discourse Theory and Practice: A Reader.* London: Sage in association with the Open University.
Wetherell, M., Taylor, S. and Yates, S.J. (eds) (2001b) *Discourse as Data: A Guide to Analysis.* London: Sage in association with the Open University.

Reading P: Analyzing Discourse (1)

Jonathan Potter and Margaret Wetherell

The label 'discourse analysis' has been applied in very different ways in the social sciences, and before attempting to explicate discourse analysis as a method it is important to be clear what we mean by it. There are at least four types of work that have commonly been described in this way. The first is influenced by speech act theory and directed at a systematic account of the organization of conversational exchange in settings such as classrooms (e.g. Coulthard and Montgomery 1981). The second is much more psychologically orientated, focusing on so-called discourse processes; for example, the effect of discourse structure on recall and understanding (e.g. van Dijk and Kintch 1983). These two kinds of work are very different from the line of work we will discuss in this chapter, which has much closer links with strands three and four.

The third type of discourse analysis developed within the sociology of scientific knowledge, partly as a response to methodological difficulties with other ways of studying science (e.g. Gilbert and Mulkay 1984). It was concerned less with the traditional sociological question of how 'social factors' influence acts such as theory choice than with exploring how scientists construct their talk and texts to display their acts as rational and warrantable in any particular setting (Mulkay *et al.* 1983). One of the conclusions of this work was that major claims of sociologists and philosophers of science may be simply retellings of scientists' own folk stories.

The fourth and final approach comes from a very different tradition of continental social philosophy and cultural analysis. While most proponents worked with the titles of semiology or post-structuralism, Foucault (1971) is notable for characterizing his 'archeology' of madness and medicine as discourse analysis. Appropriations of this work in psychology, sociology and cultural studies (e.g. Coward 1984, Henriques *et al.* 1984) have tried to show how institutions, practices and even the individual human subject itself can be understood as produced through the workings of a set of discourses. For example, Hollway (1989) has attempted to show how the psychological significance of a decision about avoiding contraception in intercourse is constructed out of a limited number of competing discourses: a male sexual drive discourse; a have and hold traditional Christian discourse; a permissive discourse developed from social changes in the 1960s; and a more recent feminist discourse.

When we use the term discourse analysis in this chapter we are signalling connections to just the latter two of these kinds of work. However, as will become clear, we are also attempting selectively to integrate some of these insights with ideas from conversation analysis (e.g. Atkinson and Heritage 1984) and rhetoric (e.g. Billig 1987). A chapter specifically on the topic of analysis is not the place for a developed survey of the theoretical ins and outs of these claims. Nevertheless, as the analytic aims are so closely tied to the general theoretical concerns in discourse analysis, it is important to give at least a thumb-nail sketch of what we see as the distinguishing features of our particular variant of discourse analysis (for more detail see Edwards and Potter 1992, Potter and Wetherell 1987, Potter *et al.* 1990, Wetherell and Potter 1992).

Three features of discourse analysis are particularly pertinent for its research practice. First, it is concerned with talk and texts as social practices; and as such it pays close attention to features which would traditionally be classed as linguistic *content* – meanings and topics – as well as attending to features of linguistic *form* such as grammar and cohesion. Indeed, once we adopt a discourse analytic approach, the distinction between content and form becomes problematic; content is seen to develop out of formal features of discourse and vice versa. Put more generally, the discourse analyst is after the answers to social or sociological questions rather than to linguistic ones.

Second, discourse analysis has a triple concern with action, construction and variability (Potter and Wetherell 1987). People perform actions of different kinds through their talk and their writing, and they accomplish the nature of these actions partly through constructing their discourse out of a range of styles, linguistic resources and rhetorical devices. One of the principal aims of discourse studies is to reveal the operation of these constructive processes. Once discourse is conceptualized in this way it becomes clear that there will be significant variation in, for example, descriptions of a phenomenon, as participants perform different kinds of actions. And, as we will show below, these variations can provide an important lever for discourse analytic work.

A third feature of discourse analysis is its concern with the rhetorical or argumentative organization of talk and texts. Rhetorical analysis has been particularly helpful in highlighting the way discursive versions are designed to counter real or potential alternatives (Billig 1991). Put another way, it takes the focus of analysis away from questions of how a version relates to some putative reality and asks instead how this version is designed successfully to compete with an alternative.

Within the style of discourse analytic work we are advocating it is possible to distinguish two broad emphases which are largely complementary to one another. On the one hand, studies have been concerned with the general resources that are used to construct discourse and enable the performance of particular actions. This style of work is most akin to the Foucauldian analysis in that it attempts to map out broad systems or 'interpretative repertoires' which are used to sustain different social practices (Potter *et al.* 1990). For example, studies of scientific discourse have shown the way it is constructed out of the combination of an 'empiricist' and a 'contingent' repertoire, and that *both* are necessary for performing the interpretative tasks that constitute scientific practice (Gilbert and Mulkay 1984, Mulkay 1985, Potter 1984). On the other hand, studies have concentrated more on the detailed procedures through which versions are constructed and made to appear factual. This style of work is closer to the concerns of conversation analysts with the interactional use of members' devices (Pomerantz 1986) and to rhetoricians' concern with the 'witcraft' (Billig 1987) through which an argument is made persuasive.

To some extent this is an artificial distinction, and we would not want to suggest that it can be sustained as much more than a convenient heuristic. Nevertheless, it usefully marks out some shades of emphasis in analysis. In this chapter, we will be concentrating on work which represents the latter tendency and will not be concerning ourselves with the identification and analysis of interpretative repertoires, which have been dealt with in detail elsewhere (Gilbert and Mulkay 1984, Potter and Mulkay 1985, Potter and Wetherell 1987, Wetherell and Potter 1988,

1992). The particular research project that we will use to illustrate our analytic practice is concerned with the way factual versions are produced in a television current affairs programme and, in particular, the ways quantification is used in the manufacture of such versions. We will try to describe how we conducted some of this research, our motivation, and the stages in analysis. Throughout we will focus on the method of analysis and thus will have as a secondary goal the explication of our research findings and conclusions. We refer readers who are interested in our conclusions about quantification in current affairs documentaries to the paper describing this work (Potter *et al.* 1991).

References

Atkinson, J.M. and Heritage, J. (eds) (1984) *Structures of Social Action: Studies in Conversation Analysis.* Cambridge: Cambridge University Press.

Billig, M. (1987) *Arguing and Thinking: a Rhetorical Approach to Social Psychology.* Cambridge: Cambridge University Press.

Billig, M. (1991) *Ideologies and Beliefs.* London: Sage.

Coulthard, M. and Montgomery, M. (eds) (1981) *Studies in Discourse Analysis.* London: Routledge and Kegan Paul.

Coward, R. (1984) *Female Desire.* London: Paladin.

Edwards, D. and Potter, J. (1992) *Discursive Psychology.* London: Sage.

Foucault, M. (1971) 'Orders of discourse', *Social Science Information* 10: 7–30.

Gilbert, G.N. and Mulkay, M. (1984) *Opening Pandora's Box: a Sociological Analysis of Scientists' Discourse.* Cambridge: Cambridge University Press.

Henriques, J., Holloway, W., Irwin, C., Couze, V. and Walkerdine, V. (1984) *Changing the Subject: Psychology, Social Regulation and Subjectivity.* London: Methuen.

Hollway, W. (1989) *Subjectivity and Method in Psychology: Gender, Meaning and Science.* London: Sage.

Mulkay, M. (1985) *The Word and the World: Explorations in the Form of Sociological Analysis.* London: Allen and Unwin.

Mulkay, M., Potter, J. and Yearley, S. (1983) 'Why an analysis of scientists' discourse is needed', in K. Knorr-Cetina and M. Mulkay (eds) *Science Observed: Perspectives in the Social Study of Science.* London: Sage.

Pomerantz, A.M. (1986) 'Extreme case formulations: a new way of legitimating claims', *Human Studies* 9: 219–30.

Potter, J. (1984) 'Testability, flexibility: Kuhnian values in psychologists' discourse concerning theory choice', *Philosophy of the Social Sciences* 14: 303–30.

Potter, J. and Mulkay, M. (1985) 'Scientists' interview talk: interviews as a technique for revealing participants' interpretative practices', in M. Brenner, J. Brown and D. Canter (eds) *The Research Interview: Uses and Approaches.* London: Academic Press.

Potter, J. and Wetherell, M. (1987) *Discourse and Social Psychology: Beyond Attitudes and Behaviour.* London: Sage.

Potter, J. and Wetherell, M. (1988) 'Accomplishing attitudes: fact and evaluation in racist discourse', *Text* 8: 51–68.

Potter, J., Wetherell, M. and Chitty, A. (1991) 'Quantification rhetoric: cancer on television', *Discourse and Society* 2: 333–65.

Potter, J., Wetherell, M., Gill, R. and Edwards, D. (1990) 'Discourse: noun, verb or social practice?' *Philosophical Psychology* 3: 207–17.

van Dijk, T.A. and Kintch, W. (1983) *Strategies of Discourse Comprehension.* London: Academic Press.

Wetherell, M. and Potter, J. (1988) 'Discourse analysis and the identification of interpretative repertoires', in C. Antaki (ed.) *Analysing Lay Explanation: a Case Book.* London: Sage.

Wetherell, M. and Potter, J. (1992) *Mapping the Language of Racism: Discourse and the Legitimation of Exploitation.* Hemel Hempstead: Harvester/Wheatsheaf.

Source: Potter and Wetherell, 1994: 47–9

Reading Q: Analyzing Discourse (2)

Jonathan Potter and Margaret Wetherell

A Qualitative Analysis of Quantification

The research project we will draw on was an intensive case study focused on the making and reception of a television current affairs programme about the effectiveness of cancer charities. The programme, called *Cancer: Your Money or Your Life*, was transmitted in 1988 as part of Channel 4's 'flagship' *Dispatches* series. The programme was described as an exposé of the way donations to cancer charities have been directed into basic research projects which have only the most tenuous links with cancer; it also made the argument that cancer charities were using hard-hitting advertising to scare people into donating money in the face of very little evidence that charity-funded cancer research has made any difference to the recovery rates for the major cancers.

One of the features of the project was that we were able to collect a number of different types of material related to the programme. Obviously we had a video of the programme itself. We also collaborated with one of the team of programme-makers, who acted as a participant observer during the entire period of its making. This enabled us to collect a range of relevant discursive materials: for example, various drafts of the script, shooting schedules and, most important, recordings of the sessions in which certain sections of the programme were edited together. We also had access to the programme-makers' interviews with the various parties who were shown on the programme (cancer scientists, charity heads, advertisers, alternative or holistic therapists); we later interviewed some of these people ourselves and recorded their reactions to the film and the way their own interviews had been edited. Finally, we interviewed some people who had worked on the programme and for the production company. The analytic value of being able to collect this range of different types of material will become clear below.

Our general interest was in current affairs television as an institutionalized arena for the construction of factual accounts, comparable to science, television news, court-rooms and various kinds of less formal everyday talk. As such our study is part of a broader concern with the way factuality can be understood as a situated product of a range of social practices, some general and some specific (Edwards and Potter 1992, Potter and Edwards 1990). In our original grant proposal to the UK Economic and Social Research Council we suggested that our study might try to accomplish for a television film what Latour and Woolgar (1986) had done for peptide research in a biochemistry laboratory, that is, to look at the procedures through which some part of reality is made to seem stable, neutral and objectively there.

This general focus and set of aims encouraged the more specific interest in the practices of quantification in television documentaries. Quantification in one form or another is one of the most important devices used in the manufacture of authoritative factual versions. Numerical accounts are often contrasted explicitly with 'vaguer', 'less precise', 'more subjective', qualitative versions of events. But should quantitative accounts be given this status? We wanted to question and explore the ideal or received image of quantification and examine how numbers are actually used in practice. This conceptualization – the questioning of an ideal or taken-for-granted story – is often very helpful in focusing one's analysis. It generates a set of questions and issues for interrogating the analytic materials. Our interest in quantification also had a *reflexive* aim. Quantification is at least as important in social scientific research as television documentaries; and this is particularly true of the research by psychologists and those other social scientists who have modelled their activities closely on images of the natural sciences. We hoped our investigations would provide a basis for intervention in methodological disputes within social science itself.

There is a relatively small amount of analytic work on this topic, although there are some ground-breaking studies of economics (Ashmore *et al.* 1989, McCloskey 1985), market trading (Clark and Pinch 1988) and 'ethnostatistics' more generally (Gephart 1988). The lack of attention to quantification in the existing literature is a double-edged sword, however. On the one hand, it suggests that a study of quantification in media settings has a guaranteed originality. On the other, the specific studies which can provide analytic start-points or be used as contrast cases are not available. As with any form of analysis or investigation, it is helpful in discourse analysis to be able to fend off and react to well-established positions based on other kinds of theoretical perspectives.

Our final motivation for selecting quantification as a topic concerned the nature of the specific materials we collected, and this was probably the overriding determinant of our interest. A quantified argument was central to what was widely seen as one of the most crucial and controversial sequences in the film we wished to study. In this sequence, cancer charity claims about their significant success in curing cancer are contrasted with the 'fact' that there has been remarkably little progress, given the huge financial outlay. This argument was picked out for attack by representatives of the cancer charities we interviewed, and it also contrasts with versions of cancer success offered in the charities' interviews with the film-makers and in their promotional materials. Importantly, we also had a complete record of the editing sessions in which this sequence was put together. The presence of a number of radically competing versions suggested that this would be a good start-point: comparison of differences between versions would be a central analytic heuristic.

We should note that, of course, all these motivations are to a greater or lesser extend *post hoc* reconstructions. We could tell the story of our research in other ways and refer, for example, to a host of contingent, subjective factors, such as parts of the film we had found interesting, our recent discussions with the author of one of the major studies of quantification (Ashmore), and the feeling that there was 'something there' that would make a good narrative. It is conventional to talk about motivations in methods chapters, but it would be counter to our practice as discourse analysts not to be self-conscious about our own methods of constructing a factual account (Ashmore 1989).

References

Ashmore, M. (1989) *The Reflexive Thesis: Wrighting Sociology of Scientific Knowledge*. Chicago: University of Chicago Press.

Ashmore, M., Mulkay, M. and Pinch, T. (1989) *Health and Efficiency: a Sociological Study of Health Economics*. Milton Keynes: Open University Press.

Clark, C. and Pinch, T. (1988) 'Micro-sociology and micro-economics: selling by social control', in N. Fielding (ed.) *Actions and Structure*. London: Sage.

Edwards, D. and Potter, J. (1992) *Discursive Psychology*. London: Sage.

Gephart, R.P. (1988) *Ethnostatistics: Qualitative Foundations for Quantitative Research*. London: Sage.

Latour, B. and Woolgar, S. (1986) *Laboratory Life: the Social Construction of Scientific Facts*, 2nd edn. Princeton, NJ: Princeton University Press.

McCloskey, D. (1985) *The Rhetoric of Economics*. Brighton: Wheatsheaf.

Potter, J. and Edwards, D. (1990) 'Nigel Lawson's tent: discourse analysis, attribution theory and the social psychology of fact', *European Journal of Social Psychology* 20: 405–24.

Source: Potter and Wetherell, 1994: 49–50

Reading R: Analyzing Discourse (3)

Jonathan Potter and Margaret Wetherell

The Facts of Cancer Death

The sequence reproduced in Extract One and the table that went with it (. . .), were thus our raw materials. We had the whole film in transcribed form as well as on video, so our initial approach was both to watch the sequence and pore over its transcript. At the same time, we tried to map the themes raised in the sequence through the rest of our materials. We could have done this quite adequately by reading all of our transcribed materials and selecting out what was relevant. To do this carefully, however, would have been a very time-consuming and laborious task – it is hard to keep the subtle analytic issues to the forefront of one's mind for hour after hour in this way. To circumvent this we took advantage of the fact that all our materials were transcribed on to a personal computer. We made a list of about a dozen key words and phrases that related to the sequence – percentage, cure rates, death rates, 1 per cent, etc. – and ran through each of the interview and interaction files looking for them with the standard word-processor (which happened to be 'Microsoft Word').

Whenever we got a 'hit' we would read the surrounding text to see if it had relevance to our target sequence. When it did we would copy it across to an already opened coding file (using the windowing facilities of the word-processor), noting the transcript page numbers at the same time. If we were not sure if the sequence was relevant we copied it anyway, for, unlike the sorts of coding that take place in traditional content analysis, the coding is not the analysis itself but a preliminary to make the task of analysis manageable. This activity resulted in a coding file of fifty-eight double-spaced pages.

Our next step was to go back to the original tapes and check the transcript for all the sections on the coding file. This not only improved the transcript but also tuned us into the sorts of voice features and sense of dynamic interaction that are not easy to render into transcript. Furthermore, by noting the appropriate sections of tape we could move between transcript and tape easily in the course of analysis to check our interpretations against the sound rather than just the words on paper. This was particularly important for the film sequence, of course, where the visuals (crucially the table of annual cancer incidence) were delicately meshed with the spoken words.

Finally, we went back to the film-makers' own interview with the charity head, which forms part of the sequence, and copied the surrounding text. This allowed us to consider some of the constructive work that went into putting the target sequence together and to compare the version in the film with sections of the talk that were not transmitted. So at the point at which we started on 'analysis proper' (and again this is a clarifying fiction rather than a fully accurate chronology) we had a manageable archive of materials: the target sequence, a section of film-makers' transcript, five sequences from our own interviews and a sequence from recording made during editing that ran to over forty pages. We will start with the target sequence and then consider some of the ways in which we went about analyzing it.

The sequence comes about half-way through the film, following interviews with scientists who question the relation of their charity-funded work to cancer treatment success.

Extract One

COMMENTARY: The message from these scientists is clear – exactly like the public – they hope their basic research will lead to cures in the future – although at the moment they can't say how this will happen. In the meantime their aim is to increase scientific knowledge on a broad front and they're certainly achieving this. But do their results justify them getting so much of the money that has been given to help fight cancer? When faced with this challenge the first thing the charities point to are the small number of cancers which are now effectively curable.

[on screen: DR NIGEL KEMP, Cancer Research Campaign]

> KEMP: The outlook for individuals suffering from a number of types of cancer has been totally revolutionized. I mean for example – children suffering from acute leukaemia – in old days if they lived six months they were lucky – now more than half the children with leukaemia are cured. And the same applies to a number of other cancers – Hodgkin's Disease in young people, testicular tumours in young men, and we all know about Bob Champion's success.

> *Scrolling table starts at this point.*
> COMMENTARY: But those three curable types are amongst the rarest cancers – they represent around 1 per cent of a quarter of a million cases of cancers diagnosed each year. Most deaths are caused by a small number of very common cancers.
> KEMP: We are well aware of the fact that erm once people develop lung cancer or stomach cancer or cancer of the bowel sometimes – the outlook is very bad and aaa obviously one is frustrated by the sss relatively slow rate of progress on the one hand but equally I think there are a lot of real opportunities and positive signs that advances can be made – even in the more intractable cancers.

As indicated, the spoken words are accompanied by the scrolling table labelled 'Annual incidence of cancer' (see Figure 1); the film-makers referred to this as a 'roller'. The table starts scrolling across the screen while Dr Kemp is first speaking and is complete at the words 'the outlook is very bad'.

One of the difficulties in writing about the process of discourse analysis is that the very category 'analysis' comes from a discourse developed for quantitative, positivist methodologies such as experiments and surveys. Analysis in those settings consists in a distinct set of procedures: aggregating scores, categorizing instances, performing various sorts of statistical analysis and so on. It is sometimes tempting to think that in discourse work there is some analogous set of codified procedures that can be put into effect and which will lead to another set of entities known as 'the results'. To see things in this way would be very misleading, although, given the authority which accrues to these procedures, it is tempting to try. We are aware that this chapter is peppered with disclaimers about what we are *not* doing; this is because, to some extent, we are writing *against* prevalent expectation about analysis (cf. Billig 1988).

	ANNUAL INCIDENCE OF CANCER
PLACENTA	20
CHILDHOOD LEUKAEMIA	350 ←
EYE	400
SMALL INTESTINE	400
PLEURA	500
BONE	550
MOUTH	900
CONNECTIVE TISSUE	900
THYROID	950
TESTIS	1,000 ←
PHARYNX	1,000
LIVER	1,200
GALL BLADDER	1,300
HODGKIN'S DISEASE	1,400 ←
LARYNX	2,000
MYELOMA	2,300
MELANOMA	2,600
BRAIN	3,200
KIDNEY	3,500
UTERUS	3,700
CERVIX	4,400
LEUKAEMIA	4,400
HODGKIN'S LYMPHOMA	4,600
OESOPHAGUS	4,800
OVARY	5,100
PANCREAS	6,400
PROSTATE	10,400
BLADDER	10,500
RECTUM	10,600
STOMACH	13,100
COLON	16,800
BREAST	24,600
SKIN	25,000
LUNG	41,400
TOTAL	243,000

Lines marked by arrows appeared in yellow (in contrast to white) on screen to mark 'curable' cancers. The figures are said in the commentary to denote cases of cancer diagnosed in a single year.

Figure 1 *Scrolling table of cancer incidence*

Another point of departure from the way analysis is understood in more traditional studies concerns the procedures through which claims about the data and the research conclusions are justified. In much traditional work, to be seen to carry out the procedure of analysis correctly and comprehensively is itself part of the justification of results. Thus the impression of the solidity of a finding is reinforced through the operationalization of the variables, the appropriate stratification of the sampling, the appropriateness of the statistical analysis and so on. In discourse analysis, in contrast, the analytic procedure is largely separate from the warranting of claims. How you arrive at some view about what is going on in a piece of text may be quite different from how you justify that interpretation.

Much of the work of discourse analysis is a craft skill, something like bike riding or chicken sexing, which is not easy to render or describe in an explicit or codified manner. Indeed, as the analyst becomes more practised it becomes harder and harder to identify explicit procedures that could be called analysis. Nevertheless, there are a number of considerations that recur in the process of analysis. We have picked out five types of analytic consideration, from a potentially longer list, to highlight here. They can be summarized as:

1   using variation as a lever;
2   reading the detail;
3   looking for rhetorical organization;
4   looking for accountability;
5   cross-referring discourse studies.

We will take them in turn, trying to illustrate how they operate in the analysis of quantification in Extract One. Before we do this we should note that they are not all of the same status. Some, such as looking for accountability, refer to features of texts that are highlighted as important by discourse theorizing (Edwards and Potter 1992, Heritage 1984); others, such as reading the detail, refer more to craft skills or analytic frames of mind. Nor are they distinct from one another; they are often overlapping concerns, and as the analyst becomes more skilled their separation becomes less and less clear-cut.

Using Variation as a Lever

We have already noted the idea that discourse is constructed in the service of particular activities which lead to variation, and that variation can, in turn, be used to help identify features of construction. This is probably the single most important analytic principle in doing discourse analysis. Attention to variation works on a range of different levels and senses. One thing it does is to focus the analyst's attention on differences within a particular text: variations within the talk of a single speaker on a single occasion (e.g. Potter and Wetherell 1988), or within a single document (e.g. Yearley 1981). For example, if we consider just the numerical formulations in the commentary sections in Extract One we read the following description of the amount of cancers that are curable: '1 per cent of a quarter of a million'. The variation here is minimal. There is not a difference between versions in a single text but merely a change in the type of quantification used in a single description: it mixes a relational description (the percentage) with an absolute quantity (x many cases). For discourse analysts, even variation as minimal as this can be used to explore questions of how the discourse is orientated to action, how it is doing different work in the text. Why does the commentary move between different kinds of quantity terms in constructing this version?

Now in this study, elucidating the sorts of activities that were going on was not the main goal. Indeed, one of the features of these materials is that, in general, activities are relatively clear-cut: cancer charity representatives are concerned to show that their work is valuable, while the film is explicitly criticizing the worth of the charity-funded work. Thus, while not taking for granted that any *specific* stretch of discourse can be characterized in this way, these different sorts of orientations provide a helpful frame for interpreting the detail. So, if we assume that the film-makers' work is here to show the lack of success of the charities, we can read the variations in numerical formulations as contributing to a description which accomplishes 'lack of success'. Following this line of thinking, we suggested that the *relational quantity* ('around 1 per cent') was used because it has an almost definitive smallness to it. It is as small a non-zero percentage as you can get without using fractions or decimals, while the *absolute quantity* ('a quarter of a million') was used because it evokes largeness; it is 'millions talk'. The *combination* of the two provides a contrast which is used as a document of failure.

We can note two things about this conclusion. First, our analytic claim concerning the numerical presentation is not a result of any mechanical procedure; it is an interpretation backed up by reference to the materials which is open to dispute by another analyst on the basis of these or other materials. Identifying this variation is not the same as making a viable interpretation of it. Second, as well as paying attention to variation in the text the analyst needs to be alive to the question of difference: why is the text this way and not that way? Why do these words or phrases appear rather than others? So we are not only comparing actual variation but also potential variation. For example, part of seeing the effectiveness of the description that appears is a result of comparing it to potential alternatives such as 'two thousand eight hundred out of two hundred and forty three thousand'. The general point is to sustain the idea that the discourse is a contingent, manufactured entity; there is nothing natural or absolute about its particular form.

In practice, variation between texts is often much more striking than variation within texts, although variations within a single text or a single speaker's talk are often more analytically revealing. Not surprisingly, people often attend to the consistency of their discourse more carefully when it is delivered in a single passage of talk or writing, while different speakers regularly produce very different constructions of the world. Something of the extent of potential variability can be seen if we consider the following untransmitted segment from Dr Kemp's interview with the film-makers, which follows directly after the passage transmitted in Extract One:

Extract Two

> KEMP: Er, one way that I find useful to look at this is that er, each year in the United Kingdom two, roughly two hundred and forty thousand people get cancer. Each year er, roughly a hundred and sixty thousand people die from cancer, so there's a difference of eighty thousand, and eighty thousand is one third of two hundred and forty thousand which is the number of people who get the disease, so one could say that one's a sort of third of the way there. It's not a totally useless way of looking at it and sometimes quite helpful. So there has been progress but we're probably not half way there yet.

If we compare the 'bottom line' figures for progress in treating cancer we can see the film-makers' figure is 'around 1 per cent' while the cancer head's figure is approaching 'half way there'.

We used the difference between this version and that in Extract One to explicate further some of the quantification practices used to justify particular claims of success and failure. The sheer scale of the contrast between these versions suggested that we needed to look for something radically different in the quantification practices of the film-makers and the cancer charities. One device we used to help reveal these different practices was to use participants themselves to get at them. In effect, we used our interviews with participants in the programme who were critical of the programme's account to perform their own analyses; we put their *interest* in rebutting it to work. The idea is not that they will provide some sort of neutral analytic account, but that they will illustrate further variability between versions, but in a particularly explicit manner.

For example, the public relations officer for the largest British cancer charity, the Imperial Cancer Research Fund, particularly objected to the construction of the table of cancer incidence used to calculate the 'around 1 per cent' statistic. In fact she characterized the table of cancer deaths (Figure 1) as 'utterly irresponsible' because many people recover from breast cancer or even lung cancer:

Extract Three

> WILKINS: I'm very angry about that [...] there isn't a form of cancer (.2) for which (.)
> no one gets cured [. . .] if you were sitting at home with breast cancer [. . .] and you
> saw that the only curable cancer was in yellow but breast cancer was in white
> [WETHERELL: Yeah] you'd think your doctor's been lying to you.[1]

This and other passages encouraged us to think of the notions of 'cure' and 'curable cancer' as fundamental to the quantification practice of making progress in treatment appear good or bad. For example, we saw moves between technical notions of 'curable cancers', which are decided by using some criterion such as 80 per cent survival for five years, and everyday notions, which might for example allow that a cancer is curable if some people can be said to be completely rid of it. We also saw flexibility over whether someone who survives cancer has been actually *cured* of cancer (as opposed to 'spontaneous recovery' or simply having a non-fatal cancer) and over whether a cure is dependent on cancer-funded research or other factors such as craft advances amongst surgeons. By taking curable cancer in its technical sense, ignoring survivals from other cancers, and taking the total of curable cancers as a percentage of those diagnosed, the programme-makers were able to generate a small figure. In contrast, by simply taking the difference between diagnosed cancers and deaths for a particular year (and thus avoiding the issue of what is a curable or incurable cancer) the charity head could produce a much bigger figure (but one which ignores questions about spontaneous recovery and craft advance).

Reading the Detail

One of the things that should be eminently clear from our discussion of variation is that the analyst needs to be attentive to the fine details of discourse. Indeed, precisely the sort of detail that is lost in more traditional quantitative analytic techniques such as content analysis, and may be obscured in forms of qualitative analysis such as participant observation or interpretive studies of interviews, is often crucial in discourse analytic studies (Potter and Wetherell 1987). This work has been strongly influenced by the insights of Harvey Sacks, developed through many studies of conversation (e.g. Atkinson and Heritage 1984, Button and Lee 1987). His argument was that all the details in a stretch of discourse – the pauses, repairs, word choice and so on – are potentially there for a purpose; they are potentially part of the performance of some act or are consequential in some way for the outcome of the interaction (Wooffitt 1990). It is worth noting, however, that our description – 'the detail' – is itself part of a set of social science presuppositions about what are 'big things' and what 'mere details'. As the researcher starts to get into the right 'analytic mentality' (Schenkein 1978) the notion of detail, at least in its trivializing sense, becomes increasingly redundant. What were details start to seem like the big things, the consequential things for making sense of actions through talk.

Our example of variation within numerical descriptions of cure rates in the previous section illustrates the value of an analytic attention to detail. We were able to show that there was a potential orderliness to the selection of 'quarter of a million' rather than, say, 'two hundred and forty three thousand'. Almost any other feature of the study would provide another example of the value of attention to detail; let us take one of the non-numerical quantifications from Extract One in which 'curable cancers' are formulated as 'amongst the rarest cancers'. The selection of the description 'rarest' for curable cancers could be seen as merely a statistical commonplace (the majority of people get other kinds of cancer); yet in addition to this there are specific inferences available from this category 'rare', which may also invoke notions such as 'unusual' or 'atypical' and which in this context may raise questions about the generalizability of research success from these cases to the more 'common' ones. That is, rather than see this term as merely a felicitious stylistic variation we can see it as subtly providing another element in the programme-makers' case. There is no formula for reading for detail; and it is surprisingly difficult to overcome years of academic training in which the goal of reading is to produce some gist or unitary summary. The process of analysis is often a long struggle with one's own tendency to read in this way (Potter 1988).

Looking for Rhetorical Organization

As we noted at the start, one of the central features of our approach to discourse is a concern with rhetoric. Again, this is best thought of as an orientation built into the analytic mentality through practice rather than the basis for any specific procedure. Nevertheless, this orientation leads us to inspect discourse both for the way it is organized to make argumentative cases and for the way it is designed to undermine alternative cases (Billig 1991). Put another way, the rhetorical orientation draws our attention away from questions about how a version relates to some putative reality (which is anyway a problematic question within discourse analysis) and focuses it on how a version relates to competing alternatives.

A concern with rhetoric in this way is often, in practice, our previous concern with variation in another guise. A comparison of differences between and within versions is frequently the best way to start to unpick their rhetorical organization. Extract One is an example where alternative versions are presented in a single construction. That is, the programme-makers are reporting the cancer charities' case for their success and undermining this version through developing their alternative. In our original study, we considered a range of devices through which the commentary version was privileged over that of the head of the cancer charity (not the least of which is the selection from Kemp's interview of the section about three cancer successes while ignoring descriptions of success with common cancers such as breast cancer and the general argument about progress given in Extract Two).

The rhetorical orientation can be seen clearly in the discourse of the programme-makers during their editing of the film. This involved developing the final form of words for the commentary and combining the words with film and graphics. These sessions presented manifest examples of the way the programme-makers were trying to make strong argumentative points with the material. For example, in the passages where they constructed the roller showing 'annual incidence of cancer' we see the team working to heighten the contrast between the (small) numbers of curable cancers and the (big) figures for total cancers diagnosed. Extract Four is from transcripts of recorded talk between the programme-makers as they edit the final version of the film; we have added emphasis to indicate those sections where this orientation is most explicit.

Extract Four

> BILLINGER: The er all the rest wipe off and total just comes up into the middle and stops by itself (.2) or (.2) conversely (.) what if you don't put total on that at all but lung – just so that (.) they all just go up and roll right off and *then I mix total up in the middle* (.2) *slightly bigger* (.8) *as if you know – as if you were doing executive producer* . . .

> FINNIS: Oh there's other bits in the programme where sort of (.) one in three people get (.) one in four people get so (.) it's not meant to demonstrate how erm (.) many people get any sort of cancer *it's meant to demonstrate that the three it's just said are incurable are a tiny (.) proportion of the lot.*
> BILLINGER: *Ye:ah it just makes – it's more impact isn't it if you if you notice that the other one going by was five and the total of all of them is two hundred and forty-five.*

The extract catches the practical film-makers' work of trying to accomplish the *bigness* of the figure for cancer diagnoses and the *smallness* of the figure for cancers which are curable.

Looking for Accountability

Concern with rhetoric is closely linked to concern with accountability. Indeed, in some respects they can be viewed as two sides of the same coin. Making one's actions and claims accountable can be viewed as constructing them in ways which make them hard to rebut or undermine, ways which make them seem fair or objective. This is perhaps a rather obvious consideration for a current affairs television programme, which has at least some institutional requirements of objectivity (Clayman 1988); however, ethnomethodologists have argued that accountability is an essential character of the design and understanding of human conduct generally (Heritage 1984, Watson and Sharrock 1991).

The analytic point that arises out of this is an important one. Traditionally, work in both sociology and social psychology has often concentrated on accounts as a discrete class of activity (Scott and Lyman 1968, Semin and Manstead 1983). From this perspective, talk is thus examined specifically for passages which contain excuses or justifications. However, the ethnomethodological perspective suggests we look for accountability as a dimension of any stretch of discourse.

If we consider our target passage, Extract One, it can be viewed as a version designed to stand up to scrutiny; its factual status is accountable (note: whether it succeeds in this is a participant's judgement; the analyst is concentrating on how accountability is done, not how well). The editing sessions show the programme-makers rehearsing various criticisms that might be made against the film and of the lines they could take arguing against them. For example, they consider whether their '1 per cent' figure can be justified as they rehearse the commentary.

Extract Five

> FINNIS: So of the quarter of a million annual cancer cases
> BILLINGER: nearly quarter million
> FINNIS: yeah cancer research can lay claim to – eighty years of cancer research can lay can – claim to having found cures for just one per cent (.2)
> CHITTY: you really want to make it that strong?
> FINNIS: If one can make it that strong(.) I'd like to make it that strong (.) it's the most surprising thing that's shown (.2)
> CHITTY: Okay what if they say that err
> FINNIS: breast cancer
> CHITTY: breast cancer Tamoxifen treatment has extended lives (.) has increased five-year survivals by 10 per cent.
> FINNIS: They couldn't say that they could <u>cure</u> breast cancer (.2)
> CHITTY: But actually they <u>might</u> (.) [*Chitty outlines a potential counter-argument.*]
> Whoo God I can't think of any others that really (.2) possible –

FINNIS: Screening the cervix.

CHITTY: Screening – screening the cervix they've dropped deaths by two thousand (.) 50 per cent erm –

FINNIS: Can we say that was cancer research though?

CHITTY: Well it certainly was.

FINNIS: Was it?

CHITTY: Yeah I mean but the pep em cervical cytology test (.) is really (.) it's not British cancer research (.) it's American thing.

FINNIS: So that's pushing it too far.

BILLINGER: Mammography would be the same (.) they say that – (.4) and only be detailed analysis of X-rays – [inaudible] they haven't *done* it yet but they –

FINNIS: Right right

BILLINGER: Yeah I think all we can say is they say these are curable (.) and these are the big claims that they make (.) for these three and yet (.2) those three are such a minute percentage of cancers.

FINNIS: So we have to keep it on the basis of their publicity as it were.

Here we see the programme-makers exploring a range of potential arguments against the claim that cancer research has had only a small (1 per cent) success. Breast cancer improvements are treated as extending life rather than actually curing (again, we see the importance for the film-makers' version of the category 'cure'). Improvements from screening for cancer of the cervix are treated as a product of American research (the film was directed at British cancer charities). Yet they decide to bypass these potential worries by focusing on 'curable cancers' and the claims the charities make about them. This is not to say that there is no concern with the 'precision' or 'truth' of the figure; rather it is that 'precision' and 'truth' are not being understood in the abstract but in the context of *arguments* where specific sorts of issues will arise. Again, this shows how collecting the right kinds of materials can make the task of analysis more straightforward.

Cross-referring Discourse Studies

The final analytic consideration that we will address concerns the way discourse studies are themselves drawn on as an analytic resource. Although discourse analysts have not been interested in the production of general laws in the more traditional social scientific sense, they have been concerned with features of discourse construction and interaction that might apply across different contexts. Indeed, conversation analysis in particular has been notable for the cumulative nature of its insights and how what were often viewed as rather trivial or uninteresting early findings have borne fruit in the analysis of subtle phenomena or complex institutional situations (Heritage and Greatbatch 1986, Levinson 1983).

Again, there is no mechanical procedure for applying prior studies in a way which will bear fruit in the current situation. Nevertheless a wide familiarity with conversation analytic and more general discourse work is undoubtedly a major resource in being able to make workable interpretations of a set of materials. At its most general level, reading other work is one of the ways of developing the analytic mentality. Indeed, it can be a very useful practice exercise simply to try to reproduce a finding with a new set of data, for this will force hidden assumptions to be confronted and provide a feel for the analytic decisions that have to be made. More specifically, earlier studies can throw light on phenomena appearing in current materials.

We can illustrate this with two examples of quantification research. The first one we used was a study of market traders (Pinch and Clark 1986). Pinch and Clark had examined the devices that traders used in making their goods appear to be bargains. The relevance of this is that it is a realm of quantification (in this case financial) where particular kinds of contrast are being produced. One technique was particularly striking, and that was the building up of the worth of some goods by selling them in collection (a pen is sold with a pencil, a case and so on). By building up this list it seems like there are a lot of goods in comparison to the selling price; by listing the goods in this way they are constituted as a bargain. We suggested that something similar was going on in the construction of the roller (Figure 1). Here the very long list of cancers, and the very big end total, serve to emphasize the smallness of the number of curable cancers.

The second example was a study of 'ontological gerrymandering' in sociologists' discourse by Woolgar and Pawluch (1985). Their argument is that in addressing the solution to 'social problems' the conclusions are often dependent on unexplicated assumptions about what is and is not a relevant realm of objects and ideas. Put another way, when conducting an argument part of the rhetorical work is to bring a particular terrain for dispute into existence and ignore or eliminate other potential terrains. Using this notion we were able to make more sense of the very wide disparities between the claims in the programme and by the cancer charities about progress. In particular, we argued that the programme-makers had selected the issue of curing cancer as a major focus of their critique while avoiding or reworking two other important issues: prevention and palliation. This helped us see how the programme-makers' 'around 1 per cent' bottom line for charity success could be seen as the product of a set of contingent decisions: to make an argument based on curing cancers, to take curability of cancers as the criterion rather than overall numbers of cured people, to calculate the number of curable cancers as a particular kind of proportion.

Conclusion

Throughout this chapter we have tried to emphasize the craft aspects of doing discourse analysis. In doing this we have not wanted to say that there are not some mechanical procedures that are often particularly helpful in doing analysis. Rather we have been wanting to undermine the idea that by simply using these procedures interesting 'results' will fall out in some way. The quality of analysis is dependent on how particular analytic interpretations can be warranted, and this depends on a whole range of factors: how well they account for the detail in material, how well potential alternatives can be discounted, how plausible the overall account seems, whether it meshes with other studies, and so on.

More than in many other kinds of social research, the evaluation of discourse analytic studies depends on the quality of the write-up. Obviously we cannot reproduce our write-up of our analysis here (see Potter *et al.* 1991) and at this point must stop our explication of method. If you are interested in our 'final' conclusions about quantification practices it is up to you to examine the published version of our work; in a sense you will need to perform your own discourse analysis to judge its persuasiveness as a critical investigation of quantification. Readers of discourse analytic studies need to be able, to an important extent, to perform their own evaluations of the analytic conclusions. Perhaps for this reason it is difficult to make a clear-cut distinction between the process of analysis and the process of writing up. Often it is only when the discipline of presenting a study publicly necessitates filling in all the steps that flaws and problems appear. We have commonly had the experience of finding that things fall apart in one way or another in the process of formal writing and we have had to go back to the materials. Because of this we have found that collaboration in analysis can be extremely advantageous: the regular attempt to make interpretations stand up publicly is a very useful discipline.

Note

1   The standard transcription scheme of conversation analysis has been used here, and in following extracts:
     [. . .] denotes omitted material;
     (.2) denotes pauses timed to a tenth of a second;
     (.) denotes a noticeable pause, too short to time;
     British: underlining denotes emphasis;
     Ye:ah Colon denotes a lengthening of the previous vowel sound;
     claim to – A dash marks a sharp cut-off in the speech.

References

Atkinson, J.M. and Heritage, J. (eds) (1984) *Structures of Social Action: Studies in Conversation Analysis*. Cambridge: Cambridge University Press.

Billig, M. (1988) 'Methodology and scholarship in understanding ideological explanation', in C. Antaki (ed.) *Analysing Lay Explanation: a Case Book*. London: Sage.

Billig, M. (1991) *Ideologies and Beliefs*. London: Sage

Button, G. and Lee, J.R.E. (1987) *Talk and Social Organization*. Clevedon, Avon: Multilingual Matters.

Clark, C. and Pinch, T. (1988) 'Micro-sociology and micro-economics: selling by social control', in N. Fielding (ed.) *Actions and Structure*. London: Sage.

Clayman, S.E. (1988) 'Displaying neutrality in television news interviews', *Social Problems* 35: 474–92.

Edwards, D. and Potter, J. (1992) *Discursive Psychology*. London: Sage.

Henriques, J., Hollway, W., Irwin, C., Couze, V. and Walkerdine, V. (1984) *Changing the Subject: Psychology, Social Regulation and Subjectivity*. London: Methuen.

Heritage, J. (1984) *Garfinkel and Ethnomethodology*. Cambridge: Polity Press.

Heritage, J. and Greatbatch, D. (1986) 'Generating applause: a study of rhetoric and response at party political conferences', *American Journal of Sociology* 92: 110–57.

Levinson, S.C. (1983) *Pragmatics*. Cambridge: Cambridge University Press.

Pinch, T. and Clark, C. (1986) 'The hard sell: patter-merchanting and the strategic (re)production and local management of economic reasoning in the sales routines of market pitchers', *Sociology* 20: 169–91.

Potter, J. (1988) 'What is reflexive about discourse analysis? The case of reading readings', in S. Woolgar (ed.) *Knowledge and Reflexivity: New Frontiers in the Sociology of Knowledge*. London: Sage.

Potter, J. and Wetherell, M. (1987) *Discourse and Social Psychology: Beyond Attitudes and Behaviour*. London: Sage.

Potter, J. and Wetherell, M. (1988) 'Accomplishing attitudes: fact and evaluation in racist discourse', *Text* 8: 51–68.

Potter, J., Wetherell, M. and Chitty, A. (1991) 'Quantification rhetoric: cancer on television', *Discourse and Society* 2: 333–65.

Schenkein, J. (1978) 'Sketch of an analytic mentality for the study of conversational interaction', in J. Schenkein (ed.) *Studies in the Organization of Conversational Interaction*. New York: Academic Press.

Scott, M.B. and Lyman, S.M. (1968) 'Accounts', *American Sociological Review* 33: 46–62.

Semin, G.R. and Manstead, A.S.R. (1983) *The Accountability of Conduct: a Social Psychological Analysis*. London: Academic Press.

Watson, D.R. and Sharrock, W.W. (1991) 'Something on accounts', *The Discourse Analysis Research Group Newsletter* 7: 3–12.

Wooffitt, R.C. (1990) 'On the analysis of interaction: an introduction to conversation analysis', in P. Luff, G.N. Gilbert and D. Frohlich (eds) *Computers and Conversation*. New York: Academic Press.

Woolgar, S. and Pawluch, D. (1985) 'Ontological gerrymandering: the anatomy of social problems explanations', *Social Problems* 32: 214–27.

Yearley, S. (1981) 'Textual persuasion: the role of social accounting in the construction of scientific arguments', *Philosophy of the Social Sciences* 11: 409–35.

Source: Potter and Wetherell, 1994: 51–64

Reading S: From the Street to the Screen: Breadline Britain *and the Semiotics of Poverty*

Ulrike Meinhof

The question of whether and how the social plight of a section of our population can, is, or should be represented is not specific to the novelist's concern, nor to other forms of fictional representation on television or film. Any form of the news and documentary media, from newspaper reports to television documentaries, reports, narrates and represents people and events involving social concerns, and, by doing so, generates further discourses. These may be in the media themselves, where programmes about programmes, and intertextual references to other media texts have become standard practice.[1] Or they may be outside the media, in the full spectrum of public and private domains; from political speeches quoting or challenging a particular programme to the reactions, narrations and discussions of viewers and readers.[2] The focus of this chapter . . . is on such discourses and representations of poverty, and how they interact with each other. As main example I have chosen *Breadline Britain* (from now on referred to . . . as *BB*), a series about poverty in the UK which coincided in two of its six parts with the period of our media search, in particular programme 1 (the definition of poverty) and programme 4 (the programme dealing with housing and homelessness).

Three different, though interconnected, perspectives will be discussed:

1   The interaction between the discourse of the social scientists alias programme makers about how to draw a poverty line, and the representation of this in televisual form.
2   The interplay between the different semiotic codes or levels of these representations, namely the interaction of words, images, and music.
3   The intervention of critical readings of these representations, in our case specifically those of *The Media Show*, and the problems this raises.

The analysis will be guided by a form of 'social semiotics', which means in the words of Halliday, 'interpreting language within a sociocultural context, in which the culture itself is interpreted in semiotic terms – as an information system' (Halliday 1978: 2). In the following brief section I want to explain what kind of methodology this implies and how it differs from other approaches to discourse.

Why Social Semiotics?

An interest in discourse means coming to terms with the vexed question of whether any of the many different theories of discourse can throw light on the problems raised by the interacting and conflicting discourses involving *BB*, and if so, how. The validity of a *theory* of discourse for our discourse analysis will thus be assessed by its effectiveness as an interpretative tool. Testing a theory by methods or practices derived from it is not the only, for some not even an important, part of the contribution which a theory has to make. However, for the purposes of a discourse *analysis* it is essential that the underlying principles of the approach are understood and their relationship to existing theories clarified, and, if possible, enhanced.

The first question to be addressed in this chapter is thus: What makes a social semiotic approach to discourse distinctive? Or in other words: Is there a difference between what social semiotics sees as its object of enquiry, and thus in the methodology which guides the enquiry and analysis and other approaches to discourse? To answer this I will draw two lines of demarcation against two competing theories of discourse which in spite of considerable overlap with social semiotics in some areas are nevertheless substantially and significantly different in others: semiotics proper on the one hand, and postmodernist/poststructuralist approaches to discourse on the other.

Semiotics and social semiotics meet in that they view all texts as communication, as 'information systems', to use Halliday's phrase (Halliday 1978: 2). 'Text' in semiotics does not restrict itself to the spoken and written words but also, most importantly, includes all the other semiotic ways of encoding meaning, such as architecture, fashion, kinship systems, traffic signs, to name but a few. In the context of our television series a semiotic analysis would be bound to include an analysis of the images and the music used in the programmes and thus differ substantially from a linguistic or sociolinguistic approach which would only capture the verbal part of the communication. But my perspective . . . is not just semiotic, but forms part of a *social* semiotic. This means that whereas in semiotics the sign is taken to be independent from its context, and meaning is established by its opposition to other signs inside a closed system of signification, social semiotics in particular explores the corrrespondence and interconnection between social practices and discourse. For the purposes of our analysis of the *BB* series, this has two implications: first, an exploration of the nature of the *context* in which the programmes were made to show how a particular view of social reality was constructed and then translated into the sequences of the television series; and secondly, in response to this, an account of the *interaction* of the different codes which are supposed to realize interdependently this construction. Each code is thus not taken as a separate system of meaning, but as interrelating. Insofar as my analysis of *BB* suggests an interpretation of the interplay between image and sound, which favours a particular view or interpretation of social reality, this resembles a kind of textual reading which I have elsewhere referred to as 'closed' (Meinhof 1993: 213),[3] and which is a familiar way of applying social semiotic theory to the interpretation of texts in contexts. But this is not sufficient. The view of social semiotics adopted here is one which has profited not only from the seminal study by Michael Halliday which made it possible to theorize the interconnection between texts and social structure; it has equally been influenced by Volosinov's and Bakhtin's notion of the 'dialogic': a dynamic, interactive view of discourse as arising between socially organized individuals, where contestation is part of any discourse (Volosinov 1973; Bakhtin 1981). Social semiotics then takes the old semiotic path from sender to message to receiver (Jakobson 1960) and explodes it into multidimensional interactive sets of relations. As a result, the meaning of discourse ceases to coincide with the interpretation of its textual strategies, relegating such readings to that of an 'implied reader' . . .

My insistence on polyphony of meaning is not a denial of potential and actual constraints on interpretation; nor am I claiming that a text has as many meanings as there are readers. There is, to answer Fish's provocative title-question, very definitely 'a text in this class' (Fish 1980). It is precisely the interplay and tension between the different kinds of meaning we have already discussed in our introduction: between the making of meaning in the making of text, and in the remaking of text in the readings.

To establish this interplay we need first of all to turn to the way the programme makers arrived at their definition of poverty.

What is Poverty? *Breadline Britain* and its Construction of Poverty

Breadline Britain is based on a Mori survey of 1,800 people commissioned by the programme makers themselves, to investigate the attitude of British people, about what in 1990 constitutes an unacceptably low standard of living. In the survey people were asked to indicate on a list of items which of those they felt to be essential. Items which more than 50 per cent of the sample listed as such were then taken into account in the definition of poverty applying the following formula: if anyone lacks three or more of these 'essential' items this is taken as an indication of deprivation. In applying this definition of poverty to the British population as a whole, the researchers discovered that in 1990 11 million people in Britain are poor. (This figure of 11 million compares to 7.5 million in 1983, when *BB* conducted its first survey for an earlier series along the same lines: an increase of 3.5 million in seven years.) The definition of poverty is thus related to lacking 'essentials' which a majority of British people feel that no-one should be without . . . Poverty is thus not a question of physical survival, although the detrimental effect of poverty on health has been established through epidemiological research (see Wilkinson 1990), and is directly addressed by the programmes; nor is it simply related to income distribution (i.e. people living on less than 50 per cent of the average national income count as poor), though people who lack such items are heavily concentrated among those with the lowest income.[4] Poverty and deprivation in *BB* are consensual definitions which shift in line with the relative expectations of society as a whole. . . .

The Semiotic Organization of *Breadline Britain*

The makers of *BB* chose the format of the documentary[5] to present their arguments about poverty in the UK. The choice of the documentary genre is not an automatic one, since television has other, frequently more popular, means of presenting a view of social reality. The much debated and highly influential television drama, *Cathy Come Home* (hereafter *CCH*), from 1966, directed by Kenneth Loach, was a fictional story, involving a script writer (Jeremy Sandford), a film producer (Tony Garnett), and actors (Carol White as Cathy and Ray Brooks as Reg). Clearly marked as television drama *CCH* was nevertheless accepted by a deeply moved mass audience as a convincing account of the situation in the UK at the time, with some consequences for the public sphere of social policy-making. Jeremy Sandford, in his introduction to the publication of his screenplay, wrote in 1976:

I wish that there had been more change in the general situation of Britain's homeless since I wrote *Cathy*. As regards its particular effect, however, I can feel pleased. It is good to know that I have altered, if only by a very small bit, the condition of life for others in my own society. As a result of the film and certain meetings we held in Birmingham afterwards, this town, and others, ceased their practice of separating three or four hundred husbands each year from their wives and children. (Sandford 1976: 14)

Dramatizations which use fictional accounts and actors to represent a particular view of social reality or figures in public life are regular features on television, with a frequent mixing of formats which often blurs the dividing line between fictional and non-fictional accounts. So-called 'factions', in particular, often mix genres by combining apparently authentic acted reconstructions of particular historical moments with genuine newsreels and other documentary material from the archives. Critical comment, too, is often favouring fictions or drama documentaries, praising reconstructions and dramatized versions as more convincing and more genuine renderings of past events than eyewitness accounts.[6] For viewers, then, the dividing line between fictional and non-fictional representation, and their respective relationship to social reality is not necessarily as clearcut and as obvious as generic descriptions seem to imply . . .

The following extract is taken from the beginning of the soundtrack of programme 1 of *BB* and introduces six individuals who reappear right through the series together with some others, and who each represent a particular aspect or aspects of poverty as defined through the criteria in section 1 of this chapter.

1(a)   Robert's room here. There's only one bed. One wardrobe. No carpets at all, curtains are second hand. As we go into the daughter's room. As you can see: one chest of drawers. Very little carpet, again. As you can see, it's absolutely bare. (Richard Winers, programme 1)

1(b)   I always have to do the washing in the bathroom with the shower water. Because I can't afford the launderette, because the cost of the washerette is astronomical. You can't possibly afford it on pension. I have a 50p meter because I couldn't afford a big electricity bill;. When the 50p is gone the meter just clicks off and you haven't got another one. You just go to bed. There's no light, and no heat, and there's no water. (Julie Smith, 77-year-old widow, programme 1)

1(c)   As you can see in the bedroom, you've got a build up of condensation. You can actually see how damp it is. Sometimes the window is actually very wet, and you got the curtain sticking to the window. In the toilet you get a lot of condensation. You get water dripping off the window. You got a lot of fungus, plus the wallpaper is lifting off. In the winter it's very very cold. (Yvonne Barnett, programme 1)

1(d)   I got my cooker off the rag and bone man, and I got it for free. I think the cooker is definitely dangerous, I mean. I'll be out for most of the day, come back in and it stinks. But I can't ring the Gas Board, because if I do they come down on the cooker and I won't be able to use it and I can't cook my meals. (John Malone, programme 1)

1(e)   <'Let's try to come down, hey. OK'>
       Before Jimmy had the accident and he was working, we could afford most things, but now, on the money we're on, you can't go out and buy what you need. It's a case of like, going into debt and get them, or doing without. And most of the time you have to do without. (Wife of disabled man, Jimmy Roberts, programme 1)

1(f)   Basically if I can't pay and I haven't got money from the Social, whatever, that means I can't buy it . . . that is nothing to eat.

It's not like Oliver Twist knocking on people's door and say 'can I have some more porridge', because they're just going to kick you out.

<'Can you spare any change, please?'> (Kim Stevens, programme 1)

Each instance stands in for a particular group of people living in poverty, as defined by the researchers on the basis of the Mori survey. Programme 1 of the series elucidates this by taking each of six clusters in turn: housing and heating; food; clothing; furniture; leisure and social activities; financial security. Each of these clusters is personified by particular individuals who are illustrating a particular category of lack and deprivation, which is then related back to the attitude of the British people that these items are essential for living. The programme ranges from the most destitute – a girl living in the street – to those who are at first sight not as dramatically poor – a disabled man forced to live with his parents again, or a young man with a broken cooker. What they are all lacking are three or more of the key items which people in the Britain of 1990 felt no-one should go without . . .

Explicitness about its thesis is thus one of the marked organizational principles of the series, with the voice-over acting as the medium for setting out the argument, and introducing each instance as part of the argument. Although television documentaries usually rely on voice-overs to interpret the instances they show, the insistence in *BB* on which particular aspect of poverty each group is representing, and how this relates to the general research findings, is unusual, and gives the series a more academic perspective than others of the same genre.

But how are the people themselves presented? Again, documentary filming has explored different options to cope with the fact that the presence of a camera or an observer will affect and alter the way people behave, from fly-on-the-wall positions which seem to suggest that the camera is not really there, to films which show cameras and camera crew, interviewer and interviewee as part of the same scene. *BB* adopted an intermediate position for most of the series. There are very few 'fly-on-the-wall', naturalistic settings, although there are some (not very successful) sequences where people are involved in make-believe encounters with officials, or just going about their daily lives as if the camera was not present. The quotes 1(a) to 1(f) illustrate this. In terms of tenor-relations[7] the addressee of the speakers is rarely another person shown on screen, or if so, as in the first line of 1(e) and the last line of 1(f), only very briefly, acting more as introduction of the clip or as transition to the next. This has consequences both for the language the speakers use and for the interaction between camera and speaker/image and text. Most often the speakers appear to be directly telling of their plight, on camera and sometimes in voice-over. No interviewer appears on screen and no questions are heard off-camera. The interviewer's role has been effaced and the subjects appear to be setting their own agenda. . . .

Very interesting in view of the absent addressee is the frequent use of phrases like 'as you can see', or similar formulations (see in particular 1(a) and 1(c) above which appear like a direct reference to an unseen camera taking its lead from the speaker) Yvonne Barnett, the single mother of three children who all sleep in one room and share one bed in 1(c) . . . uses the same phrase as Richard, 'as you can see', to draw the camera's attention to the dripping windows and the damp walls, picking up pieces of wet wallpaper and drops of water between her fingers as she speaks.

The camera is thus very much in the role of the eye-witness, seemingly acting on behalf of the individuals telling their own story. . . .

The following quotes come from the opening sequences of programme 4, and again introduce each individual by letting them speak directly to the camera, though again there are very brief sequences where the interaction is between the people shown, such as the opening remark of Alison talking to her baby.

> 4(a) *Alison to her baby son*: <'No, come and do a wee wee . . .'>
> This is my seventh month. It's just horrible. I've got no privacy, nor has he. If he's like, misbehaving, I've got nowhere I can go on my own, he's got nowhere he can go. And how I'm living it's just degrading to think that I have to live like this before I could get my flat from the Council. Otherwise they won't give me a flat.
> *Voice-over*: Alison Child is 21. With no home of her own she lives with her two-and-a-half-year-old son Ricki in this Bed and Breakfast hotel in Bayswater in London.
> *Alison*: He doesn't want sharing. He's backward in his talking, and he is just very hyperactive. If he had more children to play with, because he'd get rid of all that energy, he's got. Like, he just can't he's got so much of it.
> 4(b) *Kim [seen sitting on the street]*: It's quite dangerous sleeping out in the street. There's some weird people around, you know. I mean when you're freezing cold, and you really are cold, and you're shaking, and someone comes up and asks you for a cup of coffee and you can stay at his house, and you can sit in his car for a while. Perverts, like, take advantage of you especially if you're homeless, you know what I'm saying, and they give you money and then ask you to do them favours, and things like that.
> *Voice-over*: Kim Stevens is 17. Brought up in care, she's been sleeping rough in London for two years.
> *Kim [voice blends in slowly with camera focusing on people lying on the floor underneath blankets]*: Sleeping rough is really difficult. We used to sleep up Dean Street, and three car parks we slept in, and we got moved on from each one. Where we sleep, sometimes especially on the West End side, you sit down somewhere and they move you on before you even have your sleeping bag out. But if you're sleeping out, sometimes they wake you up, about three in the morning and then six, you hardly get any sleep. And especially when you're nice and warm in your sleeping bag, you're cuddling up in your sleeping bag and you're nice and warm. They come and kick you in the ribs, and tell you to get up, and you get all cold and wet again.

After this introduction the voice-over connects their individual narratives to the government's changes in housing policy, such as the selling off of council property, the lifting of rent controls, the withdrawal of benefits to 16- and 17-year-olds, to the lack of adequate or, indeed, absence of any housing facilities for people on low income.

> These are among the 11 million people found to be in poverty by a special survey commissioned for *Breadline Britain*. They all fall below the minimum living standard laid down by society at large. This is a rise of 3½ million since the first *Breadline Britain* survey in 1983. This found a third of those in poverty had housing problems. Since then government housing policy has radically changed. So what effect has this had on the housing of the poor? (Voice-over, programme 4)

Again, the representational nature of each selected individual is stressed, from the most destitute, Kim, who lives on the streets of London, to Alison who simply has not got a home of her own, but who is at least in a warm room in her bed and breakfast accommodation, and Yvonne Barnett, whose flat is damp and in an unsightly and dirty housing block. Ranging across all three narratives reinforces once more the sense of the relativity of poverty in the UK, in contrast to the absolute poverty familiar from Third World images of malnutrition and starvation. The consensus view of the British public as established by the survey, states that Alison and Yvonne with their children, and not just the homeless Kim, live in totally inadequate conditions: they, too, are poor. This is particularly interesting in the light of the highly critical comments made by *The Media Show* which will be discussed in the final section . . .

Breadline Britain and the Melancholia of Poverty

Apart from the different voices and different images of *BB*, there is a third semiotic layer which, in an unobtrusive way, interprets the situation of the poor in the UK: the music of the opening and closing credit sequences of each programme in the series.

In these, the camera is moving across scenes and people's faces, who are featured in the series. The images blend in and out of each other, individual faces appear as the camera pans the landscape, and each scene changes to the next without an obvious cut or transition as the faces fade away. The opening sequence begins with an industrial landscape: the smoking industrial chimneys of IBM, superimposed on which the face of a young man appears. As he is blended out, the camera moves to the tower block of a Birmingham housing estate, with the face of an older man moving across it. Next is a view of Merseyside with the face of a young woman with a child, followed by a street scene with homeless youngsters sleeping on the ground; and finally, we move from the face of a young woman to the inside of a bare room, with the face of an old man in the foreground. The sequence closes on a cracked window pane. In both, the opening and the slightly different ending sequence, the backgrounds are shot in a bluish tinted black and white which gives the film a grainy look; the faces of the people who are superimposed on these backgrounds are in grey; the look is one of great solemnity. Accompanying these images are the gentle sounds of a piano which plays an extremely simple, almost amateurish string of sounds, which lack a distinct melody and a strong foregrounded theme. Instead it is vague and wandering, a sense which the consistent use of the pedal and the consequent tonal blurring reinforces . . .

The music thus reinforces the sad and depressing nature of the images, the strong connotation that here are people resigned to their fate, and that their melancholia is a private, internalized feeling of anguish rather than one of anger at social injustice and rebellion.

To summarize the argument so far:

1 *Breadline Britain* has a thesis based on social science research relating to the poor living conditions of an increasing number of people in Britain.
2 The thesis is exemplified in the programmes through representative instances, that is through individuals whose living conditions are supposed to match the different kinds of deprivation established by the research.
3 These individuals tell their story for the programme with the help of a camera that authenticates their narratives by showing us the relevant images referred to by the speakers. The stories range from the most destitute (homeless people living on the street) to those living under impoverished but not destitute conditions, but they are similar in the tone of sadness and depression. The mood of these narratives is reinforced by the music of the credit sequences which stresses the melancholia of poverty rather than any more aggressive moods.
4 The individual narratives are related back to the general thesis by a separate commentator who is never on camera but speaks in voice-over at the beginning

and end of each section. These comments are given in a descriptive and analytical form associated with an academic 'objective' style of reporting rather than any more arousing alternative.

Such a differentiation between the discourses of individuals and their plight, and the discourse of the general thesis, the claim that these are instances of the plight of millions of other British people, is not at all unusual in the making of documentary fiction: it is one of the obvious means of blending the specific and the general into each other. What is more unusual in the structure of *BB*, though, is the total *separation* between these two discourses, which raises the question of how an audience reacts to these different appeals of credibility . . .

In the final section . . . I want to discuss another reading on the text, that presented by an episode of another television series: *The Media Show*.[8]

Breadline Britain and *The Media Show*: Whose Poor Are Telling the Truer Story?

[. . .] The sequences where Kim (called Cathy in *The Media Show*) is seen bedding down in the street together with some of her friends were picked up and critically commented on by Channel 4's *Media Show*. Broadcast in advance of the actual showing of the *BB* series and its housing episode on BBC2, the programme on *The Media Show* discussed the representation of the poor in various television genres, from news programmes to soap operas, but was particularly critical of the ways in which news and current affairs broadcasting deal with the poor.

In the usual style of *The Media Show* the programme accumulated arguments by adding Emma Freud's own analysis to a mixture of clips from interviews with broadcasters, journalists, academics, media analysts, which were, in turn, intercut with film clips from the programmes they discussed and criticized. Among these were the following types of remarks:

1   These programmes are guilty of stereotyping the poor (Chris Pond, Patrick Stoddard).
2   They are always opting for the worst possible cases rather than the typical; they are not giving the poor the opportunity to show themselves in the best possible light; they are always showing the poor as victims (Beatrix Campbell).
3   These programmes are infringing the privacy of the poor and thus deprive them of their dignity (Beatrix Campbell).
4   Programme makers merely slot the poor into narratives that they have pre-defined (Beatrix Campbell); they are not really letting the poor tell their own story.
5   People selected for television are simply playing up to the cameras, and are giving the film makers the version they wish to hear; television thus allows people to perpetuate 'myths about themselves' (Boyce).

Intercut with these comments were clips from news and documentary programmes, with one entire section devoted to the making of *BB* which included interviews with one of the programme makers, Stuart Lansley, and with the homeless young people who were featured in the *BB* series.

The technique of montage adopted by *The Media Show* makes for gripping television, and many of the points made by the interviewees are a necessary reminder of the problematic relationship between the media and its subjects. But there are problems. The way in which the views of different interviews are accumulated, cut and recast in a new argumentative context, namely that of *The*

Media Show's own, allows that potentially contradictory positions can be stated side by side without the viewers necessarily becoming aware of the fact that such views are not compatible. At the same time an argument can be constructed by cutting statements of interviewees against each other in apparent contradiction, even where these may be perfectly compatible in a different context . . .

However, the extract from *BB*, and *The Media Show*'s own version of the events, raise another issue. The instance shown in programme 4 of *BB*, where Kim and her friends are bedding down in the street is not literally the moment of the people going to sleep in a doorway, as one would assume from watching the programme, but is a moment created for television. Although there is no doubt that Kim and her friends are genuinely homeless, *The Media Show* 'discovered' some facts about them which they considered problematical, namely that Kim had already featured on three previous television programmes about homelessness, and had in the words of Emma Freud 'reached celebrity' through television. And that the young boys who were featured going to sleep on the street on that night were actually sleeping in hostels.

The following transcript is taken from a part of *The Media Show* which introduces the *BB* series by a fictional 'presenter' who supposedly advises on what it is that documentary film-makers really want. His sarcastic style contrasts with the more factual and analytic one of *The Media Show*'s own moderator, Emma Freud.

> *Presenter* [*in studio, supposedly addressing those who are about to be filmed*]: Remember, they [i.e. the documentary film-makers] are on your side, they've done their research, and they are educated people. Give them what they want; and if you're smart you give them just a little bit more.
>
> *Tommo and Michael* [*talking to* The Media Show *about being filmed for* BB]: We stood outside Centrepoint at Dean Street, and Cathy [*sic*] was there with this lady from the *Breadline* programme. And we just stood there, we just sort of asked if we could be in it, you know we just asked, and we were in.
>
> *Emma Freud* [*voice-over to pictures of* BB *editing suite*]: London Weekend Television's major new series *Breadline Britain* will look at what's happening to poverty in the UK through the lives of today's poor.
>
> [*Extract with Tommo and Michael shown on editing machine; they talk about how government has not done anything for them, how cold they were; editors of* BB *comment and cut.*]
>
> *Tommo and Michael* [*in* The Media Show *studio*].
>
> *Michael*: Well I chose the set myself, actually, because I was quite enthusiastic about the whole affair; and we went to this place just off Soho Square, and we chose a nice little alcove where we could sit and look really miserable. And we had blankets over us. [*Film shows this sequence with his voice in voice-over*]
>
> *Tommo*: For about five minutes he [the film producer?] was telling us, like, you two sit up and chat, and me I was lying down, trying to get some sleep, and they're chatting, and I'm supposed to be shouting out, you two shut up, cause I'm trying to get some sleep. You know, some things just don't happen, you never find three lads in a door way, and then two girls come up; it never happens.
>
> *Interviewer's voice*: Where were you actually sleeping that night?
>
> *Tommo*: In a hostel.
>
> *Michael*: Yeah, I was in a hostel as well.
>
> *Tommo*: Actually, in a hostel.
>
> [*Sequence with Stuart Lansley's comment about his criteria for choosing people; Boyce comments that people perpetuate myths about themselves.*]
>
> *Emma Freud*: Since this programme was completed the makers of *Breadline Britain* have issued a statement denying that they were misled by the young people they filmed. They say that these individuals regularly spent the night together on the street, and that as far as they were concerned it makes no difference to them if Michael and Tommo spent the night in a hostel, since most homeless youngsters stay in hostels from time to time. It's widespread practice for TV documentaries to try to find

> typical examples to illustrate an argument but what can be overlooked in the process are the awkward realities of everyday life. *The Media Show* has confirmed that on the night when they were pretending to sleep rough for the cameras and on subsequent nights Michael and Tommo were definitely staying in a hostel.

This critique raises two fundamental issues. First, that in response to the camera something can be created which otherwise would not exist. This does not concern us here. The poor in Britain clearly exist irrespective of the presence or absence of a camera whatever criteria for defining poverty are used.

The second point is more complicated, and concerns only the realm of representation. Does it matter if a seemingly authentic instance is a dramatized representation which may at this particular moment not account for the actual event as happening there and then, but which is nevertheless an acceptable signal of a particular aspect of social reality; that is if the relationship between the instance and what it stands for is exclusively symbolic? Issue 1 and with it the thesis of *BB* is not affected by whether or not the particular people they picked are material instances of what they are representing. If on that particular night the boys slept in the hostel, that does not devalue the fact that many other young people that night, and, indeed, the boys themselves on many other nights were sleeping in the street, and that homelessness and bad housing in the UK is a central problem for a growing number of poor . . .

Although *The Media Show* is to blame for trapping itself in a rather simplistic view of unmediated reality, this does not mean that there is no question to be answered; and this is not just in appreciation of the fact that outside the intellectual debate, with the press acting as a catalyzer for differing perspectives, issues of the 'truth-value' of representations remain central to the political debate and to political slander.

Within the dominant theoretical discourse about realism in documentaries and documentary drama, any recourse to fact versus fiction comes over as entirely simplistic because the most basic assumption behind any discussion is the impossibility of naively appealing to 'the real' as an unconstructed, unmediated slice of life. Since unmediated reality does not exist on television, the analysis of forms of representation, of the relations between various discourses within the text, and the positioning of readers in relation to them, become central concerns. In postmodern theories it is the text and its relationship to other texts which replaces the analysis of the relationship between text and a given social reality, although there are differences among postmodernists as to how extreme they are in the denial of the existence of any non-textual referent. John Frow in an excellent article on intertextuality is aware of the danger of incorporating 'broad domains of social being . . . within the single conceptual domain of textuality' (Frow 1990: 54). With a social semiotic approach to discourse this risk does not arise since it foregrounds problems of interaction between social practices and the various conflicting discursive representations as they surface in the form of the semiotic levels of media texts and in the contestation of these representations by different readings and readers. Such an approach allows not only a full semiotic analysis of any number of texts as given semiotic constructs, but equally, in the same theoretical framework, the contestation and subversion of these through the clashing worlds of the referents and respondents.

The genre of social documentary through the medium of television allows little alternative but to represent through the symbolic, so the tension and the dynamic interchange between the specific and the general will remain endemic to any of its productions.

The makers of *BB* tried to cope with this inevitable dilemma by a clear upfronting of their own thesis. In this respect the series seems to me to be far less guilty of the charges that are levelled against it than *The Media Show* itself, which pretends to be an analytical meta-perspective which is theoretically naïve, to say the least. How far these or any other semiotic presentation of social issues can convince viewers to alter pre-existing beliefs and attitudes is, however, another issue altogether, and one that cannot be argued or predicted from within these presentations . . .

Notes

1   See, for example, television review programmes such as BBC2's *Did You See?* and the now discontinued Channel 4 series discussed here, *The Media Show*; or satirical programmes such as *Spitting Image* which depends to a large extent on inter-textual references to other television programmes (Meinhof and Smith 2000).

2   For a quick review of the development of interest in the discourses of viewers see Richardson [1994] . . .

3   See also my footnote in Meinhof (1993: 222). 'With the terms "open" and "closed" I am borrowing the terminology of Eco (1981). My own usage differs from Eco's in that I am restricting the terms to different ways of interpreting texts. Eco, on the other hand, characterizes particular narratives as open or closed, depending on the range of interpretative proposals which the text validates.'

4   Income level is, of course, one of the more traditional, though not uncontroversial ways of measuring poverty. See the bi-annual, not easily accessible publication of the DHSS, *Households Below Average Income*. In contrast see P. Townsend (1979) *Poverty in the United Kingdom. A Survey of Household Resources and Standards of Living* and J. Mack and S. Lansley's own 1985 publication, *Poor Britain*.

5   See the *Guardian* leader, 8 April 1991 and New Statesman, 19 April 1991.

6   For a collection of essays on documentary broadcasting see Corner (1986).

7   Field/tenor/mode in Hallidayan linguistics are parameters of so-called 'situation types' which allow a systematic correlation to parts of grammar. Field refers to social activity including subject matter, tenor to the interrelations among participants, mode to channel or medium. Each correlates with functional components of the semantic system which, in turn, correlate with typical realizations in grammar. For discussion of this see, for example, Halliday (1978).

8   . . . *The Media Show* is a Channel 4 series, broadcast before its recent dis-continuation on prime time television on Sunday evenings. Moderated by Emma Freud who succeeded Muriel Grey in that role, the series takes as its theme aspects of media policy and practices. Programmes typically draw on a range of practitioners or analysts from the field of media studies: journalists, producers, academics, and usually present a highly critical view of their subject matter.

References

Bakhtin, M. (1981) *The Dialogical Imagination*. Austin, Texas: University of Texas Press.

Corner, J. (ed.) (1986) *Documentary and the Mass Media*. London: Arnold.

DHSS (Department of Health and Social Security) *Households Below Average Income*. London: HMSO.

Eco, U. (1981) *The Role of the Reader*. London: Hutchinson.

Fish, S. (1980) *Is There a Text in this Class?* Cambridge, Mass.: Harvard University Press.

Frow, J. (1990) 'Intertextuality and ontology'. In Warton, M. and Still, J. (eds) *Intertextuality: Theories and Practices*. Manchester: Manchester University Press.

Halliday, M.A.K. (1978) *Language as Social Semiotic*. London: Arnold.

Jakobson, R. (1960) 'Linguistics and poetics'. In Sebeok, T. (ed.) *Style in Language*. Cambridge, Mass.: MIT Press: 350–77.

Mack, J. and Lansley, S. (1985) *Poor Britain*. London: George Allen and Unwin.

Meinhof, U.H. (1993) 'Double-talk in news braodcasts.' In Graddol, D. and Boyd-Barrett, O. (eds) *Media Texts: Authors and Readers*. Clevedon: Multilingual Matters: 212–23.

Meinhof, U.H. and Smith, J. (eds) (2000) *Intertextuality and the Media: from Genre to Everyday Life*. Manchester: Manchester University Press.

Richardson, K. (1994) 'Interpreting *Breadline Britain*'. In Meinhof, U.H. and Richardson, K. (eds) *Text, Discourse and Context: Representations of Poverty in Britain*. Harlow: Longman.

Sandford, J. (1976) *Cathy Come Home*. London: Marion Boyars.

Townsend, P. (1979) *Poverty in the United Kingdom. A Survey of Household Resources and Standards of Living*. London: Allen Lane.

Volosinov, V.N. (1973) *Marxism and the Philosophy of Language*. New York: Seminar Press.

Wilkinson, R.G. (1990) 'Income distribution and mortality: a "natural" experiment', *Sociology of Health and Illness* 12: 391–412.

Source: Meinhof, 1994: 67–92

Solutions to Chapter 9 SAQs

SAQ 9.1

> *S1*: Do you know who is going to the party?
> *S2*: Who?
> *S1*: I don't know!
> *S2*: Oh, probably Pete. Jane said Phil and some of the lads might too.

We know that S1 was really asking a question – Do you know . . . But S2 hears an 'opening turn', a general day-to-day phrase that people might use to start a conversation on a topic. In fact we can see that S2 thought that S1 knew the answer to their own question! This problem is 'fixed' by S1 in their next line and they then get the answer they were looking for from S2. We know this from the structure of the interaction. In fact we can supply evidence for each of the claims made here.

SAQ 9.2

Extract 3: Diana the ambassador

1 Bashir: what role do you see for yourself in the future?

2 Diana: I'd like to be an ambassador for this country (.) I'd like to represent this country abroad.

3   (.) .hhh as I have all this media interest let's not just sit in this country (.) and be

4   battered by it let's take them (.) these people (.) out (.) and (.) to represent this country

5   and the good qualities of it abroad (1) when I go abroad (.) we've got sixty to ninety (.)

6   photographers (.) just from this country with me (.) so let's (.) use it in a-a productive

7   way, to help this country.

8 Bashir: you say you feel that your future is as some form of ambassador

  9 Diana: mmm
 10 Bashir: at whose behest is that?
 11   (2)
 12 Bashir: on what grounds do you feel that you have the right to think of yourself
              as an ambassador?
 13 Diana: I've been in a (.) privileged position for fifteen years (.) and I've got (.)
              tremendous
 14   knowledge (.) about people and how to communicate (.) I've learnt that (.)
              I've got it (.)
 15   and I want to use it (1) and when I look at people in (.) public life (1) hhh
              I'm not a
 16   political animal (.) but (.) I think the biggest disease this world (.) suffers
              from (.) in this
 17   day and age (.) is the disease of people feeling unloved (.) and I know
              that (.) I can give
 18   (.) love for a minute (.) for half an hour for a day for a month but I can give
              (.) I'm very
 19   happy to do that (.) and I want to do that
 20 Bashir: do you think that the British people are happy with you (.) in your role?
 21 Diana: I think the British people (.) need someone (.) in public life to give
              affection (.) to make
 22   them feel important (.) to support them (.) to give them light (.) in their
              dark tunnels (.)
 23   I see it as a possibly unique role (1) and (1) yes I've had difficulties (.) erm
              a-as
 24   everybody (.) has witnessed over the years (.) but let's now use the
              knowledge I've
 25   gathered (.) to help other people in distress

(*Source*: Abell and Stokoe, 2001)

Adjacency Pairs

There are a number of 'adjacency pairs' in the transcript:

- Bashir's Line 1 and Diana's reply starting on Line 2
- Bashir's Line 8 and Diana's Line 9
- At line 10 Bashir's opening gets no response – in fact a 2-second gap is a long gap in a conversation!
- Bashir's Line 12 and Diana's turn starting on Line 13 – though you could argue that Bashir has to ask the additional question at Line 20 to get the full answer he is looking for.

'Trouble' Points

There are a number of places where there is 'trouble' in the conversation. The most obvious being Diana's long pause at Line 11 – which Bashir fixes by rephrasing his question. The following answer from Diana is not very 'organised' and contains many pauses and broken sentences – this is evidence for the topic and the turn being 'troublesome' for the speaker.

Accounts

One could view Diana's turns starting at Line 13 and at Line 21 as providing 'accounts' that back up her assertion made in her turn starting at Line 2 that she wishes to be an 'ambassador'. In fact these 'accounts' are clearly responses to what are seen as 'challenges' to the claim made in Diana's first turn starting at Line 2.

Analysis

Even this very basic analysis is very different from both examples outlined in Chapter 8. In Chapter 8 we interpreted the data according to categories we generated through reading the data. Here we have a set of existing theoretical ideas such as adjacency pairs, 'trouble' and repair – based in previous studies – that we use to both make sense of the data. At the same time we use the evidence of the transcript to support our claims. We also look to see what the turns in the conversation imply about each other. For instance, Bashir's Line 12 is a reworking of a previous turn – even though it was Diana's 'turn' to speak – it was repair of a problem caused by the other speaker. This might seem trivial – but even in this case such analyses can tell us a great deal about how power and such things as ideologies (e.g. big 'D' discourses) come into play – though CA researchers tend to leave such analyses to others.

SAQ 9.3

1 (a) Studies of the 'organization of conversations'; (b) studies of the larger-scale structure of texts (e.g. narrative structure in books) on understanding and recall; (c) studies in the broad area of the sociology of knowledge; (d) studies that have made use of Foucault's ideas and writings. Potter and Wetherell note that their work ranges broadly across all these categories. In our typology (a) and (b) relate to small 'd' discourse analyses and issues whereas (c) and (d) are big 'D' issues.

2 The three most pertinent features of discourse analysis for Potter and Wetherell are:
   (a) Talk and texts as social practices: through an exploration of the linguistic features of acts of communication the discourse analyst can find answers to social questions.
   (b) A triple concern with action, construction and variability: talk and text perform actions in the world. These actions are constructed from a set of social and linguistic resources available. As such their talk and texts, their discourse, has a variable if sometimes limited range of form and content.
   (c) A focus on the rhetorical or 'argument' organisation in texts: how texts put their point or meaning across to their audience.
   In other words they wish to link broader social questions (a) (big 'D' issues)

to the specifics of actual texts and their production (b) and (c) (small 'd' issues).

3   The first of these emphases has been on studies of the sets of resources that people use in constructing discourses. Potter and Wetherell see this work as being linked to the work of Foucault. The second emphasis has been on the means by which people make texts work, in this specific case how texts are made to seem 'factual'. Potter and Wetherell link this work to CA. Again big 'D' and small 'd' combined.

SAQ 9.4

1   A video of the programme; participant observations; drafts of the script; schedules; recordings of editing sessions; interviews with a range of relevant people.

2   (a) To look at the construction of a 'factual television' programme; (b) to look at the role of 'quantification' in making factual television; (c) to consider the role of quantification in social science accounts.

3   In many respects this is akin to a combination of the studies by Okely (Readings I, J, L, N) and Yates (Reading K), with data being collected in very similar ways, and having a broad range of goals. As with these two studies, all the data were texts.

SAQ 9.5

1   (a) Using variation as a lever. This is the act of looking for differences in the way people use language and communication when referring to the same or similar things. This gives the analyst access to the different resources that are being used to construct the discourse. (b) Reading the detail. This reflects the need to focus upon the specifics of texts as all elements could be there for a purpose and serve in the construction of the discourse. (c) Looking for rhetorical organisation. By looking for rhetorical organisation the researcher can make clear how people construct knowledge or attempt to undermine the knowledge claims of others. In this example Potter and Wetherell examined how the film makers emphasised and under-emphasised various figures in the TV programme. (d) Looking for accountability. This refers to the analysts exploring people's accounts of their own actions and texts. In the example given in the extract the film makers discuss how they can 'justify' one of their statistics. (e) Cross-referencing discourse studies. Though Potter and Wetherell note that the types of discourse analysis they have focused upon have not sought to build general laws in the same sense as posited by positivism, discourse analysis studies can find interconnected results in different research contexts. These 'cross-referenced' findings can help in the process of analysis.

2   One of major similarities to the Okely material is the rejection of positivist ideas and quantitative methods. However, Potter and Wetherell were not engaged in a participant observation study. The data collection was more akin to the model in Yates's Reading K, and the analysis did not involve the total immersion in the data that Okely advocated.

3   Potter and Wetherell argue, akin to Okely, that writing down their methods in

a textbook manner is not possible. Having said that, it is clear that forms of coding took place, though this was not as formalised as the methods proposed by Strauss. Potter and Wetherell's use of key words and their focus upon certain types of communicative activity resemble axial and selective coding (see Reading R).

SAQ 9.6

There are a number of possible answers to this question. Some suggestions are analyses of:

- new mothers' conversations
- new mothers' discourse about their babies
- mothers' discourse about motherhood
- practitioners' discourse about new mothers
- nursing research discourse on motherhood

SAQ 9.7

1   Meinhof describes it as a 'social semiotic' one, based on the work of Michael Halliday, who is a 'socio-linguist'. Halliday's work is based on the premise that language was developed for social interaction purposes, especially the communication of socially and contextually linked meanings and actions. Halliday argues that the basic grammatical structure of language is orientated to these kinds of task. This position contrasts with, say, that of Chomsky, where grammar and language are seen as being innate cognitive psychological abilities. Meinhof notes that her ideas have been further influenced by Bakhtin and Volosinov, two Russian socio-linguists who worked in the first half of the twentieth century, but whose writings became readily available in Europe and the USA only in the early 1980s. These writers argue very strongly that language and communication have multiple lines of interaction that extend beyond the obvious connection between 'sender and receiver' of a communication.

2   Semiotic analysis 'proper' (as Meinhof describes it) has tended to focus on the system of signs in a text and their internal relations/oppositions to each other. Meinhof uses the idea of a 'closed' system derived from the writings of Umberto Eco, which you should not confuse with our use of the term in Part II, though they are linked. She follows Halliday, Bakhtin and Volosinov in seeking to link the system of signs to the social structures and contexts in which they are embedded. In following Bakhtin and Volosinov, Meinhof follows through the argument that texts can have multiple authors and interpretations, an argument developed strongly in post-modern theory. Meinhof falls short of the full relativism of some post-modern thinkers, whose view is that a 'text has as many readings as there are readers'. In fact, Meinhof is interested in the constraints and limitations on how texts are constructed and read because of their social contexts and role.

3   Meinhof argues that the narrative in the *Breadline Britain* documentary is based

on the claim that it was the policies of the Conservative government in the 1980s that had created and exacerbated the levels of poverty in Britain. This narrative thread was maintained by the use of a voice-over that linked the individual stories in the programmes with this 'thesis'.

4 She describes them as having a role as 'representative' examples of the types of poverty highlighted by the *Breadline Britain* survey, which allows the programme makers to highlight the issues from the survey in a meaningful, practical way. This is part of the process by which the systems of signs and meanings created in the survey become translated into the system of signs and meaning in the documentary.

5 First, there are the different 'voices' present in the narrative, including those of the participants and the narrator. These voices help to tell the narrative of poverty as experienced by people in the UK, but also articulate the overall narrative that explains the rise in poverty in relation to government policy. Second, there are the images of poverty in the programmes. This semiotic layer provides support for the voices by visually presenting the material realities of poverty. Third, there is the use of music to focus the attention on one aspect of poverty – what Meinhof calls the 'melancholia' of poverty, poverty as a sad and depressing state which engenders a feeling of hopelessness. Meinhof notes that a different use of music and images might have put forward a model of poverty as something that angers people and leads to acts of rebellion and outrage.

6 Meinhof argues that an analysis of *The Media Show*'s critique of *Breadline Britain* falls foul of its own criteria and, in fact, shows considerable naivety in relation to the role, purpose and construction of the documentary genre.

7 Meinhof argues that the combination of (a) the actual social science research base with (b) an interwoven narrative of people's experiences and (c) a clear overall thesis makes it necessary to view the series in a wider social and political discursive context.

8 Meinhof states that her work 'involved an analysis of the transposition of social scientific academic discourse into the semiotic codes of text, images and music'. I would argue that Reading S as a whole makes a clear case by developing a strong narrative of its own, supported by material from the documentary. Having said that, the actual process of data analysis is hidden from the reader. This is often the case in qualitative and discourse analytic work, reflecting the problem of presenting an analysis based upon a large body of textual data.

PART IV
SELECTING AND EVALUATING METHODS

10   *Selecting and Evaluating Methods*

This book has been a basic introduction to social research. In working through it you have encountered the following types of research and analysis:

- survey research
- experimental research
- statistical analysis
- interview research
- ethnographic research
- qualitative data analysis
- discourse analysis

You should now have a reasonable grasp of what using each of these methods involves, as well as their basic relationship to arguments in the philosophy of social science. When doing social research we are often faced with two situations where we need such understandings. First, and most obviously, is when we are designing a research project. Here we need to apply our knowledge in order to select the most appropriate method. Second, in any social science work we need to read and evaluate the research conducted by others, and in evaluating the usefulness of this research for yourself you will need to deploy your understanding of the methods used. The rest of this chapter points out some of the issues in selecting and evaluating methods.

Selecting a Research Method

While there are a number of ways in which you can go about selecting a method, they can be put into two categories. First, you can select a method by taking a position in relation to a specific philosophy of the social sciences. If, for instance, you are in agreement with a broadly positivist position, you might decide that surveys or experiments are the best method; conversely, if you feel more comfortable with idealist or relativist positions then you may choose an ethnographic approach. In many cases such decisions reflect the dominant research 'paradigm' of the area of social science in which the research is situated. Second, you can select a method on more pragmatic grounds. You might look at the research idea, the resources and time available, the purpose or goals of the research and the intended uses of the results and use these criteria as a basis for your decision.

These two approaches to choosing a method are of course related. If one is working in a specific area of social research, which has a dominant paradigm and a general philosophic orientation, then the two sets of criteria will often merge. A good example of this might be cognitive psychology which has a strongly experimental tradition, an essentially positivist position, and an object of study (mental processes such as memory, perception, problem solving, etc.) that lends itself most readily to study in these ways. This contrasts with social anthropology, where ethnographic methods are the tradition and where idealist and relativist models hold sway. Having said this, such things are never absolute. There are a large number of social anthropologists interested in cognitive issues, for example, the psychology of literacy. One clear way in which philosophical and pragmatic issues combine is in the outcomes of research. Very often these are published accounts that range from articles in learned journals and academic books, through policy documents, to journalistic and popular writings. Different disciplines of the social sciences have their own traditions of publishing, and researchers generally have to tailor the presentation of their results to the requirements of specific journals, publishers or policy bodies.

Table 10.1 lays out some of the basic aspects of the four methods we have concentrated on in this book, and relates these to some philosophical and pragmatic issues. Bear in mind that these are simplifications and do not reflect some of the complexities that you have already started to encounter.

Table 10.1 *Basic features of four research methods*

Method	Surveys	Experiments	Ethnography	Discourse analysis
Types of control	Sampling	Experimental, possibly sampling	Case selection, possibly sampling	Text selection, possibly sampling
Data collection	Questionnaires/ measures	Observations/ measures	Observation, interviews, collection of objects/ artefacts, etc.	Collection of relevant texts, possibly including interviews
Type of data	Numerical, some short texts	Numerical, some short texts	Textual, some numerical	Textual
Numbers of cases/ participants	100s to 1000s	10s to 100s	Single people to large communities	Single texts to very large corpora
Type of analysis	Statistical	Statistical	Coding, commenting (might even include theory building, thick descriptions, statistics)	Coding, linguistic, CA
Types of results	Models, theories, statistical explanations	Models, theories, statistical explanations	Textual descriptions, theories, models, explanations	Textual descriptions, theories, explanations

SAQ 10.1

Using Table 10.1, select a research method appropriate to each of these studies:

1 The effectiveness of two different teaching methods
2 People's attitudes to government education policy
3 The impact of pit closures on community life in a mining village
4 Representations of scientists in newspapers

Once you have done this, try it again, but this time assume the roles described below and decide what method you might choose. In some cases you may decide that no appropriate method can be found.

(a) You are a psychologist working in a very experimental and positivist-based research unit and must publish your work in journals that value statistical explanations.
(b) You are an anthropologist working in another culture who takes arguments about cultural relativism very seriously and you expect to publish your work as a book.

From SAQ 10.1 you can see that selecting a method can be a complicated process. You may have noticed that we described the process as one of selecting the 'appropriate' method rather than the 'right' or 'correct' method. This reflects the issues you will have faced in tackling SAQ 10.1. The choice of a method has to be supported by a good argument that combines elements of both philosophical positions and pragmatic issues.

Evaluating Social Research

Reading and assessing research publications when you are conducting literature reviews or developing a new theory or research project is the other way in which you will encounter social research methods. In order to evaluate fully the research you will need to consider the three factors outlined in Chapter 1:

1 the philosophy of the social sciences;
2 previous related research;
3 the practical context in which the research took place.

There are two main ways in which you can go about evaluating and understanding the work of social researchers. First, you can evaluate it from a philosophical standpoint. In this sense you would apply the broad range of arguments developed against a specific type of social research to the project under scrutiny. If you look back at the Okely readings in Part III you will find that she engages in a critique of this kind by making a number of general arguments against 'positivist' methods, especially survey research. As we have not dealt with these philosophical issues in depth (in the main we have pointed to the relationship between methods and the philosophy of the social sciences) we will not explore these types of critique further. Second, you can evaluate social research by examining both why the methods were chosen and the actual deployment of the method itself. In this case you need to use the knowledge you have gained about specific methods to consider if they were appropriately chosen and properly executed.

To do this you must bear in mind the important elements of each method. Table 10.2 lists some of the main questions on experimental and discourse analytic methods that you might want to consider when evaluating these types of research. These are of course only suggestions; there are many other ways in which you can address the evaluation of research projects and publications. (For a thorough review see Hart, 1998.)

Table 10.2 *Evaluating experimental and discourse analytic research*

	Issues	
Area	Experiments	Discourse analysis
Design/approach	How well was the experiment designed? Do the experimental conditions control for all of the independent variables? How well has the choice of an experiment and the specific design been argued for?	What analytic approach was taken to the data? Has the analyst kept to this approach? Has the best data been selected for this approach? How well has the choice of analytic approach/ framework been argued for?
Data selection	How well were the participants chosen? Were relevant factors (e.g. age, gender, education) controlled for?	Which texts were selected and why? How were the texts collected? Could other material have been selected?
Analysis	Have the right/best statistical methods been used and applied correctly?	How well has the analysis been executed? Has the analyst made clear how the approach/framework was applied to the data? If the data has been coded how was this done?
Results	Are all the important results clearly presented? How well have the results been linked to the hypotheses? How well and clearly have the results been interpreted? Are other interpretations possible?	Are all the important results clearly presented? Has the analyst provided clear examples of texts/coding to support their arguments? Do you agree with the interpretations of these texts? What other interpretations might be put forward?

SAQ 10.2

Now that you have considered Table 10.2, try to fill in some similar questions for survey and ethnographic research methods in Table 10.3.

Table 10.3 *Evaluating survey and ethnographic methods*

	Issues	
Area	Surveys	Ethnography
Design/approach		
Data selection		
Analysis		
Results		

From SAQ 10.2 you will have noticed that evaluating social research is not a clear-cut process. In many cases you will have actively to consider the context in which the research took place and the implications of this for the types of research design and practice that were available to the researchers.

Conclusion

In this book you have studied:

- survey research and related issues such as sampling, measures and questionnaires;
- experimental designs and the control of independent variables;
- statistical analyses and the types of explanation that such numerical analyses make possible;
- interview and ethnographic methods and related methods such as focus groups;
- examples of discourse analysis and the processes of qualitative or textual data analysis;
- some issues surrounding the selection and evaluation of social research methods.

In Part I it was claimed that one can be empirical – that is, base one's claims upon the analysis of data collected from the social world without being empiricist – by this I mean to follow the very narrow social philosophical research position of empiricism. For each method you have encountered we have made some effort to link the practical issues and research practices back to the philosophy that informed them, even if the practice might fall short of the philosophical goals. It is our hope that you will now be able to develop the understandings you have gained here in your own social research, whichever method you find most useful and appropriate.

Solutions to Chapter 10 SAQs

SAQ 10.1

1   This question is classically answered experimentally with two similar groups being taught via the two methods. You could also consider using a survey if whole schools or even educational regions were using different teaching methods. You could conduct this as an ethnographic study where you observed the teaching method 'in action'. You could even approach this from a discourse perspective, possibly looking at the discourse of children being taught by the two systems, or by looking at the educational discourse in academic journals and the press about the methods. In the last two cases measuring 'effectiveness' might prove more difficult.

2   This question would most likely be approached from a survey perspective, with a large representative sample of people being surveyed using a questionnaire that might include attitude measures. At the same time you could think up a number of ethnographic studies that might address this issue by exploring a specific group's (e.g. teachers or parents) attitudes to government education policy. Once again you might consider a discourse perspective in which you analysed teachers' or parents' discussions of government policy, or in which you analysed media coverage of policies. Conducting an experiment in this case would be difficult.

3   This is a classic example of an ethnographic study context. By living in the community the ethnographer would be able to develop complex understandings of the impacts of such change on day-to-day life. You could, of course, do this research using a survey, though you would be likely to survey more than one village. Once again you might consider a discourse perspective in which you analysed residents' discussions of the pit closure, or in which you analysed media coverage of the community. Conducting an experiment in this case would be difficult.

4   This is a classic discourse analytic question, in which you would analyse the content of newspapers covering science and related stories. You could possibly conduct a survey, though you would most likely ask about people's interpretations of the images. Such a study might best be done using focus groups based on actual newspaper images of scientists. Conducting an experiment in this case might be difficult, and an ethnographic study would probably look at the production of the newspaper rather than the newspaper texts themselves.

(a)   This question has mostly been answered above. In the teaching methods case you would most likely conduct an experiment. In the government policy case you might try to think up a novel experiment, though you would most likely choose to conduct a survey based upon a set of attitude measures. The pit village case is more difficult, and once again you would be likely to resort to a questionnaire survey containing relevant measures. In the case of scientists in newspapers, you would be unlikely to choose to conduct the project.

(b)   In this case we have provided four ethnographic examples above: (i) an ethnographic study where you observed the teaching method 'in action'; (ii) a number of ethnographic studies that might address this issue by exploring a specific group's (e.g. teachers' or parents') attitudes to government education policy; (iii) living in the community and developing complex understandings of the impacts of such change on day-to-day life; (iv) an ethnographic study would most likely look at the production of the newspaper rather than the newspaper texts themselves. All of these would fit into the constraints we have laid down, though in all except (iii) you would not be working exactly in the area laid down by the question.

SAQ 10.2

Some possible questions to complete Table 10.3 might be:

Area	Surveys	Ethnography
Design/approach	What types of question or measure were used? How was the questionnaire administrated?	How did the ethnographer choose the context and gain access? To what people and places did they have access?
Data selection	How good was the sample? How well designed were the questions and measures?	How representative was the case? What types of data did the ethnographer collect?
Analysis	Have the right/best statistical methods been used and applied correctly?	How well has the analysis been executed? Has the analyst made clear how the approach/framework was applied to the data? If the data have been coded, how was this done?
Results	Are all the important results clearly presented? How well have the results been linked to the hypotheses? How well and clearly have the results been interpreted? Are other interpretations possible?	Are all the important results clearly presented? Has the analyst provided clear examples of texts/coding to support their arguments? Do you agree with the interpretations of these texts? What other interpretations might be put forward?

Answering this SAQ may have made you realise the extent to which the various aspects of a research project are always interlinked and how weaknesses or strengths in one area might lead to weaknesses or strengths in another. Often you need to take note of the context of the research (see second part of SAQ 10.1) in order to make the best kinds of evaluation. You may also have noticed that the level of detail of your evaluation might depend upon the use you will make of a study. If you were attempting to replicate an experiment or survey you might ask very specific and detailed questions about the design. If you are simply reviewing the overall results you might just check that the design was good enough to make you confident of the general outcome.

References

Abell, J. and Stokoe, E.H. (2001) 'Broadcasting the royal role: constructing culturally situated identities in Princess Diana's "Panorama" interview', *British Journal of Psychology*, 40: 417–35.

Billig, M. (1991) *Ideology and Opinions*. London: Sage.

Bryman, A. and Cramer, D. (1990) *Quantitative Data Analysis for Social Scientists*. London: Routledge.

Bulmer, M. (1982) 'The merits and demerits of covert participant oservation', in M. Bulmer (ed.) *Social Reseearch Ethics*. London: Macmillan, pp. 217–51.

Cannel, C.H. and Kahn, R.L. (1968) 'Interviewing', in Lindzey, G. and Aronson, E. (eds) *Handbook of Social Psychology*, vol. 2. Reading, MA: Addison–Wesley.

Cohen, G. and Faulkner, D. (1989) 'Age differences in source forgetting: effects on reality monitoring and on eyewitness testimony', *Psychology and Aging* 4(1): 10–17.

Dey, I. (1993) *Qualitative Data Analysis*. London: Routledge.

Field, J., Johnson, A., Wadsworth, J. and Wellings, K. (1994) *Sexual Behaviour in Britain*, Harmondsworth: Penguin Books.

Glaser, B.G. and Strauss, A.L. (1968) *The Discovery of Grounded Theory: Strategies for Qualitative Research*. London: Weidenfeld and Nicolson.

Goffman, E. (1959) *The Presentation of Self in Everyday Life*. New York: Doubleday.

Hart, L. (1998) *Doing a Literature Review*. London: Sage.

Meinhof, U. (1994) 'From the street to the screen: *Breadline Britain* and the semiotics of poverty', in Meinhof, U. and Richardson, K. (eds) *Text, Discourse and Content. Representations of Poverty in Britain*. Harlow: Longman.

Okely, J. (1994) 'Thinking through fieldwork', in Bryman, A. and Burgess, R.G. (eds) *Analyzing Qualitative Data*. London: Routledge.

Potter, J. and Wetherell, M. (1994) 'Analyzing discourse', in Bryman, A. and Burgess, R.G. (eds) *Analyzing Qualitative Data*. London: Routledge.

Rogan, F., Schmied, V., Barclay, L., Everitt, L. and Wyllie, A. (1997) '"Becoming a mother": developing a new theory of early motherhood', *Journal of Advanced Nursing* 25: 877–85.

Schutz, A. (1967) *The Phenomenology of the Social World*. Evanston, IL: Northwestern University Press.

Sjoberg, G. and Nett, R. (1968) *A Methodology for Social Research*. New York: Harper and Row.

Smith, H.W. (1975) *Strategies of Social Research: The Methodological Imagination*. Englewood Cliffs, NJ: Prentice-Hall.

Smith, M. (1998) *Social Science in Question*. London: Sage in association with the Open University.

Strauss, A. (1987) *Qualitative Analysis for Social Scientists*. Cambridge: Cambridge University Press.

Tomas, A. (1997) 'The visual life-history interview', unpublished paper.

Warr, P., Cook, J.D. and Wall, T.D. (1979) 'Scales for the measurement of some attitudes and aspects of psychological well being', *Journal of Occupational Psychology* 52: 285–94.

Worcester, R.M. (1995) 'Lessons from the electorate: what the 1992 British General Election taught British pollsters about the conduct of opinion polls', *International Social Science* 14(4): 539–52.

Index

Page numbers in **bold** refer to readings, (Q) and (A) indicate self-assessment questions and answers. Page numbers in *italics* refer to tables.

access to participants 160
'adjacency pairs', conversation analysis 236–7
Age differences in source forgetting (Cohen and Faulkner) 68(Q), 70, **71–6**, 76–7(A), 97(Q), 127(A)
analysing data 9(Q), **17–18**, 20(A)
  qualitative models 188–91
Analyzing discourse (Potter and Wetherell)
  (1) 240(Q), **246–8**, 275–6(A)
  (2) 240(Q), **249–51**, 276(A)
  (3) 241(Q), **251–62**, 276–7(A)
atomism *13*, 14
averages 104–12
axial coding **219**

Becoming a mother (Rogan, F. *et al.*) 192(Q), **215–27**, 232(A), 242(Q), 277(A)
bias 28
Breadline Britain (Meinhof) 243–4(Q), **262–73**, 277–8(A)
Bryman, A. and Cramer, D. *see Causality and research design*; *Data analysis and the research process*

CA *see* conversation analysis
categorical data 79–80
  analysis *see* chi-squares test
causality 112–16
Causality and research design (Bryman and Cramer) 115(Q), **117–23**, 129–30(A)
CDA *see* critical discourse analysis
chi-squares test 78, 98–104
  calculating expected values 101–3
  calculating the value (x^2) 100–1
  data preparation 99–100
  degrees of freedom 103
  looking up the significance (x^2) 103–4, *131*

observed values 102
political affiliation/union membership 100–4(Q), 127–8(A)
closed questions 33–4, 166
closed systems 10, *11*
closing interviews 171
closure methods 11–12
coding
  notes 175
  qualitative data 189–91(Q), 192(Q), **200–1**, **204–10**, **219–20**, 229–31(A)
Cohen, G. and Faulkner, D. *see Age differences in source forgetting*
comparison between groups 69
conditions
  experimental research 65–8
  t-test 108
content themes
  interviews 163–5
  self-assessment 164(Q), 183(A)
continuous data 80
  analysis *see* correlations
contracts 161–2
control condition 65
control groups 68–9
conversation analysis (CA) 136, 234, 235–9
  context and epistemology 239
  and discursive psychology 240, 241, 242
  self-assessment 236(Q), 237–8(Q), 273–5(A)
copies of interview data 162
correlation coefficients 82–3, 84–6
  self-assessment 83(Q), 85(Q), 88(Q), 91(Q), 94–5(Q), 124–7(A)
  see also Spearman rank correlation coefficient
correlations 78, 81–6
  interpretation 112–14
  negative 83–4, 91

positive 81–2, 83, 90
    see also spelling scores
critical discourse analysis (CDA) 242–4
    Breadline Britain (Meinhof) 243–4(Q), **262–73**,
        277–8(A)
critical linguistics 234, 242–3
'culture and social relations' 234
    see also critical discourse analysis (CDA)

Data analysis and the research process (Bryman
    and Cramer) 8–9(Q), **14–19**, 19–20(A)
deception 160–1
degrees of freedom 103, 111
Dey, I. see What is qualitative data?
diaries 174
direct questions 34
discourse analysis 192, 244–5, 280
    and context 234–5
    definition and types 233–5
    evaluation 282
    see also conversation analysis (CA); critical
        discourse analysis (CDA); discursive
        psychology
'discourse markers' 170
discursive psychology 233, 234, 239–42
    context and epistemology 242
    see also Analyzing discourse

educational software performance 108–11
'empirical regularity' 115
empiricism 1, 13–14, 135
ending interviews 171
epistemology see philosophical positions
ethical issues 159–61, 161(Q), 182–3(A)
ethnographic fieldwork 172–5
    see also Selecting a case; Thinking through
        fieldwork
ethnography 137, 140–1, 280
ethnomethodology 136
evaluating research 281–3, 283(Q), 285–6(A)
experimental closure 11–12
experimental research 65–77, 280
    Age differences in source forgetting (Cohen and
        Faulkner) 68(Q), 70, **71–6**, 76–7(A), 97(Q),
        127(A)
    conditions 65–8
    control 68–9
    evaluation 282
    and positivism 69–70

facts/values 13, 14
falsification 7, 112–13, 115
Field, J. et al. see Studying sexual lifestyles
findings 9(Q), **18**, 20(A)
focus groups 171–2
follow-up questions 167
Foucault, M. 234, 240

'fuzzy' language/concepts 21–2

Garfinkel, H. 235
general universe 26
Goffman, E. 161, 235
grounded theory approach 189, **201–10**
    Becoming a mother (Rogan, F. et al.) 192(Q),
        215–27, 232(A), 242(Q), 277(A)

group interviews see focus groups
Gypsy studies see Thinking through fieldwork

health issues
    Analyzing discourse (Potter and Wetherell) (3)
        241(Q), **251–62**, 276–7(A)
    Studying sexual lifestyles (Field, J. et al.)
        32–3(Q), 35(Q), **48–59**, 63–4(A)
Heidegger, M. 136
hermeneutic approach 136–7
Husserl, E.G.A. 136
hypothesis 8(Q), **16**, 19(A)
    experimental research 65–7
    workers' voting behaviour 67(Q), 76(A)
    see also null hypothesis

idealist positions 135, 156
idiographic approach 135
in-depth interviews 155–62
    conducting and managing 169–71
    contract and copies of data 161–2
    ethical issues 159–61, 161(Q), 182–3(A)
    philosophical position 156
    schedule construction 163–7, 167–8(Q),
        184–5(A)
    speakers' perspective 156–7
    topics and questions 158–9, 159(Q), 164(Q),
        166(Q), 182(A), 183–5(A)
    violence on TV 157–8(Q), 181–2(A)
    Visual life history interview (Tomas) 136(Q),
        141–6, 153(A)
indexing notes 175
inductive methods 7
informed consent 160
initial stages of interviews 169–70
initiating questions 165–6
interpretations
    qualitative 137–8
    quantitative 112–16
interval scales 80
interviewers
    focus groups 171–2
    self-presentation 161, 170
interviews see focus groups; in-depth interviews

jargon 166

Kant, E. 135

language
'fuzzy' 21–2
see also discourse analysis; linguistics
Lessons from the electorate (Worcester) 30(Q),
36–47, 62–3(A)
Likert scale 34, 80
linguistics 244
critical 234, 242–3
listening in interviews 170–1

mean 104–5, 106
'variation' around 107–8
meaning 136–7
'things that carry meaning' 138(Q), 153–4(A)
Visual life history interview (Tomas) 136(Q),
141–6, 153(A)
What is qualitative data? (Dey) 139(Q), 140,
147–53, 154(A)
measurement 21–5
work satisfaction 22–4, 24(Q), 27–8, 31, 60(A),
66
median 106, 107–8
Meinhof, U. *see Breadline Britain*
memory
Age differences in source forgetting (Cohen and
Faulkner) 68(Q), 70, **71–6**, 76–7(A), 97(Q),
127(A)
spelling scores and shape memory 96–7(Q),
126–7(A)
metaphors, natural science 10
methods, natural science 10
'minds, selves and sense making' 234
see also discursive psychology
mode 107
'moderators', focus groups 171–2
motherhood *see Becoming a mother*
multiple-choice questions 34

natural science
quantitative data analysis 10–12, 13–14
see also positivism
naturalism *12*
negative correlations 83–4, 91
negatively skewed distribution *105*, 108
nominalism *13*, 14, 25, 35, 70
nomothetic approach 135
non-parametric tests 108
non-verbal reinforcement in interviews 170
normal distribution *105*, 107, 108
note-taking
ethnographic fieldwork 174–5
interviews 169, 171, 175
null hypothesis 67
rejection of 92, 93, 94, 96, 97, 98, 111

Okely, J. *see Thinking through fieldwork*
open coding **205–7**, **219**

open questions 33, 166
open systems 11
operationalisation of concepts 9(Q), **16**, 19(A)
and measurement 21–2
ordinal scales 80
see also Spearman rank correlation coefficient

'p' values 68(Q), 94–6, 126(A)
parametric tests 79, 104–5
Pearson measure 108
phenomenalism *12*, 14, 25, 35, 70
phenomenological positions 136, 157
philosophical positions
evaluation of research 281–2
qualitative 135, 136–7, 156, 157, 189, 239, 242
vs quantitative 135–6
selection of research method 279, 280
see also positivism
political affiliations
Lessons from the electorate (Worcester) 30(Q),
36–47, 62–3(A)
union membership 100–4(Q), 127–8(A)
workers' voting behaviour 67(Q), 76(A)
positive correlations 81–2, 83, 90
positively skewed distribution *105*, 108
positivism 1, 135
causality, interpretation and prediction 115–16
experimental research 69–70
measures 25
quantitative research methods 12–14
questionnaires 35–6
sampling 31
Potter, J. and Wetherell, M. *see Analyzing
discourse*
poverty *see Breadline Britain*
practice of social research 3–4
prediction 112–16
presenting qualitative data 191–2
privacy right 161
probability and random chance 67–8
probability sampling 27–8
probes 167
purposive sampling 27

Qualitative analysis for social scientists (Strauss)
188–91(Q), **197–210**, 228–31(A)
qualitative *vs* quantitative methods 137–41,
149–52, 188
quantification **249–51**
questionnaires 31–6
design contexts 31–3
designing questions 33–6
and positivism 35–6
Studying sexual lifestyles (Field, J. *et al.*)
32–3(Q), 35(Q), **48–59**, 63–4(A)
questions, in-depth interviews 164–8
follow–up 167

initiating 165–6
probes 167

random chance/variability 66–8, 92–3, 97, 98
random sampling 27–8
rapport building 169–70
ratio scales 80
'rationalism' 135
reinforcement in interviews 170
'related' design 108
relativist positions 137, 156
reliability in sampling 30
'repairs', conversation analysis 236
representativeness in sampling 30
research contracts 161–2
Rogan, F. *et al. see Becoming a mother*

Sacks, H. 234, 235
sampling 25–31, 66–7
    Lessons from the electorate (Worcester) 30(Q),
        36–47, 62–3(A)
    and positivism 31
    probability 27–8
    purposive 27
    random 27–8
    workers' housing 29–30(Q), 60–2(A)
scaled questions 34
Schultz, A. 136, 157
scientific laws *13*, 14
Selecting a case (Yates) 174(Q), **180–1**, 186–7(A)
selection
    research method 279–80, 281(Q), 284–5(A)
    respondents/cases 9(Q), **16–17**, 20(A), 173–4
    see also sampling
selective coding **220**
self-presentation 161, 170
semi-structured interviews 165
set theory 26
setting up a research design 9(Q), **17**, 20(A)
sexual behaviour *see Studying sexual lifestyles*
shared understanding 166
skewed distribution *105*, 107–8
Smith, M. 2, 3, 4, 5–6, 10–11, 12, 22, 34, 35, 70,
        112, 116, 134, 135, 138, 139, 192, 233
'social constructivist' approach 242
social interaction *see* conversation analysis (CA)
speakers' perspective in interviews 156–7
Spearman rank correlation coefficient 86–92
    calculating rho (r_2) 89–91
    data preparation 86
    looking up the significance $(r2)$ 95–6, *130*
    rho (r_2) 88
    see also correlation coefficients
spelling scores
    and reading 81–2(Q), 83, 86–93, 94–5(Q), 113,
        114, 123(A), 126(A)
    and shape memory 96–7(Q), 126–7(A)

and truancy 114(Q), 129(A)
stages of social research 3–4
standard deviation 107
statistical analysis 86–92
statistical closure 11–12
statistical significance 92–8
    level of 93–5
    looking up 95–7
        chi-squares test 103–4, *131*
        rho (r_2) 95–6, *130*
        t-test 111, *132*
    'p' values 68(Q), 94–6, 126(A)
statistical software 79, 112
statistical tests
    data types 79–80
    types 78–9
    see also chi-squares test; correlations; t-test
Strauss, A. *see Qualitative analysis for social
    scientists*
structured interviews 165
structured *vs* unstructured methods **151–2**
Studying sexual lifestyles 32–3(Q), 35(Q), **48–59**,
        63–4(A)
subjectivity 137–8, 156–7
survey research 70, 280
    and experimental research 66–7, 70
    see also measurement; questionnaires;
        sampling

t-test 78–9, 108–12
    data preparation 108–9
    degrees of freedom 111
    looking up the significance of t 111, *132*
    t value 109
    workers' performance using manual 111(Q),
        128–9(A)
television
    Selecting a case (Yates) 174(Q), **180–1**, 186–7(A)
    violence 157–8(Q), 181–2(A)
texts 139, 189, 192, 241
theoretical closure 11
theory 8(Q), **15–16**, 19(A)
Thinking through fieldwork (Okely)
    (1) 172–3(Q), **175–9**, 185(A)
    (2) 173(Q), **179–80**, 185(A)
    (3) 188–91(Q), **193–6**, 228–31(A)
    (4) 191–2(Q), **211–15**, 231–2(A)
Tomas, A. *see Visual life history interview*
two-way questions 34

'unrelated' design 108
unstructured interviews 165
unstructured *vs* structured methods **151–2**

values/facts *13*, 14
variability/random chance 66–8, 92–3, 97, 98
variables 65–6

'variation' around the mean 107–8
Visual life history interview (Tomas) 136(Q), **141–6**, 153(A)

Wetherell, M.
    Taylor, S. and Yates, S.J. 233
    see also Analyzing discourse
What is qualitative data? (Dey) 139(Q), 140, **147–53**, 154(A)
withdrawal right 161
'within subjects' design 108
Worcester, R.M. *see Lessons from the electorate*

work satisfaction 22–4, 24(Q), 27–8, 31, 60(A), 66
work types 22(Q), 60(A)
workers
    housing 29–30(Q), 60–2(A)
    performance using manual 111(Q), 128–9(A)
    voting behaviour 67(Q), 76(A)
working universe 26

Yates, S.J.
    Wetherell, M., Taylor, S. and 233
    see also Selecting a case